Economic Policy and Performance in Industrial Democracies

This book considers the joint choice of monetary and fiscal policy by monetary and fiscal authorities, the central bank and the government, which are separate entities with differing objectives insofar as the former is independent of the latter. It considers the combination of multiple characteristics of these governments and their institutional-structural environments – left/right partisanship, fractionalization, labour-market organization and institutions, and election-year incentives – in explaining these policy choices. No previous work in political science of which I am aware gives as serious and sustained attention to this political economy of the joint fiscal/monetary choices of policymakers in as richly contextualized institutional-structural environments.

(Robert J. Franzese, Jr., Associate Professor of Political Science, University of Michigan)

This book is the first systematic study of how the interdependence of fiscal and monetary policies and the interaction of party governments and central banks affect the fiscal-policy mix in 18 industrial democracies in North America, Western Europe, Japan, and Oceania. Sakamoto argues that central banks' influence on economic policy is far more extensive than has been conventionally believed. He demonstrates that central banks systematically affect fiscal policy that is conducted by party governments, and that independent central banks restrain the latter's fiscal policy.

This book also examines how government partisanship affects economic policy, and shows that partisan impact is contingent on policy instruments, time periods, and the political–economic environment in which partisan governments make policy. Sakamoto also demonstrates that the economic policy of industrial democracies did really change from the 1960s–1970s to the 1980s–1990s and became conservative as a result of the globalization of the economy and governments' response to it. But he argues that despite the neoliberal policy shift, globalization has not diminished the role of domestic politics in economic policy.

This book will be fascinating reading for students and researchers engaged with the comparative political economy of industrial democracies and comparative economic policy. It will also be of interest to policy researchers at such international organizations as the OECD, the World Bank, and the IMF.

Takayuki Sakamoto is assistant professor of political science at Southern Methodist University (USA).

Routledge frontiers of political economy

Economic Policy and Performance in Industrial Democracies

Party governments, central banks and the fiscal–monetary policy mix

Takayuki Sakamoto

LONDON AND NEW YORK

First published 2008
by Routledge
2 Park Square, Milton Park, Abingdon, Oxon OX14 4RN

Simultaneously published in the USA and Canada
by Routledge
270 Madison Ave, New York, NY 10016

Routledge is an imprint of the Taylor & Francis Group, an informa business

Transferred to Digital Printing 2009

© 2008 Takayuki Sakamoto

Typeset in Times by Wearset Ltd, Boldon, Tyne and Wear

British Library Cataloguing in Publication Data
A catalogue record for this book is available from the British Library

Library of Congress Cataloging in Publication Data
A catalog record for this book has been requested

ISBN10: 0-415-77414-4 (hbk)
ISBN10: 0-415-57227-4 (pbk)
ISBN10: 0-203-93072-X (ebk)

ISBN13: 978-0-415-77414-7 (hbk)
ISBN13: 978-0-415-57227-9 (pbk)
ISBN13: 978-0-203-93072-4 (ebk)

For my parents, Naoyoshi and Misako, and
my brother Yasuyuki

Contents

Figures

Tables

Acknowledgments

Many individuals helped me in my research and completion of this book, as is usual with everything else in my life. I benefited from the insightful and helpful comments and advice of many generous individuals on various aspects and phases of this research. I thank Robert Franzese, Thomas Fomby, and Neal Beck for patiently and generously teaching me about time-series and pooled analysis. I would also like to thank William Bernhard, Carles Boix, Geoffrey Garrett, Dennis Quinn, and Duane Swank for sharing their data and suggestions. Most of all, their data showed me how I should go about constructing my dataset and its component variables. I also thank Rob Franzese, Thomas Cargill, Nobuhiro Hiwatari, and Martin Schulz for helping me think about different subjects of this research. I am grateful to anonymous reviewers for their helpful, detailed comments. I owe intellectual debts to many more scholars, whose names appear in the text and references of this book.

I would like to thank Haruhiro Fukui and Jim Hollifield for their moral as well as logistic support, guidance, and friendship. I express my thanks to Chad Sheinbein who provided excellent research assistance. I also thank Terry Clague and Thomas Sutton of Routledge for their support for this project.

A preliminary stage of this research received financial support from the Japanese Ministry of Education (Grant-in-Aid for Scientific Research), while I was at Nanzan University. I also gratefully acknowledge financial support by the John G. Tower for Political Studies at Southern Methodist University.

Finally, I thank Barbara and Miku for being what they are. They make my life rewarding.

1   Introduction

This book is a study of the economic policy and performance of industrial democracies of North America, Europe, Japan, and Oceania.[1] It seeks to explain how distinct characteristics of different governments in these countries affect economic policy, and whether and how the different government attributes affect their economic performance, such as economic growth, unemployment, and inflation. It further examines whether and how the changes in the international and domestic economies of the recent decades – such as economic globalization and increased economic competition – have changed the economic policy and performance of these industrial countries.

More specifically, this book is guided by the following three broad sets of questions:

1   How does the interaction of party governments (fiscal policy makers) and central banks (monetary policy makers) affect economic policy and outcomes? Do different party governments operating under different central banks have varying effects on economic policy and outcomes? What effects do party governments have on the fiscal–monetary policy mix which they fashion with central banks? How do the incentive and ability of governments to generate a certain fiscal–monetary policy mix with central banks vary across different party governments?

2   Has governments' economic policy changed over time? Has change in the international and domestic economies in the recent decades brought about change in policy and outcomes? Have governments ever affected economic outcomes? If they have, has their impact on outcomes changed over time in the new globalized economy?

3   If politics ever affects economic policy and outcomes, do the presence and nature of political impact vary across different policy areas and instruments?

This book is a systematic analysis of the political–economic determinants of economic policy and outcomes. It yields many interesting findings about how the political economy of industrial democracies works. But above all, the main findings that are of particular importance are the following:

1   *Central banks systematically affect party governments' fiscal policy.
    Independent central banks restrain party governments' fiscal policy.*
    The role of central banks has become a frequently studied subject. Political
    economists have explained that central banks' independence from party
    governments produces low inflation. There is no surprise that central banks
    affect monetary policy, because they control monetary policy if they are
    independent from party governments. But this book demonstrates that
    central banks also affect fiscal policy that is made by party governments.
    Central banks' influence on economic policy is far more extensive than pre-
    viously believed by scholars. Fiscal policy is made by party governments,
    and central banks do not have direct control over it. Thus, central banks'
    influence on fiscal policy takes place through their influence on the policy
    decision and action of party governments. That is, party governments take
    central banks' preferences and actions into account in making fiscal policy.
    Furthermore, central banks' influence on economic policy is affected by the
    types of party governments they face.

2   *Government partisanship does exert influence on economic policy and out-
    comes, contrary to some recent findings that show otherwise. Yet the pattern
    of partisan impact is also significantly different from what has been
    described by the conventional partisan explanation.*
    First, contrary to the conventional explanation that right governments
    conduct a conservative (disciplined) fiscal policy, this book shows that their
    fiscal policy was relatively expansionary for most of 1961–2001 and
    particularly so in the 1980s and 1990s. Their fiscal policy was expansionary
    because they taxed less than left and center governments (as consistent with
    the standard explanation), but when it comes to spending, they were often
    higher spenders than the left or center (counter to the standard explanation).
    Second, the impact of government partisanship on economic policy and out-
    comes depends partly on governments' interaction with central banks. Dif-
    ferent party governments have different preferences, characteristics, and
    incentives. These differences affect their willingness and ability to fashion a
    fiscal–monetary policy mix with central banks. Third, partisan impact can
    be time-variant. For instance, center and left governments' economic policy
    changed from a somewhat expansionary fiscal policy regime of the 1960s
    and 1970s to a disciplined policy regime in the 1980s and 1990s.

3   *The economic policy of industrial democracies generally shifted in a
    conservative (disciplined) direction in the 1980s and 1990s as a result of
    changes in the international and domestic economies.*
    In an increasingly globalized economy, governments of all stripes came
    under the competitive pressure to discipline their economic policy and
    improve the efficiency and competitiveness of their economies. As a result,
    governments' economic policy generally became disciplined and more com-
    patible with the (conservative) policy prescriptions preferred by central
    banks. The neoliberal policy shift was particularly visible among countries
    with political–economic actors whose economic policy was considered

unrestrained or who were considered a source of economic inefficiency and uncompetitiveness, such as coalition governments, center and left governments, and strong labor. Thus, these allegedly weak-performing governments and institutions had the ability to adjust to the imperatives of the globalized economy and new economic conditions.

However, the policy shift also differs from that which was described by the convergence thesis. Despite the conservative shift in economic policy across countries, globalization has not diminished the role of domestic politics in economic policy. Politics continues to affect economic policy and outcomes. Although economic forces may put pressure on governments to make similar policy adjustments, it is still politics that determines the terms of the adjustments. I will provide evidence to show both the conservative policy shift and the continuing impact of politics in economic policy and outcomes.

The entire book is devoted to the explanation of these and other patterns in the economic policy and outcomes of industrial democracies and to the analysis of empirical data to corroborate the arguments.

Industrial democracies, globalization, challenges, and policy response: the setting

Industrial democracies of North America, Europe, Japan, and Oceania face many economic difficulties today. Prior to the two oil shocks that hit the world economy in the 1970s, industrial democracies had enjoyed a period of steady economic growth, low unemployment, and only mild inflation. They had built an extensive welfare state (to varying degrees) in this favorable economic environment. But when the oil crises took place, the postwar period of stable growth, low unemployment, and low inflation came to an end. Since the 1970s, economic growth has steadily been much lower for most industrial democracies, and unemployment has been higher even in traditionally low-unemployment social democratic countries in Scandinavia. Inflation also became higher and remained so until the governments of industrial democracies came resolutely to combat inflation in the 1980s and their economic policy turned conservative (i.e. antiinflationary).

Slow economic growth and high unemployment (in tandem with the aging of the population and decline of birth rates) have posed a problem in the context of the generous welfare state built in the postwar period. They helped create expansions of government spending in most countries, and it put strains on government finance. The end of the fast growth period meant that governments could no longer count on an ever-growing economy and resulting tax revenue increases to finance extensive redistributive welfare states and to provide workers and families with as generous social protection as before. Questions such as how governments can solve the fiscal problems resulting from economic stagnation and previous fiscal overcommitments and promote economic growth in today's competitive, interdependent world have become increasingly important. The proper role of government in the provision of social protection has become a subject of more intense policy debate from the perspectives of both the normative responsibility of government and economic rationality.

Industrial democracies have also experienced the internationalization of capital and trade. Capital became increasingly mobile, moving freely across national borders. Governments of all stripes came to feel that in order to attract mobile international capital, they needed to show firm commitment to price stability and fiscal discipline and to make their economic policy consistent with the goals of maximizing the competitiveness and efficiencies of their economies. The competitive pressure has led many governments to lower tax rates as well as broaden tax bases, and liberalize their product and labor markets. At the same time, the openness of trade has increased, and the volume of international trade has dramatically expanded. Industrial democracies have now been exposed to competitive pressures from newly emerging economies where labor costs are low as well as from other industrial economies. Increased trade has reinforced the pressures on governments to make their economies competitive and efficient.

Political scientists have studied the determinants of economic policy and outcomes from several perspectives. Those who emphasize the constraining effects of globalization argue that the competitive pressures created by globalization and other changes in the domestic economies have led to the convergence of economic policy pursued by governments of various ideological stripes and by different countries (Kurzer, 1993; Scharpf, 1991). In this view, the globalized economy pressures all countries to make their economies and industries competitive to promote and sustain economic growth. It is argued that governments' latitude in choosing economic policy contracted, and they had little choice but to attach importance to price stability and fiscal restraint, because capital interests are averse to inflation and fiscal expansionism. Mobile capital is not friendly to large government spending, heavy taxation, deficits, price instability, and heavy social protection, any of which can potentially lead to lower returns on investment, market distortions, and economic inefficiencies. As a result, they argue, globalization and resulting convergence have diminished the role of politics in economic policy.

Other recent studies, in contrast, argue that the extent of convergence is not as large as claimed by the convergence thesis, and that the domestic political–economic institutions still matter even in a globalized economy (Boix, 1998, 2000; Franzese, 2002a; Garrett, 1998; Kitschelt *et al.*, 1999b; Pierson, 2001; Schmidt, 2002; Swank, 2002). Regardless of the veracity of convergence or divergence, today's governments feel the pressure to give priority to price stability and achieve fiscal discipline, improve the competitiveness and efficiency of the national economy, liberalize the domestic product and labor markets to increase competition and enhance efficiency, and restructure the welfare system to reduce labor costs, increase workers' incentives, and curb welfare spending. Governments – particularly social democratic ones – face the difficult problem of how they should mitigate the economic dislocation experienced by their populations and keep a balance between the competitiveness of the national economies and the social protection of their citizens. Achieving equality and economic growth does not have to conflict with each other (Boix, 1998; Kenworthy, 2004). Nordic countries, for instance, have in the past decade been relatively successful in achieving both. But it is still a challenge for all governments, nevertheless.

In a similar vein, scholars have studied political impact on economic policy and outcomes under the specific constraints of capital mobility and exchange rate mechanisms (these factors are conventionally considered "international" factors). Clark (2003) argues that electoral cycles in fiscal deficits, money supply, output growth, and unemployment take place only when politicians have sufficient control over policy instruments, and their control over policy instruments is determined by capital mobility, exchange rate regimes, and central bank independence. He argues further that government partisanship never affected economic policy or outcomes. In contrast, Oatley (1999) and Boix (2000) argue that partisanship did affect fiscal and monetary policies when capital mobility and exchange rate mechanisms kept policy tools available and effective.[2]

Political scientists have also studied the roles of political and institutional factors in economic policy and outcomes – such as government partisanship (social democratic, Christian democratic, conservative governments), attributes of individual governments (e.g. the number of governing parties, majority status, stability of governments), structure of the political system (electoral system, fragmentation of party system, the structure of the legislature, federalism, central bank independence), organization of labor (centralization of labor unions, coordination of wage bargaining), and the mode of interest aggregation (pluralist and corporatist systems).[3] Some of these scholars have claimed that certain types of governments and institutions are unconducive to fiscal discipline and good economic outcomes – such as multiparty coalition governments, minority governments, and pro-welfare interventionist governments. Many studies came out on their effects on the economy, but their findings are mixed.[4]

These previous studies have greatly advanced our knowledge of the role of politics in the economy. But we are still in the midst of the struggle to understand better the ways politics affect economic policy and outcomes (if at all). Previous findings are mixed. We also do not know whether and how political impact varies across time or across different policy tools (e.g. public services, government investment, social security, public subsidies).

This book is an effort to shed light on some of these unresolved questions. I believe that the mixed findings of previous studies and puzzles that remain in our understanding of political impact on economic policy and outcomes are partly due to previous studies' insufficient attention to three factors – (1) the interdependence of fiscal and monetary policies, and the interaction of fiscal and monetary policy makers; (2) the possible time-variance and context-specificity of the effects of political factors on economic policy and outcomes; (3) the different impact of political factors across different policy tools. The incorporation of these factors into analysis will not solve all problems. But I believe it will help us better understand political impact on economic policy and outcomes and gain insights into some of the workings of the political economy that have not previously been explored or uncovered.

The interdependence of fiscal and monetary policies and the interaction of party governments and central banks

The role of central banks is a popular subject in the study of comparative political economy. Political economists explain that central banks' independence from party governments produces low inflation, because independent central banks committed to low inflation can reduce the inflationary expectations that wage bargainers build into wage negotiations in anticipation of future inflation (Cukierman, 1992; Grilli *et al.*, 1991; Rogoff, 1985).[5] Likewise, the role of partisan governments in economic policy has been frequently examined (e.g. Hibbs, 1977; Goldthorpe, 1984; Alesina *et al.*, 1997; Boix, 1998, 2000; Garrett, 1998; Clark and Hallerberg, 2000; Franzese, 2002a, 2002b; Clark, 2003).

But very few studies have examined systematically and explicitly the implications of the interdependence of fiscal and monetary policies and the effects of the strategic interaction of party governments and central banks. Partial exceptions are game-theoretic expositions by economists (Nordhaus, 1994; Bennett and Loayza, 2002; Demertzis *et al.*, 1998; Dixit and Lambertini, 2002).[6] But these studies in economics are highly abstract (contextually thin) and purely theoretical, and the picture they describe of fiscal and monetary policy makers does not do justice to their real-life interaction and the real structural environment under which they operate.

An investigation of the interdependence of fiscal and monetary policies is important because: (1) both fiscal and monetary policies affect the macroeconomy; (2) the effectiveness or consequences of fiscal policy hinge on monetary policy concurrently implemented, and vice versa; (3) as a result, fiscal and monetary policy makers need to take into account each other's policy intentions and actions in deciding what policy they should respectively pursue and assessing what effects their policies will have on the economy, given the other's policy; and therefore (4) party governments' implementation of fiscal policy is constrained by the monetary policy conducted by central banks, and also monetary policy control depends on whether central banks are independent from political control or not. Thus, an analysis of the fiscal and monetary policy interaction is the task I undertake in this book.

Party governments wish and seek to produce good economic outcomes for the goals of control of government and reelection (as well as for the welfare of society). They try to achieve as favorable economic conditions as possible, setting aside the issue of how different parties conceive of "favorable" conditions. Consequently, they seek to pursue economic policy compatible with the goal of good economic performance. Since certain combinations of fiscal and monetary policies are unconducive to economic performance, they try to pursue a fiscal–monetary policy mix that is compatible with the goal of promoting economic performance.

But the compatibility of the policy preferences of party governments and central banks can be problematic, as the former tend to value economic growth and employment, and the latter price stability. In economists' game-theoretical models, if they did not cooperate or coordinate, central banks would raise interest rates to maintain price stability and to undermine party governments' expansionary fiscal policy, while party governments would increase their fiscal spending to boost output and employment even at the expense of higher inflation and to undermine central banks' deflationary monetary policy (Nordhaus, 1994; Bennett and Loayza, 2002; Demertzis *et al.*, 1998; Dixit and Lambertini, 2002). The result of this non-cooperative game, in their models, is high interest rates and high deficits, or lower output and higher inflation.

This policy conflict and the undesirable outcome of high interest rates and high deficits could certainly be a realistic scenario if party governments and central banks did not communicate, cooperate, or coordinate their economic policies. But such a non-cooperative situation is hardly a realistic representation of the policy interaction between the two actors.

I argue that this "high interest rates–high deficits" result does not have to be a necessary outcome. Party governments and central banks share the goal of good economic outcomes – good economic growth, low unemployment, and low inflation, though they conceive of the trade-offs among them differently. Furthermore, they communicate, cooperate, and coordinate with each other with an eye toward achieving desirable economic outcomes and avoiding a deleterious fiscal–monetary policy mix. This kind of quasi-coordination (intentional or not) takes place, partly because party governments and central banks are jointly responsible for the management of the national economy and both want to achieve good economic outcomes, including price stability, growth, and employment.

But even though all party governments would like to achieve certain combinations of good economic outcomes and to avoid a deleterious fiscal–monetary policy mix that results in negative economic outcomes, they differ in their incentive and capacity to fashion a fiscal–monetary policy mix compatible with the goal of good economic performance. They also differ in their incentive and capacity to conduct a fiscal policy compatible with a given central bank monetary policy, whether it be a result of explicit or implicit coordination. Thus, the incidence and nature of policy coordination depend on the attributes of party governments. Different partisan governments have different sets of constituencies with distinct interests and policy preferences, which makes different governments have different policy preferences and pursue different policies. Party governments' policy choice, in turn, is affected by the particular central banks they face. In this book, I explore how the interdependence of fiscal and monetary policies affects economic policy and outcomes.

Change across time

The second issue that requires analytical attention is the time-variance or invariance of political effects on economic policy and outcomes. Studies in comparative political economy have long used the Hibbsian assumptions of the policy preferences and behavior of left and right party governments in studying economic policy and outcomes – left governments are more concerned about employment and growth, and right governments about price stability (Hibbs, 1977). Left (social democratic) governments have been purported to be fiscally expansionary and to build an expansive welfare state.[7] Countries with strong Christian democratic parties should suffer similar economic problems, in this view, because Christian democratic parties also have large transfer payments (e.g. social security and unemployment benefits).[8] In contrast, it has conventionally been argued or assumed that conservative (right) parties care more about price stability than unemployment and tend to implement a low inflation, low spending policy even at the cost of higher unemployment.

Previous studies typically analyze the role of partisanship (as well as other factors), for the most part, by treating the entire period under analysis as one homogeneous period where the effects of political factors or lack thereof are assumed to be constant during the entire period (i.e. typically between around 1960 and a time point somewhere in the 1990s). This is an efficient assumption for the purpose of parsimonious theory building. But why should we assume the time-invariance of political effects on economic policy and outcomes? If partisan effects are time-variant, the conventional explanations that presume a single constant policy preference scheme for political parties for an extended period of time covering three or four decades can be misleading (be they the Hibbsian thesis or the rational partisan thesis). Some political factors may affect policy and performance at some times, but may not at other times. Even if statistical analysis examining the entire period (for instance, 1961–2001) does not find significant effects, an analysis may find significant effects if it entertains the possibility that their effects can be time-variant and/or differ across different policy instruments. The conventional partisan explanations assuming their fixed, time-invariant policy preferences may not be an accurate or sufficient description of partisan effects.

Time-invariance is indeed a theoretically convenient assumption that makes possible a parsimonious explanation of political effect. But it can be an erroneous assumption, if political impact changes over time. When one glances at the recent international and domestic economies, there is abundant evidence that the environment for economic policy making has changed in the past few decades. Of course, it is a different issue whether such structural change in the policy making environment has also altered the impact of political factors and actors on economic policy and outcomes. But there is no reason to assume a priori that structural change has not affected economic policy making or the behavior of policy makers. In political science, scholars widely believe that structure or an environment affects behavior. The importance of structure on individual behavior is also seen in game theory. While there is no good reason to assume a priori that partisan governments' policy does change, the transition from the 1960s and 1970s to the 1980s and 1990s represents a case where it did.

It is not too much of a leap of faith to speculate that political actors' preferences and behavior change, when political or economic conditions surrounding them change. Our world changes over time. So do our economy, technology, and knowledge. As they change, the economic positions and preferences of socioeconomic actors and constituencies change. If constituent interests change, political parties adjust their policies. Further, our ideas about how the economy works and what policy is effective in solving economic problems also change, and it may lead to policy change. If so, it is not realistic to assign the goals of employment and economic growth to left parties and the goal of price stability to right parties for an entire time period encompassing as much as four decades, such as the time period of this study (1961–2001).

From our history, we intuitively know that during the 1940s–1970s, Keynesian demand management was the economic policy orthodoxy among policy makers, and most industrial governments – conservative and social democratic – carried out economic policy along the lines of a Keynesian welfare state, albeit to varying degrees. We also intuitively know that economic policy in many industrial countries started shifting (to varying degrees) in a more market-conforming, neoliberal direction, when Keynesian policy was called into question by both the experience of the 1970s stagflation and the theoretical development in economics (rational expectation theory). So we casually know that political parties change their policy as the political–economic environment changes. To take into account the time or context contingencies, I investigate the potentially period- and context-variant effects of political–economic factors.[9]

There is another methodological reason to examine the potential time-variance of political impact. As Kittel (1999) explains, pooled analysis typically applied in comparative political economy averages out time- and country-specific effects. The coefficient in a pooled-analysis model represents the combined average partial effect of both the time-series and cross-section dimensions, and the averaging of information could mask time-specific effects that may actually exist (Kittel, 1999). It may be the case that previous studies either produced mixed findings or found no political–economic effects because in their methodological designs, the effects of those factors cancel each other out when estimated over the entire period under study. Estimating the political–economic variables across two periods, as I do in my empirical analysis, does not solve the conceptual problems of pooled analysis, but it does mitigate them. And my analysis reveals significant political effects on economic policy and outcomes that we could not detect in studies that treat the entire period under study as one homogeneous period where effects do not change.

Different properties of policy instruments

The third issue is the possible divergence of political impact across different policy tools. That is, the choice of different economic policy tools as dependent variables is one of the reasons why previous studies either have found no evidence of political impact or have produced divergent findings about political effects on economic policy. Many previous studies analyzed only aggregate indicators of macroeconomic policy instruments – such as total government spending and revenues, and fiscal deficits or gross debt. In other studies, scholars chose to examine only a few disaggregate policy tools – such as government final consumption (e.g. Bearce, 2002) or social security transfers. There have been relatively few studies that systematically examine the disaggregated spending and revenue items and investigate the effects of political–economic factors across different policy instruments (Alesina *et al.*, 1997; Garrett, 1998; Lane, 2002; Perotti and Kontopoulos, 1998; Clark, 2003).

A potential problem with the studies examining only aggregate data is that different disaggregate economic policy tools – e.g. government consumption expenditure, government fixed capital formation, public subsidies to industries, social security payments – have different characteristics and effects and may be used by party governments and politicians in different ways. Lane (2002), for instance, shows that different disaggregate spending and revenue items behave in different ways.

If party governments or politicians use economic policies to promote their power, electoral prospects, or whatever other goals, they do so because of the specific effects they expect those policies produce. If different policy tools have different properties and create different outcomes, politicians should use the policy tools that will produce desirable effects from their point of view. Then, there may be important partisan differences in such disaggregate economic policies, even when differences do not manifest themselves in aggregate data such as total spending and fiscal deficits.

Furthermore, studying only one or two selected disaggregate policy tools can also be misleading because there is no guarantee that the results obtained about one policy tool also apply to another policy tool. Thus, in this book, I analyze a variety of disaggregate policy instruments as well as aggregate ones. The empirical results show that partisan differences do exist and differ across policy instruments.

Plan of the book

The rest of this book is devoted to the theoretical exposition of economic policy and performance and empirical analysis. In Chapters 2 and 3, I offer a theoretical explanation of the interdependence of fiscal and monetary policies, party governments' economic policy behavior, and their interaction with central banks. I show how their strategic considerations and interaction produce certain fiscal and monetary policies. In Chapters 4 and 5, I present the empirical analysis.

In Chapter 2, I explain what kind of incentives party governments have in interacting with and responding to central banks. I explain how their interaction produces certain fiscal and monetary policies. Then, I show that different party governments have different incentive and capacity in deciding their interaction with and response to central banks, and explain how the difference affects economic policy. I explain why different governments – such as coalition governments, single-party governments, left governments, right governments, center governments – have different incentive and capacity and produce distinct impact on economic policy. I also consider the possibility of electoral cycles and the factors that may affect the presence of electoral cycles.

In Chapter 3, I explain that changes in the international and domestic economies were some of the factors that led governments to adjust their economic policy. I show what those economic changes were and how they changed the environment for governments' economic policy making. I then consider in more detail the role of political factors in economic policy and performance and why politics affects economic policy and performance. In doing so, I review the arguments set forth by previous scholars claiming that certain types of governments and political–economic factors are unconducive to good economic policy and outcomes. I present theoretical considerations that lead us to expect that those allegedly weak performers do not have to perform poorly, and that even if they performed poorly at one time or another, they had good reason to correct their policy behavior and improve performance.

Chapters 4 and 5 analyze empirical data to examine whether and how political and economic factors affect economic policy and outcomes in industrial democracies, and whether and how the impact of governments and other political actors has changed in the past few decades, as well as how policy and outcomes have changed. I present empirical evidence to corroborate my theoretical arguments described in Chapters 2 and 3.

Chapter 4 presents the basic results of the empirical analysis of the determinants of economic policy and performance, focusing mostly on the general patterns of the impact of political factors on economic policy and outcomes. The basic analysis seeks to understand the individual effects of the uninteracted political and economic factors examined in the previous chapters so as to grasp the general patterns of the political–economic factors at issue. The chapter also examines the empirical validity of the conventional arguments about the weaknesses in economic policy and performance among governments and institutions that are traditionally considered fiscally undisciplined and/or low-performers. It also lays the foundations for the empirical analysis of interactive effects in Chapter 5.

Chapter 5 analyzes the interactive effects of political and economic factors. I investigate how multiple factors or institutions in tandem affect policy and performance.

Chapter 6 concludes by discussing the implications of the study of the book. I discuss what the study explains and which questions it leaves unanswered. I suggest the avenues of future research that should be followed in order to understand better economic policy and outcomes.

2 Party governments–central banks interaction

The fiscal–monetary policy mix

The role of central banks has become one of the most frequently studied subjects in comparative political economy. Political economists explain that central banks' independence from party governments produces low inflation, because independent central banks committed to low inflation can reduce the inflationary expectations that wage bargainers build into wage negotiations in anticipation of future inflation (Cukierman, 1992; Grilli *et al.*, 1991; Rogoff, 1985). Independence from political control gives credibility to central banks' commitment to antiinflationary monetary policy. As a result, wage settlements will be lower than those that would be agreed upon in the absence of independent central banks, creating less inflationary pressure. Studies have also found that independent central banks restrain the behavior of labor unions (Iversen, 1999). Other studies show that the effects of central banks are, in turn, conditional upon labor wage coordination (Franzese and Hall, 2000; Iversen, 1999) or government partisanship (Way, 2000).

Many governments moved to increase the independence of central banks in the 1990s, as they became convinced of the macroeconomic benefits (price and exchange rate stability) of central bank independence and as economists' theoretical underpinning of the effects of central banks became elaborated. Figure 2.1 shows that all industrial countries (except Norway) that had previously had dependent central banks increased their independence by the end of the 1990s. Between 1971 and 2001, there is no instance of reduction in central bank independence. The shift in scholars' and policy makers' attitudes toward monetary policy can also be seen in the establishment of the Economic and Monetary Union (EMU) by European Union countries (1999), involving the introduction of the single currency (euro) and the concentration of monetary policy making power in the union-wide European Central Bank (ECB).

There is no surprise that central banks affect monetary policy. Central banks have control over monetary policy if they are sufficiently independent from party governments. Independent central banks have been argued to enhance the antiinflationary credibility of monetary policy and facilitate price stability. Such credibility may even make it possible for central banks to maintain interest rates relatively low, because credibility induces low-inflation expectations among market actors and central banks do not have actually to raise interest rates to

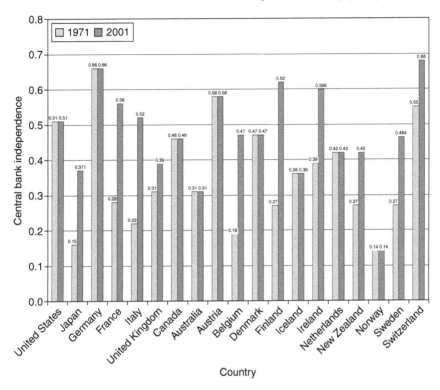

Figure 2.1 Central bank independence, 1971 and 2001 (sources: the data are Cukierman's
(1992) index of legal central bank independence (LVAU), updated by William
Bernhard and David Leblang for Belgium, France, Italy, and New Zealand,
and by the author for Finland, Ireland, Japan, Sweden, and the United
Kingdom to incorporate the changes resulting from central bank reforms in the
1990s).

create low-inflation expectations. In addition to the economic benefits of price
stability (discussed later), positive investment and output benefits can be
expected from low interest rates because they boost investment and output, and
this in turn can have positive effects on employment.

One of the main findings of this book is that central banks' influence on
economic policy goes beyond the area of monetary policy and is far more
extensive than previously thought by scholars. Namely, central banks affect
not only monetary policy but also fiscal policy, and restrain electoral expansion in fiscal policy. Fiscal policy is made by party governments, and central
banks do not have direct control over it. Thus, if central banks ever affect
fiscal policy, it has to be through their impact on the policy decision and
action of party governments and other fiscal policy makers. I will explain in
this chapter how central banks' influence on party governments' fiscal policy
takes shape. This book addresses important issues in several strands of the

literature in comparative political economy – the roles of central banks, party governments, and political–economic institutions in economic policy making and performance.

The primary feature of central banks' influence on fiscal policy is that independent central banks, for the most part, restrain fiscal policy. They also restrain electoral expansion engineered by politicians in some spending policy instruments. Central banks also affect economic policy and performance through their interaction with other political–economic actors, such as multiparty coalition governments, various partisan governments, and labor organization. In this book, I explain how central banks affect fiscal policy, monetary policy, and a fiscal–monetary policy mix through their interaction with party governments and other political actors. In doing so, I also illustrate how central banks are affected by party governments and politicians.

I will first explain why the particular combinations of fiscal and monetary policies (fiscal–monetary policy mix) are important in understanding how and what economic policy is made and how policy affects economic outcomes. Later in the chapter, I explain the interaction of party governments and central banks in economic policy making and elucidate their strategic policy making environment and the opportunities and constraints they face. Then, I explain how their policy making environment and interaction affect their fiscal and monetary policy making. I also show how the changes in the international and domestic economies in recent decades have altered the dominant fiscal–monetary policy mix used by governments and central banks. I then go on to explain the effects of interaction between fiscal and monetary policy makers on policy by focusing on the incentive and capacity of different partisan governments and of governments with distinct attributes in fashioning fiscal and monetary policies with central banks. I show that depending on the independence of central banks, different partisan governments produce distinct economic policy and performance because they have different incentive and capacity in interacting with central banks and responding to their monetary policy. At the end of the chapter, I explore the presence of electoral cycles in economic policy and performance. I particularly discuss in what form electoral cycles should manifest themselves. I explain that electoral cycles are time-variant. I also argue that electoral cycles differ across different policy tools because different policy tools have distinct properties in terms of their effects, effectiveness in achieving economic or political goals, and ease of political use.

The fiscal–monetary policy mix

The particular combination of fiscal and monetary policies – the fiscal–monetary policy mix – is important in understanding economic policy making and outcomes for mainly three reasons. First, both fiscal and monetary policies affect the macroeconomy. Second, the effectiveness of fiscal policy depends on the monetary policy concurrently implemented, and vice versa. Third, as a result, fiscal and monetary policy makers need to take into account each other's policy moves and intentions in deciding what policy they should respectively pursue and assessing what effects their policies will have on the economy in tandem with the other's policy.

Governments pursue multiple macroeconomic goals – economic growth, employment, and price stability. The three goals can conflict with each other. High growth and low unemployment, much of the time, can go together and thus can be attainable at the same time. But they are likely to put upward pressures on prices. Different governments conceive of the trade-offs among the three goals they prefer in slightly different ways (Hibbs, 1977), and seek to achieve the combinations of the three goals in accordance with their political and economic needs.

Economic policy makers (party governments and central banks) manage the macroeconomy by using two policy tools – fiscal and monetary policies. Both fiscal and monetary policies affect the economy. Fiscal and monetary policies may be used to balance each other (a loose fiscal–tight monetary policy mix or a tight fiscal–loose monetary mix) or to complement each other (a loose fiscal–loose monetary policy mix or a tight fiscal–tight monetary policy mix). Since both fiscal and monetary policies affect the economy and a particular fiscal policy may be undermined by a particular monetary policy and vice versa, fiscal policy makers need to take monetary policy into account in making fiscal policy, and monetary policy makers need to consider fiscal policy in making monetary policy.

It is important to consider particular combinations of fiscal and monetary policies also because fiscal and monetary policies tend to move in relation to each other; that is, they tend to move in a way to respond to each other. The movement of fiscal and monetary policies in relation to each other is still a contentious issue in economics and political economy. There are not many studies that empirically investigate their movements, but Melitz (1997) finds that fiscal and monetary policies tend to move in opposite directions. This book finds similar patterns of movements of the two economic policy tools. They move in a way to balance each other much of the time – when one is tight, the other tends to be loose or neutral. In this book, I elucidate which policy mix was used across different periods, why it was used, and how change in the policy mix came about.

When governments boost economic output and employment with expansionary fiscal policy, it may create inflationary pressures, so they may have to carry out overall economic policy in such a way as not to cause inflation. Since fiscal policy is already used to boost the economy, monetary policy needs to be employed to control inflation. This results in a loose fiscal–tight monetary policy mix. If, on the other hand, governments use expansionary monetary policy to stimulate output and employment, fiscal policy needs to be employed in such a way as to mitigate inflation pressures. This generates a tight fiscal–loose monetary policy mix. In addition, governments also sometimes use a loose fiscal–loose monetary policy mix to fight recessions, or a tight fiscal–tight monetary policy mix to control inflation. In these cases, both fiscal and monetary policies are used in a compatible, complementary manner to achieve economic goals.

Even though party governments and policy makers may like to achieve high economic growth and low unemployment, they cannot afford to have high inflation for a long time because high inflation can cause economic problems through multiple channels and eventually impair output and employment and undermine their economic goals. Inflation disturbs price signals and causes market distortions and resource allocation inefficiencies. It also creates economic uncertainties that can discourage investment and suppress growth. High inflation also means high nominal wages and product costs, which will in turn push down demand, output, and employment unless central banks accommodate the high wages and prices with a non-restrictive monetary policy (Iversen, 1999). Since wages do not quickly adjust downward, wages can remain higher than market-clearing levels, and this can create unemployment. Inflation can also invite capital outflows and subsequently currency depreciation. In order to stem capital flight and currency depreciation, governments will have to raise interest rates, which will depress investment and output. They will also have to raise interest rates to control inflation, which again depresses investment and output. Therefore, party governments need to pursue output growth and employment with an eye also toward price stability, because inflation creates economic problems and eventually will be unconducive to output growth and employment.

Central banks and party governments: fiscal–monetary policy interaction

Party governments are goal-seeking actors that wish and seek to produce good economic outcomes for the purposes of reelection and government control. Economic conditions and the incumbent government's economic management figure in citizens' voting decision. Even if economic conditions were not a crucial factor for citizens' voting decision, political parties and politicians would fear that they might importantly affect citizens' voting decision. Even if we assumed that electoral incentives were entirely missing in party governments' and politicians' motivations, most of them would still probably seek to achieve good economic conditions most of the time because of their normative sense of politicians' responsibility for protecting the well-being of citizens. So they would try to achieve as favorable economic conditions as possible, setting aside the issue of how different parties conceive of "favorable" economic conditions. Thus, party governments try to pursue economic policy compatible with the goal of good economic outcomes.

Certain combinations of fiscal and monetary policies can be detrimental to economic performance. As a result, party governments try to carry out a fiscal–monetary policy mix that is compatible with the goal of promoting economic performance, other things being equal. I will later explain how different political–economic actors may conceive of good economic performance and how their conceptions affect economic policy making and performance.

Party governments' policy choice and central bank independence

But party governments in different countries differ in their control of economic policy instruments available to them. One of the factors that affect the availability of policy instruments is the independence of central banks. Some countries have independent central banks, and others dependent ones (Cukierman, 1992). If central banks are not independent from party governments, party governments retain control over both fiscal and monetary policies, and can fashion a fiscal–monetary policy mix they like (that is, setting aside the constraints from exchange rate regimes and capital mobility for the moment). Party governments can maneuver both fiscal and monetary policies in different combinations as they see fit. For instance, they can use expansionary fiscal policy to boost output and employment, and tight monetary policy to keep inflation in check, or vice versa. They can also countercyclically use a both loose fiscal–loose monetary policy mix to ride out recessions or a tight fiscal–tight monetary policy mix to control inflation, if they decide to mobilize both policy tools to solve particular economic problems.

Dependent central banks still pursue price stability, and that is their primary goal. But since party governments have power over them, their antiinflationary monetary policy can be compromised more often or to a larger extent (than in the case of independent central banks), if party governments wish not to use a contractionary monetary policy. So I expect their monetary policy to have the tendency to be less restrictive and more accommodative. But this does not mean that dependent central banks' monetary policy is always loose, because depending on the economic or policy making conditions, party governments also want to employ monetary policy to control inflation, particularly when they use an expansionary fiscal policy for political or electoral purposes.

If, on the other hand, central banks are independent, party governments only have control over fiscal policy for the most part (the degree of central banks' monetary policy autonomy depends on exactly how independent they are from party governments). Independent central banks may pursue a monetary policy that party governments do not prefer. But if the central banks are truly independent, party governments are incapable of changing the monetary policy they do not like. Party governments can still potentially try to override central bank policy by changing the statutory status of central banks. Central bank independence is accorded by law, and if politicians wish and can agree, they can try to reduce central bank independence legislatively.[1] But in practice, that does not happen, if ever, once party governments and politicians grant independence to their central banks, because of the transaction costs involved in changing the statutory status of central banks and the economic benefits of central bank independence.[2] Many countries increased central bank independence in the 1990s, but no country has reduced it (see Figure 2.1). Because of the importance market actors attach to price stability and central bank independence, it is now increasingly difficult for governments to keep central banks dependent or reduce their independence, if governments wish to maintain credibility in their commitments to price stability and to promote their economic performance and stability in today's globalized economy. In the current study, since it does not often happen empirically and it does not affect the contentions of this book, I do not consider the possibility that politicians seek to deprive statutorily central banks of their independence because of the transaction costs and the potential economic costs of doing so.

Potential conflict of the goals of fiscal and monetary policy makers

If central banks are independent and party governments do not have control over monetary policy, the next strategy party governments can take is to implement a fiscal policy in a way that it will produce desirable economic outcomes given the monetary policy pursued by independent central banks. As a result, party governments' goal-seeking can create a fiscal–monetary policy mix that has the potential to produce favorable economic outcomes such as high economic growth, low unemployment, or low inflation. Again, the exact choice of preferred outcomes can vary between different partisan governments as the three goals may not be simultaneously attainable and there are trade-offs among them.

But the compatibility of the policy positions of party governments and central banks can be problematic. Many economists argue that there exists inherent conflict between party governments' and central banks' policy goals, which leads to undesirable economic outcomes – high interest rates and high deficits, or lower output and higher inflation (Nordhaus, 1994; Bennett and Loayza, 2002; Demertzis *et al.*, 1998; Dixit and Lambertini, 2002). Economists' explanation generally goes as follows. Central banks' priority is price stability. Central banks value employment and output less than politicians because they do not face elections. Party governments, in contrast, value output and employment because they face periodic elections, though their relative preferences for the three goals of output, unemployment, and inflation vary across different partisan governments. As a result of the difference in policy goals, central banks and party governments use their policy instruments – monetary and fiscal policies, respectively – to counter each other's policy action. In economists' non-cooperative game-theoretic models, this results in a policy mix that is not conducive to economic performance. Central banks raise interest rates to maintain price stability and to undermine party governments' expansionary fiscal policy. Party governments increase their fiscal spending to boost output and employment even at the expense of higher inflation and to undermine central banks' deflationary monetary policy, resulting in high deficits.[3] The degree of policy conflict increases when party governments are left-leaning because their policy preferences and the monetary authority's positions diverge more than those of right governments and central banks, resulting in more undesirable outcomes.

This policy conflict and the undesirable outcome of high interest rates and high deficits could certainly be a realistic scenario if party governments and central banks did not communicate, cooperate, or coordinate their economic policies. But such a non-cooperative situation is hardly a realistic representation of the policy interaction between the two actors.

Possibility of policy coordination between party governments and central banks: an optimistic view

I argue that this "high interest rates–high deficits" result does not have to be a necessary outcome because both party governments and central banks share the goal of good economic outcomes – good economic growth, low unemployment, and low inflation, though they conceive of the exact levels of these three indicators and trade-offs among them differently. Further, they communicate, cooperate, and coordinate with each other with an eye toward achieving desirable economic outcomes and avoiding a deleterious fiscal–monetary policy mix. Price stability is central banks' primary policy goal, but even they cannot ignore the other goals of growth and employment. They manage the national economy along with or in cooperation with party governments. They are jointly responsible for economic management with party governments. That is why we observe central banks countercyclically adjusting their monetary policy when recessionary signals become strong (though they still try not to invite inflation). While we observe that antiinflationary central banks can sometimes be willing to invite recession to control inflation as in Germany in the 1970s or in the United States in the early 1980s, they also actively relax monetary policy to stimulate the economy to avoid recession or when in recession.

Central banks attach importance to economic growth and unemployment also for the purposes of self-preservation and the maintenance of institutional reputation. If party governments, politicians, and the public experience recessions, they will demand central banks' countercyclical monetary intervention. As these actors' calls for countercyclical monetary loosening become strong, it may become difficult for central banks to resist such monetary policy demands, and the degree of freedom in running their own monetary policy may become increasingly small. If this situation worsens, central banks' monetary policy autonomy may even be impaired. Independent central banks may have the legal authority and capacity to pursue antiinflation monetary policy even at the expense of recession. But even they would have difficulty carrying out their own monetary policy without the support of politicians and the public. Even independent central banks need certain levels of support and approval by politicians and the public if they wish to preserve their monetary policy autonomy. Otherwise, central banks might lose support and legitimacy among politicians and the public.[4] They might lose trust and reputation as one of the major domestic institutions to manage the economy. In the worst case, political parties and politicians could take statutory action to deprive central banks of monetary policy autonomy.[5] So at times, it can be in central banks' interest to cooperate with party governments and politicians in order to preserve their monetary autonomy and institutional reputation. Bernhard (2002) documents instances of the German Bundesbank's such strategic calculations in their monetary policy making, where they carefully assess the political and economic conditions surrounding them in deciding their stance against party governments on economic policy issues. He argues that central banks' willingness to accommodate or reject party governments' monetary policy demands hinges on the political conditions and strategic considerations (including whether central banks' policy can gain support from political parties), which affect the credibility and therefore likelihood of party governments' threat to punish central banks.

Party governments and politicians face similar circumstances, which encourage them to cooperate with central banks. Or it should at least discourage party governments from pursuing a fiscal policy that is inconsistent with central bank monetary policy or that has deleterious consequences for economic performance when employed with a given monetary policy. Party governments and politicians would wish to boost economic growth and employment by running expansionary fiscal policy, if the economy is in recession or major elections are upcoming. But as we have seen above in economists' conceptualization of the economic policy competition between party governments and central banks, if party governments and central banks were in a non-cooperative game where they did not cooperate or coordinate, fiscal expansion by party governments would meet with central banks' contractionary monetary policy. This would place serious deflationary pressure on the national economies. The worst outcome that could result from this would be recession (low growth, high unemployment) with fiscal deficits. (Contractionary monetary policy exerts deflationary pressure: high interest rates suppress investment and consumption and consequently output; high interest rates also lead to currency appreciation with a flexible exchange rate, which in turn depresses net exports and output, and this deflationary pressure from currency appreciation persists until increased demand for foreign products and resultingly foreign currencies push the exchange rate down back in equilibrium; low money supply similarly suppresses investment and consumption through increased demand for money, high real interest rates, and tight credit.)

But neither party governments nor central banks would like to bring about this outcome. So this potential deflationary reaction by central banks and its harmful macroeconomic consequences should deter party governments from resorting to an undisciplined fiscal policy. If governments withhold an expansionary fiscal policy, central banks do not have to run a contractionary monetary policy, avoiding the deflationary pressure that would otherwise be created by their contractionary monetary policy. This helps improve economic performance. Furthermore, party governments' restrained fiscal policy releases monetary policy for use as a countercyclical tool rather than as a tool to control inflation. Freed from the inflationary concerns from party governments' expansionary fiscal policy, central banks can actively use monetary policy to promote economic growth in exchange for party governments' fiscal restraint. Thus, central banks do not have to conduct a contractionary monetary policy, and governments do not have to run high deficits that could drive up interest rates and suppress investment and growth.

H₁: *Independent central banks should generally deter party governments from implementing an expansionary fiscal policy, because the latter want to avoid a contractionary monetary policy response by the former and resulting deflationary pressures. Thus, independent central banks should facilitate fiscal discipline.*

H₂: *If independent central banks discipline party governments' fiscal policy, they generally should also facilitate economic outcomes (lower inflation, lower unemployment, and higher output growth) or not negatively affect outcomes (no effect on outcomes).*

This is so because fiscal discipline keeps inflationary pressures low and independent central banks can use monetary policy as a countercyclical tool rather than as a tool to control inflation. In the absence of a contractionary monetary policy, interest rates stay low, facilitating investment and output. Fiscal discipline keeps government deficits low, and low deficits also keep interest rates low.

Central banks or their potential contractionary response has been argued to also restrain other political–economic actors than political parties and party governments. Scholars argue that independent central banks restrain labor unions' behavior in wage negotiations (e.g. Iversen, 1999; Franzese, 2002a; Franzese and Hall, 2000). For instance, in Germany, labor's anticipation that the Bundesbank would tighten monetary policy to counter inflationary wage increases deters labor from demanding high wage increases. The same constraint and deterrence should work on party governments. Knowing central banks' unwillingness to compromise price stability, party governments should restrain their fiscal policy because their expansionary fiscal policy could invite a deflationary monetary policy response by central banks, and such a monetary policy in turn could suppress investment, output, and employment. Party governments have an even greater incentive than labor to ensure that their fiscal policy and central banks' monetary policy do not conflict with each other so much as to impair economic performance, because both of them are responsible for the conditions of the national economy. Party governments can also internalize the costs of expansionary fiscal policy and of a resulting negative policy mix better than labor unions because the former are much smaller in number and can more directly trace the negative results of their fiscal policy than the latter. Labor unions may be able to foresee the potential negative consequences of their inflationary wage behavior, but individual unions still may not have a great incentive to restrain their wage behavior unless their wage determination is highly centralized and coordinated at the national level (Calmfors and Driffill, 1988; Iversen, 1999). Even when labor is coordinated, labor unions' large size can constrain their ability to internalize the costs of inflationary wage demands and to restrain their wage behavior. The effects of party governments' fiscal policy are also more directly traceable.

Thus, I expect fiscal and monetary policies to show certain discernable patterns in their relation to each other, which should make sense in terms of their strategic interaction and of their effects on economic outcomes. The relationship between central banks and party governments should also produce interactive effects on economic policy. But the ability and willingness of party governments to fashion a fiscal policy compatible with central bank monetary policy vary across different party governments, because their ability and willingness to do so depend on their policy preferences, their institutional environment, and thus their incentive in economic policy making. Thus, the interactive effects of party governments and central banks should also vary, depending on which party governments are in office, the structure of particular governments, and what kind of structural environment they face. I will discuss what kind of differences these factors make in the next part of this chapter.

Form of fiscal–monetary policy coordination

Implicit or explicit cooperation and coordination between party governments and central banks can bring about fiscal restraint by party governments or a fiscal–monetary policy mix conducive to positive economic outcomes. Coordination of fiscal and monetary policies can most directly be obtained from explicit communication and discourse between party governments and central banks. Between party governments and central banks, there exist communication and policy discussion on how macroeconomic policy should be handled at a given time. Bernhard's (2002) study cites instances where party governments and central banks listen to each other, negotiate, and try to persuade each other and gain each other's support for their respective policies. Through such dialogue, independent central banks may be able to persuade party governments of the adverse effects of an expansionary fiscal policy and talk them out of a loose fiscal policy. Or central banks may be able to agree to use monetary policy to stimulate the economy during a recession in exchange for party governments' fiscal restraint. If party governments agree not to use an inflationary fiscal policy, central banks will not have to worry about inflation and can loosen monetary policy for economic stimulus. Alternatively, central banks can threaten a tightening of monetary policy to undermine fiscal expansion if party governments resort to such a fiscal policy. Or party governments may be able to persuade central banks to relax monetary policy to accommodate an expansionary fiscal policy during recession.

Even in the absence of explicit coordination, cooperative policy selection by the two policy authorities can be achieved from implicit communication and coordination. Both party governments and central banks publicly express their views on what policy should be pursued and what policy action the other policy authority should take. Their views and warnings thus publicly expressed can function as implicit communication and, as a result, restrain each other's policy action and deter an uncoordinated fiscal–monetary policy mix unconducive to economic performance. Both party governments and central banks are strategic actors that decide their actions according to their assessment of the other policy maker's intentions and potential action. In a policy environment like this, it is reasonable to see the relative movements of fiscal and monetary policies that indicate coordination.

The incidence of a beneficial compatible policy mix

The coordination (implicit or explicit) of fiscal and monetary policies by party governments and central banks that are compatible with the goals of good economic performance should be better achieved if central banks are independent from party governments. This is so because party governments can still get tempted to pursue an expansionary fiscal policy for political reasons (e.g. upcoming elections), no matter how well they know of the potentially inflationary consequences of certain fiscal policy. If central banks are dependent, party governments can pursue such a fiscal policy without fearing a deflationary monetary counter-response by central banks and may even obtain desired economic effects, because they also control monetary policy. By contrast, if central banks are independent, party governments will have a harder time implementing an expansionary fiscal policy because it will invite a contractionary monetary policy by central banks and result in recessionary pressures. Independent central banks will pursue whatever monetary policy they deem necessary to maintain price stability regardless of the preferences of party governments. The incidence of such coordination also hinges on the types of party governments central banks face since as I will show in the next part of this chapter, the ability and willingness of party governments to produce certain fiscal policy depend on their policy positions, organizational characteristics, and policy incentive.

There is another mechanism by which party governments' fiscal policy can be restrained. An important component of the measure of central bank independence is legal restrictions on central banks' purchase of government securities and their lending to government and the public sector (Cukierman, 1992). Thus, by definition, in countries with independent central banks, it should be legally more difficult for governments to run deficits, which lead them to restrain their fiscal policy.

Temptation for economic policy manipulation

There is an alternative explanation that would also be consistent with the results showing a relationship between central bank independence and disciplined economic policy. This is the explanation that in countries where central banks are independent, there was greater prior agreement among party governments and politicians on fiscal discipline, and party governments and politicians granted independence to central banks exactly because they intended to bring fiscal discipline in their economic policy. In this explanation, it is not that central bank independence made fiscal discipline possible, but that party governments and politicians were predisposed toward fiscal conservatism in the first place and granted independence to their central banks as part of their effort at fiscal discipline. I believe that this story must be, to a certain extent, true especially in the countries that granted independence to central banks in the 1990s where reform was an explicit result of political parties' and politicians' knowledge of the positive economic effects of central bank independence. For instance, Bernhard (2002) writes that in joining the European Monetary System (EMS) in 1979 and making the Bank of Italy more independent in 1981, Italy's Christian Democratic reformers hoped that monetary reforms "would enforce discipline on the party and provide a consistency to economic policy that would improve the macroeconomic environment" (Bernhard, 2002: p. 133).

But once created, independent central banks begin to have a life of their own and exert independent effects on party governments' economic policy. If central banks were not independent, party governments and politicians could still be tempted to run expansionary economic policy during a recession or an election year. Bernhard (2002) recounts, for instance, that the conservative Thatcher administration of the United Kingdom – which had been willing to invite a deep recession to control inflation right after coming to power in 1979 – conducted expansionary fiscal and monetary policies and caused high inflation in the late 1980s (the Bank of England was not independent at the time). The succeeding Major administration also ran a loose monetary policy in 1992–1993 to boost electoral support and again in 1995–1997 (Bernhard, 2002). This shows that party governments do resort to expansionary economic policy if central banks are not independent, and even a conservative government (which is allegedly antiinflationary) may not be sufficient to maintain economic policy discipline without an independent central bank. Political parties and politicians should also be more easily tempted to expand the economy at the expense of inflation than central bankers who do not face elections. A jump in fiscal deficits under the U.S. Bush administration (2001–2004) is another example of conservative party governments' recourse to expansionary fiscal policy. (In this case, the U.S. Federal Reserve Board is independent and should restrain party governments' fiscal expansion. But as I will explain later, conservative (right) governments are actually fiscally less disciplined than left or center governments and have difficulty generating a favorable fiscal–monetary policy mix compatible with central bank monetary policy.)

If central banks are independent, in contrast, party governments do not have access to monetary policy and would have to resort to fiscal policy for economic expansion. In this case, party governments would also have difficulty loosening fiscal policy too much because they would know that such a move would meet with central banks' contractionary monetary response and invite negative economic consequences. Politicians can actually try to eliminate leeway in their economic policy making by giving independence to central banks and making it difficult to expediently resort to unrestrained economic policy making. The Italian politicians' monetary reform mentioned above is such a case. And I suspect that many countries that carried out central bank reform in the 1990s had this goal in mind.

The two explanations – one that central bank independence induces fiscal discipline, and the other that politicians or governments that want to increase fiscal discipline create independent central banks – are not necessarily mutually exclusive and do not have to conflict with each other.[6] I believe both are true to a certain extent. Politicians realized that their governments needed to achieve fiscal discipline and, as a means to achieve the goal, increased the independence of their central banks. And in order to overcome the temptation to expand the economy for electoral reasons and continuously preserve fiscal discipline, they actually needed the presence of or constraints from independent central banks.

The dominant policy mix and its shift

In the 1960s, fiscal policy was relatively expansionary, as Keynesian expansion was an accepted policy tool, and as governments of industrial democracies did not yet have large accumulated debt.[7] While low discount rates during the decade (Figure 2.2) make monetary policy look loose at a glance, monetary policy was neutral to sufficiently tight, because governments did not yet face high inflation and did not need to use a tighter monetary policy to control inflation (Figure 2.3). Thus, governments had a policy mix comprising a relatively loose fiscal policy and a neutral to sufficiently tight monetary policy in the 1960s.

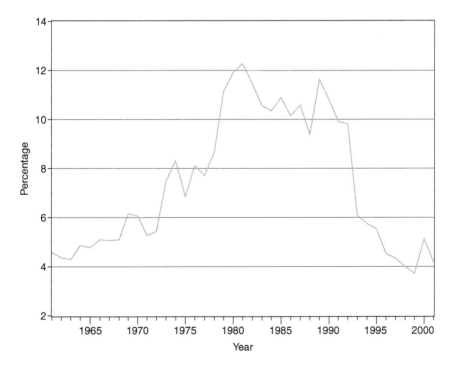

Figure 2.2 Central bank discount rates, 18-country averages, 1960–2001 (sources: see variables, definitions, and sources in Tables 4.1 and 4.2).

Figure 2.3 Monetary policy stance, 18-country averages (+ tight/– loose) (sources: see variables, definitions, and sources in Tables 4.1 and 4.2).

In the 1970s, governments responded to stagflation and recession caused by the oil crisis with Keynesian deficit spending to stimulate the economy. As a result, fiscal policy became very expansionary, and deficits increased (Figure 2.4). Governments (or central banks) progressively tightened monetary policy to contain inflation and continued to raise discount rates for much of the 1970s. By 1981, discount rates hit the highest in recent history. But in light of the large magnitude of inflation, monetary policy was not tight enough (Figure 2.3).[8] This is why governments had to keep raising discount rates until 1981. So monetary policy was tightened progressively, but was not tight enough in terms of outcome (inflation). The dominant policy mix in the 1970s was a loose fiscal–loose monetary policy mix (though monetary policy was tightened toward the end of the decade).

The 1980s was a transitional period, where the dominant policy mix gradually shifted away from a loose fiscal–loose monetary policy mix of the 1970s (and a loose fiscal–tight monetary policy mix of the beginning of the 1980s) and toward a tight fiscal–neutral monetary policy mix characteristic of the 1990s. Although the 1980s started with a loose fiscal policy, fiscal policy became progressively tighter during the 1980s, because this is a period when governments gradually abandoned Keynesian deficit spending and adopted neoliberal economic policy prescribing fiscal discipline and less government intervention.

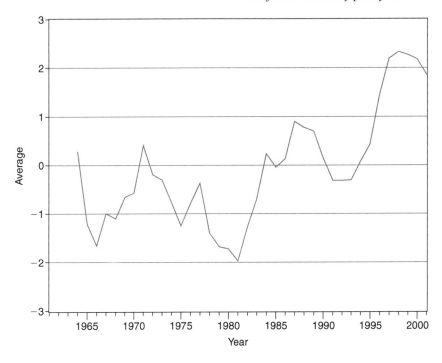

Figure 2.4 Primary balance, 18-country averages (+ surplus/– deficit) (sources: see variables, definitions, and sources in Tables 4.1 and 4.2).

Monetary policy was generally tight in the 1980s, because the 1970s ended with the antiinflationary monetary policy adopted by central banks to control high inflation. But toward the end of the 1980s, the further tightening of monetary policy was ended, and monetary policy was gradually relaxed (less contractionary), as governments successfully contained inflation. Also, governments did not have to keep tight monetary policy because their fiscal policy became more restrained from the second half of the 1980s on. So the policy mix in the 1980s started with a loose fiscal–tight monetary policy mix and moved toward a tight fiscal–neutral monetary policy mix.

In the 1990s, the economic policy of industrial governments shifted to a tight fiscal–neutral monetary policy mix. Fiscal spending was restrained, and deficits were reduced; and discount rates were progressively lowered. Governments did not have to keep a tight monetary policy, because price stability (low inflation) was achieved, and fiscal restraint and the reduced inflationary pressure from fiscal policy made a tight monetary policy unnecessary.

There were also cross-national differences in economic policy among industrial democracies (which are uncovered in the statistical analyses of Chapters 4 and 5). During the 1960s and 1970s, countries with independent central banks had a tighter monetary policy than countries with only dependent central banks. Independent central banks tightened monetary policy to respond to the inflationary effects of expansionary fiscal policy by party governments and to inflation itself. It implies that dependent central banks did not or could not do the same due to their lack of independence from party governments.

But this contractionary response by independent central banks disappeared in the 1980s and 1990s. The reason is that the economic policy of industrial democracies generally became antiinflationary, regardless of the independence of central banks. Party governments' fiscal policy during the period became restrained, and central banks did not have to keep tight monetary policy to offset inflationary effects of fiscal policy. It is also because industrial democracies successfully controlled inflation and did not have to resort to a tight monetary policy. Thus, monetary policy during the second half of the 1980s and the 1990s was neutral, compared to the 1970s and the first half of the 1980s. Fiscal restraint released monetary policy from its role as a tool of inflation control to a certain extent, and central banks could now use it for countercyclical actions as well as price stability; thus, a tight fiscal–neutral monetary policy mix in the second half of the 1980s and in the 1990s.

Why is there more neoliberal compatibility between fiscal and monetary policies in the second half of the 1980s and the 1990s?

The economic policy preferences of party governments and central banks became closer to each other in an antiinflationary conservative direction in the 1980s and 1990s than in the 1960s and 1970s. The shift in the fiscal–monetary policy mix is roughly consistent with the expectations of open-economy macroeconomics. As open-economy economics tells us, the effectiveness of fiscal and monetary policies in stimulating aggregate demand is constrained by the combination of a country's level of capital mobility and exchange rate regime (Mundell, 1963). Under perfect capital mobility, fiscal policy is an effective countercyclical tool if a country has a fixed exchange rate mechanism since central banks have to accommodate fiscal expansion by party governments in order to maintain a fixed exchange rate. Under this condition, monetary policy is ineffective because it is tied by the exigency of defending a fixed exchange rate. In contrast, if a country has a floating exchange rate system, monetary policy is an effective countercyclical tool, and fiscal policy is not, as the expansionary benefits of fiscal expansion are sapped by currency appreciation and subsequent reductions in net exports.

Fiscal policy was a preferred countercyclical policy tool among industrial democracies during the 1960s and 1970s, partly because Keynesian policy enjoyed popularity and credibility and partly because fiscal policy was an effective demand management tool under conditions both of less capital mobility and of the Bretton Woods' fixed exchange rate system. Capital restrictions were much more common among countries, and all industrial countries had a fixed exchange rate under the Bretton Woods system. Even under the condition of perfect capital mobility, the fixed rate system should make fiscal policy an effective countercyclical policy tool according to open-economy macroeconomics. As a result, industrial governments extensively used Keynesian expansion for countercyclical economic actions. The task of price stability was assumed more by monetary policy.

But in the early 1970s, the Bretton Woods system collapsed, and many countries shifted from a fixed rate mechanism to a floating rate system.[9] At the same time, capital mobility increased in the course of the 1980s and 1990s. Under the conditions of capital mobility and a floating rate system, monetary policy is effective in stimulating the economy, but fiscal policy is not. Further, the stagflation following the oil crises and governments' actual failures at reversing recessions with Keynesian policy called into question the effectiveness of Keynesian demand management. Consequently, governments in industrial countries used Keynesian expansion much less in the 1980s and 1990s. Instead, monetary policy had to assume the role of a countercyclical policy tool for economic stimulation. In order to make monetary policy available for countercyclical measures, governments had to keep a relatively tight fiscal policy because otherwise, they would have to use monetary policy to control inflation. Thus, we observe a tight fiscal–neutral (or relaxed) monetary policy mix in the second half of the 1980s and the 1990s.

Why was there more neoliberal (conservative) compatibility between fiscal and monetary policies in the 1980s and 1990s? Why did party governments' fiscal policy thinking go in a neoliberal direction during the period? That is because learning about economic thinking had to take place among party governments and politicians (Hall, 1993; McNamara, 1998). Fiscal and monetary policy makers had to come to share an understanding of how the economy works. Prior to the oil crises of the 1970s, economic policy makers in industrial democracies had had relative consensus on the effectiveness of Keynesian demand management. But Keynesian economics did not explain stagflation (simultaneous occurrence of high inflation and high unemployment) that appeared in the 1970s after the oil crises. At first, governments tried to ride out the recessions with Keynesian policy, but it was not effective in ending recessions and controlling high inflation and unemployment. Following the experience with inflation and its negative economic repercussions, price stability became the policy priority among central bankers. The spread of antiinflationary economic thinking came later and to a lesser extent among party governments and politicians who also had the electoral needs to create economic growth and employment and for whom spending their way out of a recession with Keynesian fiscal expansion had presented an attractive policy option. Party governments and central banks needed to experience these new economic conditions and be led to a common understanding of their cause and solution.

The neoliberal shift in economic policy first became visible in the U.K. Thatcher and the U.S. Reagan administrations in the 1980s. It then spread to other industrial democracies gradually since, and the neoliberal policy shift deepened in the 1990s. In the past decade or so, politicians and policy makers have increasingly spoken of their economic policy needs in terms of increasing market competition and economic efficiency, achieving fiscal restraint, and attracting international capital. Thus, learning had to take place among party governments and politicians. Party governments and central banks also had to learn how to manage jointly the macroeconomy using fiscal and monetary policies, deciphering which policy works and which does not.

Different incentive and capacity of partisan governments, and their interaction with central banks

We have so far considered the possible policy coordination (explicit or implicit, intentional or unintentional) between fiscal and monetary policy makers as if all party governments were identical in their policy positions and government structure, and as if their effects on economic policy were the same regardless of their partisanship or government composition. But the degree to which party governments are able and willing to cooperate or coordinate with central banks also varies across different governments, which have different characteristics and face different incentives. Party governments come in different shapes and sizes. Government economic policy is conceivably affected by which political parties control government and by how the institutional structure of government constrains their decision making. At a minimum, party governments take into account the policy preferences of their constituents in making policy because their electoral support affects political parties' control of government. Different political parties have different electoral bases and need to meet different policy demands, which can potentially lead them to pursue different policies. Further, government action is affected by other political–economic actors that constrain or encourage certain policy actions.

This part of the chapter examines the interaction between fiscal and monetary policy makers by focusing on the incentive and capacity of different party governments in fashioning fiscal and monetary policies with central banks. The analysis of the independent effects of government partisanship and government structure will be presented in Chapter 3. The questions such as "Do left and right governments really pursue different policies and exhibit different performances, as stipulated by partisan theory?" and "Do different characteristics of party governments – such as single-party vs. multiparty coalition governments, majority vs. minority governments – affect economic policy and outcomes?" are deferred to Chapter 3.

Different attributes, incentive, and capacity

Political scientists have paid analytic attention to political and institutional factors in studying economic policy and outcomes, such as government partisanship (social democratic, Christian democratic, conservative governments), attributes of individual governments (e.g. the number of governing parties, majority status, stability of individual governments), structure of the political system (electoral system, fragmentation of party system, the structure of the legislature, federalism, central bank independence), organization of labor (centralization of labor unions, coordination of wage bargaining), and the mode of interest aggregation (pluralist and corporatist systems) (see, for instance, Goldthorpe, 1984; Grilli *et al.*, 1991; Alesina *et al.*, 1997; Boix, 1998, 2000; Garrett, 1998; Lohmann, 1998; Kitschelt *et al.*, 1999a; Iversen, 1999; Iversen *et al.*, 2000; Poterba and von Hagen, 1999; Hall and Soskice, 2000; Pierson, 2001; Franzese, 2002a, 2002b; Swank, 2002; Clark, 2003; Hallerberg, 2004).

Political and economic actors pursue their goals whatever the goals may be (e.g. reelection, control of government, economic gains, good public policy). Different actors may share certain goals but may also have different goals. Different actors also have different capacity for performing certain functions and achieving their goals due to their divergent characteristics. Or they may use different means to achieve similar goals.

In this part of the chapter, we consider how different partisan governments or multiparty coalition governments – facing independent or dependent central banks – affect economic policy making and performance. Depending on the independence of central banks, different partisan governments produce distinct economic policy and outcomes because they have different incentive and capacity in interacting with central banks and responding to their monetary policy. What effects do partisan governments have on the fiscal–monetary policy mix that they fashion with central banks? Do different partisan governments operating under certain central banks have varying effects on policy and performance? Are the ability and incentive of governments to generate certain fiscal–monetary policy mixes with central banks identical across different partisan governments, or do they differ?

Even though all party governments would like to achieve certain combinations of good economic outcomes – growth, employment, and price stability – and to avoid a deleterious fiscal–monetary policy mix that results in negative economic outcomes, they differ in their incentive, willingness, and capacity to fashion a fiscal–monetary policy mix compatible with the goal of good economic performance. They also differ in their incentive, willingness, and capacity to conduct a fiscal policy compatible with a given central bank monetary policy, whether it be a result of explicit or implicit coordination. The differences in their incentive and capacity result from the fact that different party governments have different traits. They have different sets of constituencies that have distinct political or economic interests and diverse policy preferences. Different governments or their constitutive political parties also have their own organizational characteristics that give them distinct constraints and opportunities, and incentive and capacity for policy action. Party governments in different countries also operate under particular political and economic environment and institutions, which again give them different constraints and opportunities.

Some party governments have little incentive to relinquish monetary policy control to central banks because they find it in their interest to retain monetary policy control.[10] Other governments have an incentive to delegate monetary policy making power to central banks, because they think the benefits of policy control delegation exceed its costs. Some governments may also have a great incentive to coordinate with central banks or to implement a fiscal policy compatible with a given central bank monetary policy. And some of them may have the capacity to do so, while others may not even if they want to. Thus, if party governments differ in their incentive and capacity to engineer a policy mix conducive to economic performance or coordinate with central banks, different combinations of party governments and central banks should have different effects on economic policy and performance.

Central banks themselves also respond to party governments in different ways, depending on the partisanship or composition of the governments. Bernhard (2002) shows that central bank independence – the degree to which central banks can pursue monetary policy that they prefer and/or that party governments do not want – is not necessarily just a constant but also depends on political conditions and strategic environments surrounding the party governments and central banks, such as the partisan composition of government and of parliament (see also Lohmann, 1998). Central banks are strategic actors that determine their course of action against or in support of party governments by cautiously assessing the strategic conditions in which party governments and central banks find themselves and the possibility of negative consequences of going against party governments for central banks themselves. If central banks are such strategic actors, it is natural for their policy and response to vary, depending on which party governments they face.

In sum, different partisan governments should produce distinct economic policy and outcomes, because they have different incentive and capacity in interacting with central banks and responding to their monetary policy. Their policy and performance should also depend on the independence of central banks.

Veto players: single-party and multiparty governments[11]

Two factors affect different governments' incentive and capacity – (1) the number of governing parties (veto players) in government, which affects the possibility of intra-government policy conflict, and (2) government partisanship, which is the policy positions and differences of party governments and affects the possibility of policy conflict and the difficulty or ease of policy shift in certain directions.

Scholars argue that an increase in the number of veto players within party governments (multiparty coalition governments) or in the political system (constitutional checks and balances, federalism, etc.) increases the discretion of central banks in choosing monetary policy and makes central banks' policy more credible and effective (Bernhard, 2002; Lohmann, 1998; Moser, 1999; Keefer and Stasavage, 2003; Hallerberg, 2003).[12] In this view, the presence of multiple veto players makes it difficult for party governments to override central bank monetary policy because it requires approval by multiple veto players, and central bank policy cannot be overturned as long as there is one veto player who prefers the central bank policy to the policy that would be implemented by party governments. In contrast, they argue, if party governments have only a fewer veto players (as in single-party governments), they have an easier time agreeing to override central bank policy. This is so because the number of veto players is small whose approval is required for overriding central bank policy. As a result, single-party governments have a relatively easier time running fiscal policy that runs counter to the economic policy envisioned by central banks, than multiparty coalition governments.

If single-party governments can more easily implement a fiscal policy that conflicts with the policy preferences of central banks, it makes it difficult for central banks to conduct a monetary policy that would constitute a favorable fiscal–monetary policy mix, given the fiscal policy implemented by single-party governments. Thus, the combination of single-party governments and independent central banks creates a situation of an incompatible fiscal–monetary policy mix envisioned by economists' game-theoretic models, where central banks and party governments use their policy instruments (monetary and fiscal policies, respectively) to counter each other's policy action. Namely, central banks raise interest rates to maintain price stability and to undermine party governments' expansionary fiscal policy, and party governments increase fiscal spending to boost output and employment and to undermine central banks' deflationary monetary policy, resulting in undesirable economic outcomes – high interest rates and high deficits, or lower output and higher inflation (Nordhaus, 1994; Bennett and Loayza, 2002; Demertzis *et al.*, 1998; Dixit and Lambertini, 2002).

Coalition governments' larger number of governing parties means that there is a greater chance that their policy positions diverge and that they have more sources of internal disagreement, other things being equal. Multiple political parties in a coalition government have different sets of constituencies with distinct economic interests and policy preferences. The divergence in interests and policy preferences increases the number and magnitude of potential sources of policy conflict within coalition governments than in single-party governments (Bernhard, 2002). Coalition governments want to keep internal policy disagreement under control because such discord and conflict can trigger a collapse of government and shorten their tenure in office. Because of this greater potential for policy conflict, coalition governments have the greater incentive to seek to control policy conflict. Bernhard (2002) argues that coalition governments delegate monetary policy control to central banks in order to remove this particular source of intra-government conflict from the list of their potentially contentious policy issues and thereby to reduce the chance of conflict over monetary policy within government. He writes,

> Systems in which legislators, coalition partners, and government ministers share similar incentives over policy or in which the government's position in office is secure have a low potential for intraparty conflict over monetary policy. [Under such a condition,] [p]arty politicians have less incentive to limit the cabinet's policy discretion with an independent central bank.
>
> (Bernhard, 2002: p. 97)

In contrast, multiparty governments or federal systems give politicians an incentive to create independent central banks in hopes that the delegation of monetary policy to central banks will help politicians balance diverse constituent interests and policy demands and minimize the chance of internal conflict over monetary policy.

A case of Italy's monetary policy change, for instance, illustrates the incentives coalition governments face (at these times, Italy had coalition governments). Bernhard (2002) writes that Italian Christian Democratic reformers hoped that monetary reforms (joining the EMS in 1979 and making the Bank of Italy more independent in 1981) "would enforce discipline on the party and provide a consistency to economic policy that would improve the macroeconomic environment" (p. 133). This suggests that political parties under certain conditions can be willing to delegate monetary policy control to central banks so as to improve the economic environment and outcomes and be willing to pursue economic policy consistent with central bank monetary policy to improve economic performance. It also shows that coalition government politicians have the willingness to make economic policy consistent with the policy preferences of central banks, a policy considered to be conservative and market-conforming.

H_3: *Coalition governments are more willing to pursue economic policy consistent with central bank monetary policy to improve economic performance (especially in the new globalized economy of the 1980s and 1990s); that is, a conservative fiscal policy or fiscal discipline.*

In contrast, single-party majority governments are often considered "strong" governments in terms of their ability to pursue their policy (e.g. Weaver and Rockman, 1993). They comprise member politicians of the same party whose policy positions are relatively homogeneous and cohesive, when compared to those of coalition government members. Thus, single-party governments have higher policy cohesion and a fewer veto players within themselves than coalition governments. Since all member politicians come from the same one party, the economic interests and policy positions of their constituencies also diverge less than those of coalition governments. As a result, single-party governments have fewer potential sources of policy conflict within themselves (Bernhard, 2002). This makes it easier for single-party governments to conduct a fiscal policy that runs counter to the policy preferred by central banks. Single-party governments can also carry out their own policy more decisively because they do not have to yield to demands by their coalition partners or opposition parties and because the economic interests and policy preferences of their constituencies are less diverse. Their strength and decisiveness can be carried into their policy coordination or competition with central banks, and can make them less willing to heed policy prescriptions by central banks.

If single-party governments are strong governments that can pursue their own economic policies even by overriding central banks' policy preferences, they have the greater potential and ability to act on their temptation for an expansionary fiscal policy, when central banks strongly oppose it for inflationary concerns. If single-party governments have these tendencies, the combination of decisive single-party majority governments and independent central banks can, if their policies diverge, result in a conflictive or unconducive policy mix and, as a result, poor economic outcomes. I expect single-party governments to have less fiscal discipline and to cause an unfavorable fiscal–monetary policy mix (or poor economic performance or both), when their central banks are independent. I expect independent central banks to conduct a tight (contractionary) monetary policy to offset inflationary pressures created by single-party governments' expansionary fiscal policy. Therefore, the combination of single-party governments and independent central banks should produce a macroeconomic policy mix consisting of an expansionary fiscal policy and a tight monetary policy.

H₄: *Single-party governments have less fiscal discipline and produce an unfavorable fiscal–monetary policy mix, when their central banks are independent. Independent central banks conduct a tight (contractionary) monetary policy to offset the inflationary pressures created by single-party governments' expansionary fiscal policy. The tight monetary policy creates deflationary pressures, slowing down output growth and increasing unemployment.*

When central banks are dependent, conversely, I expect single-party governments to produce a relatively tight fiscal policy. When central banks are not independent, single-party governments can afford to conduct a conservative fiscal policy, because they have control over monetary policy and do not have to rely only on fiscal policy for economic stimulus and expansion. That is, since central banks are not independent, they can also use monetary policy to promote output growth and employment, and their fiscal policy does not have to be expansionary. Thus, I expect to observe a relatively tight fiscal policy, and a loose monetary policy under single-party governments when they do not have independent central banks.

H₅: *When central banks are dependent, single-party governments conduct a tighter fiscal policy than when central banks are independent. Monetary policy is more neutral or relaxed than when central banks are independent.*

Note, however, that the effectiveness of fiscal and monetary policies is affected by capital mobility and exchange rate mechanisms (Mundell, 1963), and the willingness of governments to use fiscal or monetary policy is affected by the economic policy orthodoxy of the time, so their choice of policy (fiscal or monetary) and stance (tight or loose) is also affected by these additional factors, as we will see later.

Not all coalition governments relinquish monetary policy control to central banks, as other factors than the potential for intra-government policy conflict and policy differences also affect the incidence of politicians giving independence to central banks. Some coalition governments have dependent central banks and retain monetary policy control. If coalition governments retain monetary policy autonomy, they face the temptation to expand economic growth and employment, which can create inflationary pressures. When coalition governments control monetary policy, they can more easily resort to an expansionary economic policy since they do not have to worry about deflationary monetary counteraction by central banks and can also use monetary or fiscal policy or both to stimulate real demand. So I expect coalition governments to have less fiscal discipline and a less favorable fiscal–monetary policy mix, when they do not have independent central banks. If fiscal policy is expansionary this way, coalition governments and their dependent central banks may need to mobilize monetary policy to offset the inflationary pressures created by the former's expansionary fiscal policy. Coalition governments' use of fiscal policy – rather than monetary policy – for economic expansion under dependent central banks is more likely, because fiscal policy is more suited for targeted political or electoral distribution of government resources than monetary policy, and coalition parties with diverse interests and constituencies need to deliver exactly that kind of diversified, targeted policy benefits. Thus, I expect the combination of coalition governments and dependent central banks to produce a loose fiscal–tight monetary policy mix.

H_6: *When central banks are not independent, coalition governments' fiscal policy becomes expansionary. Monetary policy becomes tighter under coalition governments and dependent central banks. As a result, output growth is lower, and unemployment higher.*

In the absence of independent central banks, coalition governments' fiscal policy becomes relaxed, and single-party governments' fiscal policy becomes restrained, because coalition governments have a greater propensity to spend, all else equal, as a result of the multiplicity of governing parties with different constituents and policy positions and their electoral desire.

   In contrast, in countries with independent central banks, coalition governments should be better able to conduct a restrained fiscal policy, because they can anticipate central banks' contractionary monetary response to an expansionary fiscal policy and like to avoid recessionary pressures that such a contractionary monetary policy would create; so coalition governments are more capable of fiscal restraint and of possibly realizing the economic benefits associated with it, if central banks are independent and control monetary policy (countries where party governments have delegated monetary policy control to central banks). If fiscal policy is disciplined and not expansionary, central banks do not have to conduct a contractionary monetary policy to mitigate inflationary pressures from fiscal policy. Independent central banks may even be able to mobilize monetary policy for countercyclical economic action. So if coalition governments have independent central banks, they should be better able to achieve fiscal discipline, and they and central banks together can fashion a tight fiscal–neutral (or loose) monetary policy mix.

H₇: *When central banks are independent, coalition governments' fiscal policy is disciplined, and as a result, monetary policy does not have to be restrictive. Fiscal discipline and the availability of monetary policy for economic stimulus lead to higher output growth and lower unemployment.*

In sum, coalition governments have more potential veto players and have more sources of policy conflict due to their diverse constituencies and economic interests. As a result, they have the greater urge to control policy conflict, enhance discipline in economic policy, and improve economic outcomes. In countries where coalition governments have delegated monetary policy to central banks, they are likely to have more fiscal discipline and possibly better economic performance that can be promoted by fiscal discipline. In contrast, in countries where central banks do not have monetary policy autonomy, it should be more difficult for coalition governments to achieve fiscal discipline and good economic outcomes.

Incentives of partisan governments (left vs. center vs. right) facing central banks

We have just seen that single-party and multiparty governments have different incentives in dealing with central banks and crafting a fiscal–monetary policy mix. But the number of governing parties is not the only dimension of government attributes that affect party governments' economic policy. Governments' incentive is also affected by their partisanship (social democratic, Christian democratic, and conservative).[13]

Scholars have long used the assumption that left governments are more concerned about employment and growth, and right governments about price stability (Hibbs, 1977). In this conventional assumption, left (social democratic) governments are fiscally expansionary and build an expansive welfare state. Center governments (mostly Christian democratic) are similar in this respect, since they have large transfer payments (e.g. social security and unemployment benefits).[14] Christian democratic governments also receive electoral support from Christian sections of labor unions, which demand large public spending and welfare programs. Economists point out that large public spending by these governments is likely to lead to high deficits, high inflation, and high interest rates, which suppresses investment and output and creates market distortions. Government intervention also reduces market competition and economic efficiency, and impairs the competitiveness of the national economy. These interventionist governments also usually have extensive product and labor market regulations, and these regulations stifle economic activities and reduce economic efficiencies. Right (conservative) governments, in contrast, care more about price stability than unemployment and tend to implement a restrained fiscal policy. Right governments allegedly cater to financial interests, mobile capital, and employers. Mobile capital is averse to big government, high taxation, high public deficit, inflation, or exchange rate instability because of their negative effects on the national economy and on the returns on their investments. Right governments are thus hypothesized to implement a low inflation, low spending policy even at the cost of higher unemployment. Right governments prefer a small state because they believe that government involvement in the private economy causes market distortions, suboptimal resource allocation, and economic inefficiency.

As we will see closely in Chapter 3, the economies of industrial democracies have been subjected to various changes in the past few decades, including the internationalization of capital and trade and increased international competition among others, and the economic environment for governments and economic actors has changed. As a result, governments of all stripes came under the competitive pressure to shift economic policy in a market-conforming and efficiency-enhancing direction. The influence of neoliberal economic thinking grew with its emphasis on market principles, competition, and efficiency, and by the 1990s, even left governments could not ignore the logic of market economy. According to the globalization thesis, in a globalized economy, mobile capital is not friendly to large government spending, heavy taxation, deficits, price instability, and heavy social protection, any of which can cause low returns on investment, market distortions, and economic inefficiencies. Capital will flee a country with non-market-conforming economic policies and practices in search of a market-conforming country with potential for higher returns. In order to attract mobile capital and promote economic competitiveness, governments with a prior reputation of fiscal expansionism and/or high deficits (e.g. left and center governments, coalition governments) particularly needed to show their commitment to price stability, restrain fiscal policy, and retrench or restructure the welfare system to reduce labor costs and curb welfare spending.

In this economic environment, different partisan governments have the different kinds and strengths of incentives in approaching (or working with) central banks and fashioning a fiscal–monetary policy mix with them. Some partisan governments had a greater incentive than others to seek to achieve fiscal discipline and improve economic performance by granting independence to central banks and/or by implementing a fiscal policy compatible with central banks' monetary policy. There are three related factors that gave governments the incentive to conduct a more market-conforming fiscal policy compatible with a monetary policy or policy prescriptions pursued by central banks.

First, partisan governments with a record of fiscal indiscipline or poor economic performance had a great incentive to achieve fiscal discipline and good economic performance by using independent central banks and gaining antiinflationary credibility or by conducting a market-conforming fiscal policy. Second, partisan governments with a reputation for fiscal indiscipline needed to erase the reputation and to show the market their commitments to fiscal discipline and price stability in order to attract mobile capital and improve economic performance, even when there is a question whether such a reputation was warranted. An actual record of indiscipline can be damaging to investment and output, but the market's expectations of indiscipline can also be equally damaging because the market reacts to its expectations and the expectations materialize as a self-fulfilling prophecy. Granting independence to central banks helps build anti-inflationary credibility among market actors.

Third, center and left governments faced more potential sources of policy conflict than the conservative right, because the distance was larger between their traditional interventionist policy and the neoliberal market policy toward which they needed to shift their policy in recent decades. That is, center and left governments had to move their economic policy farther away from their traditional positions toward the right to make their policy more market-conforming. This greater potential for policy conflict led them to seek to achieve fiscal discipline and make a market-conforming policy shift by delegating monetary policy to central banks. In other words, they faced the prospect of more resistance from their traditional constituencies and the politicians who drew votes from them, because the policy change would have to be greater to them than to conservative party constituencies and the politicians who protected them. Thus, they used independent central banks to make a neoliberal policy shift and fiscal austerity palatable to their pro-intervention and pro-welfare constituencies and the politicians who relied on their votes. The delegation of monetary policy to independent central banks makes it easier for center and left governments to justify their market-conforming policy shift, because they could explain to their constituencies that the governments had no room for policy maneuvering in the presence of independent central banks and of the competitiveness and efficiency pressures of the global economy.

This explanation is somewhat similar to the argument explained previously when discussing coalition governments that had the incentive to delegate monetary policy to central banks because of the presence of multiple parties and constituencies with diverse interests and policy preferences and because of a larger number of potential sources of policy conflict. In the case of coalition governments, the government attribute that had the effect of increasing sources of conflict was the number of veto players (governing parties) in government. But here, my explanation is about partisan governments (social democratic, Christian democratic, and conservative). It stipulates that center and left governments faced more sources of policy conflict because their conventional economic policy positions were on the left of the policy spectrum, and they had to move their policy rightward farther away from their traditional positions in order to gain the confidence of mobile capital and markets, make their economic policy market-conforming, and improve economic performance.

Traditionally interventionist governments faced a larger number of potentially severer sources of policy conflict, because their constituencies are the kind of socioeconomic groups that supported and benefited from interventionist Keynesian policy and the generous welfare state. They were likely to oppose a rightward policy shift in a market-conforming direction, and it would pose a greater obstacle to center and left governments' efforts to make their economic policy market-conforming. These constituencies would need to endure a larger rightward policy shift than conservative constituencies, exactly because their conventional policy position was at the left of the policy spectrum. A neoliberal market-conforming policy shift would impose larger costs on these constituencies. As a result, it could produce a larger number of and/or severer policy conflicts for center and left governments than the right.

Granting independence to central banks helps party governments achieve fiscal discipline and gain antiinflationary credibility, because party governments do not have control over monetary policy and cannot manipulate it to meet constituents' demands, and antiinflationary central banks make sure that price stability will be maintained. By relinquishing their monetary policy control, party governments can remove monetary policy from their list of potentially contentious policy issues (Bernhard, 2002). Further, although party governments could still use fiscal policy to expand the economy, they cannot easily do so because they know that inflationary fiscal expansion would meet with central banks' contractionary monetary response and invite recessionary pressures. In other words, politicians can reduce their leeway in economic policy making by giving independence to central banks and by making difficult easy recourse to fiscal expansion.

The competitiveness pressure from the global economy and mobile capital and a resulting market-conforming policy shift create more conflict for left and center governments that have relatively pro-intervention and pro-welfare constituencies. In contrast, the policy preferences of conservative right governments' constituencies were closer to neoliberal market economic policy. Because of this, conservative constituencies did not have to incur as large a policy shift as leftist or centrist constituencies. As a result, conservative governments had a weaker need to use central bank independence to manage economic policy. They had less to gain from giving independence to central banks and following conservative economic policy prescriptions by central banks, since they had better antiinflationary credibility than left and center governments (even though as I will show in the empirical analysis in Chapter 4, right governments are high spenders much more than previously thought). Thus, they had less incentive to increase the independence of central banks or to run a fiscal policy compatible with a given monetary policy pursued by central banks. Center and left governments, on the other hand, had much to gain from borrowing price stability credibility from independent central banks and from the fiscal constraints central banks impose, so they took advantage of the merits of independent central banks. Thus, they had greater incentive to grant independence to their central banks and conduct a fiscal policy compatible with the policy prescriptions by central banks.

We should expect that center and left governments are better able to achieve fiscal discipline and relatively good economic performance when they have independent central banks, because they are more willing, and have the incentive, to run a fiscal policy compatible with a monetary policy pursued by central banks. So they should be better able to craft a fiscal–monetary policy mix conducive to fiscal restraint and economic performance when central banks are independent. We expect that, in contrast, the combination of right governments and independent central banks either does not produce favorable results in terms of fiscal discipline and economic performance or even may result in fiscal indiscipline and negative outcomes.[15] Thus, when central banks are independent, center and left governments should be better able to achieve fiscal discipline and favorable economic outcomes than conservative governments.

H_8: *Under independent central banks, center and left governments better achieve fiscal discipline than when central banks are not independent, and monetary policy need not be restrictive. Fiscal discipline and the availability of monetary policy for economic stimulus improve their output growth and unemployment.*

H_9: *If central banks are not independent, however, center and left governments have difficulty achieving fiscal discipline, and monetary policy needs to be tight. Fiscal indiscipline and a contractionary monetary policy produce negative economic outcomes (low output growth, high unemployment).*

H_{10}: *Under independent central banks, conservative governments' fiscal policy is not as disciplined, and as a result, monetary policy may be restrictive, possibly producing lower output growth and/or higher unemployment. (This is so because the relatively lower incentive of conservative governments to conduct a fiscal policy compatible with central banks' monetary policy leads the former to run an expansionary fiscal policy, and the latter need to implement a tight monetary policy to offset the inflationary pressures from the former's fiscal policy.)*

Electoral cycles, central banks, and policy attributes

Electoral cycles

We have so far discussed the potential for central banks to restrain other political–economic actors' policy action through their policy positions, intentions, and actions on the management of the macroeconomy. What about party governments' electoral manipulation of economic policy? Do or can they use fiscal or monetary expansion for electoral purposes in election years? Studies examining the existence of electoral cycles are numerous.[16] The results of previous research are mixed on the existence of electoral cycles. For instance, Alesina *et al.* (1997) detect some electoral cycles in both fiscal and monetary policies among the Organization for Economic Cooperation and Development (OECD) countries. Franzese (2002a) show that electoral cycles exist in transfer payments and fiscal deficits. Clark and Hallerberg (2000), in contrast, argue that electoral manipulation by party governments are subjected to the constraints imposed by capital mobility, exchange rate mechanisms, and central bank independence as stipulated by open economy macroeconomics. They argue that electoral cycles exist only when and where these constraints do not interfere with the availability and effectiveness of fiscal and monetary policies as tools of economic manipulation.

There are two considerations that should go into our thinking about electoral cycles, on top of those addressed by previous studies – the potential time-variance of electoral cycles, and the properties of the policies that are expected to have electoral cycles.[17] Most previous studies sought to examine electoral cycles by inspecting the entire period under study (e.g. 1960–1995, 1980–2000). These studies, by design, assume that electoral cycles are time-invariant. But one of the reasons why previous studies did not find electoral cycles (if they did not) may be that electoral cycles are time-variant and may exist in some periods, but not others. As I explain in Chapter 3, the environment for governments' economic policy making has changed in the past decades, and if that is the case, it will not be a surprise to find that such structural changes in the international and domestic economy have affected the presence, strength, or frequency of electoral cycles. So this book examines the existence of electoral cycles by inspecting both the entire period of 1961–2001 and two sub-periods (the 1960s–1970s, and the 1980s–1990s). The analysis of electoral cycles (or any other factor) across the sub-periods is prudent also because pooled analysis averages out time-specific effects, and averaging may conceal time-specific effects that may actually exist (Kittel, 1999).

The other important consideration is that different economic policy tools have distinct properties. Different policy tools have different effects and may affect different segments of the economy differently. If so, the effectiveness of different policies in achieving certain political or economic goals may be distinct. Some policy tools may be easier for politicians to use or manipulate than other policy tools. Some policy tools may be more suited for boosting electoral support than others. Or some policy tools may be more effective in bringing desired economic outcomes. If so, it is natural that party governments choose the policy tools that they expect will have positive effects on their electoral prospects or achieve desired economic outcomes or the tools that are easy to use. What this implies is that electoral cycles may exist in some policy tools, but not in others. This logic should apply not only to electoral cycles but also to the use of different policies by partisan governments (i.e. left, center, and right) regardless of election years or the combined effects of partisanship and election years. We now turn to the potential effects of the properties of different policy tools.

Properties of policy

Different fiscal policies have certain properties that make them more or less suitable for use as a tool of electoral or political manipulation. I expect party governments to use policy tools that they believe will promote their goals, whether they be electoral or economic. For instance, public subsidies are relatively suited for electoral manipulation because they are easy to target to particular industries or regions. Public works (approximately government fixed capital investment) are also a useful tool of electoral manipulation as they, too, are easy to target at particular regions or constituent groups.

Social security benefits may not be a particularly useful tool of short-term electoral manipulation, because their benefits levels and eligibility are more difficult to manipulate in the short term and their changes usually need to be accompanied by broader institutional changes that take a longer time to agree on and implement. Electoral use of social security may happen once in a while, but it would be hard to do on a regular basis in election years that come around periodically and frequently. One potential benefit of using social security benefits for electoral purposes would be that the size of recipients of social security is relatively large, and they are likely to be aged citizens who tend to pay attention to political issues and to vote regularly. In this sense, politicians might potentially derive large gains in votes they receive by increasing social security benefits. But social security spending has steadily been rising in industrialized countries, so the room has been small for politicians' electoral use of social security benefits in recent years. Thus, I do not expect strong electoral cycles in social security benefits.

Government final consumption expenditure – which is approximately the provision of public services by government such as health care, education, and welfare, and the wages for the personnel to provide them – could be an attractive tool of electoral manipulation because voters – particularly low income groups – would favor increases in government services and public employment that would directly benefit them with more public services and public-sector jobs (if they are inclined to support big government and expansive welfare programs). On the other hand, if sizeable voters (e.g. the wealthy and conservative) opposed expansive government services and employment, increases in this spending category would not be a desirable electoral strategy. In addition, if voter turnout tends to be low among low-income workers and families who are likely supporters of government services, it also would make this spending increase a less attractive tool for politicians. Further, once governments increase public services and employment, it is not so easy for them to scale them down even when elections are over. Then, from this perspective, party governments may not be able to use frequently this spending item as a tool of electoral manipulation. Increases in government final consumption should also have been difficult to use for electoral purposes in the 1980s and 1990s, because this was the largest government spending item (19 percent of GDP or 43 percent of total disbursement, when its wage and non-wage components are combined) and a large portion of the budget deficit reduction carried out in the 1980s and 1990s by industrial democracies came from this spending category (particularly its wage component) (Figures 2.5 and 2.6). It must have been easier for party governments to use this spending item in election years before the two oil crises in the 1970s when they still had a degree of freedom in expanding expenditures. But in the 1980s and 1990s, these governments had much smaller room for fiscal maneuvering, because of their conservative policy shift and the need to achieve fiscal discipline.

Tax policies are relatively useful and attractive tools for electoral manipulation. Personal income tax cuts are particularly attractive to party governments, because they directly benefit voters and are highly visible. Very few voters oppose personal income tax cuts unless there are well-publicized concerns about large government debt and deficit or inflation, and unless there are

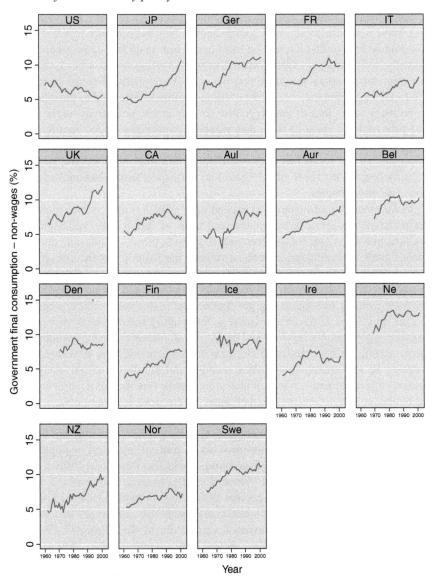

Figure 2.5 Government final consumption as a percentage of GDP, non-wages (sources: see variables, definitions, and sources in Tables 4.1 and 4.2).

politicians who successfully capitalize on it to oppose such tax cuts. Corporate tax cuts may be a slightly less attractive tool because the size of corporate managers, owners, stock holders, or general investors who directly benefit from them is more limited than the beneficiaries of personal income tax cuts. Corporate employees benefit indirectly from low corporate taxes and their

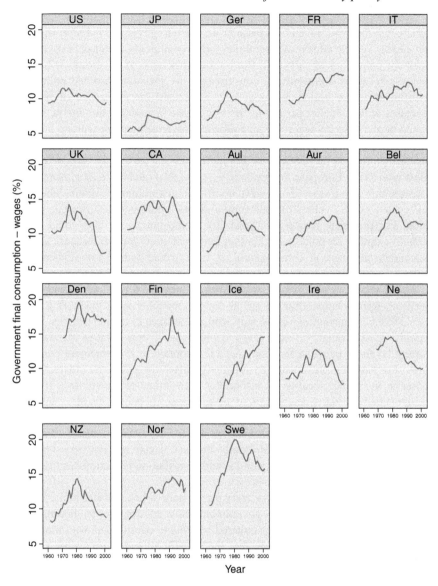

Figure 2.6 Government final consumption as a percentage of GDP, wages (sources: see variables, definitions, and sources in Tables 4.1 and 4.2).

positive effects on the performance of their firms, but the benefit is indirect and not easily perceptible by individual workers. Corporate tax cuts, when they happen, may be more driven by party governments' need to lower corporate tax to attract mobile capital and their economic policy positions than by electoral calculations.

What about consumption (sales) tax? Consumption tax is relatively visible to voters, and they can trace its increase or decrease to government action with relative ease. For the reason of traceability, consumption tax increases may be difficult for politicians to carry out. But on the other hand, if governments have to increase taxes by some means, consumption tax increases provide politicians with an attractive option, because they can secure the same size of revenue increases with a smaller percentage point increase in consumption tax rates than would be the case for achieving an equivalent revenue increase with an increase in income tax rates. Thus, if politicians want to avoid personal income tax increases for electoral reasons, a consumption tax increase may offer a feasible substitute. Many European countries rely a great deal (and more increasingly) on consumption tax (rather than direct taxes) for government revenues, and this reflects such effectiveness of consumption tax as a policy tool of revenue generation. For the same reason of traceability, consumption tax cuts could be an attractive option for politicians, but they rarely (if ever) happen, because a small percentage decrease in consumption tax rates would reduce government revenues significantly.

Social security contributions are hard to manipulate for the same reason that the short-term manipulation of social security benefits is difficult. If governments reduce contribution levels, they would also have to reduce benefits, which would not be popular, or incur revenue shortfalls. If they want to maintain the current levels of benefits, they may need to maintain or even increase contributions. For this reason, it may be relatively easier for politicians to justify an increase in social security contributions than other tax increases, if it is accompanied by the preservation of or increases in benefit levels. Thus, we should not observe strong downward electoral manipulation in social security contributions. We expect the absence of downward electoral manipulation of social security contributions, especially because social security spending has constantly been rising in most countries and contribution reduction has been difficult to carry out (Figures 2.7 and 2.8).

In contrast to fiscal policy, monetary policy may not be a useful tool of electoral manipulation (even if party governments have control over it), because it is difficult for politicians to deliver targeted benefits to constituents with monetary policy. Voters also do not easily feel the benefits of monetary policy easing, when compared to fiscal policy manipulations like tax cuts and spending increases (unless they are buying houses or starting businesses). Besides, if central banks are independent and have monetary policy control, party governments cannot exploit monetary policy for political purposes. The electoral use of monetary policy may also be difficult because of exchange rate and inflation concerns.

Thus, the presence and magnitude of electoral cycles should vary across different policy instruments (and time periods), because different instruments have distinct properties and thus should differ in their effectiveness in achieving politicians' economic and political goals, the nature of their effects, and their utility as tools of political manipulation.

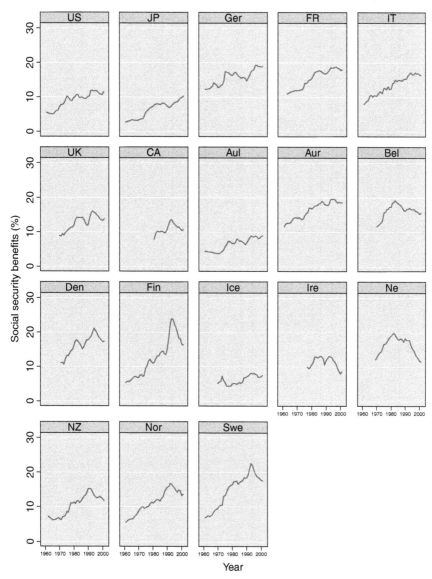

Figure 2.7 Social security benefits paid by government as a percentage of GDP (sources: see variables, definitions, and sources in Tables 4.1 and 4.2).

The results of the empirical analysis of this book indicate that electoral cycles exist in some economic policies and performance indicators during certain periods. Thus, electoral cycles are period- and/or policy category-specific. In election years, holding central bank independence constant, GDP growth is higher (the 1980s and 1990s) than in non-election years, unemployment is lower

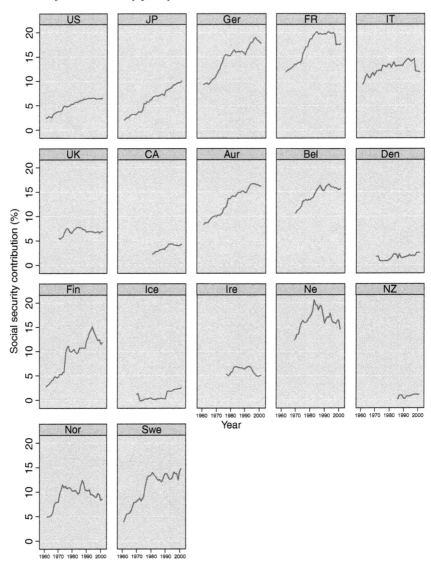

Figure 2.8 Social security contributions received by government as a percentage of GDP
(sources: see variables, definitions, and sources in Tables 4.1 and 4.2).

(the 1980s and 1990s), total tax revenues are lower (the 1980s and 1990s and the entire period), personal income tax is lower (the 1980s and 1990s and the entire period), government subsidies are higher (the 1960s and 1970s), and deficits are higher (the 1980s and 1990s and the entire period). Thus, party governments implemented spending increases and tax cuts in election years in some fiscal policy categories, and were apparently successful in expanding output and employment in the 1980s and 1990s. As expected, there are electoral cycles in public subsidies to industries and businesses. Contrary to the conceptual ease and benefits, public works do not show electoral cycles. As expected, personal income tax has electoral cycles. As consistent with the conceptual difficulty of electoral use, consumption tax and social security contributions do not have electoral cycles. Total tax revenues, total disbursement, and primary balance also experience certain electoral cycles.

Electoral cycles are concentrated in the 1980s and 1990s rather than in the 1960s and 1970s, as we will see in Chapter 4. During the 1960s and 1970s, we do not observe systematic electoral cycles except for a few policy tools. These results suggest that previous studies did not find electoral cycles (if they did not), maybe because they did not take into account the possibility that electoral cycles may exist in some policy tools but not in others and that they are present during some periods but not during others. Different policy tools have distinct properties and vary in their usefulness as tools of electoral competition. If so, it is natural that party governments choose the policy tools that they expect will have desirable effects on their electoral prospects or economic outcomes.

The stronger presence of electoral cycles in the 1980s and 1990s than in the 1960s and 1970s runs counter to the views suggesting that politicians' degree of freedom and capability in manipulating economic policy and outcomes have become progressively small in the recent decades due to globalization, convergence, the rise of neoliberal economic orthodoxy, or central bank independence. The literature on comparative political economy, to the best of my knowledge, does not provide an explanation for the stronger presence of electoral cycles in the 1980s and 1990s, and I also do not have a prior theory to explain it. But one possible explanation is the following. During the pre-oil crisis period, governments had steady and high economic growth and, as a result, government resources were relatively abundant when compared to the post-oil crisis period. Government debt was also much smaller. As a result, governments were generally able to provide fiscal expansions regardless of whether or not they faced upcoming election, possibly mitigating the need to generate large-scale expansions particularly in election years.[18] In the post-oil crisis period, however, governments' finance was much tighter, and they made a transition to the conservative economic policy regime. As a result, any fiscal expansions generally became harder to carry out. That means that it became more difficult for party governments to please voters and constituents with expansionary fiscal policy on a regular basis. This fiscal austerity in the 1980s and 1990s may have accentuated the need for politicians to generate expansions in election years to court their constituents. That is, party governments used electoral expansions more in the 1980s and 1990s because they could not afford to do so in non-election years.

Another possible explanation would be that electoral competition among political parties became more intense in the 1980s and 1990s than the 1960s and 1970s, and it led political parties to use electoral expansions to bolster their electoral prospects. Or even if there was no objective increase in the intensity of electoral competition over time, political parties' perception of harsher electoral competition may have changed in that direction, moving them to use electoral expansions. A related explanation would be that economic performance among industrial democracies deteriorated after the 1970s oil crises (lower growth, higher unemployment, higher inflation), and economic conditions became more important as a determinant of electoral outcomes or as an election issue (or political parties may have just felt that way), compelling political parties to use electoral expansions.

Yet another possibility would be that political parties were restrained from using monetary policy for electoral purposes in the 1980s and 1990s – due to central bank independence (or as with the EMU countries, which delegate monetary policy making power to the supranational European Central Bank) or other restrictions on the use of monetary policy such as the need for economic discipline to attract capital and to erase inflationary concerns – and thus had to resort, instead, to fiscal policy. In other words, in the 1980s and 1990s, political parties may have had only fiscal policy to use for political purposes, as the use of monetary policy was restricted. This is what Gali and Perotti (2003) find in studying the cyclicality of macroeconomic policy during the preparation period for the EMU in the 1990s and after the establishment of the EMU. They argue that the countercyclical use of fiscal policy should increase under the EMU or under other restrictions on monetary policy, because governments do not have control over monetary policy.

In contrast to fiscal policies that experienced electoral expansions, monetary policy experienced electoral contraction during the period under study. Monetary policy was significantly tighter in election years (holding central bank independence (CBI) constant). This is what my policy mix argument expects – party governments' fiscal policy tends to get expansionary in election years, and central banks offset it by conducting a contractionary monetary policy to mitigate inflationary pressures. And the electoral contraction in monetary policy was stronger during the 1960s and 1970s when party governments' fiscal policy in industrial democracies was more expansionary than in the 1980s and 1990s. The stronger electoral monetary contraction in the 1960s and 1970s would, at a glance, appear to contradict my policy mix argument because, one might argue, electoral monetary contraction should be stronger during the 1980s and 1990s when electoral fiscal expansions were clearer than in the 1960s and 1970s. But we need to keep in mind that electoral expansions in fiscal policy during the 1980s and 1990s took place in an environment of the conservative fiscal policy regime, as I explain in Chapter 3 and empirically demonstrate in Chapter 4. Party governments' fiscal policy became conservative and disciplined in the second half of the 1980s and the 1990s, and central banks' monetary policy subsequently became less restrictive than in the 1960s and 1970s, because central banks did not have to conduct a contractionary monetary policy in the absence of expansionary fiscal policy by party governments and resulting inflationary pressure.

Do independent central banks affect electoral cycles?

What about central banks' influence on electoral cycles? Do independent central banks affect electoral cycles in economic policy and outcomes? If central banks generally have disciplining effects on party governments' fiscal policy as we have seen earlier in this chapter, it is reasonable to expect that independent central banks also restrain party governments' electoral expansions. If central banks are not independent from party governments, party governments can potentially use fiscal or monetary policy or both to expand the economy if they decide to. But if central banks are sufficiently independent, party governments can only use fiscal policy. In this case, we should observe electoral expansion only in fiscal policy, if any expansion should be attempted by governments.

H_{11}: *Independent central banks should restrain party governments' fiscal expansions in election years. In the absence of independent central banks, we should observe fiscal expansions.*

H_{12}: *Independent central banks should restrict monetary expansions in election years. In the absence of independent central banks, we should observe monetary expansions.*

If central banks restrain party governments' electoral manipulation of fiscal policy, countries with independent central banks should experience less of fiscal expansion in election years than those without independent central banks, because a potential contractionary monetary response by central banks and its negative economic consequences would restrain party governments' easy recourse to fiscal expansions. Electoral expansion in monetary policy should also be absent as independent central banks control monetary policy. Or we may even see electoral monetary contraction as central banks try to counterbalance fiscal expansion by party governments. Non-elected central bankers do not have electoral incentives for themselves, so are free to use deflationary monetary policy even in election years in accordance with their own perception of monetary policy needs (setting aside their strategic action vis-à-vis party governments and political pressures). By contrast, if central banks are dependent and not free from political control, party governments are more capable of stimulating aggregate demand with fiscal as well as monetary policies in or prior to election years. If central banks are not independent, politicians should be better able to use economic policy for electoral purposes because they do not have to worry about central banks' contractionary response. And they could potentially use fiscal or monetary policy or both if central banks are not independent.

What do the empirical results tell us? Consistent with my theoretical conception presented earlier of central banks' disciplining effects on fiscal policy, independent central banks do restrain electoral expansion in some fiscal policy tools during some periods. Independent central banks restrained electoral expansion (that would have otherwise existed) in government consumption (non-wages) (the entire period and the 1980s and 1990s), public subsidies (the entire period and the 1960s and 1970s), and total government disbursement (the entire period). But in other fiscal policy items, central banks' restraining effect on electoral expansion is not observable.

Independent central banks also restrained electoral expansions in monetary policy in the 1960s and 1970s. But the pattern is a bit more complicated than in the cases of fiscal policy. The results show that monetary policy was tighter under independent central banks in both election and non-election years. Interestingly, however, when central banks were dependent, monetary policy got tighter in election years than non-election years. This is probably because when central banks were dependent, party governments' fiscal policy was expansionary, and the latter needed to offset it with a somewhat tighter monetary policy to control inflation. While independent central banks' monetary policy in election years was still tighter than dependent ones, the former experienced a small expansion in election years. This is because party governments' fiscal policy was relatively tight under independent central banks and the latter did not have to conduct a monetary contraction.

Do coalition governments or fragmented party systems cause electoral expansions?

We also observe electoral expansions in other fiscal policy tools when we inspect whether certain types of governments or party systems generate electoral cycles. In the empirical analysis in Chapter 5, we will examine whether coalition governments or fragmented party systems create electoral cycles – the types of governments and party systems that some scholars have portrayed are more prone to opportunistic fiscal indiscipline (Roubini and Sachs, 1989a, 1989b; Grilli *et al.*, 1991). We will examine this by interacting the coalition government variable (the raw number of governing parties) or the party fragmentation variable (the effective number of parties) with election years. As we will see in Chapter 5, multiparty coalition governments created electoral expansions in government consumption (both wage and non-wage components) and social security benefits in the 1980s and 1990s. Here again, electoral cycles exist mostly in the 1980s and 1990s. Fragmented party systems experienced electoral expansions in government consumption (wages, the 1980s and 1990s), total government spending (the 1980s and 1990s), corporate income tax (the 1960s and 1970s), and fiscal balance (the 1960s and 1970s). However, the evidence showing that coalition governments or fragmented systems experienced more electoral expansions is not strong. Other than the electoral expansions listed here, coalition governments and fragmented systems did not produce expansions in economic policy and outcomes. Less fragmented systems actually had electoral expansions in government consumption (non-wages, the 1980s and 1990s), public subsidies (the 1960s and 1970s), and GDP growth (the 1980s and 1990s and the entire period).

3 Change in the economic environment, political actors, and adjustment

Environment for economic policy making

Political actors and institutions make an imprint on economic policy and performance. But their behavior and effects are contingent on the environment under which they operate, such as the domestic and international economic environment, domestic political structure, and party competition, among others. The effects of political actors and institutions can be environment-specific. Politics and institutions matter, but they matter in the context of their interaction with the environment and other political–economic actors. We saw in Chapter 2, for instance, that party governments' fiscal policy is affected by the independence and monetary policy of central banks they face, since the effectiveness of fiscal policy can hinge on monetary policy implemented by central banks. In this example, party governments need to take into account central bank monetary policy in pursuing their objectives.

The behavior and effects of political–economic actors on economic policy change when their environment changes. Change in the environment (such as the international and domestic economies) can alter their opportunities and constraints and thus their incentive structure. Change in the environment can also induce change in actors' preferences and goal-seeking behavior, in the way they interact with other actors, and in the policy decisions and economic outcomes they produce. A new environment gives actors different incentives from those they received from the previous environment, and induces them to adjust or adapt to it.[1]

It is important to study the environment under which economic policy making takes place. The development of political–economic actors, institutions, behavior, and events are highly path-dependent (North, 1990). Political–economic actors and institutions are a product of their origin and evolutionary path. They are also a result of their interaction with other actors, the environment, and external events. They are the way they are now, because they came into being at a certain time in history and interacted with their particular environment and other actors in it. They exert the influence they do, partly because of the particular environment and systemic forces they have encountered in the past.[2] Therefore, it is important to inspect under what economic environment political actors operate and how they respond to it.

Important changes took place in the international and domestic economies approximately after the two oil crises in the 1970s. As a result of the changes in the economic policy-making environment, the roles of political–economic factors in economic policy making changed in the 1980s and 1990s. The economic policy of government of many types and stripes changed in a conservative, market-conforming direction. Political actors and institutions with a prior reputation or record of fiscal expansionism and inflationary policy particularly came to feel the need to achieve discipline in fiscal and monetary policies and gain antiinflationary credibility. They felt that they needed to make their economic and social policies "market-friendly" to attract capital and promote the national economy's wealth. The changes in the economic environment also altered their constituencies' interests and policy preferences and the way they pursued their goals and the way they conceived of their policy preferences and priorities. The change in the preferences and demands of constituencies, in turn, encouraged further change in party governments' policy positions.

In the next part of the chapter, I explain how the environment for economic policy making in industrial democracies has changed due to changes in the global and domestic economies since the two oil crises in the 1970s. I then show how the new faces of the global and domestic economies have altered the economic policy behavior of political actors and the effects of political institutions. I argue that the economic policy of different types of governments became more market-conforming and efficiency-enhancing in the 1980s and 1990s, and thus more compatible with the policy prescriptions preferred by central banks, as a result of changes in the international and domestic economic environment.

The economic policy-making environment is not the only political factor that affects economic policy and outcomes. The properties and nature of political actors that operate under the given economic environment also affect policy and outcomes. My analysis in Chapter 2 focused on the interaction of party governments and central banks and its consequences for the fiscal–monetary policy mix, and mostly treated party governments as if they were identical, regardless of partisanship and their structural composition. But in reality, party governments come in different shapes and sizes. Economic policy is affected by which political parties control government and how the institutional structure of government constrains their decision making. Different party governments have different constituencies with distinct interests and policy preferences. In making policy, they take into account the policy preferences of their constituencies because the latter's electoral support affects political parties' control of government. The second task of this chapter is to set the stage for the empirical analysis in Chapters 4 and 5 by shifting attention to the properties of individual party governments and other political–economic actors and their effects on economic policy and outcomes. Specifically, we briefly review the government attributes and other institutional factors that have previously been argued to affect negatively economic policy and outcomes (fiscal indiscipline and poor economic performance associated with it).

The new economic environment, policy adjustments, and adaptation

The environment for economic management facing industrial democracies has changed considerably in the past few decades. Several important changes took place in the international and domestic economies to alter the economic environment: (1) a new economic environment after the two oil crises in the 1970s, which ended the golden postwar period of high economic growth, low unemployment, and low inflation among industrial democracies, and which ushered in a new era of slow growth and high unemployment; (2) the decline of Keynesian policy in credibility and effectiveness; (3) the internationalization of capital and trade, and the competitiveness and efficiency pressure it imposed on domestic market actors and governments; (4) the decline of employment in the manufacturing sector and the rise of employment in the service sector; (5) change in the dominant mode of production from the Fordist mode based on mass production and semi-skilled workers to a post-Fordist mode based on diversified production of high-quality products and high-skilled workers; and (6) change in the interests and policy preferences of socioeconomic coalitions and constituencies as a result of the changes in their economic environment.

New era of slow growth and high unemployment, and the decline of the Keynesian orthodoxy

Prior to the two oil shocks in the 1970s, industrial democracies enjoyed a period of steady economic growth, low unemployment, and only mild inflation. Keynesian demand management was their preferred economic policy tool during the period and worked reasonably well. Keynesian policy enabled governments to overcome negative economic shocks. In this environment, governments built an extensive welfare state and provided social protection, while the size of the welfare state varied across countries. But the two oil shocks and ensuing stagflation (simultaneous occurrence of high inflation and unemployment) ended the postwar golden period of high growth and ushered in the period of slow economic growth and high unemployment. The newly emerged economy set the stage for the gradual collapse of the postwar consensus among policy makers and societal actors on the maintenance of full employment, social protection against economic dislocation, and Keynesian demand management. Slow economic growth, high unemployment, and the aging of the population in the context of the generous welfare state helped fuel increases in government spending in many countries, and the increases put strains on government finance. The end of the fast growth period also meant that governments could no longer simply count on an ever-growing economy and resulting tax revenue increases to finance extensive redistributive welfare states and to provide workers and families with as generous social protection as before. Further, governments could not easily maintain social peace by distributing the fruits of rapid growth to various segments of society.

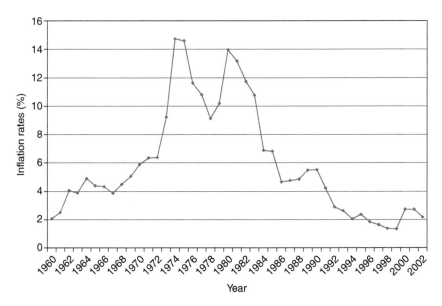

Figure 3.1 Inflation, 19-country averages, 1960–2002 (sources: see variables, definitions, and sources in Tables 4.1 and 4.2).

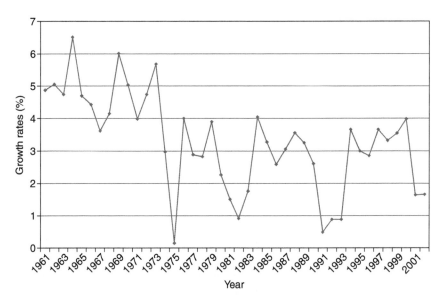

Figure 3.2 Real GDP growth rates, 19-country averages, 1961–2002 (sources: see variables, definitions, and sources in Tables 4.1 and 4.2).

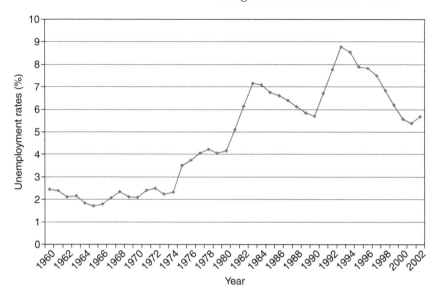

Figure 3.3 Unemployment, 19-country averages, 1960–2002 (sources: see variables, definitions, and sources in Tables 4.1 and 4.2).

At first, governments tried to weather the economic difficulties resulting from the oil crises and stagflation with a familiar policy tool, Keynesian expansion. But this time, Keynesian policy did not solve the problems of stagnant growth, high unemployment, and inflation. If anything, governments accumulated large gross debt from Keynesian fiscal expansion without alleviating the economic problems. As a result, Keynesian policy began losing its credibility among scholars and policy makers alike in the course of the 1970s. Keynesian theory was called into question also by the emergence of stagflation, which Keynesian economics did not expect and by the theoretical developments in economics (rational expectations theory) that rejected the existence of the long-term inflation–unemployment trade-offs envisioned by Keynesian economics. The new economic environment thus deprived industrial governments of the ability to stimulate the domestic economy by resorting to conventional countercyclical Keynesian policy.

The end of the 1970s and beginning of the 1980s witnessed a growing influence of neoliberal economic thinking in economic policy with emphasis on market principles, competition, and efficiency. The rise of the neoliberal orthodoxy facilitated the arrival of the conservative Thatcher administration in the United Kingdom and the Reagan administration in the United States, which in turn bolstered the influence of neoliberal economic policy in the two countries. Then, it gradually spread to other industrial democracies. By the 1990s, even leftist social democratic governments could no longer dismiss the economic logic of market principles and started shifting their economic policy rightward toward market reform and fiscal discipline. Kitschelt (1999) describes the widespread market-conforming policy changes by many European leftist governments as follows. The Spanish Social Democratic Party (PSOE) carried out economic austerity and liberalization programs after coming into power during a recession in 1982. (The PSOE subsequently suffered gradual electoral decline because of its economic policy.) The French Socialist Party (PS) implemented expansionary fiscal and monetary policies upon coming to power in 1981, but when they led to capital flight and increased exports, the PS turned its policy in a market-conforming direction. The Dutch PvdA (Dutch Workers' Party) abandoned its leftist economic position and adopted a more centrist position in the second half of the 1980s. The German SPD similarly made a centrist shift in 1998. The Swedish SAP made a market-conforming turn and ran austerity programs in the late 1980s in the middle of a recession. Leftist parties in Austria and the United Kingdom likewise made a market-conforming shift.[3]

As a result of the rightward policy changes by leftist governments, it became increasingly difficult to distinguish the economic policies of right and left governments. Thus, the rise of the neoliberal orthodoxy helped create an environment for policy changes by political parties and other actors that were previously considered fiscally expansionary (e.g. coalition governments, center and left governments). The new economic environment, particularly, moved the economic policy of center and left parties that aspired to regain public support by showing their competence and viability for the management of the national economy. But these competitive pressures were also placed on other political–economic actors and institutions.

Globalization of capital and new constraints on governments

Industrial economies experienced the globalization of capital and the rise of the neoclassical policy orthodoxy as a dominant source of policy ideas. Capital became increasingly mobile, and governments of all stripes came to feel the need to make their economic policy consistent with the goals of maximizing the competitiveness and efficiencies of their economies to attract capital. Governments' latitude in choosing economic policy contracted, and they had little choice but to attach more importance to price stability and fiscal restraint because capital interests are averse to inflation and fiscal expansionism. According to the globalization thesis, in a globalized economy, mobile capital is not friendly to large government spending, heavy taxation, deficits, price instability, and heavy social protection, any of which can potentially lead to lower returns on investment, market distortions, and economic inefficiencies. In the view of capital interests, large public spending can generate fiscal deficits. Deficits can then cause high taxes and inflation. Deficits can also invite high interest rates and low savings, which in turn depress investment and growth. Inflation also creates price distortions and resource allocation inefficiencies. It also increases economic uncertainty, which again suppresses investment and growth. Mobile capital will flee a country with non-market-conforming economic policies and practices in search of a more market-conforming country with potential for higher returns. As a result, governments of all stripes have no choice but to make their economies market-conforming and carry out efficiency-enhancing economic policies. Industrial countries' economic policy became increasingly antiinflationary (Franzese, 1999) as well as fiscally conservative.

In order to attract mobile capital and promote international competitiveness, governments and other political–economic actors with a prior reputation of fiscal expansionism (left and center governments, coalition governments, organized labor) particularly needed to show their commitment to price stability and restrain their fiscal policy to build credibility for their antiinflationary stance. As a result, many of the governments in which left or center parties participated made efforts to increase credibility by granting independence to their central banks (Belgium, 1993; Finland, 1998; France, 1993; Italy, 1981, 1992; New Zealand, 1990; Sweden, 1998; the United Kingdom, 1997) and adopting fixed exchange rates (Austria, 1996; Belgium, 1979, Maastricht; Denmark, 1979; Finland, 1996, Maastricht; France, 1991, Maastricht; Germany, 1979; Italy, 1991, Maastricht, 1996; the Netherlands, 1991, Maastricht; Norway, 1994; Sweden, 1996), thereby abandoning monetary policy autonomy.[4] Most of these governments were also multiparty coalition governments. Governments with a reputation for fiscal expansionism had much to gain from borrowing price stability credibility from independent central banks and from the fiscal constraints central banks indirectly impose, so they took advantage of the merits of independent central banks. The delegation of monetary policy to independent central banks also makes it easier for governments to justify their market-conforming policy shift, because they could explain to their constituencies that the governments had no room for policy maneuvering in the presence of independent central banks and of the competitiveness and efficiency pressures of the global economy (Bernhard, 2002; Bernhard and Leblang, 2003).

As the face of the international and domestic economies changed, economic policy now needed to be managed in different ways as well. Governments now need to: give priority to price stability even if it may come at some expense of employment; achieve fiscal discipline; improve the competitiveness and efficiency of the national economy; deregulate and liberalize the domestic product markets as well as the labor market to increase competition and enhance economic efficiency; and retrench or restructure the welfare system to reduce labor costs, increase workers' incentives, and curb welfare spending. Firms and workers now (particularly in the traded sector) need to contain wages within ranges where they can maintain their international competitiveness or below productivity gains. They also need to lower employee benefits and protection to curb labor costs for the same reason. Negotiated wage restraint is a reasonable approach to achieving the goals above, but is not so easy in the face of the new divisions between high- and low-skilled workers and between the exposed and sheltered sectors and of labor's declining capacity for wage coordination because of the new divisions among workers and sectors.

I am not implying that fiscal austerity, welfare retrenchment, and labor cost reduction are the best or the only approach to a nation's wealth. Nor am I suggesting that government spending is counterproductive across the board. To the contrary, public spending on education, health care, job training, and active labor market policy can be designed to enhance the quality of human capital to facilitate growth and productivity gains. Effective public policy on education and research and development can also facilitate technological advances. As endogenous growth theory in economics implies, government spending in these areas can assist a nation's effort to promote economic growth. If a country can improve its physical and human capital and promote technological advances by using public policy, mobile capital does not necessarily have automatically to react negatively to high government spending and taxes per se (Boix, 1998; Manow, 2001). The benefits of government spending on physical and human capital and technology can exceed its costs. If government spending can help provide a good environment for economic activities and investment, mobile capital may not avert high public spending and taxation or labor costs. I am only suggesting that setting aside these economic benefits of public policy, governments are under significant pressure to enhance economic efficiency and competitiveness and achieve stability in prices and exchange rates. As a result, governments and politicians of not only the right but also the left and center now speak of the economy and policy increasingly in efficiency and competitiveness terms.

Change in the modes of the economy: the decline of manufacturing and rise of services, and the mode of production

The dominant mode of production and economic activities in the industrial economies changed (see, for instance, various chapters in Kitschelt *et al.*, 1999a; Iversen *et al.*, 2000). Employment in traditional manufacturing and agriculture declined, and employment in the service sector (where productivity growth is lower than in the manufacturing sector) expanded. This poses a new problem to economies and governments because slow productivity growth in the service sector makes employment creation more difficult than during the days of manufacturing dominance. Iversen and Wren (1998) explain it as follows. In the manufacturing sector, productivity growth is higher. Productivity growth increases employment as long as wages do not completely absorb productivity growth (and if demand for manufactured products is price elastic), because lower product prices achieved by productivity growth increase demand. But in the service sector, which has been the alternative source of employment in the past few decades, productivity growth is slower. In the absence of fast productivity growth, employment growth needs to rely on lower wages in order to achieve lower prices and higher demand. This means that in services-dominant economies, job creation can be more difficult, wages can be low even if there are jobs, and firms and workers are under great competitive pressures to achieve efficiency.

Alternatively, the employment problem could be solved by increases in public employment, as Scandinavian social democratic governments did. But this can create other equally serious problems of fiscal deficits, high taxes, inefficiencies, or high wage pressures. Wages in the public sector would have to be maintained sufficiently low, but wage containment might not be so easy to achieve since the public sector is usually not exposed to international competition. If governments cannot maintain low wages in the public sector, it will become more difficult to restrain wages in the private sector much of which is exposed to international competition, and high wages in the private sector will reduce the international competitiveness of national economies.

Industrial economies also experienced a transition from a Fordist mode of production based on the mass production of standardized products and semi-skilled workers to a production mode based on the flexible, diversified production of high-quality products and skilled labor, partly reflecting market saturation and the diversification of consumer preferences (see, for instance, various chapters in Kitschelt *et al.*, 1999a; Iversen *et al.*, 2000). More than before, employers needed high-skilled workers and flexible labor markets to allow flexible production of high-quality, diversified products. To secure high-skilled labor, employers needed to differentiate wages for high- and low-skilled workers. This helped create a division between high- and low-skilled workers, whereas their division had previously been reined in by solidaristic wage policy. Increased international competition also widened the division between the traded sectors that were exposed to competition from foreign firms and products and thus needed to restrain wages to maintain international competitiveness, on the one hand, and the sheltered domestic sectors (including the public sector) for which the issue of international competitiveness was not so pressing, on the other. This division pitted the workers and employers in the exposed sectors against those in the sheltered sectors. These new divisions widened the fissures within workers and within employers along industry lines, and weakened the foundation of the postwar corporatist arrangements based on tripartite cooperation and a Keynesian welfare state. Wage restraint – which had been a corner-stone of the price stability and full employment policy for many, especially social democratic, countries – became more difficult than before. If wage restraint cannot be achieved by labor's wage coordination, employers and governments will increasingly need to leave wage determination to market forces and bring market principles into the labor market in order to maintain competitive wages. This facilitates a neoliberal policy shift in the political–economic system because it moves governments and employers to reduce worker protection and deregulate the labor market to reduce wage rigidities.

Change in dominant socioeconomic coalitions and political parties' policy adjustment

What these changes in the economic environment did was to convince political–economic actors that change in their policy was inevitable or desirable. The internationalization of capital and trade changes the policy preferences of domestic political–economic actors with diverse economic interests (Rogowski,

1989; Frieden, 1991; various chapters in Keohane and Milner, 1996; Garrett, 1998). Change in the international economy also affects dominant domestic actors and coalitions, whose policy preferences, in turn, affect a country's economic policy profile (Gourevitch, 1986; Katzenstein, 1985). In an integrated economy, certain domestic groups become more subject and vulnerable to world economic fluctuations and economic dislocations resulting from world economic conditions and international competition. Multiple cleavages arise between socioeconomic groups advocating free trade and those demanding trade protection; between those pushing liberalization and deregulation and those dislocated by economic changes and demanding social protection by government along the lines of a Keynesian welfare state; and between exporters who prefer a depreciated currency, importers who may prefer an appreciated one, and investors and international traders who prefer exchange rate stability.

If the economic conditions surrounding socioeconomic actors – who are political parties' constituencies – change in such a way as to alter their economic policy preferences and interests, it alters the way they pursue their goals. It can also alter their relative power in the domestic political economy. To mitigate the erosion of their economic interests and political power, declining constituencies will be driven to change their behavior and strategies or develop new preferences in the new environment. If they fail to adjust or adapt, they will decline and may perish.

Change in constituents' interests and policy preferences leads political parties to adjust their economic policy so long as they wish to win elections and gain control of government. Otherwise, they will fail to capture votes and to survive electoral competition. It is thus natural for political parties to adjust their economic policy, as the international and domestic economies change and it changes their constituents' economic interests and policy preferences. Thus, political parties are compelled to alter their policy positions if dominant domestic coalitions realign or are transformed as a result of economic changes.

Take the example of labor unions and left and Christian democratic parties that support labor. Labor unions' power started to decline at about the same time policy makers' confidence in Keynesian demand management and in an expansive welfare state started to be shaken. The economies with big government and a big welfare state also started displaying poor economic performance. Persistently high unemployment also weakened the power of labor in Europe. With the poor records of economic management, political parties on the left and center supporting a welfare state lost electoral support, and the 1980s saw the inauguration of conservative governments among industrial democracies. In the United Kingdom, for instance, the conservative Thatcher government consciously sought to undermine the power of labor by changing the labor laws and by implementing neoliberal market reform. With the rise of neoliberal thinking in economic policy making, left and center governments and labor faced the crisis of their electoral and political power. The internationalization of capital also shifted power away from labor to capital. The new division within labor between workers in the sheltered and export sectors and between high-skilled and low-skilled workers also weakened the power of labor as a whole. As a result, left and center governments and labor faced the need to change their electoral and political strategies and shift their economic policy positions rightward for self-preservation. When left governments returned to power in the 1990s, they did not revert the neoliberal economic policy installed by outgoing conservative governments back to their traditional Keynesian policy, and instead they pursued neoliberal economic policy not too different from that of conservative governments.

It is reasonable for political actors and institutions with a prior reputation for fiscal expansionism and inflationary policy to feel a particularly strong need to achieve discipline in fiscal and monetary policies and gain antiinflationary credibility. These governments feel that they need to make their economic and social policies "market-friendly" to attract capital and promote the national economy's wealth. After all, it is market actors' expectations that help shape prices and wages and affect economic decisions about consumption and investment. Not surprisingly, we observe economic policy adjustments most clearly among coalition governments, left and center governments, and labor, which had conventionally been perceived by investors and academics to be prone to fiscal expansionism or economic indiscipline, as we will see in the empirical analysis of Chapters 4 and 5.

Katzenstein (1985) shows that, in response to the crises of the 1930s and 1940s (the Depression and World War II), small open European countries reorganized their political economy and developed democratic corporatism characterized by flexible economic adjustments and compensation based on consensual social partnership and interest coordination. Their adjustment was an effort to ensure survival in the world economy. I argue that industrial countries (not limited to small European countries) made adjustment again in the past two decades in response to the economic crises starting in the 1970s and the new reality of the economic environment. Governments and other political–economic actors that were considered poor economic performers made adjustments, and their economic policy became more conservative and market-conforming. But since different governments' incentive and capacity for economic policy adjustment were different, their trajectories or speed of adjustments were also different.

New economic environment and policy adjustment

As a result of the economic changes and resulting adjustments reviewed above, significant change took place in the roles of political–economic factors in economic policy making in the 1980s and 1990s. One of the findings of this book is that the economic policy of governments of many types and stripes changed in a conservative, market-conforming direction as a result of changes in the international and domestic economic environment since the 1970s. The changes in the economic environment altered the constituencies' economic positions and the way they pursued their goals and the way they conceived of their policy preferences and priorities. The change in the preferences and demands of constituencies, in turn, induced change in party governments' policy positions. The governments and institutions, which had previously been considered the sources of fiscal profligacy or economic inefficiencies, made a transition toward a more market-conforming policy regime. Their economic policies now became more conservative, and thus more compatible with the neoliberal policy prescriptions embraced by central bankers. The change in economic policy also improved the economic performance of governments and institutions in the 1980s and 1990s that had previously been considered unconducive to healthy economic performance. They learned, adjusted, and adapted.

Also necessary in this policy shift was the development and acceptance of dominant policy ideas in support of neoliberal economic policy. Neoliberal thinking gained influence after the oil crises of the 1970s. Party governments came to realize in the course of the 1980s and 1990s that their inflationary fiscal expansion might invite central banks' contractionary monetary policy and result in recessions, and that fiscal discipline was desirable for the goal of attracting mobile capital and achieving good economic outcomes. These economic policy ideas about how fiscal policy should be conducted and about whether they should pursue fiscal policy compatible with central bankers' policy preferences needed to develop among party governments and fiscal policy makers to make the policy shift more likely.

The adjustment was a process of the development of policy conflict between party governments and central banks and of their learning how each side acted and responded and what needed to be done and how. In the 1960s, although party governments' fiscal policy was somewhat loose, there was little policy conflict between them and central banks, because inflation was low. Central banks did not have to counter party governments' relaxed fiscal policy, because their policy goal (price stability) was met. In the 1970s, policy conflict arose, because the oil crisis caused high inflation and party governments responded to the recession caused by the crisis with expansionary Keynesian spending, adding inflationary pressures. Consequently, central banks had to counteract with a contractionary monetary policy to neutralize the inflationary effects of party governments' expansionary fiscal policy. This was a period when central banks had to learn that they needed to implement resolutely a disinflationary monetary policy to control inflation and confront party governments' fiscal policy. It was also a period when party governments' learning had to start about the detrimental effects of inflation on the economy and the negative consequences of fiscal indiscipline.

During the 1980s, party governments learned and gradually disciplined their fiscal policy. Although central banks' monetary policy was still tight, they were able gradually to relax their monetary policy, now that inflation was declining and party governments' fiscal policy was becoming less expansionary. In the 1990s, party governments and central banks came to share the ideas about how the economy works and how they should manage it. Party governments' fiscal policy became more restrained. Inflation was well controlled. As a result, central banks did not have to conduct a tight monetary policy.

However, the conservative shift in the economic policy of different types of governments does not mean that globalization has undermined the role of politics in the economy. If anything, it has accentuated the impact of politics. As I will show in the empirical analysis, political and partisan factors continued to exert influence on economic policy and performance in the 1980s and 1990s, when the globalized economy put competitiveness and convergence pressure on all governments and institutions and the effects of political factors had allegedly diminished. The empirical evidence runs counter to the convergence thesis that expects convergence in economic policy and thus the diminishing role of politics.

Weak-performing governments and institutions?: myth

Poor-performing governments and institutions?

Scholars have argued that certain government attributes and institutional features of the political economy are unconducive to the performance of the national economies.[5] This "weak government" (or "weak institution") argument emerged when industrial democracies experienced economic problems arising from the two oil crises of the turbulent 1970s and their after-effects. During the 1970s, governments conducted expansionary deficit spending to ride out economic recessions characterized by stagflation. The result was accumulated government debt and declining macroeconomic performance. By the beginning of the 1980s, many governments reduced expansionary Keynesian deficit spending, but those economic problems continued well into the 1980s. Though most governments faced similar problems, the problems were more serious in some countries than others. Scholars started claiming in the 1980s that they observed certain characteristics in countries where the problems of fiscal deficit and economic stagnation were more severe. Many studies have come out on this topic of the economic effects of political institutions and actors, but their findings are mixed. And there have been a few studies that study their effects across distinct disaggregate economic policy tools systematically. So a systematic empirical examination of the effects is one of the tasks I carry out in this book. The empirical results will be presented in Chapters 4 and 5. In the remainder of this chapter, I review those "weak government" arguments to set the stage for the subsequent empirical analysis.

Four factors stand out, of all the factors that scholars have claimed cause fiscal indiscipline and/or poor economic performance: multiparty coalition governments, minority governments, left and Christian democratic governments, and strong labor unions. I now review these previous arguments.[6]

Multiparty coalition governments

Scholars have argued that multiparty coalition governments are unstable, because the multiplicity of governing parties makes it more difficult to secure policy agreement among coalition parties than in the case of single-party governments that have only one governing party. In this view, the larger the number of political parties in government, the higher the probability of disagreement among the governing parties. The multiplicity of governing parties increases the chance that they will face difficulty agreeing on important policy issues and will collapse as a result of being unable to agree on government policy. Consequently, the average durability of the tenure of multiparty governments in office will be shorter than single-party governments. As a result, in this view, coalition governments produce economic policy that is myopic, inconsistent, or fiscally irresponsible (e.g. Roubini and Sachs, 1989a, 1989b; Grilli *et al.*, 1991).[7] Roubini and Sachs (1989a) explain that the fast turnover of coalition governments shortens the time horizon for repeated plays among political parties, and unstable governments discount their future and act myopically. The likely policy outcomes are large public spending, high deficit and debt, or unstable and/or frequent economic policy reversals, which create economic uncertainties and market distortions and discourage investment, among others.[8]

In this view, multiple veto players in government increase the potential difficulty coalition parties face in agreeing on policy changes. The likelihood of policy conflict should be high particularly with policy changes that impose costs on various constituents and socioeconomic groups – policy innovations entailed by the pressure for neoliberal reforms, globalization, increased international competition, the maturation of advanced economies and slow economic growth, and the unsustainability of the generous welfare state. The result is policy immobilism and maladjustment. The implication is that multiparty governments are less capable of carrying out economic policy that is required to meet the challenges posed by the national and global economies but that entails the imposition of (short-term) economic losses on societal groups that are important constituents for the coalition parties. Neoliberal economic reforms carried out by many governments in the past few decades are those kinds of policies that have such short-term costs.

Coalition governments' lesser capabilities for policy innovation, in this conventional view, are linked to electoral system. The likelihood of multiparty governments increases in countries with proportional representation (PR) electoral systems, where it is difficult for a single party to win a majority of parliament and form a single-party government, because PR allows multiple small parties to survive electoral competition.[9] Examples of countries with frequent coalition governments and large public debt that inspired this argument were Italy, Belgium, and Denmark.

Scholars apply the same logic to the effects of political institutions such as federal systems and divided government. A federal system increases the number of veto players (federal and state governments) whose approval is required for policy implementation and thus increases the difficulty of securing policy agreement. Divided government created by separation of powers, like the U.S. presidential system, also increases the number of veto players. The U.S. president and both of the two houses of the Congress are powerful actors in policy making and can veto each other's policy attempts. Most other industrial countries have a

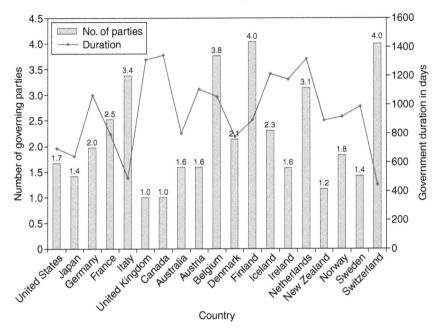

Figure 3.4 The number of governing parties and government duration, 1961–2001 averages (sources: see variables, definitions, and sources in Tables 4.1 and 4.2).

parliamentary system where the prime minister is usually the leader of the majority party in the lower house of parliament and has relatively tight control over the action of party members in the house. Therefore, in a parliamentary system, the legislature most of the time does not serve as an independent veto player as much as in the United States and does not pose a serious threat to the prime minister's policy initiatives.[10]

As these previous scholars speculate, coalition governments may have more sources of potential policy conflict and problems. But if they are aware of their policy-making problems, it is natural for them to acquire the desire to improve on the inferior results that they would otherwise face. Then, they have an incentive to seek to prevent the potential problems from becoming real problems and impairing their economic management and performance. They can, for instance, seek to bring economic discipline in their policy making by delegating monetary policy control to central banks (Bernhard, 2002). I argued in Chapter 2 that coalition governments' economic policy and performance should depend on the independence of central banks. Coalition governments, in the presence of independent central banks, should conduct a disciplined fiscal policy and produce good economic outcomes. They can also seek to achieve the same objective by other means than central bank reform. Then, coalition governments need not show poorer performance in the form of fiscal indiscipline or negative economic outcomes.

Moreover, there is only weak theoretical reason to assume that coalition governments are, as previous scholars argue, more myopic and irresponsible than single-party governments. After all, they, too, face elections and need to secure reelection. Voters may have difficulty identifying the location of responsibility for economic mismanagement, when they have coalition governments. But that does not need to keep governing coalition parties from worrying that voters might hold all or some of them accountable. Besides, in many countries that usually have coalition governments and frequent government changes, the same parties tend to stay in the incoming coalition governments after their outgoing ones collapse. In these cases, such dominant parties that stay in successive coalition governments are visible to voters. Voters may even erroneously attribute economic mismanagement to the dominant parties, even when the fault was with their coalition partners, not them. Or the dominant parties may just fear that voters may make such wrong inferences, even if voters actually do not. If so, dominant parties have even stronger reason to fear electoral retribution for the economic mismanagement of their coalition governments.

Furthermore, as I argued in Chapter 2 and at the beginning of this chapter, the changes in the international and domestic economies put pressure on governments to make their economic policy disciplined and market-conforming and to improve economic efficiency and competitiveness in the 1980s and 1990s. The pressure was particularly strong for governments or actors with a prior reputation for fiscal indiscipline and poor economic performance, such as coalition governments. Then, there is even weaker reason to assume that coalition governments have continued to produce fiscal indiscipline and remained weak economic performers.

In sum, the weak government explanation set forth by previous scholars expects coalition governments to produce fiscal indiscipline and possibly also poor economic outcomes (if fiscal indiscipline is unconducive to good economic outcomes). Thus, their hypothesis is:

H_{13a}: [Weak government thesis] *Coalition governments produce higher spending and/or fiscal deficit than single-party governments. Coalition governments may also suffer higher inflation, lower growth, and/or higher unemployment.*

Conversely, if my conjectures above have any merit, the following hypothesis may hold:

H_{13b}: [Counter-weak government argument] *Coalition governments do not produce higher spending and/or fiscal deficit than single-party governments. They also do not suffer poorer economic outcomes.*

Or,

H_{13c}: *Coalition governments' fiscal discipline improved (lower deficit or lower spending) in the recent decades, as the new international and domestic economies put pressure on governments to achieve fiscal discipline (while they may have had high spending or deficit in the previous period).*

To preview the findings of my empirical analysis in Chapter 4, there is little evidence that coalition governments systematically produced economic indiscipline or inferior economic outcomes. In fact, it shows that coalition governments' economic policy became very disciplined in the 1980s and 1990s. Thus, it appears that coalition governments were in a good position to see the prospects of the potential policy-making problems that could arise from the diversity of their interests and policy positions, and that, as a result, they made conscious efforts to achieve economic policy discipline and positive economic outcomes in the recent decades.

The results of my empirical analysis (Chapter 4) provide another indirect piece of evidence that coalition governments were restrained and responsible economic policy makers. The results show that although coalition governments did not suffer fiscal indiscipline or poor economic outcomes, *countries with fragmented party systems did* in the 1960s and 1970s. That is, it is *many parliamentary parties in the whole party system* that impaired economic policy discipline and caused negative economic outcomes in the 1960s and 1970s, *not many coalition parties in government*. Thus, governing coalition parties can be responsible policy makers. It is probably partly because their economic mismanagement would be attributed to their government action and they could fear electoral retribution. It is also partly because the fact that they are the managers of the national economy does not give them many choices but to act more or less responsibly. In contrast, parliamentary parties in fragmented party systems either did not face as strong concerns unless they were in government, or suffered from collective action problems. But in the 1980s and 1990s, even the countries with party fragmentation restrained their economic policy and improved outcomes, as we will see in Chapter 4. Thus, the competitive pressure coming from the new economic environment in the 1980s and 1990s was also on countries with party fragmentation, and those countries adjusted accordingly.

Minority governments

Another government attribute discussed by previous scholars that potentially affects governments' economic policy making capabilities is their majority status (Roubini and Sachs, 1989a, 1989b; Edin and Ohlsson, 1991). Minority governments cannot pursue their policy without some other parties' support outside the government. As a result, it is speculated, minority governments are less able to carry out a contested policy if it is opposed by opposition parties. Or they are more likely to make concessions to opposition parties, compromising the integrity of their policy (Blais *et al.*, 1993). In order to obtain opposition parties' cooperation, minority governments may use side payments in the form of shares of government budget or tax cuts, which may make minority governments prone to fiscal indiscipline and its negative economic consequences. The result would be poorer economic performance than strong majority governments. Examples of countries with frequent minority governments are Denmark, Sweden, Ireland, and Norway (Figure 3.5).

So according to this view by previous scholars, the following hypothesis should hold:

H$_{14}$: [Weak government thesis] *Minority governments produce higher fiscal deficit and/or spending than majority governments. (The former may also suffer poorer economic outcomes.)*

Certainly, lack of a majority imposes constraints on a government. Yet the theoretical justification to believe a priori minority governments perform poorly is weak. First, a majority government may be better able to carry out economic policy decisively even in the presence of a minority opposition (the market reforms in the United Kingdom and New Zealand in the 1980s are examples of such decisiveness by single-party majority governments in policy implementation). But a majority government can also better pursue *bad* policy if it decides to do so. For instance, if it wants to pursue ill-advised deficit spending, it has the greater ability to do so. It has the ability also to act on their temptations to expand the economy for political purposes, even if it means inflation.

Second, majority governments may also have difficulty carrying out unpopu-

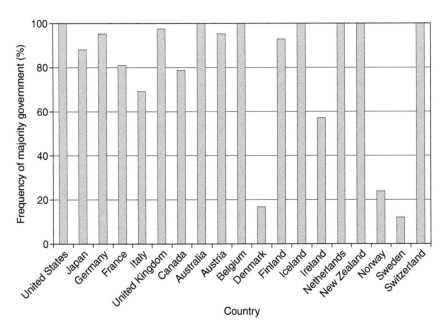

Figure 3.5 Frequency of majority governments, 1960–2001 averages (%) (sources: see variables, definitions, and sources in Tables 4.1 and 4.2).

lar policies required for the long-term health of the economy, because the immediate, negative impacts of such policies are more easily attributable to majority governments than in the case of minority governments. Third, to the extent that minority governments are single-party governments more often than not, it could be easier for them to agree on policy than for coalition majority governments (Borrelli and Royed, 1995; Strom, 1990; Woldendorp *et al.*, 1993). Moreover, minority governments are not necessarily significantly weaker than majority ones in durability, government cohesion, and electoral performance, particularly when compared with multiparty majority governments (Strom, 1990). The differences in the performance of majority and minority governments are thus not conclusive at the theoretical level.

Empirically, as presented in Chapter 4, the data suggest that majority status often does not affect policy and outcomes. Even when it does, the pattern of the effects is not systematic. The effects are also very weak. So if I can put trust in the results of my empirical analysis, majority status is not an important factor for economic policy or outcomes, and the argument about the weak performance of minority governments is not supported.

Pro-welfare interventionist partisan governments

Left (social democratic) governments have been purported by economists to be fiscally expansionary and to build an expansive welfare state.[11] In this conventional view, large public spending by left governments (e.g. Sweden, Norway, Denmark, Finland) is likely to lead to high deficits, high inflation, and high interest rates, which suppresses investment and output and creates market distortions. Large-scale government intervention reduces market competition and economic efficiency, and impairs the competitiveness of the national economy.

Of course, we know that this view in its most simplistic form is not well supported by the recent empirical cases of Scandinavian countries. In the past decade, Scandinavian countries have successfully produced very favorable economic outcomes and achieved economic competitiveness, despite their large welfare state and high spending levels. Their governments have actively promoted economic growth and the well-being of citizens through the government provision of public services – high-quality education, health care, active labor market policy, job (re)training, and investments in knowledge-intensive industries and R&D.

But the point is that economists view that large public spending and government intervention, in general, lead to economic inefficiency and poor economic performances. Countries with strong Christian democratic parties should suffer similar economic problems, in this view, because Christian democratic parties also have large transfer payments (e.g. social security and unemployment benefits).[12] Christian democratic parties also receive electoral support from Christian sections of labor unions, which usually tend to demand large public spending and welfare programs (e.g. Germany, Italy). Countries with strong Christian democratic parties have large spending on transfer payments, whereas social democratic governments have expansive government services spending (see the Appendix at the end of this chapter). These interventionist governments also usually have extensive product and labor market regulations, and these regulations stifle economic activities and reduce economic efficiencies.

In contrast, it has conventionally been argued or assumed that conservative (right) parties care more about price stability than unemployment and tend to implement a restrained fiscal policy (Hibbs, 1977). Right governments allegedly cater to financial interests, mobile capital, and employers because they draw electoral support from these constituents. Mobile capital is averse to big government, high taxation, high public deficit, inflation, or exchange rate instability because of their negative effects on the national economy and on the returns on their investments. Right governments are thus hypothesized to implement a low inflation, low spending policy even at the cost of higher unemployment. According to this partisan explanation, right governments prefer a small state because they believe that government involvement in the private economy causes market distortions, suboptimal resource allocation, and economic inefficiency. Thus, they try to reduce government intervention and to let market forces operate as freely as possible so as to maximize returns on investments by corporations and consumers and exploit the potential of the domestic economy (Boix, 1998).

Studies in comparative political economy have long used these Hibbsian assumptions of the policy preferences and behavior of left and right party governments – left governments are more concerned about employment and growth, and right governments about price stability (Hibbs, 1977). The patterns of postwar empirical data seemed to justify the assumptions until recently – i.e. left governments appeared to have higher spending and expansionary fiscal and welfare policy than right governments.[13]

So the hypothesis of the conventional partisan model is:

H_{15a}: [Conventional partisan model] *Left and center governments lead to higher spending and/or fiscal deficit than right governments (and potentially to negative outcomes, such as high inflation and low growth).*

The standard partisan model also implicitly or explicitly holds that left governments conduct economic policy to achieve high growth and low unemployment, and that right governments make economic policy to achieve low inflation. So we will test if these governments can or do successfully achieve their goals:

H_{15b}: [Conventional partisan model] *Left governments produce higher growth and/or lower unemployment than right governments. Right governments achieve lower inflation than the left.*

However, my analysis in this book shows that the conventional partisan explanation is not an accurate or sufficient description of partisan effects on economic policy and performance, although government partisanship does exert influence on economic policy and outcomes. First, as I argued in Chapter 2, the impact of partisan governments should depend on central banks that they face. So my broad hypothesis here is:

H_{15c}: *Partisan governments' impact on policy and outcomes should vary, depending on whether they face independent or dependent central banks.* (More specific hypotheses about interactive effects are explained in Chapter 2.)

Second, partisan impact also can be time-variant. For instance, the internationalization of capital and the new global and domestic economies have put competitiveness and efficiency pressure on governments to achieve fiscal discipline and liberalize their economies. The pressure should be particularly strong on left and center governments that had either a record or a reputation of large fiscal spending resulting partly from their extensive Keynesian welfare state. It is then reasonable to suspect that they have made efforts to achieve fiscal discipline by reducing spending and deficit in the 1980s and 1990s, as the globalization of the economy progressed and deepened and as they needed to increase the competitiveness and efficiency of their economies and show their commitment to antiinflationary economic policy. My hypothesis is:

H_{15d}: *Left and center governments improved fiscal discipline (lower spending and/or lower deficit in the recent decades than in the previous 1960s and 1970s).* (If so, their fiscal discipline may have also improved their economic outcomes.)

As we will see in the empirical analysis, center and left governments' economic policy indeed changed from a somewhat expansionary fiscal policy regime of the 1960s and 1970s to a disciplined policy regime in the 1980s and 1990s. Thus, partisan explanations assuming their fixed, time-invariant policy preferences are insufficient. Governments' policy can change when the environment changes, when economic conditions change, when their constituencies' policy preferences change, or when policy ideas about how the economy works change. I explain the reason for center and left governments' policy shift later in the chapter under "Were these allegedly 'weak' actors really poor economic performers, or are they still?" The empirical evidence will be presented in Chapter 4.

Third, the expectation of the standard partisan theory that the left is expansionary and the right is fiscally conservative simply does not hold empirically, especially in the 1980s and 1990s. In taxation, the standard explanation holds – i.e. right governments tax less. But when it comes to spending levels, right governments are often higher spenders than left or center governments. I explain why we obtain this result in "An anomaly: conservative governments" below, and present the empirical results in Chapter 4. Government partisanship affects both economic policy and outcomes. But the effect is contingent on time periods and on the policy-making environment in which partisan governments make policy.

Left governments and labor: social democratic corporatist regimes

Political scientists have countered the claim about left governments' poor eco-nomic performance, and pointed to their economic benefits. They argued that social democratic governments promote full employment and a redistributive welfare state, and centralized unions can achieve wage restraint in exchange for such favorable policy, helping to sustain employment and economic growth while containing inflation (Goldthorpe, 1984). Garrett (1998) likewise shows that left governments with encompassing labor under trade and capital openness produce low unemployment and high growth with higher inflation. In this view, thus, coherent economic policy made possible by left governments and encom-passing labor leads to good economic performance.[14] Boix (1998) argues that left governments are fiscally conservative because large fiscal deficits would decrease domestic savings and impair their supply-side growth strategy of public investment in fixed and human capital. But a recent study claims that social-democratic neocorporatism does not affect economic policy or performance at all (Clark, 2003).

These theses yield many more nuanced hypotheses than we can deal with here. But, roughly, if the social democratic corporatist regime thesis is valid, the combination of left governments and coordinated labor should produce low unemployment and good economic growth, though government spending levels and inflation may be high. If the opposite view (e.g. Clark, 2003) is valid, we should not observe the effects of left-corporatist regimes. We will test these theses in Chapters 4 and 5.

Labor unions

Strong labor unions have been cited by economists as a factor unconducive to good economic performance. A common explanation is that strong labor can distort the price and market mechanisms, drive up wages and prices above market-clearing levels, and make the labor market rigid, rendering firms' eco-nomic adjustments to business cycles difficult and increasing unemployment. This problem is magnified by the fact that countries that have strong labor tend to have strong left parties that are allegedly also fiscally expansionary and promote labor's interests, and vice versa. In such social democratic corporatist regimes, it has been pointed out, governments run an expansionary fiscal policy and increase social spending to facilitate labor's wage restraint, to create employment (particularly, in the public service sector), or to provide a safety net for the unemployed and the weak as the social wage (Iversen, 1999). This fiscal expansionism can produce high deficits, inflation, and high interest rates. High interest rates, in turn, suppress investment, economic growth, and employment. Government deficits also drain resources from the private economy. Inflation creates resource allocation inefficiency and economic uncertainties, which impair investment and stifle growth.[15] So when labor is considered alone:

H_{16}: [Conventional explanation in its simplest form] *Strong labor leads to inflation, low growth, and high unemployment.*

Another line of labor explanation calls attention to the interaction of central banks' monetary policy and labor's wage coordination. Iversen (1999) explains that when monetary policy is accommodating, unemployment increases at the intermediate level of wage bargaining centralization, and becomes low toward the high level of centralization. But when monetary policy is nonaccommodating, unemployment is low at intermediate centralization and becomes high at high levels of centralization. In his view, when the government accommodates higher nominal wages through demand expansions and higher inflation, unions leaders can enforce real wage restraint that will keep unemployment low. But if monetary policy is nonaccommodating, higher nominal wages will translate into higher real wages and unemployment. In intermediately coordinated systems with nonac-commodating policy, unemployment will be low because bargainers will have an incentive to restrain wage demands for fear of high unemployment resulting from militant wage increases. In contrast, Franzese and Hall (2000) contend that the antiinflationary effects of central bank independence hinges on the effectiveness of a signaling process between central banks and wage negotiators, and the effec-tiveness of the signaling mechanism in turn depends on the degree of wage coordination. They argue that although central bank independence always lowers inflation regardless of the organization of wage bargaining, it does so only at the cost of increasing unemployment with deflationary monetary policy under unco-ordinated systems. These theses will be tested in Chapters 4 and 5.

Were these allegedly "weak" actors really poor economic performers, or are they still?: the myth of weak performers and the effect of globalization

What do the empirical data tell us about the validity of the previous explanations reviewed above, which stipulate fiscal indiscipline or weak economic perform-ance for those governments and institutions? Were they really weak economic performers? Today's integrated international and domestic economies exert competitive pressures on domestic governments and economic actors. Have the allegedly weak actors and institutions continued to perform as poorly, despite the strong pressures for competitiveness and efficiency? Or if they ever previ-ously exhibited poor performance, have they made successful adjustments and improved performance when the nature of the international and domestic economies changed?

As we will see in the empirical analysis (Chapters 4 and 5), the evidence does not support the arguments that so-called weak governments and actors (e.g. coalition governments, interventionist center and left governments, minority governments, or labor) had undisciplined economic policy and negative economic outcomes. There are some sporadic signs of fiscal expansionism by some of these actors in some cases in the 1960s and 1970s. Some of these actors may even have exhibited some weakness in one performance indicator or another. But even then, the supposedly weak governments and actors restrained their economic policy and improved their economic outcomes in the 1980s and 1990s. Most of these weak government arguments are exaggerated or are not sufficient explanations for their policy and performance. These actors have never been as weak performers across policy and performance categories as has been conventionally believed.

Furthermore, these actors' economic policy made a shift in a conservative, market-conforming direction in the 1980s and 1990s, and displayed economic discipline and favorable outcomes. The actors whose policy regime made a conservative shift include coalition governments, center governments, left governments, and countries with fragmented party systems. The fiscal policy of countries with high levels of wage coordination became more conservative and their economic outcomes improved.

The conservative (neoliberal) shift in the economic policy of these governments came as a result of changes in the international and domestic economic environment since the 1970s. In an increasingly globalized economy, governments of all stripes came under the competitive pressure to make their economic policy market-conforming and efficiency-enhancing. Governments with a record of fiscal indiscipline or poor economic performance had a particularly strong incentive to achieve fiscal discipline and good outcomes by, for instance, granting independence to central banks and gaining antiinflationary credibility. Governments with an unwarranted reputation for fiscal indiscipline also needed to obliterate the reputation and to show the market their commitments to fiscal discipline and price stability in order to attract mobile capital and improve economic outcomes.

Coalition, center, and left governments had a greater incentive to conduct disciplined economic policy in the 1980s and 1990s because of their reputation for fiscal indiscipline or an actual prior record of it. The incentive to adjust economic policy and behavior was stronger for governments or institutions that had previously performed poorly (especially in the new environment) or whose poor performance had weakened their economic positions, organizational power and reputation, or political power.[16] These actors thus had a compelling reason to discipline their economic policy, make their policy more market-conforming, and improve economic performance in a globalized economy. Some of these governments or institutions may have exhibited some fiscal indiscipline and/or poor economic outcomes in the earlier decades of the 1960s and 1970s, but their policy and performance improved in the 1980s and 1990s. As I will show in this book, this neoliberal shift took place across different types of political–economic actors and institutions. And these actors' policy adjustment is a story of their learning and adaptation.

Changes in the economic environment altered the economic positions and interests of constituencies and the way they pursued their goals and the way they conceived of their policy preferences and priorities. Change in the preferences and demands of constituencies, in turn, induced change in party governments' policy preferences because of electoral incentives. The actors and institutions that had previously been thought unconducive to healthy economic performance were no longer poor performers in the 1980s and 1990s. They even became fiscally more conservative than right governments. As the new economic environment changed the economic interests of constituencies, the incentive structure of those governments changed, and they adjusted. But the ways these governments adjusted their economic policy varied across different types of governments, as we will see in Chapters 4 and 5. So it was a convergence of their economic policy, but also was a "divergent" convergence.

The direction and timing of change in the behavior and effects of political actors in the 1980s and 1990s are consistent with what we expect from the effects of competitive pressures brought on by globalization. Change in the environment for the economy and policy making can become a catalyst to subsequent change in the policy preferences and behavior of political–economic actors and in the influence they exert on economic policy and outcomes. Actors pursue goals under a certain environment, and different environments give them different constraints and opportunities and thus different incentives. Change in the economic environment can alter the way actors pursue goals or may even lead them to redefine their interests and policy preferences themselves. Such change can also alter the political and/or economic power of actors.

An anomaly: conservative governments

In contrast to coalition, center, and left governments, right governments did not experience as much conservative policy shift. This is not because right governments' fiscal policy was already conservative and did not have to be shifted rightward. Contrary to the conventional partisan explanation that right governments' fiscal policy is conservative, the empirical analysis of this book shows that their fiscal policy was relatively expansionary for most of 1961–2001 and particularly so in the 1980s and 1990s. As we will see in Chapter 4, conservative governments' fiscal policy was loose because when it comes to taxation, they taxed less than the left and center, as consistent with the conventional partisan explanation. But when it comes to spending, they were high spenders, naturally resulting in fiscal deficits. So the conventional partisan explanation is correct about right governments' lower taxation, but inaccurate about their spending levels.

Why were conservative governments fiscally less disciplined? Several factors contribute to this. The first factor is the affinity between conservative governments and single-party majority governments. Countries with frequent conservative governments are often found in countries with frequent single-party majority governments, and single-party governments' economic policy tends to be less disciplined, as we have seen in Chapter 2. Single-party majority governments (as opposed to coalition ones) tend not to delegate their monetary policy control to central banks and, as a result, their antiinflation policy can be less credible or effective (Bernhard, 2002).[17] They have less incentive to increase the independence of central banks or to conduct a fiscal policy compatible with a given monetary policy pursued by central banks. They face fewer veto players within government (than coalition governments), and the policy positions of their member politicians are relatively homogeneous and cohesive. As a result, they have less difficulty agreeing to go against central banks than coalition governments, and central banks consequently have a harder time going against them (than against coalition governments). Central banks are strategic actors that determine their course of action against or in support of party governments by assessing the strategic conditions they find themselves in and the possibility of negative consequences of going against party governments (Bernhard, 2002; Lohmann, 1998). This constricts the discretion of central banks in choosing monetary policy and makes monetary policy less credible and effective. As I argued in Chapter 2, single-party governments can also afford less fiscal discipline, because they do not face as strong constraints on their fiscal policy from central banks' contractionary monetary response.

Conservative governments suffer from an identical problem because they are often single-party majority governments. As Table 3.1 shows, there is a

Table 3.1 Correlations among government partisanship, single-party governments, and central bank independence

	Left	Center	Right	Single-party majority govts	CBI	Number of governing parties	Majority
Left	1.0000						
Center	−0.3570 0.0000	1.0000					
Right	−0.6425 0.0000	−0.4580 0.0000	1.0000				
Single-party majority govts	−0.0673 0.0543	−0.1343 0.0001	0.1899 0.0000	1.0000			
CBI	−0.0301 0.3962	0.1379 0.0001	−0.0919 0.0094	−0.0849 0.0177	1.0000		
Number of governing parties	−0.0832 0.0173	0.1917 0.0000	−0.0954 0.0063	−0.5343 0.0000	0.0572 0.1108	1.0000	
Majority	−0.2990 0.0000	0.1542 0.0000	0.1617 0.0000	0.2705 0.0000	0.1829 0.0000	0.2559 0.0000	1.0000

Note
The number in the second line is statistical significance.

positive correlation between conservative governments and single-party majority governments, and a negative correlation between conservative governments and central bank independence. Thus, conservative governments are more likely to be single-party majority governments and to have fewer independent central banks than left or center governments.[18] As a result, conservative governments did not face as strong constraints on their fiscal policy imposed by their central banks, and could conduct loose fiscal policy because they did not have to worry about a contractionary monetary response by central banks. Conservative governments also already had a reputation of fiscal discipline (setting aside the issue of whether they were really disciplined). As a result, they had less incentive to give independence to central banks because they had less to gain from borrowing anti-inflationary credibility from independent central banks.

Single-party majority governments are often found in countries with strong conservative (right) parties, such as the United States, United Kingdom, Australia, New Zealand, Canada, and Japan. Most of these countries with strong conservative parties have Westminster systems with single-member district (SMD) systems, which produce a party system with close to two major parties, and thus frequent single-party majority governments. The only partial exceptions are Japan, which had a multimember district system until 1994 and a mixed SMD–PR system after that, and New Zealand since 1994, which changed the electoral system from an SMD to a mixed member system.

In another study, I have shown that right governments' fiscal policy does not change between when having independent central banks and dependent central banks (Sakamoto, 2003). That is, conservative governments do not let their fiscal policy be affected by central banks, as consistent with my observation above that conservative governments had less incentive to conduct a fiscal policy compatible with a given monetary policy pursued by central banks or to give independence to central banks.[19]

The second factor that contributes to right governments' relative lack of fiscal discipline is that the countries that are conventionally considered social-democratic dominant or Christian-democratic dominant actually have relatively frequent conservative party participation in the executive branch. Conservative cabinet portfolios (1961–2001 averages) are as high as 40 percent in Denmark, 45 percent in France, and 33 percent in the Netherlands (see Figure 3.6 and Appendix tables). This means that if these social-democratic dominant or Christian-democratic dominant countries ever have high levels of fiscal spending, chances are it will also show in the empirical results for conservative party governments in these countries, as government spending tends to change only incrementally.

Third, right governments' relative lack of fiscal discipline is consistent with some anecdotal instances of expansionary fiscal policy implemented by conservative governments. Some conservative governments in the last two decades were fairly expansionary. The U.S. Reagan administration accumulated a large deficit in the 1980s. Japan's successive governments controlled by the conservative Liberal Democratic Party also conducted an extremely expansionary policy to end successive recessions and deflation throughout the 1990s, which pushed Japan's gross

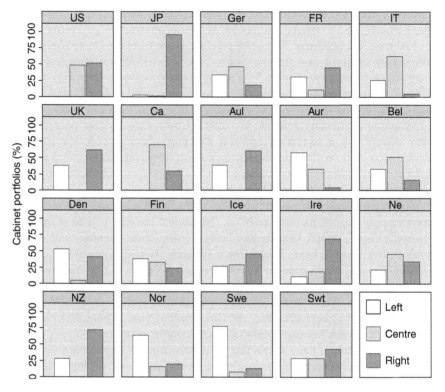

Figure 3.6 Partisan composition of governments, 1961–2001 averages (sources: see variables, definitions, and sources in Tables 4.1 and 4.2).

debt to the highest level among industrial countries.[20] Conservative governments that occasionally replaced social democrats in Nordic countries also were unable to reduce spending. In the United States, the centrist Clinton administration reduced fiscal deficit, and the succeeding conservative Bush administration increased it (though the latter is outside the sample of this book). The conservative Thatcher administration of the United Kingdom conducted expansionary fiscal and monetary policies and caused inflation in the late 1980s (Bernhard, 2002).

Fourth, while it is true that when we examine only cross-sectional data on various spending items and partisan cabinet portfolios averaged across years (without controlling for other factors), right governments tend to have lower spending than left or center governments, the often-discussed differences between right governments and the left and center are exaggerated. When we review these data averaged across years (see the Appendix to this chapter), the spending levels in conservative-dominant countries (liberal market economies) are only marginally lower than the left or center across spending items.

Right governments' loose fiscal policy also remains statistically significant after controlling for economic conditions, including GDP growth, unemployment, and inflation. The relationship between the right and policy remains after controlling for single-party governments. The partisan explanation that the right is fiscally conservative and does not spend as much as the left simply does not hold in the 1990s and beyond, no matter how cogent or elegant the original partisan hypothesis was. Traditional partisan theory needs a revision with respect to right governments' policy preferences and action.

Sum

The domestic economies of industrial democracies have been subjected to various kinds of change – the internationalization of capital and trade, resulting competitiveness and efficiency pressures, the end of the postwar rapid growth era and the rise of the period of slow growth and high unemployment, the decline of the Keynesian orthodoxy and rise of neoliberal policy, and change in the dominant mode of production. These changes in the economic environment altered the economic positions and interests of constituencies and the way they pursued their goals and the way they conceived of their policy preferences and priorities. Change in the policy preferences and demands of constituencies, in turn, induced change in party governments' policy preferences. When structural conditions change, economic policy and behavior that worked in the past may no longer work well, and governments may have to change their behavior and even policy preferences and priorities, in order to achieve their goals in a new environment. As we will see in the empirical analysis (Chapters 4 and 5), political actors changed their policy behavior and, as a result, exerted different influence on economic policy and outcomes in the 1980s and 1990s than they had in the previous decades.

The economic policy and behavior of the allegedly undisciplined and uncompetitive political–economic actors (coalition, center, and left governments, and labor) clearly changed in the 1980s and 1990s. Their economic policy now became more disciplined and more compatible with the kind of policy prescriptions preferred by central banks. Prior to the 1980s and 1990s, these purportedly uncompetitive actors were either associated with expansionary fiscal policy to a certain degree, or had a reputation for fiscal expansion among market actors and observers. But many governments reversed their policy in the 1980s, and their policy shifted rightward in a neoliberal, antiinflationary direction.

These allegedly weak-performing governments and institutions had the ability to adjust to the imperatives of the globalized economy and new economic conditions and change the practices and systems that no longer worked well. This suggests that institutions may produce various constraints, but political actors that operate under those institutional constraints have the ability to mitigate or change the secondary consequences of those institutions. PR may produce multiparty system and coalition governments, and political actors may have little they can do about this institutional effect (except for changing their electoral system or going against electoral incentives). But they can try to alter the secondary consequences of the institutions and mitigate the negative effects of multiparty coalition governments on policy and performance. The record of economic policy by the governments of industrial democracies is, thus, partly a story of political–economic actors' learning, adjustment, and adaptation.

I am not making a conventional convergence argument, despite my suggestion in the preceding paragraphs that the systemic forces from globalization and other economic changes altered political–economic actors' incentives, strategies, and policy behavior. While I agree that those systemic forces have put significant competitive pressure on domestic political–economic actors, I also argue that those actors adjusted in different ways depending on their goals, characteristics, incentives, and resources, which affected their ability, willingness, and potential to change or not change. Thus, it is *a convergence* in that most actors have moved in conservative directions for the most part, but it is (if the reader allows me to use an oxymoron) *divergent convergence* that happened in economic policy and performance among industrial democracies. In this respect, I agree with Kitschelt *et al.* (1999b) who make a similar argument that the adjustment or evolutionary paths of the three different market economies continue to differ (i.e. liberal market economies, sector coordinated market economies, and national coordinated market economies).

Partisan governments' economic policy changes over time. When constituencies' policy preferences change, political parties adjust their economic policy. Change in the economic environment alters the economic position and policy preferences and priorities of constituencies. This change in the preferences and demands of constituencies, in turn, leads to change in party governments' policy positions and, as a result, policy. The kind of policy shift that took place in the 1980s and 1990s has happened before. We know, for instance, that between the 1940s and 1970s, even conservative governments' economic policies leaned more or less toward Keynesian demand management, employment creation, and a welfare state. Political parties including conservatives supported these policies in the early postwar period because there was relatively wide public consensus on the Keynesian welfare state, and the parties had to keep their policy around the consensus. Prior to that, conservative governments' economic policy followed neoclassical prescriptions (Gourevitch, 1986).

The change that started at the very end of 1970s and early 1980s was another change of a similar kind. Public opinion and governments' dominant economic policy started shifting rightward toward the neoliberal position pointing to the economic benefits of market principles. Political–economic actors' understanding of how the economy works and what hinders or promotes economic performance changed between the 1960s–1970s and the 1980s–1990s. As a result, their preferences and action changed accordingly, mostly in the neoliberal, market-conforming direction. Party governments came to realize in the course of the 1980s and 1990s that fiscal discipline was desirable for the goal of attracting mobile capital and achieving good economic outcomes.

There is no reason to assume a priori that political parties have fixed, time-invariant policy positions. Their policy changes when the environment changes, when economic conditions change, when their constituencies' policy preferences change, and when policy ideas about how the economy works change. In this sense, the assumption of the conventional partisan theory that presumes partisan governments' time-invariant or context-invariant policy preferences is too restrictive. Government partisanship affects both economic policy and outcomes. But the effect of partisanship is contingent on time periods and on the political–economic institutional setting in which partisan governments make policy, as we have seen in this chapter and Chapter 2.

Appendix

Table 3.a.1 Economic and political indicators of 18 OECD countries, 1961–2001 averages

Country[a]	Real GDP growth (%)	Unemployment (%)	Inflation (%)	Primary balance as % of GDP (–deficit/+ surplus)	Left cabinet portfolio (%)[b]	Center cabinet portfolio (%)[b]
National coordinated market economies						
Denmark	2.7	4.5	5.9	2.1	52.9	4.6
Finland	3.3	5.9	6.1	1.9	38.0	32.6
Norway	3.7	2.8	5.7	2.8	64.1	15.8
Sweden	2.7	3.2	5.7	–0.2	77.4	7.7
Industry-coordinated market economies						
Austria	3.2	3.1	3.9	0.2	57.9	33.0
Belgium	3.1	5.8	4.2	1.0	33.1	51.5
France	3.0	7.2	5.4	–0.1	30.8	10.9
Germany	2.8	3.9	3.1	0.2	34.2	46.5
Italy	3.3	7.1	7.7	–2.0	25.7	62.3
Netherlands	3.3	5.2	4.1	0.7	21.0	45.0
Switzerland	2.2	1.1	3.4		28.6	28.6
Liberal market economies						
Australia	3.7	5.8	5.8	0.0	38.8	0.0
Canada	3.7	7.6	4.6	–0.4	0.0	70.3
Ireland	5.0	9.6	7.2	–0.4	10.9	18.9
New Zealand	2.6	3.5	7.1	1.1	27.7	0.0
United Kingdom	2.5	5.6	6.8	0.2	37.8	0.0
United States	3.4	5.9	4.5	0.0	0.0	48.4
Japan	4.9	2.3	4.3	–0.5	2.4	1.2

Source: see variables, definitions, and sources in Tables 4.1 and 4.2.

Notes

a The classification of countries in the three types is from Kitschelt *et al.* (1999a).

b As a percentage of all cabinet portfolios.

c Cukierman's (1992) index of legal central bank independence (LVAU), updated by William Bernhard and David Leblang for Belgium, France, Italy, and New Zealand, and by the author for Finland, Ireland, Japan, Sweden, and the United Kingdom to incorporate the changes resulting from central bank reforms in the 1990s.

d Laakso/Taagepera's (1979) index of the effective number of parliamentary parties, showing the fragmentation of the party system.

e Social security contributions received by government.

f Exports + imports of goods and services as a percentage of GDP.

Right cabinet portfolio (%)[b]	Government wage consumption expenditure as % of GDP	Government non-wage consumption expenditure as % of GDP	Government fixed capital formation as % of GDP	Social security transfers as % of GDP	Government employment as % of total employment
40.8	17.4	8.3	2.4	16.4	24.4
23.9	13.1	5.7	3.5	12.5	19.2
20.1	12.4	6.7	3.8	11.4	23.9
13.1	16.5	10.0	4.0	14.9	27.2
4.1	11.0	6.7	3.9	16.4	11.8
15.7	11.9	9.4	3.1	16.2	16.5
45.1	12.2	8.8	3.5	15.4	20.5
18.3	9.0	9.1	3.3	15.7	12.6
4.9	11.0	6.4	2.9	13.5	14.5
33.7	12.4	12.5	3.8	16.3	12.5
42.9					
61.2	10.8	6.2	3.4	6.4	16.3
29.7	13.3	7.0	3.3	10.9	20.8
69.4	10.4	6.1	3.8	11.3	12.5
72.2	10.9	7.0	2.7	10.5	15.8
62.2	11.0	8.7	3.0	12.7	24.6
51.6	10.4	6.3	3.9	9.0	15.4
95.6	6.5	6.5	5.1	6.3	8.3

Table 3.a.2 Economic and political indicators of 18 OECD countries, 1961–2001 averages

Country[a]	Central bank independence[c]	Raw number of governing parties	Effective number of parties in parliament[d]	Gross debt as % of GDP	Current disbursement as % of GDP
National coordinated market economies					
Denmark	0.5	2.1	5.0	71.7	54.2
Finland	0.3	4.1	5.8	31.6	43.7
Norway	0.2	1.8	4.3	35.4	45.5
Sweden	0.3	1.4	3.7	55.4	55.9
Industry-coordinated market economies					
Austria	0.6	1.6	2.7	46.4	50.2
Belgium	0.2	3.8	7.4	99.9	53.2
France	0.4	2.5	5.2	45.9	47.4
Germany	0.7	2.0	3.3	34.4	44.8
Italy	0.3	3.4	4.9	83.7	43.9
Netherlands	0.4	3.1	5.0	59.8	51.8
Switzerland	0.6	4.0	6.1		
Liberal market economies					
Australia	0.3	1.6	3.0	30.4	33.5
Canada	0.5	1.0	3.2	66.9	46.8
Ireland	0.4	1.6	3.2	72.6	45.2
New Zealand	0.3	1.2	2.9	53.1	39.5
United Kingdom	0.4	1.0	2.9	57.6	43.3
United States	0.5	1.7	2.1	57.6	33.8
Japan	0.2	1.4	3.6	65.2	30.9

Source: see variables, definitions, and sources in Tables 4.1 and 4.2.

Notes
a The classification of countries in the three types is from Kitschelt *et al.* (1999a).
b As a percentage of all cabinet portfolios.
c Cukierman's (1992) index of legal central bank independence (LVAU), updated by William Bernhard and David Leblang for Belgium, France, Italy, and New Zealand, and by the author for Finland, Ireland, Japan, Sweden, and the United Kingdom to incorporate the changes resulting from central bank reforms in the 1990s.
d Laakso/Taagepera's (1979) index of the effective number of parliamentary parties, showing the fragmentation of the party system.
e Social security contributions received by government.
f Exports + imports of goods and services as a percentage of GDP.

Current receipt as % of GDP	Public subsidies as % of GDP	Personal income tax as % of GDP	Corporate income tax as % of GDP	Social security contribution as % of GDP[e]	Indirect tax as % of GDP	Trade openness (%)[f]
54.0	2.1	22.7	2.0	2.3	17.2	55.8
45.9	2.8	13.3	2.2	9.8	13.4	46.0
50.4	3.9	11.4	4.9	10.0	15.7	61.3
56.0	2.6	17.6	1.9	11.6	14.1	54.5
48.3	2.7	9.8	1.8	13.8	15.6	58.3
46.9	2.2	12.1	2.5	15.2	12.3	102.4
45.9	2.1	5.6	2.2	17.8	15.5	32.2
43.3	1.7	9.1	1.9	15.4	11.9	45.5
36.7	2.0	7.9	2.2	13.3	10.3	34.6
49.3	1.6	10.4	3.1	17.3	10.4	80.8
31.1	1.2	11.0	3.5		11.3	28.5
42.3	1.5	10.8	3.7	4.3	13.4	47.7
40.4	2.1	11.1	2.2	6.7	15.1	92.1
40.1	1.1	17.3	4.4	1.5	11.5	42.4
40.8	1.2	12.8	2.9	7.6	12.8	44.7
31.3	0.4	10.2	3.1	5.8	8.2	15.2
28.9	1.0	5.5	4.1	6.8	7.3	13.1

4 The political–economic determinants of economic policy and outcomes

Basic empirical results

This and the next chapters analyze empirical data to investigate whether and how political and economic factors affect economic policy and performance in industrial democracies and whether and how the impact of governments and other political actors on economic policy and outcomes have changed in the past few decades. I also show which economic policy and outcomes these political and economic institutions and factors affect. I present empirical evidence to corroborate my theoretical arguments described in Chapters 2 and 3.

Chapter 4 presents the basic results of the empirical analysis of the determinants of economic policy and outcomes, focusing mostly on the general basic patterns of the impact of political and economic factors on economic policy and outcomes. The basic analysis seeks to understand the individual effects of the *uninteracted* political and economic factors examined in the previous chapters so as to grasp their general patterns. The examination of the interactive effects of multiple political factors is deferred to Chapter 5. Chapter 5 analyzes the *interacted* effects of the political–economic institutions – I investigate how multiple institutions or factors jointly affect economic policy and outcomes. Since more findings that are significant from the theoretical perspective of this book regarding the central bank–party government connection are found in the analysis of interactive effects presented in Chapter 5, the primary goals of Chapter 4 are to (1) understand how political–economic factors affect economic policy and outcomes when considered independently without their interaction, (2) test the empirical validity of the conventional arguments about the weaknesses in economic policy and performance among governments and institutions that are traditionally considered fiscally undisciplined and/or weak performers, and (3) lay the foundations for the empirical analysis of interactive effects in Chapter 5.

In both Chapters 4 and 5, I present the results of the statistical analysis of the entire period of 1961–2001 and the results of the statistical analysis conducted by dividing the entire period into two sub-periods (1961–1981 and 1982–2001) to explore the possibility that economic policy and outcomes and their determinants have changed in recent decades. The two-period analyses are conducted to decipher any time-variant effects of political and economic factors and to see if their effects are constant throughout the entire period of 1961–2001. More importantly, I investigate the roles of political–economic factors between the two periods to identify how their impacts changed between the two periods, if they have ever existed. This is a prudent approach also because we need to take measures to reduce the possibility that the design of pooled time-series cross-sectional analysis masks time-specific effects that may actually exist. As Kittel (1999) points out, pooled analysis averages out time- and country-specific effects, and the coefficient in a pooled-analysis model represents the combined average partial effect of both the time-series and cross-section dimensions.

As we will see, when we analyze the two periods separately, we observe that significant time-variant effects of political and economic factors exist, which are not detected in pooled analyses covering the entire 1961–2001 period where their impacts are assumed or treated as constant. In addition, the two-period analysis is important because the nature and conditions of the international and domestic economies changed in the past few decades and it often led governments and political–economic actors to adjust their economic policy and altered their impact on economic outcomes, as I argued in Chapter 3.

This chapter starts by explaining the data, variables, and the methods of empirical analysis. I then begin to present the results of the basic empirical analysis. The analysis starts with individual disaggregate economic policy items (e.g. government consumption, government investment, personal income tax, corporate tax) and move on to more aggregate policy indicators (total government spending and revenues). Then, the analysis examines two broad aggregate indicators of macroeconomic policy stances, government primary balance and the monetary policy stance. Lastly, it investigates economic performance indicators – economic growth, inflation, and unemployment. Thus, the analysis moves from disaggregate policy to aggregate policy, and from economic policy to performance. The analysis in Chapter 5 also follows this order.

As I argue in this book, a useful understanding of economic policy and outcomes and the roles of political–economic factors therein requires an overall understanding of the general patterns of different policy instruments and economic performance indicators. To gain such an understanding requires us to go back and forth between different policy tools and economic outcomes because we need to understand how individual parts are related to each other and to the whole. Parts that at a glance may not make sense individually can make sense when they are understood as parts of the whole.

Data, variables, and methods

Data and variables

To study the determinants of economic policy and performance, I examine data from 18 industrial democracies between 1961 and 2001.[1] All data are annual data. The definitions and sources of the variables are summarized in Tables 4.1 and 4.2. I explain below our principal variables.

Table 4.1 List of dependent variables

Variables	Definitions	Sources
Total spending	Total government disbursement as a percentage of GDP.	OECD (2003).
Total revenues	Total government receipt as a percentage of GDP.	OECD (2003).
Spending		
Government wage consumption	Government final consumption expenditure (wages) as a percentage of GDP.	Calculated from OECD (2003).
Government non-wage consumption	Government final consumption expenditure (non-wages) as a percentage of GDP.	Calculated from OECD (2003).
Government fixed investment	Government fixed capital formation as a percentage of GDP.	Calculated from OECD (2003).
Government subsidies	Government subsidies to industries as a percentage of GDP.	Calculated from OECD (2003).
Social security payments	Social security benefits paid by government as a percentage of GDP.	Calculated from OECD (2003).
Supplement		
Government employment	Public employment as a percentage of total employment.	Calculated from OECD (2003).
Tax		
Individual income tax	Individual income tax as a percentage of GDP.	Calculated from OECD (2003).
Corporate income tax	Corporate income tax as a percentage of GDP.	Calculated from OECD (2003).
Consumption tax	Indirect tax as a percentage of GDP, including excise taxes.	Calculated from OECD (2003).
Social security contributions	Social security contributions received by government as a percentage of GDP.	Calculated from OECD (2003).
Macroeconomic policy stance		
Primary balance (fiscal policy stance)	Cyclically adjusted primary balance as a percentage of potential GDP (+ surplus/– deficit).	OECD (2003).
Discount rates (monetary policy stance)	Cyclically adjusted monetary policy stance by central banks (+ tight monetary policy/– loose policy). Calculated as discount rates minus Taylor-rule implied discount rates. Taylor-rule implied discount rate$_{(t)}$ = 2 + inflation$_{(t-1)}$ + 0.5* (inflation$_{(t-1)}$ – π*) + 0.5*output gap$_{(t-1)}$ where the constant term (2) is the assumed long-run equilibrium	Computed from IMF (2003) and OECD (2003).

continued

Table 4.1 continued

Variables	Definitions	Sources
	real rate, and π* is the central bank's inflation target rate, and it is assumed to be 2%. The Taylor-type rule calculates a price-stability-conforming discount rate target from the past inflation rate, central banks' inflation target rate, the long-term real interest rate, and the gap between real and potential GDP. See the text for justification.	
Primary balance (unadjusted)	Government primary balance as a percentage of GDP (+ surplus/– deficit). Cyclically unadjusted.	OECD (2003).
Discount rates (unadjusted)	Central bank discount rates. Cyclically unadjusted (+ tight monetary stance/– loose stance).	IMF (2003).
Economic performance		
GDP	Real GDP annual growth rates.	Calculated from OECD (2003).
Inflation	Inflation rates – consumer price index.	OECD (2003), IMF (2003).
Unemployment	Unemployment rates.	OECD (2003).

Dependent variables We have altogether about 17 economic policy and performance indicators for our dependent variables, as shown in Table 4.1. For fiscal policy, we examine both expenditure and revenue sides. For aggregate measures, we have total government disbursement, total receipt, and primary balance as percentages of GDP. We also study disaggregate spending and tax items, including both wage and non-wage components of government final consumption expenditures, government fixed investment, government subsidies, and social security payments on the spending side, and individual income tax, corporate income tax, indirect tax (mostly sales and consumption taxes), and social security contributions on the revenue side. We also study the size of public employment as a percentage of total employment to explore government policy toward job creation and maintenance through provision of government employment. For monetary policy, we have central bank discount rates. When observations for discount rates are missing in a small number of cases, the data are augmented by money market rates and then by treasury bills rates.

For indicators of economic performance, we have real GDP growth, inflation, and unemployment. *GDP* is real GDP annual growth rates. *Unemployment* is unemployment rates as a percentage of total labor force. *Inflation* is annual inflation rates (annual change in consumer price index). The data for all dependent variables come or are computed from the OECD (2003) and IMF (2003).

Political–economic variables   Our main independent variables are summarized in Table 4.2. *CBI* is a measure of central banks' independence from party governments (the executive and legislative branches) and captures their ability to pursue monetary policy without or despite political interference by the latter (the values range from 0 to 1). The data are Cukierman's (1992) index of legal central bank independence (LVAU). To incorporate the recent changes resulting from central bank reforms in the 1990s, the data are updated by Bernhard and Leblang for Belgium, France, Italy, and New Zealand, and by the author for Finland, Ireland, Japan, Sweden, and the United Kingdom.[2]

   Coalition, Majority, and *Fragmentation* are political variables measuring the attributes of governments that may affect governments' policy-making capabilities, strength, or stability. *Coalition* is the raw number of governing parties.[3] The conventional argument by previous studies is that a larger number of governing parties makes policy making difficult and causes undisciplined economic policy. I will show in the empirical chapters that this conventional view is too simplistic. *Majority* is a dummy variable representing the majority status of governments (majority = 1, minority = 0). In addition to *Coalition*, which measures how many political parties share the control of government (the executive branch), I also enter the variable *Fragmentation*. *Fragmentation* is Laakso and Taagepera's (1979) index of the effective number of parliamentary parties, which shows the degree of the fragmentation of the party system. It shows how many political parties exist in the party system after taking into account their vote shares as well as the simple number of parties. I investigate the potential impact of *Fragmentation* as well as *Coalition* to examine whether it is the fragmentation of the government or of the party system that affects economic policy making and outcomes. As we will see in the empirical analysis, *Coalition* and *Fragmentation* affect economic policy and performance in different ways, producing interesting results. I examine the effect of *Coalition* and *Fragmentation* by entering them separately and together in the models to avoid drawing erroneous conclusions as a result of possible multicollinearity. (The correlation between *Coalition* and *Fragmentation* is 0.72.)

   Left, Center, and *Right* are three separate government partisanship variables. They measure cabinet portfolios held respectively by leftist, centrist, and rightist parties as a percentage of all cabinet portfolios. Left parties include social democratic and labor parties. Center parties include Christian democratic and Catholic parties and other centrist parties, and right parties conservative and liberal parties. The data are from Armingeon *et al.* (2002).[4]

   In the regression analysis, I alternately enter each of the three partisan variables in all regression models one at a time, instead of entering all of them at the same time. The reason I separate government partisanship into three separate variables and measure their separate effects is the following. Most previous studies typically examine the effects of government partisanship by using a

Table 4.2 Independent variables: definitions and sources

Variables	Definitions	Sources
Political–economic variables		
CBI	Central bank independence (Cukierman's index of legal central bank independence (LVAU)). Range: 0–1.	Cukierman (1992); updated by Bill Bernhard and David Leblang for Belgium, France, Italy, and New Zealand, and by Takayuki Sakamoto for Finland, Ireland, Japan, Sweden, and the United Kingdom.
Coalition	The number of governing parties.	Woldendorp *et al.* (1993, 1998), Mackie and Rose (1991, 1997), *European Journal of Political Research, Political Data Yearbook* (various years), and *Keesing's Record of World Events* (various years).
Majority	Majority status of governments (a dummy variable: majority = 1, minority = 0).	Woldendorp *et al.* (1993, 1998), Mackie and Rose (1991, 1997), *European Journal of Political Research, Political Data Yearbook* (various years), and *Keesing's Record of World Events* (various years).
Stability	The degree of the stability of government measured as the average duration of the most recent three governments in days prior to the current year.	Calculated from Woldendorp *et al.* (1993, 1998), Mackie and Rose (1991, 1997), *European Journal of Political Research, Political Data Yearbook* (various years), and *Keesing's Record of World Events* (various years).
Fragmentation	Laakso and Taagepera's (1979) index of the effective number of parliamentary parties, which shows the degree of the fragmentation of the party system after taking into account both the number of political parties and their vote shares.	Armingeon *et al.* (2002).
Left	Left party cabinet portfolios as a percentage of all cabinet portfolios.	Armingeon *et al.* (2002).
Center	Center party cabinet portfolios as a percentage of all cabinet portfolios.	Armingeon *et al.* (2002).

continued

Table 4.2 continued

Variables	Definitions	Sources
Right	Right party cabinet portfolios as a percentage of all cabinet portfolios.	Armingeon *et al.* (2002)
Election	A dummy variable for election years. 1 = election years, 0 = otherwise. For the United States, both presidential and congressional elections were coded. For France, similarly, both presidential and National Assembly elections were coded. For all other countries, national elections to the lower house of the parliament were coded.	Woldendorp *et al.* (1993, 1998); *Keesing's Record of World Events* (various years); Mackie and Rose (1991, 1997); *European Journal of Political Research, Political Data Yearbook* (various years).
Labor	Kenworthy's index of wage setting coordination. Range: 1 (low coordination) to 5 (high coordination).	Kenworthy (2001).
Economic variables (controls)		
Capital mobility	Capital mobility, an index of financial openness. Range: 0 (low mobility) to 14 (high mobility).	Quinn (1997), supplemented by his recent data.
Exchange rate	Exchange rate mechanisms under which governments operate (1 = a floating exchange rate system, 0 = a fixed system).	IMF (various years).
Trade openness	Trade openness measured as the sum of the exports and imports of goods and services as a percentage of GDP.	Calculated from OECD (2003).
Economic size	The size of the national economy measured as real GDP in U.S. dollars, 1995 constant PPP.	OECD (2003).
Pop65	Population 65 years and over as a percentage of total population.	OECD (various years).
Output gap	Output gap – the percentage deviation of real GDP from a trend line measuring potential real output.	OECD (2003).

similar version of a single partisan variable that measures the impact of left party cabinet portfolios (i.e. using *Left* without using *Right* or *Center*), thereby measuring the impact of right party cabinet portfolios with low left values. Such a unidimensional or dichotomous conception of the impact of government partisanship assumes, for instance, that if the left (social democratic) causes low unemployment, that means by design the right (conservative) causes high unemployment. This conceptualization also assumes that the impact of centrist parties – often represented by Christian democratic parties – must be halfway between that of the left and right.

Yet as some scholars show (e.g. Esping-Andersen, 1990; Huber and Stephens, 2001), Christian democratic parties constitute a separate cluster of political parties from the left and right in terms of their welfare and economic policies. Christian democrats' general economic policy may be conservative and similar to the right's. But in welfare policy, their welfare provision is generous; their welfare spending levels are almost as high as those of left parties due to their strong sense of social responsibility that dictates that it is the responsibility of state and society to take care of the weak and poor in society. The form of Christian democrats' welfare provision does differ from that of social democrats; the latter's welfare provision is more universalistic and implemented through provision of public services such as health care, education, and daycare, whereas the former's is more occupationally segregated and relies on cash transfers such as pensions, unemployment benefits, and income assistance, instead of providing public services (Esping-Andersen, 1990). But at least in terms of welfare spending levels, Christian democrats are more similar to left than right parties, and it may affect their impact on economic policy and performance in ways that cannot be captured by the notion of Christian democrats being halfway between the left and right. In other words, a dichotomous conception of the impact of government partisanship may not always allow us to understand accurately the role of partisanship in economic policy and performance.

Does a negative impact of left governments really mean a positive impact of right governments? Or does it mean a positive impact of center governments? It depends. A low left score means a strong right sometimes and a strong center at other times, and a strong center-right at yet other times, depending on the partisan composition of those non-left party governments. In short, this is not something one can assume a priori. If there really are three distinct clusters of partisan governments in their economic policy making and performance, then, we may get different results from measuring their effects separately if partisanship does make a difference to policy and performance. For this reason, I examine the impacts of left, center, and right governments separately. The empirical evidence in this and the following chapters indeed shows that we can better understand the impacts of partisan governments by using the three different partisan variables. Furthermore, the three different partisan governments behave differently in managing economic policy along with central banks. Either central banks affect different partisan governments differently or different partisan governments respond to central banks differently, or both. Using three different partisan variables increases the number of models we have to estimate and thus time demands on researchers. But it is a productive approach in deciphering partisan influence on economic policy and outcomes.

Election is a dummy variable for election years (1 = election years, 0 = otherwise). For the United States, both presidential and congressional elections were coded. For France, similarly, both presidential and National Assembly elections were coded. For all other countries, national elections to the lower house of the parliament were coded.

Labor is a variable capturing the degree of wage coordination. I use Kenworthy's (2001) wage setting coordination index for this variable. His index is coded based on the institutional features of the wage bargaining process that are likely to generate high wage coordination. The index consists of annual observations that vary across time. The values range from 1 (least coordinated) to 5 (most coordinated).[5] This wage coordination index is similar to, but differs from a group of similar scores of the strength or centralization of labor (e.g. Cameron, 1984; Golden and Wallerstein, 1994; Lange *et al.*, 1995; OECD, 1993; Traxler, 1994; Boix, 2000). Kenworthy's index emphasizes the institutional attributes of wage bargaining that facilitate wage coordination, whereas the others focus on the organizational power of labor measured by factors such as union density and the centralization and power of labor in wage bargaining. They are also different in that the former is time-variant, but the latter is largely time-invariant. But since the components of their scores overlap, the correlation between Kenworthy's index and Boix's (2000) index of the organizational power of labor, for instance, is reasonably high (0.70).[6] I decided to use Kenworthy's index in my empirical analysis because as Soskice (1990) notes, we are, most of the time, interested in wage coordination in analyzing the economic effects of labor, not merely the centralization of labor organizations, and also because his index is time-variant and sensitive to fluctuations across time.[7]

Globalization variables   *Capital mobility*, *Exchange rate*, and *Trade openness* are entered to control for the effects of economic globalization and integration. *Capital mobility* is Quinn's (1997) index of financial openness, supplemented by his recent data (ranging from 0 to 14).[8] It is an approximate measure of how freely capital can move in and out of a country. Larger scores indicate higher capital mobility. *Exchange rate* is a dummy variable measuring exchange rate mechanisms under which governments operate (1 = a floating exchange rate system, 0 = a fixed system).[9] *Trade openness* is a variable that measures trade openness – the level of a country's exposure to international competition due to trade liberalization – and is operationalized as the sum of the exports and imports of goods and services as a percentage of GDP.

Estimation

Certain estimation problems can exist in time-series cross-section data, like the data of this book – serial correlation, panel heteroskedasticity, and contemporaneous correlation of errors. How I deal with these potential problems will be discussed below. But in addition to them, there are at least two other methodological and estimation issues that need to be addressed – a unit root problem, and the use or non-use of fixed effects. I discuss these first.

Unit root and spurious correlation   Many economic and policy time-series are suspected to have a unit root. If they have a unit root, the results of regression estimation can be misleading. If time-series are nonstationary, we may detect a spurious relationship between nonstationary times-series and conclude erroneously that there is a significant relationship between the two nonstationary variables. That is, even when two time-series are independent of each other, we can detect statistically significant t-statistics if they are nonstationary. So if there is a unit root problem, it needs to be remedied to derive correct results and conclusions. As I describe shortly below, some of my time-series under analysis also have a unit root. There are several approaches one can adopt in dealing with a unit root problem.

The first method is to difference nonstationary time-series variables. First differencing usually makes nonstationary time-series stationary. After first differencing, we can interpret the regression results without worrying about a unit root. This is usually the approach taken by many economists. This solves the unit root problem, but creates a new problem. That is, when we use a first difference as a dependent variable, we are measuring the effects of independent variables on annual changes in the dependent variable, not its levels (all our data are annual data). But we are interested in the effects that the independent variables have on the levels of dependent variables. Unfortunately, models using the first difference of the dependent variables do not allow us to observe effects on levels. So I do not use this method.

The second approach is to use single-equation error correction models (ECMs) (Beck, 1992; Franzese, 2002a). The pseudo ECMs are robust to a unit root, so one can study effects on both changes (approximately, short term) and levels (approximately, long term) of the dependent variable. While the simple design of single-equation ECMs is attractive for researchers who want to study both long- and short-term effects, pseudo ECMs are not entirely free from an estimation problem because the standard errors for coefficients on other lagged level independent variables may not be appropriate (since these coefficients are on I(1) variables).[10] This book analyzes numerous time-series variables (fiscal and monetary policy items, economic performance indicators, and other political–economic variables) that can potentially have a unit root and have their own stochastic nature. The estimation method using ECMs should eventually be pursued in future research to understand both short- and long-term dynamics of policy and political–economic variables. But to do so in this book is not an economical strategy in terms of the time demands and analytical complexity it would impose, since I would have to try to estimate single-equation ECMs for all my policy and performance variables while allowing for the different stochastic nature each time-series variable has. As a result, I do not use these ECMs in this book. For similar reasons, conventional ECMs are also not used in this book. But such ECM analyses should be pursued in future research.

The results of multiple panel unit root tests (implemented in EViews5) suggest that Table 4.2 variables *GDP, Inflation, Discount rates, Capital mobility, Majority, Coalition,* and *Labor* do not have a unit root. *Primary balance, Consumption tax, Government investment, Right,* and *Center* are also most likely stationary. So for these variables, we can simply enter their level variables in regression models. In contrast, panel unit root tests do not reject the possibility of a unit root for variables *Unemployment, Discount rates, Spending, Revenues, Government employment, Government non-wage consumption, Government wage consumption, Government subsidies, Personal income tax, Corporate income tax, Trade openness, CBI,* and *Fragmentation. Primary balance* (cyclically adjusted) and *Left* may also be borderline stationary as some panel unit root tests do not reject a unit root and other tests reject it. But one thing we need to keep in mind is that the power of unit root tests is fairly weak, especially so when one has a small number of years of observations under study (in this book, it is 41 years). Because of the low power of unit root tests, there is the possibility that unit root tests fail to reject a unit root for time-series even though they are not unit root processes. That is, we may possibly mistakenly conclude that a time-series variable is nonstationary due to the low power of unit root tests, when it is actually stationary.

In light of the patterns of our time-series data and the econometric considerations mentioned above, the approach I take is, first, to estimate models with levels of dependent variables. This does not pose an estimation problem for our time-series variables that do not have a unit root, such as output growth and inflation. Second, for times-series that may potentially have a unit root (and those for which unit root tests reject a unit root), I regress their levels on independent variables and check the coefficient(s) on the lagged dependent variable(s). If the coefficient (or the sum of the coefficients) is significantly below unity (1), then, those times-series dependent variables are not likely to have a unit root problem (Alesina *et al.*, 1997). If so, we can proceed with analysis just like we interpret conventional regression results. Fortunately, the coefficient(s) on the lagged dependent variable(s) for our time-series for which unit root tests do not reject a unit root is always significantly smaller than 1. So we do not face a serious unit root problem in our time-series data. We can proceed with analysis using level variables entered in the regression equations without first-differencing. This estimation approach also makes it easier to compare the results of my empirical analysis with those of many previous studies (e.g. Garrett, 1998; Boix, 1998; Bearce, 2002; Clark, 2003; Swank, 2002; Huber and Stephens, 2001) because they use the levels of time-series variables in their regressions.[11] But when we use unemployment as an independent variable, to be cautious, we use its first difference since it is entered in the equations mostly as an economic control.

Fixed effects   Next, we need to make a decision whether to use fixed-effect models or models without country dummies. We face two potential problems:

(1) a chance of omitted variables; and (2) the possibility that country dummies soak up the cross-national variance that should instead be attributed to the independent variables under analysis. In estimating time-series cross-section models, the use of country dummies merits consideration because a failure to include independent variables that do really affect the dependent variable causes the problem of omitted variables. If we use country dummies as independent variables, the effects of political, economic, or any factors that we do not enter in the models will be captured by the country dummies. We have a sample of 18 countries with great diversity in economic, political, and social conditions, and we cannot control for all sources of divergence in the models. In this respect, country dummies provide a convenient way to control for all other factors we do not model.[12]

But the inclusion of country dummies can create another problem. That is, country dummies modeled in the specifications can potentially soak up the effects of the other cross-nationally divergent institutional variables we specifically include in the models. If country dummies soak up the cross-national variance that should instead be attributed to the other independent variables, we can get statistically insignificant results for these institutional variables even when they actually have effects. In other words, in the presence of country dummies, the differences that should be attributed to the cross-national institutional differences we explicitly model can be erroneously imputed to the country dummies. This factor can be a serious concern especially when models have institutional variables that have small cross-time variance.

Estimation with and without country dummies both has strengths and weaknesses. It can be premature to a priori favor one over the other, and it is good to estimate models both with and without country dummies to take advantage of the strengths of the two approaches and minimize the chance of errors. I estimate all models both with and without country dummies. The results stay the same sometimes, and change at other times. When the results change between fixed models and models without country dummies, I explain the difference. In presenting the numerical regression results in the tables in Chapter 4, I report the results of fixed effect models in principle to avoid clutter. But I explain in the text when the results of fixed-effect and no-dummy models differ. In Chapter 5, I utilize the results of fixed-effect and no-dummy models.

Estimation   The estimation method is ordinary least squares (OLS) with panel-corrected standard errors (PCSEs) and country and period dummy variables to correct for the estimation problems prevalent in panel data of this kind – serial correlation, panel heteroskedasticity, and contemporaneous correlation of errors (Beck and Katz, 1995, 1996). When Lagrange multiplier tests suggest that the models show a sign of autocorrelation, lags of the dependent variable are entered in the equations as independent variables until autocorrelation is eliminated. All independent variables except for the election year dummy are lagged one year to allow for the time lag between policy making and implementation and to mitigate the endogeneity problem.

I analyze the effects of political–economic factors across different time periods to explore the possibility that the effects may be time-variant. Scholars have argued that because of economic globalization, governments lost latitude in choosing their economic policy or the effectiveness of their policy was lost, and as a result, their policies converged (e.g. Kurzer, 1993; Scharpf, 1991). If this convergence thesis is valid, we may observe effects of political–economic factors during the 1960s and 1970s, but such effects should disappear in the 1990s and maybe the 1980s.

In addition to the analysis of the entire period of 1961–2001, I divide the entire period into two sub-periods (1961–1981 and 1982–2001) and run the same analysis for each of the sub-periods to examine time-variant effects of political–economic factors.[13] The first period (1961–1981) is one in which the link between government attributes and economic policy was supposedly strong with the dominance of Keynesian economic policy. Toward the end of the period, the link started to loosen, and Keynesian policy eventually would be replaced by the neoliberal policy regime in the second period. As we reviewed in Chapter 3, the economic environment for industrial democracies changed toward the end of the first period after two oil crises and the collapse of the Bretton Woods monetary system. Many governments first tried to ride out stagflation after the oil crises with Keynesian policy in the 1970s, but their economic policy gradually started to shift toward neoliberal antiinflationary policy when Keynesian policy did not alleviate the economic problems. The collapse of the Bretton Woods also ended the days of a fixed exchange rate regime, and many industrial countries shifted to a floating rate system. As open-economy economics tells us, the effectiveness of fiscal and monetary policies in stimulating demand hinges on the exchange rate regime and capital mobility (Mundell, 1963). In tandem with capital mobility, which was to increase dramatically in the 1980s and 1990s, a change in the exchange rate mechanism should affect the effectiveness of macroeconomic policy and governments' economic policy behavior into the 1980s and 1990s. Thus, the second period (1982–2001) is one in which the globalization of capital and trade deepened, and market pressures and competitiveness imperatives allegedly diminished room for governments' economic maneuvering. The influence of neoclassical economic policy also became widespread and more dominant.

The choice of the two-period analysis – rather than analysis of three or four periods – was made partly for the theoretical reasons explained above and in the previous chapters, and also partly for the reason of methodological practicality. For one, the use of more time periods reduces the number of observations for each model and limits the power of our regression models. For another, the values for some institutional variables do not change much during some periods, and a time-invariant variable and country dummies together cause perfect multicollinearity, making it impossible to estimate fixed models with country dummy variables. As a result, the more time periods we create, the larger the number of models or institutional variables we cannot estimate. There was thus the need to carry out the period-specific analysis while minimizing the number of time periods so as to estimate models for all variables and all time periods at the same time.

A note is in order with regard to the presentation of the results about government partisanship (left, center, right governments). I first report the results of the basic models with only left partisanship entered (i.e. without center or right governments) and explain the findings about all other political–economic factors. Then, I present in separate tables the results that show the effects of left, center, and right governments. As mentioned before, in order to understand accurately how partisanship affects policy and performance, I enter only one of the three partisan variables at a time and run all the models for each of the three partisan variables. Since the magnitude and statistical significance of the rest of the independent variables rarely change across models with left, center, and right, I omit the results of the other independent variables in reporting the results of partisanship and report only the coefficients, standard errors, and *p*-values of the government partisanship variables side by side. The reader can safely assume that the results of the other independent variables remain very close to those in the basic models. I follow the same presentation style in reporting the results about the number of governing parties vs. the number of effective parliamentary parties.

Spending policy

We first examine spending policy, then tax policy, and economic outcomes.

Tables 4.3–4.8 report the results of model estimation of various spending items – the wage and non-wage components of government final consumption expenditure (government services), government investment, government subsidies to industries, social security transfers, and government employment. The models include a lagged dependent variable(s) to eliminate autocorrelation. Some models also have a second, or a second and a third, lagged dependent variable when they are necessary to eliminate autocorrelation. Autocorrelation is eliminated when appropriate lagged dependent variables are entered. For all models, the sum of the coefficient(s) on the lagged dependent variable(s) is significantly below unity (1), so we do not have unit root concerns.

Economic controls   Before proceeding to examine the political–economic factors of our greatest interest, let us first look at the effects of economic controls. For most of the spending items, the effects of inflation are positive, indicating that spending increases with inflation. This is probably because of inflation's upward effect on prices, including the costs of government operations and services, wages for government employees, the goods and services governments purchase, inflation-indexed social transfers, and so on. It may also be caused partly by economic expansions (that are often accompanied by rises in prices) that usually increase government revenues and therefore the economic resources governments can use.

The effects of economic growth are countercyclical for government subsidies in 1982–2001, social security in 1961–1981 and 1982–2001, and government employment in 1961–1981 and 1982–2001. This matches the conventional understanding that during economic downturns, social security spending (e.g. unemployment benefits) increases, and governments respond to downturns with increases in public employment. At the same time, however, the data also indicate that economic growth has procyclical effects on government investment in 1961–1981 and subsidies in 1961–1981. This pattern of procyclicality and countercyclicality across different spending items matches the pattern found by Lane (2002), though he and I use different datasets and specifications. Lane explains procyclicality in some spending items as a result of political actors' competition for shares of increased government resources during economic upturns. The cyclical response of government spending is, thus, not uniform for different spending items, and this shows the analytical merit of studying different disaggregate spending items, instead of studying only total spending. As we will see later, when we look at only total spending, total spending responds countercyclically to economic growth. So if one studied only total spending, one would conclude that spending generally moves countercyclically – a generalization that does not hold uniformly for disaggregate spending items.

Unemployment never achieves significance in the second period (indicating that spending is not sensitive to unemployment during the period), but the signs of its coefficients show an interesting pattern if the results are to be trusted. The signs indicate that (with the exceptions of government wage consumption and subsidies) governments responded countercyclically to unemployment during the second period, but procyclically during the first period. This is contrary to the conventional wisdom that governments widely used Keynesian countercyclical policy in the 1960s and 1970s and (more procyclical) neoliberal policy in the 1980s and 1990s. *Unemployment* achieves significance only in the first period (procyclical), so the evidence for countercyclicality in the second period is weak. But if the results are to be trusted, they run counter to the conventional wisdom and also to the globalization thesis that while there was room for governments' countercyclical maneuvering in the first period, globalization and competitive pressure eliminated such room for governments' use of countercyclical policy in the second period.[14] As we will see throughout the empirical analysis of this book, the impacts of political factors on economic policy were stronger in the 1980s and 1990s. At the least, the negative coefficient (indicating procyclicality) during the first period is significant for the spending items except for government subsidies and public employment, calling into question the view that governments responded countercyclically to unemployment during the height of the Keynesian orthodoxy. This same pattern is also observed for total government spending, as we will see later.

One might wonder if this happens because *Unemployment* is a lagged first difference and if it may be the case that spending is sensitive to the level of unemployment, but not its change from the previous year. (Note that I use the difference of unemployment for unit root concerns.) To check the possibility, I also ran the models with the lagged level, but the results show that unemployment still shows procyclicality (results not reported). While this issue should be pursued further, I defer it to future research partly because unemployment is for the most part an economic control in this book and it is beyond the scope of this book to examine the precise role of unemployment in policy. Let me note just that there are three possibilities. One is that different partisan governments respond differently to unemployment, which can be revealed by the use of the interactive terms between unemployment and government partisanship. Cusack (1999), for instance, finds that left governments run larger deficits when unemployment is high. The second is that when unemployment is high (a sluggish economy), government revenues fall, and it reduces governments' means to finance spending increases. This is consistent with the observation above that some spending items respond procyclically to fluctuations in economic growth. The other is simply that spending is not as sensitive to unemployment as previously considered.

Globalization variables   We now look at the roles of the economic globalization variables (*Trade openness*, *Capital mobility*, *Exchange rate*). On the effects of the openness of the economy, Cameron (1978) argues that trade dependence (openness) increases public spending because governments try to mitigate the economic dislocations caused by the international economy that is beyond their control (the compensation thesis; see also Garrett, 1998; Katzenstein, 1985). The results in Tables 4.3–4.8 (*Trade openness*) show that trade openness indeed produced higher government spending during the first period (positive signs), but in the second period, it actually led to lower spending (negative signs). Thus, the compensation thesis holds for the first period, but the convergence thesis – which claims reduced spending and policy convergence as a result of competitive pressures of globalization – explains various spending items in the second period (except for government investment). The same pattern also holds for total government spending. This result for *Trade openness* suggests that in the 1980s and 1990s, open-economy governments' spending policy made a competitive turn, and open economies had lower government spending levels to make their spending policy more market-conforming and improve their economic efficiency and competitiveness, which are a more serious concern for trade-dependent countries.[15] As we will see in the section on tax policy, trade openness has a somewhat different effect on tax revenues.

Moving to *Capital mobility*, the popular view would expect greater capital mobility to move governments to reduce public spending (and tax revenues), because of their concern that mobile capital is averse to high government spending and taxation, which squeeze returns on investment, and to the negative economic consequences of expansionary spending, such as high deficits, high interest rates and/or inflation that can suppress investment and growth, as well as averse to all the economic inefficiencies and uncompetitiveness entailed by large government intervention. In this view, governments try to reduce spending and taxation in order to prevent capital flight and attract investment. But as shown in Tables 4.3–4.8, *Capital mobility* rarely has a negative sign (lower spending), and is negative and significant only in one model (public subsidies in the entire period). With higher capital mobility, governments particularly have higher social security spending (significant in all the first, second, and entire periods), which lends support to the compensation hypothesis (Cameron, 1978; Katzenstein, 1985; Garrett, 1998) arguing that governments provide social protection to mitigate the economic dislocations caused by the international economy or globalization. Capital mobility induces higher government wage consumption, social security transfers, and public employment during the second period (1982–2001), which is exactly when a greater influence of neoliberal economic policy should have moved governments to reduce spending and taxation to compete for mobile capital in a globalized economy. As we will see later, capital mobility also induces higher spending in total government expenditure in all the first, second, and entire periods (all significant). This result suggests that, at least with regard to the effects of capital mobility, the convergence thesis is overstated. The result is also the opposite of the austerity effects of trade openness during the second period where it induced lower spending.

With regard to the exchange rate mechanism, there is reason to expect that governments with a flexible exchange rate system not show high spending, *if* capital mobility is perfectly free. Under perfect capital mobility, fiscal policy should not be effective as a countercyclical economic tool if a country has a floating exchange rate regime (Mundell, 1963). If governments know this, they may not resort to countercyclical Keynesian spending to boost the economy. The result at a glance seems to support this explanation as the signs of *Exchange rate* are negative (lower spending) for almost all models. (*Exchange rate* is a dummy variable where 1 = a flexible rate, and 0 = a fixed rate.) As we will see later, a floating exchange rate mechanism also induces low total spending for the first, second, and entire periods. The result suggests lower spending for governments with a flexible rate. But capital mobility in these models is not fixed to be perfectly free, so we would need to add an interactive term of capital mobility and exchange rate systems to examine the empirical validity of this explanation (which this analysis does not pursue). But it must be easier for governments and politicians to resort to fiscal expansion under a fixed rate system in hopes of stimulating the domestic economy since they do not have to worry about currency appreciation causing reductions in net exports and output and offsetting the economic benefits of the demand stimulus.

On the other hand, politicians should not have to give up entirely spending increases and tax reductions, since they can still be an effective electoral tool, even if they are not an effective countercyclical tool. Politicians and political parties can still try to boost their electoral support among certain constituencies by offering them spending hikes or tax cuts. They could still try to improve electoral prospects with an expansionary fiscal policy even if it were not an effective demand management tool. The regression models here are, unfortunately, not designed to provide us with evidence to test this hypothesis. All we can tell is that governments with a flexible exchange rate have lower spending levels. Research into this issue is highly desirable.

Political variables   If various arguments set forth by previous scholars – that certain types of governments and political–economic institutions produce undisciplined economic policy and negative economic outcomes (reviewed in Chapter 3) – have validity, the results should show that such actors as multi-party coalition governments, pro-welfare interventionist left and center governments, and strong labor had expansionary or undisciplined economic policy and/or poor economic performance. If, on the other hand, my argument about the neoliberal shift in economic policy in industrial democracies is valid, we should observe a policy shift toward conservative economic policy toward the second period (1982–2001). We should observe that even if those actors may have had poor policy or performance records in the first period (1961–1981), their economic policy became disciplined and outcomes improved in the second period.

   I argued in Chapter 2 that the effects of different governments and institutions are contingent upon the institutional setting in which they operate. More specifically, I argued that even weak actors such as coalition or center governments should be better able to discipline their economic policy and improve economic outcomes if they are accompanied by independent central banks. The empirical analysis of this interaction between various political actors and central banks is deferred to Chapter 5, but the results there show that such was indeed the case.

Government wage consumption expenditures

Table 4.3 shows the results of government wage consumption spending. Coalition governments had higher spending than single-party governments during 1961–1981. An increase of governing parties by one caused a spending increase by 0.07 percent of GDP (0.6 percent of total government wage consumption: the average government wage consumption = 11.5 percent of GDP). When the number of parties increases from one to six (the lowest to highest in the sample), spending increases by 0.35 percent of GDP (or 3 percent of total government wage consumption). Thus, during 1961–1981, coalition governments put upward pressure on government wage consumption. However, the coefficient of coalition turns negative (lower spending) and insignificant in 1982–2001, indicating that increases in the number of coalition parties did not increase or decrease spending. Thus, the result shows that though coalition governments were high spenders in the first period, they were not any more in the second, supporting my argument that coalition governments' fiscal policy became restrained in the second period. Further, *Coalition* is negative and significant when *Right* is entered instead of *Left* in 1982–2001, providing some, though weak, evidence that coalition

Table 4.3 Determinants of government wage consumption

Model	Government wage consumption		
	1961–1981	*1982–2001*	*1961–2001*
Independent variables			
Gov. wage consumption$_{t-1}$	1.139***	1.218***	1.255***
	(0.102)	(0.084)	(0.060)
Gov. wage consumption$_{t-2}$	−0.386***	−0.547***	−0.499***
	(0.143)	(0.119)	(0.089)
Gov. wage consumption$_{t-3}$	0.093	0.188***	0.134**
	(0.092)	(0.075)	(0.057)
GDP$_{t-1}$	0.011	0.0040	0.012
	(0.016)	(0.0159)	(0.010)
Inflation$_{t-1}$	0.039***	0.049***	0.034***
	(0.009)	(0.011)	(0.008)
ΔUnemployment$_{t-1}$	−0.168***	−0.033	−0.079***
	(0.044)	(0.033)	(0.028)
Economic size$_{t-1}$	0.322	0.680**	0.554***
	(0.302)	(0.336)	(0.193)
Majority$_{t-1}$	−0.068	0.0065	0.0011
	(0.084)	(0.0962)	(0.0565)
Coalition$_{t-1}$	0.070**	−0.033	0.0072
	(0.036)	(0.029)	(0.0218)
CBI$_{t-1}$	−0.111	0.335	0.336
	(0.977)	(0.317)	(0.312)
Labor$_{t-1}$	−0.027	−0.043	−0.0022
	(0.027)	(0.031)	(0.0201)
Left$_{t-1}$	−0.00150	0.00046	0.00019
	(0.00112)	(0.00070)	(0.00054)
Election	0.0069	0.0041	0.017
	(0.0473)	(0.0400)	(0.032)
Trade openness$_{t-1}$	0.015*	−0.014***	−0.011***
	(0.009)	(0.003)	(0.002)
Exchange rate$_{t-1}$	−0.266***	−0.125	−0.259***
	(0.082)	(0.131)	(0.058)
Capital mobility$_{t-1}$	0.00027	0.077***	0.015
	(0.03367)	(0.028)	(0.016)
R^2	0.999	0.999	0.999
Observations	260	338	598

Notes
OLS estimates with panel-corrected standard errors in parentheses.
Country and time dummy variables not reported.
***Significant at the 0.01 level.
**Significant at the 0.05 level.
*Significant at the 0.10 level.

governments had restrained spending in government wage consumption in the second period (results not reported). Thus, the argument that coalition governments are profligate may hold up in the 1960s and 1970s, but not in the 1980s and 1990s, and they may have even become lower spenders than single-party governments.

The other political variables – *Majority*, *CBI*, *Labor*, and *Election* – are not significant, indicating that those factors did not affect this spending item. There is no evidence that minority governments were profligate, denying one version of the weak government arguments. Electoral cycles are also not observable in this spending category. Meanwhile, *Labor* has a negative sign and is close to significance in 1982–2001. It also becomes significant (negative) when *Center* is entered instead of *Left*, suggesting that there is some (though weak) evidence that coordinated labor contributed to reduced spending in 1982–2001, which runs counter to the claim that labor puts upward pressure on government consumption and supports my argument that labor contributed to restrained spending in the 1980s and 1990s.[16]

Partisan impact and fragmentation   Table 4.3b shows the results about the effects of government partisanship. They show that center governments had lower spending in government wage consumption in 1982–2001 than other partisan governments. Thus, center governments' spending in this category was restrained in 1982–2001, contrary to the popular view that center governments suffered fiscal indiscipline. Furthermore, the results also show that conservative (right) governments had *higher* spending in both the first and second periods. This refutes the standard partisan argument that conservative governments' spending is more restrained than their counterparts. Thus, as far as government wage consumption is concerned, the conventional partisan thesis fails.

Substantively, when center cabinet portfolios increased from 0 to 100 percent (no center-party representation to all-center cabinets) during 1982–2001, government wage consumption decreased by 0.3 percent of GDP (2.4 percent of

Table 4.3b Partisan impact on government wage consumption

Model	Government wage consumption		
	1961–1981	*1982–2001*	*1961–2001*
Independent variables			
Left$_{t-1}$	–0.00150	0.00046	0.00019
	(0.00112)	(0.00070)	(0.00054)
Center$_{t-1}$	–0.00046	–0.00273***	–0.00165***
	(0.00095)	(0.00080)	(0.00054)
Right$_{t-1}$	0.00168*	0.000995*	0.00073
	(0.00102)	(0.00062)	(0.00052)

Notes
Only the results of the three government partisanship variables that were alternately entered in the basic models are reported. The full results of the models are not reported. The statistical significance and substantive effects of the rest of the independent variables do not change enough to alter the full results reported in Table 4.3.
OLS estimates with panel-corrected standard errors in parentheses.
***Significant at the 0.01 level.
**Significant at the 0.05 level.
*Significant at the 0.10 level.

Table 4.3c Impact of party fragmentation on government wage consumption

Model	Government wage consumption		
	1961–1981	*1982–2001*	*1961–2001*
Independent variables			
Fragmentation$_{t-1}$	0.062*	0.054	0.043*
	(0.036)	(0.036)	(0.025)
Coalition$_{t-1}$	0.051	−0.040	−0.003
	(0.039)	(0.030)	(0.023)

Notes
Only the results of the two government variables that were entered in the basic models are reported. The full results of the models are not reported. The statistical significance and substantive effects of the rest of the independent variables do not change enough to alter the full results reported in Table 4.3.
OLS estimates with panel-corrected standard errors in parentheses.
***Significant at the 0.01 level.
**Significant at the 0.05 level.
*Significant at the 0.10 level.

total government wage consumption). By contrast, when right cabinet portfolios increased from 0 to 100 percent during 1982–2001, spending increased by 0.1 percent of GDP (0.9 percent of total government wage consumption). In 1961–1981, a similar jump in right party portfolio led to a 0.17 percent increase in spending (1.5 percent of total consumption).

Table 4.3c reports the results for the impact of party fragmentation and the number of governing parties. I estimated all models with *Fragmentation* only and with both *Fragmentation* and *Coalition*. The results do not change between the specifications, and there is no indication of multicollinearity. So I only report the models with both variables. I follow the same procedure for all other dependent variables.

The results show that an increase in the effective number of parliamentary parties increased government wage consumption spending in 1961–1981, though the number of coalition parties did not affect spending. The coefficient for 1982–2001 is positive and close to significance. This suggests that a large number of parties existing in the party system as a whole had the effect of putting upward pressure on spending, but the number of governing parties did not. Thus, the weak government hypothesis is correct about the number of parliamentary parties, but wrong about governing parties. The size of its effect is not so small. When the effective number of parliamentary parties increased from two to ten (lowest to highest in the sample) in 1961–1981, this spending increased by 0.5 percent of GDP (4.3 percent of total wage consumption spending).

This result about the effective number of parties is a general pattern also among other spending and tax items and economic outcomes, as we will see below. That is, an increase in the effective number of parliamentary parties puts upward pressure on spending and tax revenues and negatively affects economic outcomes. But there is little evidence that an increase in the number of governing parties has similar negative effects. Furthermore, despite its general negative economic impact, the evidence (explained below) shows that the economic policy of countries with a large number of parliamentary parties became generally disciplined in 1982–2001 (though not in wage consumption).

Government non-wage consumption expenditures

Table 4.4 reports the results of government non-wage consumption expenditures. They show that central bank independence put upward pressure on this spending item in 1961–1981. The reason for this is not immediately clear. In the second period, the sign of *CBI* becomes negative. It is not significant, but becomes significant in the models without country dummies (results not reported). If the result is to be trusted, CBI's disciplining effect kicked in during the second period, as it did for other spending and tax items.

Coordinated labor contributed to restrained (low) spending in this item in 1982–2001, the same pattern with government wage consumption. This suggests that coordinated labor facilitated fiscal restraint in the 1980s and 1990s, pointing to the conservative policy shift I discussed in Chapters 2 and 3. Majority governments also had lower spending in 1982–2001. But the sign turns positive and significant in models without country dummies. There is no evidence that multi-party coalition governments put upward spending pressure on government non-wage consumption in any period (the signs are positive but not significant). If anything, in the model with *Right* instead of *Left* and without country dummies, *Coalition* becomes negative (lower spending) and significant for the second period, suggesting that coalition governments' spending was disciplined in the 1980s and 1990s. There is also no electoral cycles in this spending category.

Partisan impact and fragmentation   Table 4.4b shows the results about the role of government partisanship. The coefficients for left governments are all positive, as expected from the partisan thesis that left governments have large spending on government services. But none of them are statistically significant, indicating that they were not high spenders in this policy category. But in the models without country dummies, *Left* becomes significant for 1961–2001, providing some evidence that left governments may have been high spenders (the substantive size of their spending is very small: a 0.07 percent of GDP increase with a 0 to 100 increase in left cabinet portfolios).

The signs of *Center* show that center governments' spending was high in 1961–1981, but became restrained (negative = low) in 1982–2001. *Center* is not significant for 1982–2001 but is close to significance ($p = 0.12$), and it becomes significant ($p = 0.04$) in the models without country dummies. Thus, although center governments had large spending in the first period, they restrained their spending on government services in the second, suggesting a conservative policy shift among center governments. Substantively, an increase in center cabinet portfolios from 0 to 100 (the lowest to highest in the sample) pushed up

Table 4.4 Determinants of government non-wage consumption

Model	Government non-wage consumption		
	1961–1981	*1982–2001*	*1961–2001*
Independent variables			
Gov. non-wage consumption$_{t-1}$	0.780***	0.879***	0.895***
	(0.059)	(0.037)	(0.023)
GDP$_{t-1}$	0.0016	−0.015	0.0009
	(0.0134)	(0.014)	(0.0094)
Inflation$_{t-1}$	0.018**	0.011	0.0042
	(0.008)	(0.008)	(0.0068)
ΔUnemployment$_{t-1}$	−0.100***	0.017	−0.022
	(0.037)	(0.028)	(0.023)
Economic size$_{t-1}$	0.069	0.866***	0.267*
	(0.215)	(0.284)	(0.161)
Majority$_{t-1}$	−0.0001	−0.150**	0.010
	(0.0637)	(0.074)	(0.044)
Coalition$_{t-1}$	0.014	0.013	0.0058
	(0.028)	(0.025)	(0.0175)
CBI$_{t-1}$	1.274*	−0.029	0.217
	(0.736)	(0.261)	(0.232)
Labor$_{t-1}$	−0.017	−0.058**	−0.024
	(0.023)	(0.027)	(0.018)
Left$_{t-1}$	0.00050	0.00044	0.00074
	(0.00093)	(0.00066)	(0.00050)
Election	−0.028	−0.015	−0.0058
	(0.044)	(0.033)	(0.0288)
Trade openness$_{t-1}$	0.023***	−0.0011	−0.0030*
	(0.009)	(0.0025)	(0.0017)
Exchange rate$_{t-1}$	0.011	−0.220***	−0.062
	(0.083)	(0.086)	(0.049)
Capital mobility$_{t-1}$	0.018	0.0026	0.018
	(0.025)	(0.0234)	(0.014)
R^2	0.998	0.999	0.998
Observations	278	338	616

Notes
OLS estimates with panel-corrected standard errors in parentheses.
Country and time dummy variables not reported.
***Significant at the 0.01 level.
**Significant at the 0.05 level.
*Significant at the 0.10 level.

spending by 0.12 percent of GDP (1.6 percent of total government non-wage consumption: the average total non-wage consumption = 7.46 percent of GDP) during 1961–1981. During 1982–2001, the same increase in center cabinet portfolios decreased spending by 0.11 percent of GDP (1.5 percent of total non-wage consumption). Meanwhile, there is no evidence that right governments had low spending in any of the periods, as nothing is significant. The signs suggest that their spending was low in 1961–1981, but increased in 1982–2001.

Table 4.4b Partisan impact on government non-wage consumption

Model	Government non-wage consumption		
	1961–1981	*1982–2001*	*1961–2001*
Left$_{t-1}$	0.00050	0.00044	0.00074
	(0.00093)	(0.00066)	(0.00050)
Center$_{t-1}$	0.00122*	−0.00111	0.00008
	(0.00073)	(0.00073)	(0.00047)
Right$_{t-1}$	−0.00133	0.00022	−0.00071
	(0.00086)	(0.00054)	(0.00048)

Notes
Only the results of the three government partisanship variables that were alternately entered in the basic models are reported.
OLS estimates with panel-corrected standard errors in parentheses.
***Significant at the 0.01 level.
**Significant at the 0.05 level.
*Significant at the 0.10 level.

Table 4.4c Impact of party fragmentation on government non-wage consumption

Model	Government non-wage consumption		
	1961–1981	*1982–2001*	*1961–2001*
Fragmentation$_{t-1}$	−0.033	−0.074**	−0.027
	(0.045)	(0.030)	(0.022)
Coalition$_{t-1}$	0.022	0.023	0.013
	(0.028)	(0.025)	(0.018)

Notes
Only the results of the three government partisanship variables that were entered in the basic models are reported.
OLS estimates with panel-corrected standard errors in parentheses.
***Significant at the 0.01 level.
**Significant at the 0.05 level.
*Significant at the 0.10 level.

Table 4.4c reports the results about the roles of party fragmentation and the number of governing parties. Only *Fragmentation* in 1982–2001 is significant, suggesting that government non-wage consumption spending in countries with fragmented party system was lower and restrained during the period. (The sign for 1961–1981 is negative in the fixed models and positive in those without country dummies, but neither is significant.)

Government investment

Table 4.5 presents the results of government investment (fixed capital formation). The results indicate that majority governments had lower spending in

Table 4.5 Determinants of government investment (fixed capital formation)

Model	Government fixed investment		
	1961–1981	*1982–2001*	*1961–2001*
Independent variables			
Government investment$_{t-1}$	0.765***	0.868***	0.889***
	(0.049)	(0.039)	(0.026)
GDP$_{t-1}$	−0.0001	0.031***	0.012
	(0.0128)	(0.011)	(0.008)
Inflation$_{t-1}$	−0.0026	0.011**	−0.0024
	(0.0083)	(0.006)	(0.0056)
ΔUnemployment$_{t-1}$	−0.100***	0.020	−0.045**
	(0.039)	(0.020)	(0.021)
Economic size$_{t-1}$	0.074	0.101	0.034
	(0.252)	(0.260)	(0.158)
Majority$_{t-1}$	−0.092	−0.108*	−0.047
	(0.073)	(0.059)	(0.043)
Coalition$_{t-1}$	−0.0038	0.041	0.0036
	(0.0308)	(0.028)	(0.0173)
CBI$_{t-1}$	1.350	−0.176	0.259
	(0.874)	(0.184)	(0.254)
Labor$_{t-1}$	0.012	0.016	0.014
	(0.026)	(0.019)	(0.016)
Left$_{t-1}$	0.00006	−0.00054	−0.00012
	(0.00088)	(0.00041)	(0.00037)
Election	0.034	−0.0063	0.019
	(0.043)	(0.0240)	(0.025)
Trade openness$_{t-1}$	−0.00195	0.00150	−0.00271
	(0.00790)	(0.00229)	(0.00210)
Exchange rate$_{t-1}$	−0.115*	−0.091	−0.028
	(0.063)	(0.061)	(0.042)
Capital mobility$_{t-1}$	−0.0028	0.015	−0.0034
	(0.0297)	(0.016)	(0.0115)
R^2	0.994	0.995	0.994
Observations	272	338	610

Notes
OLS estimates with panel-corrected standard errors in parentheses.
Country and time dummy variables not reported.
***Significant at the 0.01 level.
**Significant at the 0.05 level.
*Significant at the 0.10 level.

1982–2001 than minority ones, lending support to one version of the weak government arguments.[17] Coalition governments did not affect this spending positively or negatively. Neither did central bank independence, although it has an expected sign (negative) in 1982–2001, suggesting that CBI had disciplining effects on spending during the second period. But *CBI*'s negative sign becomes significant in models without country dummies. The results show that an increase in central bank independence from 0.14 to 0.68 (the lowest to highest in the sample) reduced this spending by 0.12 percent of GDP (3.4 percent of total government investment: the average government investment spending = 3.54 percent of GDP). Labor did not affect government investment in any period. There is no electoral cycle in this spending.

Partisan impact and fragmentation   The results of partisan effects on government investment run completely counter to the conventional partisan theory (Table 4.5b). Center and left governments had lower government investment than the right in the 1980s and 1990s, supporting my argument that the fiscal policy of the governments previously considered expansionary became disciplined in the second period. Right governments had higher spending during the same period, contrary to the partisan explanation that right governments are fiscally more conservative than the left or center. Only *Center* and *Right* for 1982–2001 are significant (*Left*'s *p*-value = 0.19), but in models without country dummies, *Left* also becomes significant for 1982–2001. The insignificant coefficients for 1961–1981 mean that center and left governments did not have higher or lower spending (though their signs are positive). In models without country dummies, *Right* becomes significant and positive (higher spending) for 1961–2001, as well.

Substantively, an increase in center cabinet portfolios from 0 to 100 (the lowest to highest in the sample) lowered government investment by 0.07 percent of GDP (2 percent of total government investment) in 1982–2001. A comparable increase in right cabinet portfolios pushed up spending by 0.1 percent of GDP (2.4 percent of total government investment) for the same period. As we can see in Figure 4.1, government investment declined in almost all countries from the early 1970s on. In light of the general trend among OECD countries toward low

Table 4.5b Partisan impact on government investment

Model	Government fixed investment		
	1961–1981	*1982–2001*	*1961–2001*
Left$_{t-1}$	0.00006	−0.00054	−0.00012
	(0.00088)	(0.00041)	(0.00037)
Center$_{t-1}$	0.00119	−0.00072*	−0.00017
	(0.00086)	(0.00042)	(0.00042)
Right$_{t-1}$	−0.00078	0.00084**	0.00026
	(0.00074)	(0.00037)	(0.00034)

Notes
Only the results of the three government partisanship variables that were alternately entered in the basic models are reported.
OLS estimates with panel-corrected standard errors in parentheses.
***Significant at the 0.01 level.
**Significant at the 0.05 level.
*Significant at the 0.10 level.

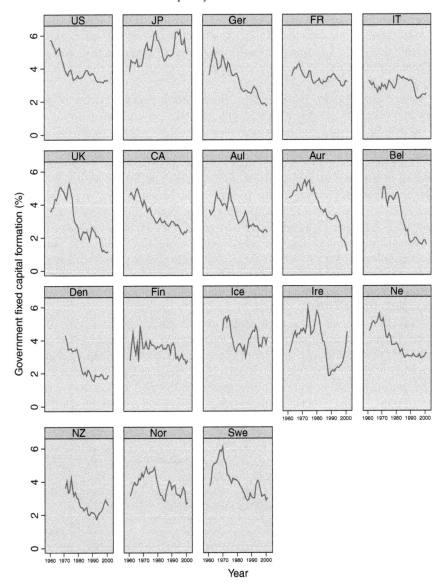

Figure 4.1 Government investment (fixed capital formation) as a percentage of GDP (sources: see variables, definitions, and sources in Tables 4.1 and 4.2).

public investment, right governments' higher government investment spending is notable.

The results for party fragmentation are reported in Table 4.5c. They show that a larger number of parliamentary parties (fragmentation) caused higher spending in 1961–1981, but lower spending in 1982–2001 (both significant),

Table 4.5c Impact of party fragmentation on government investment

Model	Government fixed investment		
	1961–1981	*1982–2001*	*1961–2001*
Fragmentation$_{t-1}$	0.068*	−0.052**	−0.039**
	(0.042)	(0.023)	(0.020)
Coalition$_{t-1}$	−0.020	0.048*	0.014
	(0.034)	(0.028)	(0.019)

Notes
Only the results of *Fragmentation* and *Coalition* that were entered in the basic models are reported.
OLS estimates with panel-corrected standard errors in parentheses.
***Significant at the 0.01 level.
**Significant at the 0.05 level.
*Significant at the 0.10 level.

the same pattern found in government non-wage consumption. During 1961–1981, an increase in parliamentary parties by one raised government investment by 0.068 percent of GDP (1.9 percent of total public investment). But in 1982–2001, the same one-party increase reduced spending by 0.05 percent of GDP (1.5 percent of total investment). Thus, a large effective number of parties put upward pressure on this spending during 1961–1981, but downward pressure during 1982–2001, suggesting a conservative policy shift in countries with fragmented party system. The results also show that coalition governments had higher spending for 1982–2001. This is the only piece of evidence in the entire dataset suggesting their upward spending pressure during the 1980s and 1990s.

Government subsidies

Table 4.6 reports the results of public subsidies. During 1961–1981, public subsidies were higher in election years (0.06 percent of GDP higher or 3.1 percent of total government subsidies: the average total subsidies = 1.92 percent of GDP), suggesting that governments used this spending item for electoral purposes in the first period. Most of *Majority, Coalition,* and *CBI* have positive signs, but nothing is significant, showing these factors did not affect public subsidies.[18] The results also show that coordinated labor pushed down public subsidies during the first period of 1961–1981 and the entire period of 1961–2001. There is no evidence that coordinated labor put any upward pressure on this spending item for any period. Overall, political factors generally did not affect this spending item much, partly because public subsidies spending represents only 1.9 percent of GDP (the average in the sample) and partly because most industrial countries significantly reduced public subsidies since around the 1970s (see Figure 4.2), so there was not much room or attraction for governments to use this spending item for electoral purposes.

Table 4.6 Determinants of government subsidies to industries

Model	Government subsidies		
	1961–1981	*1982–2001*	*1961–2001*
Independent variables			
Gov. subsidies$_{t-1}$	0.759***	0.814***	0.812***
	(0.060)	(0.046)	(0.029)
GDP$_{t-1}$	0.027**	−0.019*	0.011
	(0.011)	(0.011)	(0.007)
Inflation$_{t-1}$	0.016***	0.016**	0.0071
	(0.006)	(0.007)	(0.0048)
ΔUnemployment$_{t-1}$	−0.015	−0.0040	0.0050
	(0.033)	(0.0221)	(0.0185)
Economic size$_{t-1}$	0.226	0.047	−0.048
	(0.213)	(0.168)	(0.097)
Majority$_{t-1}$	0.022	0.018	0.033
	(0.060)	(0.074)	(0.042)
Coalition$_{t-1}$	0.00800	0.00771	0.00401
	(0.02154)	(0.02152)	(0.01470)
CBI$_{t-1}$	−0.606	0.013	−0.053
	(0.900)	(0.213)	(0.203)
Labor$_{t-1}$	−0.059**	−0.0076	−0.030*
	(0.025)	(0.0260)	(0.016)
Left$_{t-1}$	−0.00109	−0.00054	−0.00070*
	(0.00081)	(0.00041)	(0.00036)
Election	0.060*	−0.028	0.016
	(0.037)	(0.023)	(0.022)
Trade openness$_{t-1}$	0.00595	−0.00090	−0.00203
	(0.00586)	(0.00247)	(0.00139)
Exchange rate$_{t-1}$	0.065	−0.251***	−0.113***
	(0.060)	(0.058)	(0.036)
Capital mobility$_{t-1}$	−0.0020	−0.0009	−0.027**
	(0.0286)	(0.0169)	(0.011)
R^2	0.985	0.991	0.987
Observations	272	338	610

Notes
OLS estimates with panel-corrected standard errors in parentheses.
Country and time dummy variables not reported.
***Significant at the 0.01 level.
**Significant at the 0.05 level.
*Significant at the 0.10 level.

Partisan impact and fragmentation   The results of partisan effects are reported in Table 4.6b. There is some indication that left governments had lower spending, and center and right governments had higher spending. The signs of *Left* are all negative, and significant in the entire period of 1961–2001 (p-value = 0.17 for 1961–1981, and = 0.18 for 1982–2001). The sign of *Center* is negative for 1961–1981 and positive for 1982–2001. The coefficients are both close to significance, but do not quite attain it (p-value = 0.11 for 1961–1981, and = 0.16 for

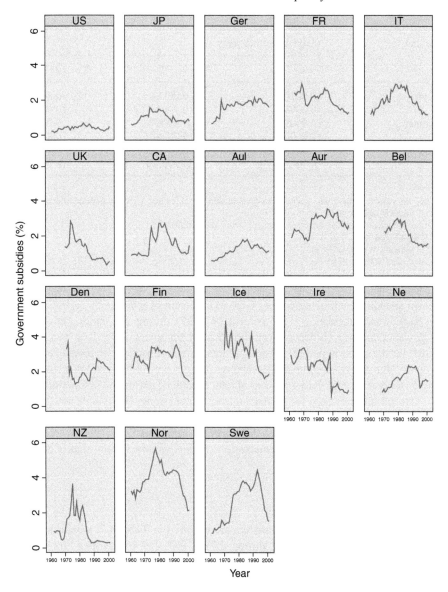

Figure 4.2 Government subsidies as a percentage of GDP (sources: see variables, definitions, and sources in Tables 4.1 and 4.2).

1982–2001). But in models without country dummies, *Center* is positive and significant for 1961–2001, and positive and close to significance in 1982–2001 (*p*-value = 0.13). Right governments had higher spending in 1961–1981 (significant) while the other signs are also positive, though not significant. Substantively, an increase in left cabinet portfolios from 0 to 100 pushed

Table 4.6b Partisan impact on government subsidies to industries

Model	Government subsidies		
	1961–1981	*1982–2001*	*1961–2001*
Left$_{t-1}$	−0.00109	−0.00054	−0.00070*
	(0.00081)	(0.00041)	(0.00036)
Center$_{t-1}$	−0.00097	0.00067	0.00027
	(0.00062)	(0.00048)	(0.00037)
Right$_{t-1}$	0.00156**	0.00004	0.00046
	(0.00072)	(0.00043)	(0.00037)

Notes
Only the results of the three government partisanship variables that were alternately entered in the basic models are reported.
OLS estimates with panel-corrected standard errors in parentheses.
***Significant at the 0.01 level.
**Significant at the 0.05 level.
*Significant at the 0.10 level.

down spending by 0.07 percent of GDP (3.6 percent of total public subsidies: the average total subsidies = 1.92 percent of GDP) during the entire period. An equivalent increase in center portfolios pushed up spending by 0.06 percent of GDP for the entire period (3.1 percent of total public subsidies) (in models without country dummies). A comparable increase of right portfolios raised this spending by 0.16 percent of GDP (8.1 percent of total subsidies) during the first period.

Overall, the evidence for partisan impact is not strong. But it does not support the standard partisan model, since the results (where significant) show that left governments had lower spending than right governments.

The results about party fragmentation (*Fragmentation*) show that it did not affect public subsidies.

Social security transfers

The results of social security transfers are reported in Table 4.7. Coalition governments had higher spending during 1961–1981, but lower spending in the second period than single-party governments. Thus, coalition governments restrained social security spending in the second period, as consistent with my argument in Chapter 3. But the substantive size of the effect is small. During the first period, an increase of coalition parties by three pushed up spending by 0.3 percent of GDP (2.1 percent of total social security transfers: the average total transfers = 12.2 percent of GDP). The signs of CBI and labor are in the expected directions – these factors helped governments reduce spending in the second period – but not significant. There is no observable electoral cycle, either. There is also no evidence that minority governments had undisciplined spending, not supporting one of the weak government arguments. If anything, the sign of the coefficient is positive (higher spending for majority governments).

Table 4.7 Determinants of social security transfers

Model	Social security transfers		
	1961–1981	*1982–2001*	*1961–2001*
Independent variables			
Social security transfers$_{t-1}$	0.887*** (0.114)	1.182*** (0.088)	1.175*** (0.065)
Social security transfers$_{t-2}$	−0.019 (0.117)	−0.328*** (0.086)	−0.297*** (0.064)
GDP$_{t-1}$	−0.00030 (0.00019)	−0.00055** (0.00027)	0.00003 (0.00015)
Inflation$_{t-1}$	0.00072*** (0.00010)	0.00033* (0.00018)	0.00056*** (0.00011)
ΔUnemployment$_{t-1}$	−0.00169*** (0.00059)	0.00018 (0.00059)	0.00035 (0.00044)
Economic size$_{t-1}$	0.0054 (0.0034)	0.021*** (0.006)	0.0036 (0.0026)
Pop65$_{t-1}$	−0.00051 (0.00104)	0.00038 (0.00047)	0.00039 (0.00029)
Majority$_{t-1}$	0.00110 (0.00117)	0.00002 (0.00140)	−0.00001 (0.00093)
Coalition$_{t-1}$	0.00095** (0.00044)	−0.00096** (0.00048)	0.00024 (0.00034)
CBI$_{t-1}$	0.021 (0.014)	−0.0033 (0.0061)	0.0020 (0.0049)
Labor$_{t-1}$	0.00001 (0.00041)	−0.00036 (0.00041)	−0.00026 (0.00032)
Left$_{t-1}$	−0.0000033 (0.0000103)	−0.0000129 (0.0000092)	−0.0000070 (0.0000068)
Election	0.00009 (0.00062)	−0.00014 (0.00057)	0.00011 (0.00045)
Trade openness$_{t-1}$	0.021 (0.016)	−0.021*** (0.006)	−0.014*** (0.004)
Exchange rate$_{t-1}$	−0.00240** (0.00111)	−0.00384** (0.00187)	−0.00348*** (0.00081)
Capital mobility$_{t-1}$	0.00087*** (0.00035)	0.00097*** (0.00037)	0.00084*** (0.00021)
R^2	0.999	0.999	0.999
Observations	232	336	568

Notes
OLS estimates with panel-corrected standard errors in parentheses.
Country and time dummy variables not reported.
***Significant at the 0.01 level.
**Significant at the 0.05 level.
*Significant at the 0.10 level.

Table 4.7b Partisan impact on social security transfers

Model	Social security transfers		
	1961–1981	*1982–2001*	*1961–2001*
Left$_{t-1}$	−0.0000033	−0.0000129	−0.0000070
	(0.0000103)	(0.0000092)	(0.0000068)
Center$_{t-1}$	−0.00214*	−0.00141	−0.00111
	(0.00129)	(0.00119)	(0.00084)
Right$_{t-1}$	0.0000174	0.0000167**	0.0000132**
	(0.0000115)	(0.0000086)	(0.0000066)

Notes
Only the results of the three government partisanship variables that were alternately entered in the basic models are reported.
OLS estimates with panel-corrected standard errors in parentheses.
***Significant at the 0.01 level.
**Significant at the 0.05 level.
*Significant at the 0.10 level.

Partisan impact and fragmentation   The results show that conservative governments had higher social security transfers than the center or left in potentially both first and second periods (Table 4.7b). The signs of *Right* are all positive, and though the first period is not significant, it is not far from significance ($p = 0.13$). This runs counter to the conventional partisan theory, though the substantive effects are not large. The signs of *Center* and *Left* are all negative. Center governments had lower spending than the others in the first period, but did not affect spending in the second period since the second period is not significant. Substantively, an increase in center cabinet portfolios from 0 to 100 reduced spending by 0.2 percent of GDP during the first period (1.7 percent of total social security transfers). No coefficient for *Left* is significant, suggesting left governments did not affect the spending either way.

   Why does the analysis turn up the results showing that right governments were fiscally less disciplined than the left or center, when partisan theory has pointed out the opposite? Conservative governments' high spending is not limited to social security, but is the overall finding that emerges from the empirical analysis of this book. Conservative governments' higher spending is also detected in government wage consumption, government investment, public subsidies, total disbursement, and primary balance. There are three reasons. First, while it is true that when we examine only cross-sectional data on various spending items and partisan cabinet portfolios averaged across years (without controlling for other factors), right governments tend to have lower spending than left or center governments, the often-discussed differences between right governments and the left and center are overly exaggerated (see Appendix in Chapter 3, which shows the cross-national data averaged across years). The spending levels in conservative-dominant countries (liberal market economies) are only marginally lower than the left or center across spending items. So when we examine only cross-sectional data without controlling for other factors, conservative governments' spending is only slightly lower, which can be eliminated once we control for other factors in regressions.

Second, anecdotal episodes also suggest that many conservative governments in the last two decades have been fairly expansionary. The U.S. Reagan administration accumulated large deficit in the 1980s. Japan's successive governments controlled by the conservative Liberal Democratic Party also conducted an extremely expansionary policy to end successive recessions and deflation throughout the 1990s, which pushed Japan's gross debt to the highest level among industrial countries.[19] Conservative governments that occasionally replaced social democrats in Nordic countries also were unable to reduce spending. In the United States, the centrist Clinton administration reduced fiscal deficit, and the succeeding conservative Bush administration increased it, though the latter is outside the sample of this book. As we will see below, there is some evidence that conservative governments had lower tax revenues than the left and center. So the standard partisan explanation that the right prefers small government may be correct about tax revenues, but when it comes to spending levels, the explanation does not hold up at all in the 1990s.

Third, as Figure 3.6 (Chapter 3) shows, the countries that are conventionally considered social-democratic-dominant and Christian-democratic-dominant actually have sizeable conservative-party representation in the executive branch. Conservative cabinet portfolios are as high as 40 percent in Denmark, 45 percent in France, and 33 percent in the Netherlands. So if those countries have high spending, it will be reflected in conservative governments' spending, as well.[20]

Government employment

Table 4.8 reports the results of government employment. Coalition governments had higher public employment during 1961–1981, but the upward pressure on public employment disappears in 1982–2001, supporting my argument that coalition governments' fiscal policy became restrained in the second period. The substantive effect is small. So are the substantive effects of all political variables on public employment, partly because this variable is expressed as public employment as a percentage of total employment. There is evidence that majority governments had lower public employment during 1982–2001 though the theoretical justification for lower public employment by majority governments is weak. CBI and labor did not affect public employment.[21] The social democratic neocorporatist model expects that countries with strong labor organizations, if accompanied by social democratic parties, have high public employment. But when labor is considered alone, there is no such effect. Further, even when the interactive effects of left governments and coordinated labor are examined, social democratic corporatist regimes (left governments + coordinated labor) actually produced lower public employment for both periods, as we will see in Chapter 5. There is no electoral cycle.

Table 4.8 Determinants of government employment

Model	Government employment		
	1961–1981	*1982–2001*	*1961–2001*
Independent variables			
Gov. employment$_{t-1}$	1.002***	1.039***	1.213***
	(0.112)	(0.090)	(0.060)
Gov. employment$_{t-2}$	−0.011	−0.113	−0.246***
	(0.114)	(0.088)	(0.060)
GDP$_{t-1}$	−0.00022***	−0.00054***	−0.00028***
	(0.00008)	(0.00015)	(0.00008)
Inflation$_{t-1}$	0.00011*	0.00032***	0.00019***
	(0.00006)	(0.00009)	(0.00006)
ΔUnemployment$_{t-1}$	−0.00037	0.00033	−0.00010
	(0.00030)	(0.00033)	(0.00023)
Economic size$_{t-1}$	0.00232	0.00649***	0.00566***
	(0.00179)	(0.00263)	(0.00154)
Majority$_{t-1}$	−0.00050	−0.00179**	−0.00049
	(0.00075)	(0.00086)	(0.00057)
Coalition$_{t-1}$	0.00043**	0.00019	0.00016
	(0.00022)	(0.00033)	(0.00017)
CBI$_{t-1}$	0.00793	−0.00350	0.00053
	(0.00812)	(0.00257)	(0.00219)
Labor$_{t-1}$	−0.00037	0.00006	0.00010
	(0.00029)	(0.00034)	(0.00020)
Left$_{t-1}$	0.0000136*	0.0000074	0.0000144***
	(0.0000078)	(0.0000061)	(0.0000050)
Election	−0.0000037	0.00020	0.00023
	(0.0003747)	(0.00039)	(0.00029)
Trade openness$_{t-1}$	0.00313	−0.00792***	−0.00662***
	(0.00426)	(0.00263)	(0.00156)
Exchange rate$_{t-1}$	−0.00321***	−0.00129	−0.00218***
	(0.00071)	(0.00109)	(0.00057)
Capital mobility$_{t-1}$	−0.00012	0.00048*	−0.00007
	(0.00022)	(0.00027)	(0.00013)
R^2	1.000	1.000	1.000
Observations	279	338	617

Notes
OLS estimates with panel-corrected standard errors in parentheses.
Country and time dummy variables not reported.
***Significant at the 0.01 level.
**Significant at the 0.05 level.
*Significant at the 0.10 level.

Partisan impact and fragmentation   We now turn to partisan effects. Table 4.8b shows that left governments had higher public employment during 1961–1981 and the entire period of 1961–2001. Right governments, meanwhile, had lower public employment in the first period of 1961–1981 and 1961–2001. The substantive effects are all small. But this result is consistent with the partisan theory that left governments have high public employment to provide jobs for low-income,

Table 4.8b Partisan impact on government employment

Model	Government employment		
	1961–1981	*1982–2001*	*1961–2001*
Left$_{t-1}$	0.0000136*	0.0000074	0.0000144***
	(0.0000078)	(0.0000061)	(0.0000050)
Center$_{t-1}$	0.0000096	–0.0000071	–0.0000062
	(0.0000075)	(0.0000076)	(0.0000058)
Right$_{t-1}$	–0.0000176**	–0.0000023	–0.0000086*
	(0.0000082)	(0.0000053)	(0.0000052)

Notes
Only the results of the three government partisanship variables that were alternately entered in the basic models are reported.
OLS estimates with panel-corrected standard errors in parentheses.
***Significant at the 0.01 level.
**Significant at the 0.05 level.
*Significant at the 0.10 level.

Table 4.8c Impact of party fragmentation on government employment

Model	Government employment		
	1961–1981	*1982–2001*	*1961–2001*
Fragmentation$_{t-1}$	0.00015	–0.00059*	–0.00005
	(0.00031)	(0.00033)	(0.00018)
Coalition$_{t-1}$	0.00039	0.00027	0.00018
	(0.00024)	(0.00034)	(0.00019)

Notes
Only the results of *Fragmentation* and *Coalition* that were entered in the basic models are reported.
OLS estimates with panel-corrected standard errors in parentheses.
***Significant at the 0.01 level.
**Significant at the 0.05 level.
*Significant at the 0.10 level.

low-skilled workers, and union workers, and right governments have the opposite characteristics. This is one of the only few results found in this book supporting the standard partisan theory. However, left governments' upward pressure on public employment disappeared in the second period. It supports my argument that the economic policy of previously expansionary governments became restrained in the second period.

Next, party fragmentation has a positive sign (high public employment) for the first period of 1961–1981, but a negative sign (low public employment) for the second period of 1982–2001 (Table 4.8c). Only the second period is significant. Thus, fragmented party systems contributed to lower public employment in the second period, lending support to my argument in Chapter 3 that the effects of previously expansionary political actors shifted in the conservative direction in the 1980s and 1990s.

Tax policy

Tables 4.9–4.12 report the results of the regression estimation of various tax revenues – individual income tax, corporate income tax, consumption tax, and social security contributions. As with the spending models in the previous part of the chapter, the tax models include lagged dependent variables to eliminate auto-correlation. Autocorrelation is eliminated when the first and second lagged dependent variables are entered in the specifications. For all models, the sum of the coefficients on the lagged dependent variables is significantly below unity (1), suggesting that we do not have to worry about unit root. Before investigating the political factors, let us first review the effects of economic controls.

Economic controls   Economic growth (*GDP*) contributed to higher revenues during 1961–1981 except for social security contributions. But according to these results, growth did not affect tax revenues in either way in 1982–2001. This is somewhat surprising since the conventional wisdom is that economic growth increases tax revenues by expanding the tax bases of personal and corporate income taxes and consumption. One possibility is that in the second period, gov-ernments implemented tax reductions as part of broader tax reform during eco-nomic upturns, offsetting the upward effects of high economic growth on revenues, because they could cut taxes without incurring fiscal deficit more easily in high-growth periods than during economic downturns. In the 1980s and 1990s, as has been widely documented, industrial countries carried out large-scale tax reform and, in general, cut tax rates, reduced the number of brackets, and broad-ened tax bases.[22]

Inflation increased revenues from individual income tax and social security contributions, and reduced corporate income tax revenues in the first period of 1961–1981. Inflation did not affect tax revenues in the second period (no coeffi-cient is significant for the second period). Consumption tax was not affected by inflation. The upward impact of inflation on personal income tax revenues during the first (but not the second) period was probably due to the fact that during the first period (prior to extensive tax reform in the 1980s and 1990s), many countries had a larger number of tax brackets, and inflation pushed income earners into higher brackets more easily and tax rates were also higher. But tax reform in the second period reduced the number of brackets as well as tax rates, mitigating the upward effect of inflation on personal income tax revenues.[23] The possible reason for the absence of inflation's upward effect on corporate tax rev-enues may be that corporate tax had fewer tax brackets than personal income tax, lessening the impact of bracket creep. Turning to unemployment, most of the signs are in the expected direction (negative), suggesting that tax revenues dropped with high unemployment. But no coefficient is significant except for social security contributions in the first period, which responded negatively to high unemployment. In contrast, the results suggest that consumption tax rev-enues increased with high unemployment in the first period, which has no imme-diate answer.

Economic globalization   Let us now look at the effects of the economic globalization variables (*Trade openness, Capital mobility, Exchange rate*). On the
effects of the openness of the economy (*Trade openness*), the results of the
individual income tax and social security contributions models follow those of
most spending items – trade openness induced higher tax revenues in the two
categories during the first period (positive signs), but in the second period, it
led to lower revenues (negative signs). This suggests that during the 1960s and
1970s, governments in open economies raised large tax revenues in these categories to finance their high public spending, which they employed to mitigate
the negative consequences of the economic dislocations caused by the international economy, but in the 1980s and 1990s, they had lower tax revenues
probably for international competitiveness concerns. Thus, the compensation
thesis is supported in the first period, but the convergence thesis – which
expects reduced revenues and policy convergence as a result of competitive
pressures from globalization – explains the two tax items in the second period.
As we will see, total government revenues also follow the same pattern.

But corporate income tax shows the opposite pattern. Governments in open
economies had lower revenues in 1961–1981 and higher revenues in
1982–2001. The results of the models without country dummies also show that
open-economy governments taxed firms more than low trade-dependent governments in the 1980s and 1990s. Setting aside explanatory validity, lower
corporate tax revenues during the first period could be explicable as a result of
the efforts by governments in open economies to reduce tax burdens on
export-sector industries and firms that are exposed to international competition. The higher corporate tax revenues in the second period could potentially
be explained by the compensation thesis as a result of governments' efforts to
enhance the competitiveness of their economies by spending public money to
develop and improve human and physical capital or provide a favorable economic environment for domestic firms. As has previously been suggested,
high corporate tax does not have to drive away mobile capital, if governments
can provide firms with high-quality human and physical capital and other
favorable economic conditions because of public spending made possible by
high tax (Garrett, 1998; Boix, 1998). The present data seem to support this
explanation. If this is the case, it suggests that, contrary to the convergence
thesis, open-economy countries collected higher corporate tax revenues to
assist domestic firms and maybe workers by using government policy in the
second period. Thus, open-economy governments' use of corporate income tax
is different from individual income tax and social security contributions
reviewed above, and the prediction of the convergence thesis is not supported
in corporate income tax, although it explains individual income tax and social
security contributions in the second period.

Why convergence (low tax) in individual income tax and social security contributions in 1982–2001, but compensation (high tax) in corporate income tax?
One possibility would be that globalization in terms of increased capital mobility causes low corporate tax, but not globalization in terms of trade openness.

This, at a glance, would sound reasonable, and its explanation would be that capital mobility leads governments to lower corporate tax for fear that high corporate tax would drive away mobile capital because high taxes squeeze returns on investment, but trade openness by itself does not have to raise governments' same concerns with mobile capital. However, this explanation does not hold up because as you can see in the tables, increased capital mobility is also associated with high corporate tax (the signs of *Capital mobility* are all positive, and significant for 1961–1981 and 1961–2001). Thus, a "race to the bottom" (low taxes) expected by the convergence or globalization thesis not only has not happened at all in corporate income tax, but globalization has led to high corporate tax revenues. Capital mobility also significantly leads to high total government revenues in all periods.

The high corporate tax revenues by open-economy governments in the globalized economy may be possible due to the fact that the revenues from corporate tax are much lower than those from individual income tax and social security contributions. The average government revenues from individual income tax and social security contributions (10–11 percent of GDP, respectively) are four times larger than those from corporate tax (2.6 percent of GDP). Because of the significantly smaller size of corporate tax revenues, open-economy governments may be able to keep high corporate tax without worrying too much about capital flight.

The results of the consumption tax models also support the compensation thesis. Capital mobility is significantly associated with higher consumption tax revenues for 1961–1981 and 1961–2001, as with corporate tax. The higher consumption tax revenues in the first and the entire periods can be explained as a result of governments' efforts to bolster the competitiveness of their economies by spending public money to develop and improve human and physical capital or provide a favorable economic environment for domestic firms, or it may simply be governments' need to finance whatever other spending needs. A race to the bottom (low tax) expected by the convergence thesis has not taken place in countries with great capital mobility.

Personal income tax, by contrast, has a different pattern. *Capital mobility* has a positive sign in the personal tax models for the two periods, but is not significant. But in the models without country dummies, the sign becomes negative and significant for 1961–1981 and 1982–2001 and the entire period. Thus, according to the results of the models without country dummies, capital mobility induced lower personal income tax, as consistent with the convergence thesis. It is not clear why the sign reversal happens, but it suggests that some unknown country-specific factors erase whatever downward effect of capital mobility on income tax revenues that appear when the country-specific factors are not taken into account.

Social security contributions show a yet slightly different pattern. Capital mobility induced higher contributions in 1961–1981 but lower contributions in 1982–2001. In the fixed models, the coefficient for the second period is not significant, but in the models without country dummies, it is significant for both periods. This pattern suggests that governments with high capital openness followed the compensation path during the first period, but as the internationalization of capital deepened in the world economy during the second period and as neoliberal economic policy ideas sank in, they moved to reduce social security contributions, as consistent with the convergence thesis for the second period.

But as shown in the social security payments models of the previous part of the chapter on government spending, social security transfers by governments followed the compensation pattern during all periods, suggesting that although governments with capital openness managed to reduce social security contributions in the second period, they were unable to contain social security spending, probably due largely to spending pressures from population aging and early retirement, and to the electoral difficulty of reducing social security benefits.

As we will see later, the results of total tax revenues also show a similar pattern (Table 4.14). Capital mobility is associated with larger revenues in 1961–1981 and 1961–2001. The second period is not significant, but when the country dummies were removed, *Capital mobility* turns negative and significant in 1982–2001. Thus, in terms also of total revenues, governments with high capital openness followed the compensation path during the first period, but during the second period with the internationalization of capital and neoliberal policy ideas, they moved to reduce tax revenues, as consistent with the convergence thesis.

The exchange rate regime rarely affected tax revenues (except the negative effect on personal income tax in 1961–2001). Though not significant, the signs of *Exchange rate* suggest that in general, a floating system reduced revenues in 1961–1981 and led to high revenues in 1982–2001.

Political variables Now I explain the impact of political variables in various tax revenues.

Individual income tax

Table 4.9 reports the results of individual income tax. *CBI* contributed to high personal income tax in all periods. Judging from *CBI*'s general fiscal-conservatism effects, this should be considered the disciplining effects of independent central banks on party governments' fiscal policy – independent central banks help put pressure on party governments to raise sufficient revenues to finance their spending so that they will not create fiscal shortfalls and their fiscal policy will not be expansionary. The substantive effect is large. During 1961–1981, an increase in *CBI* from 0.14 to 0.68 (the lowest to highest in the sample) increased personal tax revenues by 1.6 percent of GDP (14 percent of total personal income tax: the average personal income tax = 11 percent of GDP). During 1982–2001, a corresponding increase in *CBI* pushed up the revenues by 0.5 percent of GDP (4.3 percent of total personal tax).

The revenues from personal income tax experienced electoral expansions in the 1980s and 1990s. In election years, the revenues from individual income tax

Table 4.9 Determinants of individual income tax revenues

Model	Individual income tax		
	1961–1981	*1982–2001*	*1961–2001*
Independent variables			
Individual income tax$_{t-1}$	0.950***	0.847***	0.980***
	(0.104)	(0.076)	(0.056)
Individual income tax$_{t-2}$	−0.142	−0.045	−0.093*
	(0.098)	(0.072)	(0.055)
GDP$_{t-1}$	0.060**	0.007	0.049***
	(0.026)	(0.025)	(0.017)
Inflation$_{t-1}$	0.030**	−0.007	0.010
	(0.014)	(0.015)	(0.011)
ΔUnemployment$_{t-1}$	−0.143	−0.050	−0.036
	(0.100)	(0.046)	(0.044)
Economic size$_{t-1}$	1.122**	0.875**	0.803***
	(0.515)	(0.399)	(0.272)
Majority$_{t-1}$	−0.151	0.273*	0.022
	(0.140)	(0.158)	(0.093)
Coalition$_{t-1}$	0.092	−0.067	0.059
	(0.059)	(0.054)	(0.037)
CBI$_{t-1}$	2.883*	0.873*	1.097**
	(1.645)	(0.456)	(0.463)
Labor$_{t-1}$	−0.038	−0.073	−0.062*
	(0.051)	(0.052)	(0.036)
Left$_{t-1}$	0.00083	0.00127	0.00131
	(0.00194)	(0.00108)	(0.00094)
Election	−0.044	−0.166***	−0.097*
	(0.091)	(0.061)	(0.055)
Trade openness$_{t-1}$	0.027*	−0.016***	−0.014***
	(0.015)	(0.004)	(0.003)
Exchange rate$_{t-1}$	−0.137	0.080	−0.146*
	(0.122)	(0.132)	(0.085)
Capital mobility$_{t-1}$	0.012	0.001	−0.032
	(0.059)	(0.046)	(0.029)
R^2	0.997	0.998	0.998
Observations	249	332	581

Notes
OLS estimates with panel-corrected standard errors in parentheses.
Country and time dummy variables not reported.
***Significant at the 0.01 level.
**Significant at the 0.05 level.
*Significant at the 0.10 level.

decreased by 0.17 percent of GDP in 1982–2001 (1.5 percent of total personal income tax revenues). Thus, party governments created electoral expansions by reducing personal income tax revenues during the second period. Personal income tax is the only tax item that shows electoral cycles. The existence of electoral expansions in personal income tax is readily understandable, because income tax cuts are probably the most visible and effective as an electoral tool for party governments and politicians.

The signs of *Labor* are all negative, indicating that coordinated labor put downward pressure on personal income tax (significant for the entire period in fixed-effect models and also for 1961–1981 in no-dummy models). This result is also easy to understand since labor coordination and labor strength are corre- lated, and union members include low- to middle-income workers that prefer and demand low income tax. Given an option between individual and corporate income tax cuts, they should prefer the former. As expected, labor does not exert any effect on corporate tax, as we will see later.

There is some evidence that coalition governments had higher revenues from personal income tax during 1961–1981 and the entire period (the coefficients are significant in no-dummy models and close to significance in fixed effect models (p-value = 0.12 for 1961–1981 and 0.11 for the entire period)). This resulted probably from their high spending in the 1960s and 1970s and the need to finance it. But their high levels of personal income tax revenues disappeared in the 1980s and 1990s, reflecting their conservative shift in fiscal policy. Majority governments also had higher revenues in 1982–2001.

Partisan impact and fragmentation   The results of partisan effect are reported in Table 4.9b. The conventional belief about taxation is that left and center governments tax more heavily than the conservative. While *Left*'s signs are positive (higher revenues), there is no evidence that left governments raised higher revenues from personal income tax, since no coefficient is significant. This does not change when we remove country dummies. By contrast, center governments may have collected higher revenues from personal income tax in both periods, though the coefficients slightly fall short of statistical significance

Table 4.9b Partisan impact on individual income tax revenues

Model	Individual income tax		
	1961–1981	1982–2001	1961–2001
Left$_{t-1}$	0.00083	0.00127	0.00131
	(0.00194)	(0.00108)	(0.00094)
Center$_{t-1}$	0.00259	0.00199	0.00073
	(0.00179)	(0.00125)	(0.00090)
Right$_{t-1}$	−0.00233	−0.00211**	−0.00173**
	(0.00174)	(0.00097)	(0.00084)

Notes
Only the results of the three government partisanship variables that were alternately entered in the basic models are reported.
OLS estimates with panel-corrected standard errors in parentheses.
***Significant at the 0.01 level.
**Significant at the 0.05 level.
*Significant at the 0.10 level.

($p = 0.15$, $p = 0.11$). Right governments collected lower revenues from personal income tax in 1982–2001 and the entire period (significant). The substantive size of the effect is not small. An increase in right party cabinet portfolios from 0 to 100 (the lowest to highest in the sample) pushed down the revenues by 0.2 percent of GDP (1.9 percent of total personal income tax revenues: the average total personal income tax = 11 percent of GDP). This result is understandable from conservative governments' preference for small government that supposedly suppress both spending and taxes. But as we will see in this chapter, though conservative governments collected lower tax revenues, they were actually higher spenders than the left or center, producing fiscal deficit. Thus, the conventional belief about conservative governments' preference for small government is correct about taxation, but inaccurate about spending.

Fragmentation did not affect personal income tax in any period, and this remains the same when we remove *Coalition* from the specifications (results not reported).

Corporate income tax

The results of corporate income tax (Table 4.10) show that no political factor, except for government partisanship, affects the revenues from this tax source (partisan effects are discussed later). But the models without country dummies show that *CBI* contributed to lower corporate tax revenues in 1961–1981, 1982–2001, and the entire period (results not reported). CBI has less time-series variance than other independent variables, and its variance is mostly cross-sectional. Therefore, it is more susceptible to the effects of country dummies soaking up the cross-national variance. So if we had to put confidence in one of the results, it would be those of no-dummy models. Substantively, an increase in *CBI* from 0.14 to 0.68 (the lowest to highest in the sample) pushed down corporate tax revenues by 0.36 percent of GDP (13.3 percent of total corporate tax revenues: the average corporate tax revenues = 2.68 percent of GDP) in 1961–1981. The corresponding figures for 1982–2001 are 0.4 percent of GDP (15.1 percent of total corporate tax revenues). This suggests that although governments with independent central banks generally raised sufficient tax revenues so as not to produce deficit and not make their fiscal policy expansionary, they kept low corporate tax revenues throughout 1961–2001. This may be a result of the influence of neoliberal economic thinking with concerns for the economic distortions caused by high taxation, a concern that should be correlated with party governments' willingness to maintain independent central banks and to conduct economic policy along the neoliberal lines.

According to the results of the models without country dummies, the number of coalition parties also put downward pressure on corporate tax revenues in the 1960s and 1970s. The substantive size is not so small: an increase of coalition parties by three pushed down the corporate tax revenues by 0.17 percent of GDP (6.3 percent of total corporate tax revenues). This may be a sign of fiscal indiscipline that coalition governments had in the 1960s and 1970s, but eliminated in the 1980s and 1990s.

Table 4.10 Determinants of corporate income tax revenues

Model	Corporate income tax		
	1961–1981	*1982–2001*	*1961–2001*
Independent variables			
Corporate income tax$_{t-1}$	0.747***	0.895***	0.906***
	(0.164)	(0.133)	(0.103)
Corporate income tax$_{t-2}$	−0.081	−0.236*	−0.185*
	(0.124)	(0.132)	(0.102)
GDP$_{t-1}$	0.027**	0.001	0.009
	(0.013)	(0.026)	(0.013)
Inflation$_{t-1}$	−0.016**	−0.007	−0.027***
	(0.008)	(0.011)	(0.008)
ΔUnemployment$_{t-1}$	0.060	−0.060	−0.019
	(0.047)	(0.043)	(0.029)
Economic size$_{t-1}$	0.685**	−1.057**	0.071
	(0.300)	(0.543)	(0.205)
Majority$_{t-1}$	0.010	−0.116	−0.108
	(0.067)	(0.167)	(0.075)
Coalition$_{t-1}$	−0.029	0.025	0.012
	(0.025)	(0.052)	(0.026)
CBI$_{t-1}$	−1.724	0.294	0.229
	(1.184)	(0.358)	(0.298)
Labor$_{t-1}$	0.026	−0.019	0.008
	(0.030)	(0.048)	(0.023)
Left$_{t-1}$	−0.00096	−0.00222**	−0.00117*
	(0.00084)	(0.00104)	(0.00069)
Election	−0.036	−0.060	−0.050
	(0.047)	(0.061)	(0.042)
Trade openness$_{t-1}$	−0.025***	0.015***	0.005**
	(0.009)	(0.005)	(0.002)
Exchange rate$_{t-1}$	−0.013	0.363	−0.010
	(0.063)	(0.232)	(0.088)
Capital mobility$_{t-1}$	0.068**	0.016	0.056**
	(0.033)	(0.045)	(0.026)
R^2	0.987	0.976	0.978
Observations	221	332	553

Notes
OLS estimates with panel-corrected standard errors in parentheses.
Country and time dummy variables not reported.
***Significant at the 0.01 level.
**Significant at the 0.05 level.
*Significant at the 0.10 level.

There was also no electoral cycle, which is understandable since the economic benefits of corporate tax cuts are not obvious to general voters and therefore the electoral benefits of low corporate tax revenues are not so large for governments and politicians. People vote, but corporations do not, so the electoral merits of corporate tax cuts are not large, maybe except for business owners and voters in management; hence, electoral use of income tax reductions, but not corporate tax. In theory and practice, corporate taxes do affect regular workers, but the effects are not obvious to workers.

Partisan impact and fragmentation   The results of partisan effects on corporate tax also run counter to conventional partisan theory. As Table 4.10b shows, *Left* has all negative signs (lower revenues), and *Center* and *Right* have positive signs (higher revenues) in all periods. *Left* is significant for the second and entire periods, and *Center* is significant for the second period. That is, left governments had lower revenues from corporate tax, and center governments higher revenues, at least in the 1980s and 1990s (with right governments in the middle since *Right* is not significant). Standard partisan theory would expect that pro-business conservative governments have lower corporate tax, and pro-labor left governments tax corporations more heavily than workers (personal income tax). But the results here suggest that during the 1960s and 1970s, such a stereotypical difference among partisan governments did not exist, and that in the 1980s and 1990s, left governments were more forthcoming in lowering corporate tax than the center or right.

Left governments' lower corporate tax revenues should probably be considered their conscious choice to create a favorable economic environment for corporate activities, attract investment, and gain the confidence of markets. Their low corporate tax is not a sign of their fiscal indiscipline, because their fiscal policy in the 1980s and 1990s was conservative (restrained). They achieved low corporate tax by depending more on consumption tax revenues and thinly distributing the fiscal burden of financing low corporate tax revenues. As we will see below, the left had higher revenues from consumption tax than other partisan governments in the 1980s and 1990s.

Table 4.10b Partisan impact on corporate income tax revenues

Model	Corporate income tax		
	1961–1981	*1982–2001*	*1961–2001*
$Left_{t-1}$	−0.00096	−0.00222**	−0.00117*
	(0.00084)	(0.00104)	(0.00069)
$Center_{t-1}$	0.00007	0.00223*	0.00078
	(0.00095)	(0.00117)	(0.00070)
$Right_{t-1}$	0.00069	0.00074	0.00045
	(0.00090)	(0.00071)	(0.00057)

Notes
Only the results of the three government partisanship variables that were alternately entered in the basic models are reported.
OLS estimates with panel-corrected standard errors in parentheses.
***Significant at the 0.01 level.
**Significant at the 0.05 level.
*Significant at the 0.10 level.

The substantive size of the partisan effect of left governments is also not small. In 1982–2001, an increase in left cabinet portfolios from 0 to 100 (the lowest to highest in the sample) decreased corporate tax revenues by 0.2 percent of GDP (8.2 percent of total corporate tax revenues). A corresponding increase in center cabinet portfolio increased the revenues by the same magnitude. Meanwhile, the effective number of parliamentary parties did not affect corporate income tax in any period with or without *Coalition* in the specifications (results not reported).

Consumption tax

The results of consumption tax are reported in Table 4.11.[24] *CBI* contributed to higher consumption tax revenues for the entire period of 1961–2001. An increase in *CBI* from 0.14 to 0.68 (the lowest to highest in the sample) pushed up the revenues by 0.34 percent of GDP (2.7 percent of total consumption tax revenues: the average total consumption tax revenues = 12.8 percent of GDP). Central banks' bias toward fiscal conservatism is consistent with the results of other taxes and spending items (i.e. they restrain spending and help secure sufficient (more) revenues for the most part).

Interestingly, the results also show that during the first period, consumption tax revenues were higher in election years. The exact reason is not clear. The only other tax item that shows significant electoral cycles is personal income tax – governments reduced personal tax revenues in election years during 1982–2001 and the entire period. If the personal tax reduction were observed during 1961–1981, higher consumption tax in election years could be interpreted as governments' attempt to finance the personal tax cuts with consumption tax increases – but we do not observe personal income tax cuts during the first period. Or if the 1960s and 1970s had experienced electoral expansions in spending, the consumption tax increases could be considered governments' way of securing a revenue source to finance the expansions. But there was no electoral cycle in spending during the 1960s and 1970s. The consumption tax hikes could still be a means to finance spending that was generally expansionary in the 1960s and 1970s. But it does not make much electoral sense to increase consumption tax in election years. Further research is necessary to understand why governments increased consumption tax revenues in election years in the 1960s and 1970s.[25] The number of governing parties, labor, and majority status did not affect consumption tax in any period.

Partisan impact and fragmentation The results of partisan effects are reported in Table 4.11b. Left governments had high consumption tax revenues, and center governments had low revenues during the second and entire periods. It is well documented that left governments have relied on consumption tax for revenues more than other governments, and this result is consistent with the conventional understanding. Combined with the results of personal and corporate income taxes, the results show that left governments relied more on indirect

Table 4.11 Determinants of consumption tax revenues

Model	Consumption tax		
	1961–1981	*1982–2001*	*1961–2001*
Independent variables			
Consumption tax$_{t-1}$	0.929***	0.866***	0.952***
	(0.090)	(0.090)	(0.057)
Consumption tax$_{t-2}$	–0.147*	–0.077	–0.100*
	(0.083)	(0.093)	(0.056)
GDP$_{t-1}$	0.023*	–0.034	0.001
	(0.014)	(0.022)	(0.013)
Inflation$_{t-1}$	–0.00391	–0.00751	0.00150
	(0.00908)	(0.01421)	(0.00916)
ΔUnemployment$_{t-1}$	0.168***	–0.054	0.026
	(0.056)	(0.041)	(0.032)
Economic size$_{t-1}$	–0.001	0.039	–0.211
	(0.287)	(0.404)	(0.228)
Majority$_{t-1}$	0.155	0.022	0.065
	(0.132)	(0.127)	(0.092)
Coalition$_{t-1}$	0.006	–0.012	0.026
	(0.041)	(0.048)	(0.028)
CBI$_{t-1}$	–2.012	0.457	0.634*
	(1.413)	(0.452)	(0.363)
Labor$_{t-1}$	–0.018	–0.041	–0.023
	(0.041)	(0.048)	(0.030)
Left$_{t-1}$	0.00037	0.00170*	0.00155**
	(0.00106)	(0.00091)	(0.00070)
Election	0.138**	–0.047	0.016
	(0.062)	(0.056)	(0.044)
Trade openness$_{t-1}$	–0.017*	–0.005	–0.006***
	(0.011)	(0.004)	(0.003)
Exchange rate$_{t-1}$	0.126	–0.110	–0.011
	(0.108)	(0.195)	(0.081)
Capital mobility$_{t-1}$	0.115***	0.009	0.039*
	(0.036)	(0.043)	(0.024)
R^2	0.999	0.999	0.999
Observations	250	337	587

Notes
OLS estimates with panel-corrected standard errors in parentheses.
Country and time dummy variables not reported.
***Significant at the 0.01 level.
**Significant at the 0.05 level.
*Significant at the 0.10 level.

taxes than direct taxes, and center governments relied more on direct than indirect taxes for revenues. No coefficient of *Right* is significant. Substantively, an increase in left cabinet portfolios from 0 to 100 (the lowest to highest in the sample) raised consumption tax revenues by 0.17 percent of GDP during 1982–2001 (1.3 percent of total consumption tax revenues: the average total

Table 4.11b Partisan impact on consumption tax revenues

Model	Consumption tax		
	1961–1981	*1982–2001*	*1961–2001*
Left$_{t-1}$	0.00037	0.00170*	0.00155**
	(0.00106)	(0.00091)	(0.00070)
Center$_{t-1}$	−0.00114	−0.00252***	−0.00212***
	(0.00132)	(0.00084)	(0.00070)
Right$_{t-1}$	0.00047	−0.00017	−0.00029
	(0.00103)	(0.00071)	(0.00061)

Notes
Only the results of the three government partisanship variables that were alternately entered in the basic models are reported.
OLS estimates with panel-corrected standard errors in parentheses.
***Significant at the 0.01 level.
**Significant at the 0.05 level.
*Significant at the 0.10 level.

Table 4.11c Impact of party fragmentation on consumption tax revenues

Model	Consumption tax		
	1961–1981	*1982–2001*	*1961–2001*
Fragmentation$_{t-1}$	0.025	0.136***	0.065*
	(0.071)	(0.056)	(0.036)
Coalition$_{t-1}$	−0.001	−0.032	0.008
	(0.048)	(0.048)	(0.030)

Notes
Only the results of *Fragmentation* and *Coalition* that were entered in the basic models are reported.
OLS estimates with panel-corrected standard errors in parentheses.
***Significant at the 0.01 level.
**Significant at the 0.05 level.
*Significant at the 0.10 level.

consumption tax revenues = 12.8 percent of GDP). During the same period, an equivalent increase in center cabinet portfolios suppressed the revenues by 0.25 percent of GDP (2 percent of total consumption tax revenues).

Party fragmentation pushed up consumption tax revenues in the second and entire periods (Table 4.11c). An increase of the effective number of parliamentary parties by three pushed up the revenues by 0.4 percent of GDP (3.2 percent of total consumption tax revenues). When considered with the effects of *Fragmentation* on other tax and spending items, this is a result partly of high spending levels in countries with fragmented party system and partly of their effort to discipline their fiscal policy in the second period by restraining spending and raising sufficient revenues so as not to create deficit.

Table 4.12 Determinants of social security contributions

Model	Social security contributions		
	1961–1981	*1982–2001*	*1961–2001*
Independent variables			
Social security contributions$_{t-1}$	0.952***	0.960***	1.040***
	(0.104)	(0.101)	(0.069)
Social security contributions$_{t-2}$	−0.173*	−0.132	−0.155**
	(0.106)	(0.102)	(0.067)
GDP$_{t-1}$	−0.022	0.004	−0.008
	(0.021)	(0.021)	(0.015)
Inflation$_{t-1}$	0.036***	0.019	0.025***
	(0.014)	(0.012)	(0.009)
ΔUnemployment$_{t-1}$	−0.213***	0.045	−0.029
	(0.079)	(0.040)	(0.036)
Economic size$_{t-1}$	−0.317	1.367***	0.452*
	(0.330)	(0.425)	(0.268)
Pop65$_{t-1}$	0.139	0.017	−0.001
	(0.130)	(0.048)	(0.028)
Majority$_{t-1}$	0.024	0.135	0.066
	(0.115)	(0.129)	(0.087)
Coalition$_{t-1}$	0.034	−0.086	0.004
	(0.047)	(0.056)	(0.039)
CBI$_{t-1}$	−2.841**	−0.139	0.013
	(1.460)	(0.506)	(0.476)
Labor$_{t-1}$	−0.012	−0.082**	−0.049*
	(0.047)	(0.042)	(0.028)
Left$_{t-1}$	−0.00268**	−0.00141	−0.00102
	(0.00126)	(0.00100)	(0.00075)
Election	0.031	−0.050	−0.017
	(0.056)	(0.053)	(0.044)
Trade openness$_{t-1}$	0.028**	−0.010**	−0.004
	(0.012)	(0.004)	(0.003)
Exchange rate$_{t-1}$	0.018	0.072	−0.016
	(0.090)	(0.128)	(0.087)
Capital mobility$_{t-1}$	0.093**	−0.029	−0.004
	(0.040)	(0.035)	(0.023)
R^2	0.999	0.999	0.999
Observations	199	310	509

Notes
OLS estimates with panel-corrected standard errors in parentheses.
Country and time dummy variables not reported.
***Significant at the 0.01 level.
**Significant at the 0.05 level.
*Significant at the 0.10 level.

Social security contributions

Table 4.12 shows the results of social security contributions received by governments. Though not significant, coalition governments had higher contributions in the first period and lower contributions in the second. There is a chance that this pattern may have been real, as the second period is not far from significance ($p = 0.12$) and in the models without country dummies, the first period becomes significant. If this result is to be trusted, it suggests that coalition governments trimmed social security contribution burdens in the 1980s and 1990s, consistent with my argument about the neoliberal policy shift in the past two decades.

CBI has a negative sign (lower contributions) for both the first and second periods, and is significant for the first. Thus, independent central banks suppressed social security contributions in the first period. *Labor*'s sign is also negative for all periods and significant in 1982–2001 and 1961–2001. The reason for this may be similar to the one for personal income tax, which was lower under coordinated labor – union members including low-income workers prefer low social security contributions, and in countries where labor is strong and coordinated, they get their wishes. This interpretation is supported by the evidence we will see in Chapter 5 – coordinated labor had the lowest social security contributions when it was accompanied by left governments (social democratic neocorporatist regimes) than any other combination of labor and government partisanship. There is understandably no observable electoral cycle in social security contributions, as most governments could not easily cut contributions, when they faced ever-growing social security payments and the need to finance them while maintaining fiscal discipline at the same time. Long-term programs such as social security are also hard to manipulate in the short run.

Partisan impact and fragmentation Table 4.12b reports the results of partisan impact. As expected from the welfare state literature (Esping-Andersen, 1990), the signs for left governments are all negative, and those for center governments are all positive. *Left* is significant for 1961–1981 (and when I add *Fragmentation* to this specification, *Left* becomes significant for 1982–2001). But no coefficient is

Table 4.12b Partisan impact on social security contributions

Model	Social security contributions		
	1961–1981	*1982–2001*	*1961–2001*
Left$_{t-1}$	−0.00268**	−0.00141	−0.00102
	(0.00126)	(0.00100)	(0.00075)
Center$_{t-1}$	0.00032	0.00009	0.00019
	(0.00137)	(0.00088)	(0.00064)
Right$_{t-1}$	0.00256**	0.00096	0.00077
	(0.00109)	(0.00073)	(0.00057)

Notes
Only the results of the three government partisanship variables that were alternately entered in the basic models are reported.
OLS estimates with panel-corrected standard errors in parentheses.
***Significant at the 0.01 level.
**Significant at the 0.05 level.
*Significant at the 0.10 level.

significant for center governments. The previous literature suggested that center governments (which are often Christian democratic governments) have high social security contributions because of their welfare system's dependence on transfer payments, while left governments have lower transfer payments because their welfare system leans toward the provision of government services and is funded by taxes more than social security contributions. But the evidence here suggests that center governments did not collect high social security contributions (although their contributions were higher than left governments in the first period). This is consistent with the results of social security benefits paid by governments (discussed earlier), where center governments had lower social security payments in the first period (the second period is also negative but not significant).

Meanwhile, the signs of *Right* are all positive (higher contributions) for all periods, and the first period is significant. This is contrary to the previous literature, but is consistent with the results of social security payments that show right governments had higher spending in this area during all periods (as discussed above). These results show that conservative governments were higher spenders than previously believed, and more expansionary than left or center governments, and consistent with my argument about right governments' relative fiscal indiscipline. The effective number of parliamentary parties (party fragmentation) did not affect social security contributions in any period (results not reported). The signs are all negative, but none is significant.

Total spending and tax revenues

Economic controls   The results of the total spending models (Table 4.13) show that total spending responds countercyclically to economic growth (*GDP*), as conventionally understood (in the models without country dummies, *GDP* is significant for both periods). Inflation pushes up spending. Somewhat surprisingly, but consistent with the results of the disaggregate spending items, total spending responds procyclically to unemployment in 1961–1981.[26] During 1982–2001, the sign of *Unemployment* is positive (countercyclical) but not significant (in the models without country dummies, the sign is negative).

The results of total revenues (Table 4.14) show that total revenues are not sensitive to output growth (not significant). This is also somewhat surprising, because tax revenues usually increase during economic booms and the results reviewed above show that the revenues from individual tax items increased with high growth at least for 1961–1981.

Total revenues increase with inflation, as expected (in no-dummy models, the coefficient is significant for both 1961–1981 and 1982–2001). Unemployment depresses total receipts, as expected, but it is significant only for 1961–1981.

Globalization   Trade dependence (*Trade openness*) increased total spending in 1961–1981 and reduced it in 1982–2001. The coefficient for 1961–1981 is not significant, but in the models without country dummies, it is significant for both periods as well as for the entire period of 1961–2001. This is consistent with the

Table 4.13 Determinants of total government spending

Model	Spending		
	1961–1981	*1982–2001*	*1961–2001*
Independent variables			
Spending$_{t-1}$	0.801***	1.026***	1.035***
	(0.120)	(0.090)	(0.069)
Spending$_{t-2}$	0.045	−0.218***	−0.194***
	(0.115)	(0.085)	(0.066)
GDP$_{t-1}$	−0.179**	−0.094	−0.047
	(0.080)	(0.064)	(0.054)
Inflation$_{t-1}$	0.157***	0.137***	0.119***
	(0.032)	(0.054)	(0.032)
ΔUnemployment$_{t-1}$	−0.839***	0.023	−0.073
	(0.210)	(0.154)	(0.131)
Economic size$_{t-1}$	0.703	4.251***	2.010*
	(1.965)	(1.329)	(1.064)
Majority$_{t-1}$	0.255	0.049	0.219
	(0.401)	(0.350)	(0.246)
Coalition$_{t-1}$	0.065	−0.021	0.072
	(0.164)	(0.115)	(0.083)
CBI$_{t-1}$	1.216	−0.506	0.425
	(4.574)	(1.499)	(1.354)
Labor$_{t-1}$	−0.067	−0.182	−0.065
	(0.126)	(0.119)	(0.088)
Left$_{t-1}$	−0.00179	−0.00380	−0.00121
	(0.00360)	(0.00257)	(0.00195)
Election	0.067	−0.024	0.044
	(0.157)	(0.156)	(0.119)
Trade openness$_{t-1}$	0.078	−0.060***	−0.049***
	(0.058)	(0.018)	(0.011)
Exchange rate$_{t-1}$	−0.784**	−1.176**	−1.228***
	(0.348)	(0.527)	(0.248)
Capital mobility$_{t-1}$	0.202*	0.304***	0.165**
	(0.121)	(0.121)	(0.074)
R^2	0.999	0.999	0.999
Observations	204	326	530

Notes
OLS estimates with panel-corrected standard errors in parentheses.
Country and time dummy variables not reported.
***Significant at the 0.01 level.
**Significant at the 0.05 level.
*Significant at the 0.10 level.

pattern observed in individual spending items. All individual spending items increased with trade openness in the 1960s and 1970s, but decreased in the 1980s and 1990s, except for government investment. Thus, open-economy governments increased spending in the 1960s and 1970s to mitigate the economic dislocations from the international economy, as argued by the compensation thesis. But in the

1980s and 1990s, they reduced total spending for concerns with mobile capital, economic efficiency and competitiveness, and the negative economic consequences of fiscal indiscipline, as expected by the convergence thesis.

Governments with great capital mobility had higher spending levels during all periods, lending support to the compensation thesis and contrary to the convergence thesis. This is also the overall pattern of the effect of capital mobility on both spending and tax items – high capital mobility causes increases in spending and tax revenues (except for government investment (1961–1981), government subsidies, and social security contributions (1982–2001)). In contrast, governments with a floating exchange rate regime had consistently lower spending throughout the periods. This is also a general pattern of the response of spending items to different exchange rate mechanisms.

The patterns of total revenues follow those of total spending. Trade openness led to higher revenues in the first period (not significant) and lower revenues in the second, and capital mobility induced higher revenues (the second period not significant). The only difference from total spending is that a floating exchange rate regime does not significantly affect total revenues, except for the entire period where it negatively affected total revenues.

Thus, although spending and revenues sometimes get out of sync with each other and produce deficit or surplus, the patterns of total revenues and spending are similar – i.e. most of the time, governments either spend what they raise or raise enough tax to finance their spending. The other difference is that as expected, total spending tends to be countercyclical, and total revenues procyclical.

Political variables   The interpretation of the results of tax revenues requires a bit of care, because one cannot a priori determine whether high taxes are a sign of a tight fiscal policy or an expansionary fiscal policy. On the one hand, high tax revenues can be a result of governments' efforts to raise sufficient revenues to finance their spending so as not to produce deficit. If revenues are raised in a way not to create deficit, then higher taxes should be considered a conservative and disciplined fiscal policy. On the other hand, higher taxes can be a sign of an undisciplined policy if they are simply a result of higher spending. Likewise, low revenues are a sign of a conservative policy if accompanied by a disciplined spending policy, because governments that do not spend much do not need large revenues. But low revenues can be a sign of an undisciplined policy if spending is not restrained, because high spending and low tax revenues obviously create deficit. Therefore, an assessment of tax revenue results needs to be made in the context of their relationships to spending policy and the fiscal balance.

The results of total revenues (Table 4.14) show that *CBI* produced high tax revenues in the second period of 1982–2001 and the entire period of 1961–2001. Coalition governments also raised higher total revenues in the entire period. In models without country dummies, coalition governments produced higher revenues (than single-party governments) in both the first and entire period. These should be interpreted as a sign of fiscal discipline (conservative fiscal policy)

Table 4.14 Determinants of total government revenues

Model	Revenues		
	1961–1981	*1982–2001*	*1961–2001*
Independent variables			
Revenues$_{t-1}$	0.768***	0.800***	0.861***
	(0.044)	(0.040)	(0.023)
GDP$_{t-1}$	−0.007	−0.037	−0.001
	(0.048)	(0.042)	(0.033)
Inflation$_{t-1}$	0.070***	0.009	0.025
	(0.024)	(0.028)	(0.020)
ΔUnemployment$_{t-1}$	−0.295*	−0.087	−0.107
	(0.174)	(0.086)	(0.081)
Economic size$_{t-1}$	2.561*	1.823**	1.935***
	(1.459)	(0.801)	(0.705)
Majority$_{t-1}$	−0.174	0.081	−0.222
	(0.281)	(0.275)	(0.190)
Coalition$_{t-1}$	0.103	−0.095	0.117*
	(0.103)	(0.099)	(0.070)
CBI$_{t-1}$	−0.401	1.858**	1.607*
	(3.216)	(0.827)	(0.846)
Labor$_{t-1}$	0.129	−0.232***	−0.055
	(0.112)	(0.089)	(0.069)
Left$_{t-1}$	−0.00007	−0.00262	−0.00013
	(0.00297)	(0.00171)	(0.00146)
Election	0.017	−0.329***	−0.160*
	(0.128)	(0.109)	(0.093)
Trade openness$_{t-1}$	0.023	−0.032***	−0.035***
	(0.035)	(0.010)	(0.007)
Exchange rate$_{t-1}$	−0.389	0.361	−0.331**
	(0.282)	(0.269)	(0.168)
Capital mobility$_{t-1}$	0.428***	0.050	0.143***
	(0.105)	(0.080)	(0.050)
R^2	0.999	1.000	1.000
Observations	211	328	539

Notes
OLS estimates with panel-corrected standard errors in parentheses.
Country and time dummy variables not reported.
***Significant at the 0.01 level.
**Significant at the 0.05 level.
*Significant at the 0.10 level.

because central banks and coalition governments did not have high spending and, as a result, contributed to budget surpluses in the second and entire periods (as we will see later in the analysis of the fiscal balance). Their substantive effects are also sizeable. An increase in *CBI* from 0.14 to 0.68 (the lowest to highest in the sample) increased total revenues by 1 percent of GDP (2.4 percent of total revenues: the average total revenues = 42.1 percent of GDP) in the second period. An increase in the number of coalition parties by three increased revenues by 0.35 percent of GDP (0.83 percent of total revenues) in the entire period of 1961–2001.

The results provide clear evidence of party governments' engineering of electoral expansions in total government revenues. During 1982–2001 and 1961–2001, total revenues were lower in election years. During 1982–2001, total revenues dropped by 0.33 percent of GDP (8 percent of total revenues) in election years. This result suggests two important things. First, although the globalization thesis stresses the progressively reduced ability of governments to manipulate fiscal policy for political, economic, or electoral purposes in recent decades, the room for governments' maneuvering of economic policy did not diminish. To the contrary, electoral cycles existed only in the recent second period. Governments could and did reduce tax revenues in election years in 1982–2001. (For explanations of the electoral cycles in the 1980s and 1990s, see "Electoral cycles, central banks, and policy attributes," Chapter 2, p. 41.) Second, the results of the fiscal balance also show that governments' budget balance worsened (higher deficit) in election years during the same periods of 1982–2001 and 1961–2001, but similar electoral cycles are not detected in total government spending. This means that governments' electoral expansions may have been created more by reducing tax revenues rather than increasing spending. The results of other individual disaggregate spending and tax items also show the same pattern – i.e. governments' electoral expansions are detected more in tax policy than in spending.

The results also suggest that coordinated labor pushed down tax revenues in the second period of 1982–2001. This represents coordinated labor's generally conservative effect on fiscal policy in the 1980s and 1990s. During the period, countries with coordinated labor decreased both spending and revenues. (But the results of the fiscal balance suggest that their spending cuts did not sufficiently keep up with revenue cuts, creating a small deterioration in the fiscal balance.) There is no evidence that minority governments had an unrestrained fiscal policy in any period.

Contrary to total revenues, total government spending was not affected much by central bank independence, the number of governing parties, labor, and the majority status of governments (Table 4.13). Though none of *CBI*, *Coalition*, and *Labor* achieve statistical significance, the signs of their coefficients show that overall, these factors reduced total spending levels as they entered the 1980s and 1990s.

So the general picture that comes out of the examination of total spending and revenues is that the fiscal policy of coalition governments and governments with independent central banks became conservative in 1982–2001, and fiscal discipline was achieved by restraining (or not increasing) spending but keeping high tax revenues (or increasing them). This result is consistent with the anecdotal reports about many industrial countries that these governments have been trying in the past 15 years to restrain spending and increase (or maintain) tax revenues in order to balance their budget and to reduce government debt. This tendency is conspicuous particularly among European countries that strove to qualify for the EMU membership by meeting the convergence criteria that stipulated that fiscal deficit be contained within 3 percent of GDP and gross debt within 60 percent of GDP. But this fiscal conservatism is also the common trend among the rest of the industrial countries after the 1980s when they began to place more policy emphasis on fiscal discipline and the reduction of the size of government.[27]

Partisan impact and fragmentation Tables 4.13b, 4.13c, 4.14b, and 4.14c report the results of the impact of partisanship and party fragmentation. The signs of *Left* are all negative in both spending and revenue models, suggesting left governments' lower spending and revenues. But none is significant, meaning that they did not put upward or downward pressure on expenditures or tax revenues. There is thus no evidence that left governments were fiscally expansionary in any period. As we will see below, there is also no evidence

Table 4.13b Partisan impact on total government spending

Model	Spending		
	1961–1981	*1982–2001*	*1961–2001*
Left$_{t-1}$	−0.00179	−0.00380	−0.00121
	(0.00360)	(0.00257)	(0.00195)
Center$_{t-1}$	−0.00199	−0.00499*	−0.00258
	(0.00378)	(0.00299)	(0.00215)
Right$_{t-1}$	0.00259	0.00568***	0.00275
	(0.00356)	(0.00223)	(0.00181)

Notes
Only the results of the three government partisanship variables that were alternately entered in the basic models are reported.
OLS estimates with panel-corrected standard errors in parentheses.
***Significant at the 0.01 level.
**Significant at the 0.05 level.
*Significant at the 0.10 level.

Table 4.13c Impact of party fragmentation on total government spending

Model	Spending		
	1961–1981	*1982–2001*	*1961–2001*
Fragmentation$_{t-1}$	0.073	−0.013	−0.055
	(0.203)	(0.149)	(0.115)
Coalition$_{t-1}$	0.046	−0.020	0.087
	(0.180)	(0.120)	(0.092)

Notes
Only the results of *Fragmentation* and *Coalition* that were entered in the basic models are reported.
OLS estimates with panel-corrected standard errors in parentheses.
***Significant at the 0.01 level.
**Significant at the 0.05 level.
*Significant at the 0.10 level.

Table 4.14b Partisan impact on total government revenues

Model	Revenues		
	1961–1981	*1982–2001*	*1961–2001*
Left$_{t-1}$	–0.00007	–0.00262	–0.00013
	(0.00297)	(0.00171)	(0.00146)
Center$_{t-1}$	0.00398	0.00407*	0.00189
	(0.00312)	(0.00219)	(0.00160)
Right$_{t-1}$	–0.00343	0.00010	–0.00135
	(0.00299)	(0.00149)	(0.00136)

Notes
Only the results of the three government partisanship variables that were alternately entered in the basic models are reported.
OLS estimates with panel-corrected standard errors in parentheses.
***Significant at the 0.01 level.
**Significant at the 0.05 level.
*Significant at the 0.10 level.

Table 4.14c Impact of party fragmentation on total government revenues

Model	Revenues		
	1961–1981	*1982–2001*	*1961–2001*
Fragmentation$_{t-1}$	–0.279*	–0.001	0.009
	(0.158)	(0.122)	(0.080)
Coalition$_{t-1}$	0.172	–0.095	0.115
	(0.119)	(0.102)	(0.075)

Notes
Only the results of *Fragmentation* and *Coalition* that were entered in the basic models are reported.
OLS estimates with panel-corrected standard errors in parentheses.
***Significant at the 0.01 level.
**Significant at the 0.05 level.
*Significant at the 0.10 level.

that they contributed to fiscal deficit according to the results of fiscal balance models.

Center governments had lower expenditures and higher revenues than other partisan governments in 1982–2001 (significant). This is a sign of their fiscal discipline in the 1980s and 1990s, which is confirmed in the primary balance models (cyclically unadjusted) showing that they produced a better fiscal balance than the left or right during the period. Thus, center governments had restrained spending but kept high revenues to improve their fiscal balance and reduce government debt in the 1980s and 1990s. There is no evidence that center governments were fiscally expansionary.

Contrary to the conventional partisan theory, right governments' fiscal policy was less disciplined than the left or center. Right governments had higher total spending than the left or center during the second period of 1982–2001. The signs in the revenue models also suggest (though nothing is significant) that their higher spending was accompanied by lower revenues than the left or right (the second period is positive, but in models without country dummies, all signs are negative, and right governments' lower revenues during 1961–2001 are significant). As a result, right governments produced higher deficit than the left or center. As we will see later in the results of the fiscal balance, the signs of *Right* are negative (higher deficit) for all of the first, second, and third periods. Only the first period is significant, but the second ($p = 0.14$) and entire ($p = 0.15$) periods are not too far from significance. And in cyclically unadjusted models, all the periods are negative and significant, suggesting that right governments were fiscally most expansionary during the entire periods.

Thus, right governments collected potentially lower revenues in 1961–2001 (without fixed effects), spent more in 1982–2001 and potentially 1961–2001 ($p = 0.12$), and produced higher deficit (or lower surplus) in 1961–1981 (or in all three periods in unadjusted models). Even if we discount the results of the unadjusted models, there is no slightest evidence that they were fiscally more disciplined than the left or center. Therefore, the standard partisan theory is not supported, at least as far as total spending, total tax revenues, and the fiscal balance are concerned.

Party fragmentation (the effective number of parliamentary parties) did not affect total spending, since no coefficient is significant (Table 4.13c). Though not significant, the coefficients suggest that it had an upward effect on total spending in the first period (1961–1981) and a downward effect in the second period (1982–2001). The signs are in the directions expected by my argument that so-called weak actors restrained their fiscal policy in the 1980s and 1990s. The tax revenue results (Table 4.14c) show that party fragmentation had a negative effect on total revenues in 1961–1981, i.e. the larger the number of parties, the lower total revenues, supporting one version of weak government arguments, which would expect fiscal indiscipline for countries with fragmented party systems. The negative effect disappears in the 1980s and 1990s (in the models without country dummies and *Coalition, Fragmentation* turns even positive and significant). This suggests that countries with fragmented party systems may have restrained fiscal policy in the second period and collected more revenues to finance their spending, lending support to my argument about the conservative policy shift.

Budget balance and monetary policy stance

We now examine governments' fiscal balance (primary balance) and monetary policy stance (for the description of the data, see the Appendix at the end of this chapter).[28]

Economic controls – fiscal balance   Table 4.15 reports the results of the fiscal balance (+ surplus/– deficit). Economic growth improved the fiscal balance in the first period of 1961–1981, as consistent with the conventional understanding –

Table 4.15 Determinants of the fiscal balance

Model	Fiscal balance		
	1961–1981	*1982–2001*	*1961–2001*
Independent variables			
Fiscal balance$_{t-1}$	0.636***	0.908***	0.973***
	(0.115)	(0.074)	(0.063)
Fiscal balance$_{t-2}$	−0.213**	−0.139**	−0.180***
	(0.105)	(0.072)	(0.061)
GDP$_{t-1}$	0.208***	0.049	0.072
	(0.069)	(0.061)	(0.049)
Inflation$_{t-1}$	0.025	−0.059*	−0.063**
	(0.034)	(0.035)	(0.029)
ΔUnemployment$_{t-1}$	0.328*	−0.066	0.033
	(0.196)	(0.123)	(0.107)
Economic size$_{t-1}$	−7.714***	−2.087*	−0.468
	(2.787)	(1.097)	(1.103)
Majority$_{t-1}$	−0.583	0.284	0.005
	(0.401)	(0.367)	(0.285)
Coalition$_{t-1}$	−0.205	−0.272**	−0.085
	(0.148)	(0.130)	(0.097)
CBI$_{t-1}$	(dropped)	1.941**	1.909*
		(0.989)	(1.102)
Labor$_{t-1}$	0.180	−0.188	−0.016
	(0.120)	(0.124)	(0.088)
Left$_{t-1}$	0.00805	0.00151	0.00181
	(0.00549)	(0.00238)	(0.00201)
Election	0.080	−0.416***	−0.319**
	(0.213)	(0.149)	(0.131)
Trade openness$_{t-1}$	0.072	0.021*	0.003
	(0.059)	(0.013)	(0.011)
Exchange rate$_{t-1}$	0.249	0.851***	0.185
	(0.446)	(0.336)	(0.267)
Capital mobility$_{t-1}$	0.663***	−0.198*	−0.032
	(0.181)	(0.107)	(0.087)
R^2	0.875	0.830	0.803
Observations	123	330	453

Notes
OLS estimates with panel-corrected standard errors in parentheses.
Country and time dummy variables not reported.
***Significant at the 0.01 level.
**Significant at the 0.05 level.
*Significant at the 0.10 level.

during economic booms, spending decreases (e.g. unemployment benefits), but tax revenues grow, as economic growth expands the tax bases for personal and corporate incomes taxes and consumption tax, producing an improvement in the fiscal balance. The sign for 1982–2001 is in the expected direction, but not significant. When we compare these results with those for total spending and total revenues (Tables 4.13, 4.14), we see that growth had this positive effect on the fiscal balance, because total spending decreased with growth in a typical Keynesian fashion in the first period, but revenues did not decline.

Inflation deteriorated the fiscal balance in the second period (1982–2001) and for the entire period (1961–2001). This matches the results of the total spending and revenues models showing that spending increased with inflation in the second period, but revenues did not. Next, unemployment has a positive sign (surplus) in 1961–1981, but a negative sign in 1982–2001, though it is significant only in 1961–1981. The common belief expects the result of the second period, that is, the fiscal balance's countercyclical response to unemployment. But it is not significant. The comparison with the total spending and revenue models suggests that the procyclical response to unemployment in the first period happened because spending decreased with unemployment more than revenues did. These results remain the same in the models without country dummies.

Economic globalization – fiscal balance   Trade openness contributed to a positive balance (surplus) in the second period of 1982–2001. This largely supports the convergence thesis and is consistent with the patterns of various spending items reviewed above – open-economy governments conducted a relatively tight fiscal policy in the second period. The comparison with the total spending and revenue models suggests that the positive balance took place, because total spending decreased with trade openness more than revenues did. The results of the first period also suggest a surplus result, but this is not significant. The result of *Exchange rate* shows that a flexible exchange rate regime improved the fiscal balance in 1982–2001. This is consistent with the results of most spending models discussed in the previous parts of the chapter, showing that a floating exchange rate served to reduce government spending. The signs are all positive, though only the second period is significant. The positive effect on the fiscal balance happened, as spending decreased with a floating system, but revenues did not.

Capital mobility has a positive sign (surplus) in the first period of 1961–1981 and a negative sign (deficit) in the second period of 1982–2001, and both are significant. The second-period result runs counter to the expectation of the globalization or convergence thesis that governments with high capital mobility conduct a tight fiscal policy to attract mobile capital. This result is consistent with the results of various spending items in my analysis, including total spending, showing that in the 1982–2001 period, governments with high capital mobility responded by increasing spending. Thus, the result of the second period supports the compensation thesis. The comparison with the total spending and revenues results suggest that in the first period, revenues increased with capital mobility more than spending did, resulting in a surplus. In the second, spending increased with capital mobility, but revenues did not; hence, a deficit.

Economic controls – monetary policy   Let us now look at the monetary policy stance (Table 4.16).[29] The signs of the coefficients for economic growth (*GDP*) show that, as consistent with the conventional understanding, governments tightened monetary policy during economic expansions (positive = high discount rates). The coefficient is not significant for the first period of 1961–1981, but in the models without country dummies, it is significant for all the periods. *Unemployment* has a positive sign (tight monetary policy) in all periods, suggesting that monetary policy tightened with unemployment (the first period not significant). As we have seen in earlier discussions, there is no immediate answer to this procyclical response to unemployment.

Economic globalization – monetary policy Moving to the globalization variables, the signs of the coefficients suggest the following (they are significant only for the entire period of 1961–2001 for *Trade openness* and *Capital mobility*). Open-economy governments (*Trade openness*) had a looser monetary policy for the entire period of 1961–2001. There are two related possibilities for this. The first is the possibility that open-economy governments provided domestic industries and firms, which were exposed to international competition, with lower interest rates to enhance their economic performance (as well as to boost the economy). This also coincides with qualitative accounts pointing out that small open economies of Europe, particularly left governments of Scandinavia, used monetary policy as a supply-side policy tool to assist domestic industries and firms (e.g. Huber and Stephens, 1998).

The second and related possibility is that open-economy governments used currency devaluation to promote their export industries, which led to an expansionary monetary policy. This also fits well with the experience of the open economies of the Nordic countries.

Note also that as the previous primary balance models show, fiscal policy became tighter with trade openness. I argued in Chapter 2 that when fiscal policy is tight, central banks do not have to implement a tight monetary policy and that fiscal and monetary policies are made with an eye toward each other and in complementary manners. The monetary policy results suggest that central banks did not have to implement a tight monetary policy in open-economy countries (greater trade openness) because fiscal policy was relatively tight, lending support to my policy mix argument.

A floating exchange rate regime had a loose monetary policy during the first period of 1961–1981 and a tight policy during the second period of 1982–2001. But none of these are significant. The signs are approximately in the direction expected by my fiscal–monetary policy mix argument, as a floating rate regime contributed to a tight fiscal policy (in the fiscal balance), and monetary policy had a negative sign (loose or not tight) except for the second period. Under a floating regime, central banks did not have to implement a tight monetary policy (the coefficient not significant or negative) because fiscal policy was relatively tight.

The signs for capital mobility are all positive, suggesting that countries with great capital mobility had a tighter monetary policy, which lends support to the globalization thesis that governments keep a disciplined monetary policy under capital mobility to maintain the market's confidence in their economic policy (though the coefficient is significant only for 1961–2001). It also supports my policy mix argument, since governments under capital mobility conducted a loose fiscal policy at least for 1982–2001, and central banks' monetary policy had to be tight in response. But all these economic globalization variables lose significance when the country dummies are removed from the specifications.

Political variables – fiscal balance   First, independent central banks restrained party governments' fiscal policy and contributed to budget surplus (Table 4.15), as I argued in Chapter 2. During the second period of 1982–2001 and the entire period of 1961–2001, an increase in *CBI* from 0.14 to 0.68 (the lowest to highest in the sample) improved the primary balance by 1 percent of potential GDP. *CBI* cannot be estimated for the first period of 1961–1981 in fixed models, because *CBI* is relatively time-invariant during the first period, and *CBI* and country dummies cause perfect multicollinearity. But in the models without country dummies, *CBI* is negative and insignificant for the first period.

The results show clear evidence of governments engineering electoral fiscal expansions – party governments conducted an expansionary fiscal policy in election years. And the evidence is found for 1982–2001 when, according to the globalization thesis, governments allegedly lost latitude in manipulating fiscal policy due to economic globalization. This result supports my argument that political impact on economic policy became accentuated in the second period. Substantively, governments' primary balance deteriorated in election years by 0.42 percent of potential GDP during the second period of 1982–2001 and by 0.32 percent during the entire period of 1961–2001.

There is a slight chance that coordinated labor contributed to budget surplus during the first period of 1961–1981 but to deficit during the second period of 1982–2001, though the coefficients do not attain significance ($p = 0.13$). The second period becomes significant in models without country dummies, suggesting that labor may have worsened the fiscal balance in the 1980s and 1990s. If this result is to be trusted, this negative effect was due to the pattern that although labor served to reduce both spending and taxation, spending decreases did not keep up with tax cuts, as we saw previously in the chapter in total spending and revenues.

The interpretation of the effects of the number of governing parties (*Coalition*) is difficult. In the fixed-effect models, the sign is negative (deficit) and significant for the second period of 1982–2001, but in models without country dummies, it is positive (surplus) and significant for 1982–2001. Though it needs further research, I am inclined to place confidence in the surplus result of *Coalition* (the models without country dummies) for the following reason. In the fixed-effects models of total spending and revenues, *Coalition* has no effect on total spending and revenues, which suggests that *Coalition* should have no effect on the fiscal balance, and thus, the deficit result of the fixed-effects models does not exactly match the results of the total spending and revenues models. In contrast, the results of the models without country dummies show that coalition governments significantly increased revenues, but had no effect on spending during the same 1982–2001 period, which should help produce surplus. Thus, the result of the models without country dummies is consistent with the results of the total spending and revenue models. If these results without country dummies are to be trusted, it means that coalition governments had a more disciplined fiscal policy than single-party governments in the 1980s and 1990s. But this conclusion is tentative.

Lastly, majority status did not affect the fiscal balance in any period, showing that there is no evidence that minority governments were fiscally profligate. (When *Fragmentation* is entered instead of *Coalition*, *Majority* is negative and significant for 1961–1981, suggesting that majority governments were fiscally less disciplined than minority ones, denying one of the claims of weak government arguments. *Majority* is also negative and significant in models with the cyclically unadjusted primary balance as the dependent variable.)

Partisan impact and fragmentation – fiscal balance   Table 4.15b reports the results of partisan effects on the fiscal balance. There is no evidence that pro-welfare left and center governments – whose economic policy has conventionally been considered expansionary – suffered fiscal indiscipline in any period. To the contrary, the directions of the coefficients suggest that both left and center governments contributed to lower deficit (or higher surplus) and thus were fiscally disciplined. Furthermore, when we use the cyclically unadjusted primary balance as the alternate dependent variable, the positive coefficient for left governments becomes significant for 1961–1981, and significant for center governments for 1982–2001 and 1961–2001 (results not reported). Thus, according to the cyclically unadjusted results, left and center governments actually had a better fiscal balance (fiscal discipline) than right governments.

Contrary to the conventional partisan theory, conservative (right) govern-

Table 4.15b Partisan impact on the fiscal balance

Model	Fiscal balance		
	1961–1981	*1982–2001*	*1961–2001*
Left$_{t-1}$	0.00805	0.00151	0.00181
	(0.00549)	(0.00238)	(0.00201)
Center$_{t-1}$	0.00491	0.00337	0.00091
	(0.00567)	(0.00319)	(0.00243)
Right$_{t-1}$	−0.00871**	−0.00303	−0.00262
	(0.00408)	(0.00207)	(0.00185)

Notes
Only the results of the three government partisanship variables that were alternately entered in the basic models are reported.
OLS estimates with panel-corrected standard errors in parentheses.
***Significant at the 0.01 level.
**Significant at the 0.05 level.
*Significant at the 0.10 level.

ments actually had a worse fiscal balance than left and center governments during the first period of 1961–1981 (significant). *Right*'s negative signs (deficit) for 1982–2001 and 1961–2001 are also not too far from significance ($p = 0.14$, 0.15). Further, when I use the cyclically unadjusted primary balance as the dependent variable, right governments' negative signs (higher deficit) turn significant for all of the 1961–1981, 1982–2001, and 1961–2001 periods, indicating that they were fiscally more profligate than left and center governments during all three periods under study.

Thus, conservative governments were fiscally less disciplined than left and center governments. These patterns of partisan difference in the fiscal balance are consistent with those of individual spending and tax items. Substantively, an increase in right cabinet portfolios from 0 to 100 (the lowest to highest in the sample) produced a deterioration (deficit) of the primary balance by 0.9 percent of potential GDP during 1961–1981.

Table 4.15c reports the results of party fragmentation (the effective number of parliamentary parties). An additional number of parliamentary parties improved the primary balance in the entire period of 1961–2001, denying one of the claims of weak governments' arguments. An increase of the effective number of parties by one improved the primary balance by 0.26 percent of potential GDP. Though not significant, the signs for the sub-periods are negative (deficit) for the first period of 1961–1981 and positive (surplus) for the second period of 1982–2001. This suggests that although countries with fragmented party systems produced higher deficit in the 1960s and 1970s, they disciplined fiscal policy in the 1980s and 1990s and contributed to fiscal surplus, consistent with my argument in Chapter 3 that governments and institutions that produced fiscal indiscipline in the 1960s and 1970s experienced a conservative shift in fiscal policy in the 1980s and 1990s, if the result is to be trusted. *Fragmentation* turns positive (surplus) and significant for both 1982–2001 and the entire period when country dummies are removed (results not reported), adding some more

Table 4.15c Impact of party fragmentation on the fiscal balance

Model	Fiscal balance		
	1961–1981	*1982–2001*	*1961–2001*
Fragmentation$_{t-1}$	–0.117	0.123	0.263**
	(0.227)	(0.150)	(0.124)
Coalition$_{t-1}$	–0.159	–0.289**	–0.149
	(0.183)	(0.132)	(0.101)

Notes
Only the results of *Fragmentation* and *Coalition* that were entered in the basic models are reported.
OLS estimates with panel-corrected standard errors in parentheses.
***Significant at the 0.01 level.
**Significant at the 0.05 level.
*Significant at the 0.10 level.

Table 4.16 Determinants of monetary policy

Model	Monetary policy		
	1961–1981	*1982–2001*	*1961–2001*
Independent variables			
Monetary policy$_{t-1}$	0.322*	0.591***	0.466***
	(0.182)	(0.084)	(0.082)
Monetary policy$_{t-2}$	−0.251	−0.053	−0.185**
	(0.196)	(0.095)	(0.090)
Monetary policy$_{t-3}$	−0.074	0.044	0.026
	(0.209)	(0.078)	(0.078)
GDP$_{t-1}$	0.388	0.296**	0.285**
	(0.287)	(0.141)	(0.136)
ΔUnemployment$_{t-1}$	0.388	0.810***	0.891***
	(0.771)	(0.260)	(0.273)
Economic size$_{t-1}$	−8.157	−3.733*	1.705
	(10.768)	(2.172)	(3.082)
Majority$_{t-1}$	−2.334	0.331	−0.816
	(1.559)	(0.817)	(0.736)
Coalition$_{t-1}$	−0.084	0.213	0.033
	(0.484)	(0.246)	(0.219)
CBI$_{t-1}$	(dropped)	−0.838	0.559
		(2.133)	(3.699)
Labor$_{t-1}$	−0.699	−0.038	−0.208
	(0.471)	(0.267)	(0.230)
Left$_{t-1}$	0.006	−0.012**	−0.008*
	(0.014)	(0.005)	(0.005)
Election	2.055***	0.157	0.596*
	(0.825)	(0.294)	(0.325)
Trade openness$_{t-1}$	−0.020	−0.014	−0.077***
	(0.219)	(0.025)	(0.026)
Exchange rate$_{t-1}$	−1.986	0.995	−0.288
	(1.829)	(0.700)	(0.740)
Capital mobility$_{t-1}$	0.994	0.270	0.625***
	(0.708)	(0.231)	(0.227)
R^2	0.768	0.546	0.641
Observations	118	346	464

Notes
OLS estimates with panel-corrected standard errors in parentheses.
Country and time dummy variables not reported.
***Significant at the 0.01 level.
**Significant at the 0.05 level.
*Significant at the 0.10 level.

support to my argument about the neoliberal shift in countries with a prior reputation for fiscal indiscipline.

Political variables – monetary policy   Now we review the results of the monetary policy models (Table 4.16). *CBI* gets dropped in the first-period model, because the low number of observations for this dependent variable (*Discount rates*) during the first period makes *CBI* time-invariant during this specific limited time period, and it is impossible to estimate the model with equally time-invariant country dummies due to perfect multicollinearity.[30] But the models without country dummies can measure the effect of *CBI*. Fortunately, the results of the models with and without fixed effects do not vary, except for CBI in the first period. So I report the results of the fixed-effect models, but I describe the results of the models without country dummies for *CBI* in 1961–1981.

CBI is positive and significant for the first period of 1961–1981 (the models without country dummies), showing that independent central banks indeed conducted a very tight monetary policy in the 1960s and 1970s. This is partly central banks' monetary response to the relatively expansionary fiscal policy conducted by party governments during this period. Thus, in tandem with the results of fiscal policy, we can see that the dominant policy mix in countries with independent central banks during the 1960s and 1970s was a loose fiscal–tight monetary policy mix (implying that the policy mix in countries with dependent central banks was a loose fiscal–loose monetary policy mix).

But during the 1980s and 1990s (1982–2001), independent central banks did not run a tight monetary policy, as the coefficient is not significant. The sign is even negative. Central banks' monetary policy in the 1980s and 1990s was not particularly tight because during this period, party governments' fiscal policy became more conservative and disciplined, and central banks did not have to use a contractionary monetary policy to mitigate the inflationary effects of an expansionary fiscal policy. It was also partly because in the 1980s and 1990s, price stability became a top priority and central banks' monetary policy became antiinflationary in most countries, regardless of the independence of their central banks.[31] Inflation was also well contained during the period, so central banks did not have to mobilize a tight monetary policy. In this sense, central banks' monetary policy during the 1980s and 1990s should be considered neutral (not tight, but tight enough to maintain low inflation). Overall, the results suggest the interdependence of fiscal and monetary policies, as I argued in Chapter 2. And the dominant policy mix governments used in the 1980s and 1990s was a tight fiscal–neutral (or relaxed) monetary policy mix (regardless of central bank independence).

There is another important result in the monetary policy models – monetary policy has electoral cycles, and central banks tightened their monetary policy in election years to counter party governments' electoral expansions during the first period of 1961–1981 and the entire period of 1961–2001. Thus, industrial democracies experienced a loose fiscal–tight monetary policy mix in election years, as central banks sought to subdue inflationary pressures from party governments' fiscal expansions. During 1961–1981, central banks' discount rates were 2.1 percent higher in election years. Their discount rates were 0.6 percent higher, when the entire period of 1961–2001 is considered. (But the higher discount rates (positive sign) during 1982–2001 are not significant.)

The sign of Labor is all negative and not significant. But there is a small chance that coordinated labor may have induced a looser monetary policy during

Table 4.16b Partisan impact on monetary policy

Model	Monetary policy		
	1961–1981	*1982–2001*	*1961–2001*
Left$_{t-1}$	0.006	−0.012**	−0.008*
	(0.014)	(0.005)	(0.005)
Center$_{t-1}$	0.012	0.008	0.001
	(0.017)	(0.007)	(0.006)
Right$_{t-1}$	−0.014	0.007	0.008
	(0.016)	(0.005)	(0.005)

Notes
Only the results of the three government partisanship variables that were alternately entered in the basic models are reported.
OLS estimates with panel-corrected standard errors in parentheses.
***Significant at the 0.01 level.
**Significant at the 0.05 level.
*Significant at the 0.10 level.

the first period of 1961–1981, as the coefficient is not too far from significance ($p = 0.13$), and attains significance when *Right* is entered in place of *Left* in the models without fixed effects (results not reported). Loose monetary policy with coordinated labor can be explained by Iversen's (1999) theory. He argues that social democratic governments under centralized labor typically accommodated higher nominal wages through demand expansions and higher inflation to facilitate real wage restraint by labor unions.[32] The result here, if it is to be trusted, suggests that such an economic policy regime in neocorporatist countries may have existed in the 1960s and 1970s (but not in the 1980s and 1990s). Lastly, there is no evidence that what scholars have called "weak governments" – minority or coalition governments – had a loose monetary policy in any period.

Partisan impact and fragmentation – monetary policy   Table 4.16b reports the results of partisan effects. Left governments had a looser monetary policy during 1982–2001 and the entire period. During 1982–2001, fully left governments (*Left* = 100) had 1.2 percent lower discount rates than non-left governments (*Left* = 0). The coefficients for center governments are positive (tight monetary policy) but none is significant, indicating that center governments did not have a loose or tight monetary policy. The sign for right governments is positive (tight monetary policy) and close to significance for the entire period of 1961–2001 ($p = 0.11$), suggesting that monetary policy may have been tighter under right governments.

The results are largely consistent with my fiscal–monetary policy mix argument (though not all coefficients are significant) – monetary policy under right governments was tight because their fiscal policy was expansionary (the results of the fiscal balance in Table 4.15b), and monetary policy needed to be tight to control inflation. Likewise, monetary policy under left governments was relatively loose because their fiscal policy was not loose, and monetary policy did not need to be mobilized to curb inflation.[33] This fits well with qualitative accounts showing that left party governments used monetary policy as a supply-side policy tool (e.g. low interest rates, cheap credit, currency devaluation) to promote economic growth and enhance the performance of the economy (e.g. Huber and Stephens, 1998). As we can see throughout the empirical analysis of this chapter, left governments' economic policy regime became similar to that typically preferred by central banks in the 1980s and 1990s. The policy positions of left governments and central banks became more compatible during the period, confirming the former's rightward shift in economic policy and willingness to conduct economic policy along the lines of central banks' policy prescriptions. The same conservative shift is also observed for center governments during the same 1980s and 1990s, and is even stronger than for left governments. In contrast, as we see in this chapter, right governments' economic policy was far from the conservative policy regime preferred by central banks.

Lastly, there is no evidence that party fragmentation (the effective number of parliamentary parties) affected monetary policy in any period, though all the signs are negative (loose monetary policy) (results not reported).

Economic performance

Economic growth   The results of the economic growth models are presented in Table 4.17. Inflation has a negative impact on output growth, consistent with the conventional understanding that inflation causes economic problems through multiple channels and eventually impairs output and employment. Unemployment had a positive effect on growth during 1961–1981. The reason is not clear. It could be some sort of reversion to the means, or could be that the previous year's increase in unemployment means progress in economic adjustments and it has a positive effect on the economy in the following year.[34]

Economic globalization   Open-economy countries (*Trade openness*) had significantly higher economic growth during all three periods. The possible reasons for this are: the positive economic benefits of free trade; the expansionary effect of somewhat relaxed monetary policy in open-economy countries (open-economy countries had relatively relaxed monetary policy: see the section on monetary policy); the economic benefits of low inflation, which enhances resource allocation efficiency and encourages investment and growth (open-economy countries had relatively low inflation); or the positive economic benefits of fiscal discipline in open-economy countries, which enables governments to avoid the negative consequences of fiscal indiscipline, such as high deficits, inflation, high interest rates, and resulting low investment and output (see the sections on the fiscal balance, total spending, and total revenues: open-economy countries had fiscal discipline). But the exact cause is not clear.

A floating exchange rate regime (*Exchange rate*) is positive and significant in the entire period of 1961–2001, suggesting that countries with a flexible

Table 4.17 Determinants of economic growth

Model	Economic growth		
	1961–1981	*1982–2001*	*1961–2001*
Independent variables			
GDP$_{t-1}$	0.101	0.439***	0.216***
	(0.106)	(0.090)	(0.064)
Inflation$_{t-1}$	−0.203***	−0.253***	−0.166***
	(0.055)	(0.056)	(0.044)
ΔUnemployment$_{t-1}$	0.869***	0.251	0.212
	(0.267)	(0.160)	(0.148)
Economic size$_{t-1}$	−5.581***	−8.772***	−4.351***
	(1.667)	(1.665)	(1.094)
Majority$_{t-1}$	0.182	0.854**	0.119
	(0.398)	(0.426)	(0.276)
Coalition$_{t-1}$	−0.156	0.167	0.023
	(0.169)	(0.124)	(0.097)
CBI$_{t-1}$	−7.809*	−1.542	−4.075***
	(4.078)	(1.578)	(1.629)
Labor$_{t-1}$	0.064	0.545***	0.134
	(0.162)	(0.146)	(0.110)
Left$_{t-1}$	0.00306	0.00114	0.00059
	(0.00542)	(0.00311)	(0.00270)
Election	0.177	0.458***	0.235
	(0.256)	(0.173)	(0.164)
Trade openness$_{t-1}$	7.814*	7.775***	6.403***
	(4.072)	(1.612)	(0.954)
Exchange rate$_{t-1}$	−0.146	0.492	0.494*
	(0.492)	(0.382)	(0.269)
Capital mobility$_{t-1}$	−0.134	−0.237*	0.027
	(0.150)	(0.128)	(0.076)
R^2	0.778	0.806	0.761
Observations	316	358	674

Notes
OLS estimates with panel-corrected standard errors in parentheses.
Country and time dummy variables not reported.
***Significant at the 0.01 level.
**Significant at the 0.05 level.
*Significant at the 0.10 level.

exchange rate system had higher economic growth. The sign is negative for the first period of 1961–1981 and positive for the second period of 1982–2001, but neither is significant. In the models without country dummies, a floating exchange rate regime is positive and significant for 1961–1981 and 1961–2001. The reason for its positive effect on growth is not clear. One possibility is that fiscal discipline – which is observed among countries with a floating exchange rate regime – was conducive to output growth. Another is an economic benefit of reduced price distortions from a floating rate system. A flexible rate system also contributed to low unemployment, as we will see later.

Capital mobility negatively affected output growth in the second period of 1982–2001 (significant). As we will see below, capital mobility also caused high unemployment (but low inflation). The low output growth and high unemployment in countries with high capital mobility are explained by my policy mix argument as follows. Countries with high capital mobility had expansionary spending and fiscal indiscipline in the 1980s and 1990s, as we have seen in the results of various spending and fiscal balance models. As a result, their central banks (or governments) had to conduct a contractionary monetary policy (as we have seen in the section on the monetary policy stance (Table 4.16)). The tight monetary policy put deflationary pressures on their economies.

Another (complementary) explanation is that low output growth and high unemployment were the negative consequences of fiscal indiscipline itself observed in countries with high capital mobility. But there is also a chance that fiscal indiscipline, conversely, was a result of their negative macroeconomic outcomes – that is, governments conducted compensation policy (large spending) to mitigate the negative effects of the poor economic outcomes caused by high capital mobility (Cameron, 1978; Katzenstein, 1985; Garrett, 1998). Still another explanation is that high capital mobility countries are vulnerable to the conditions in the international economy and the vagaries of mobile capital. Capital mobility gives countries a chance to attract foreign capital, but also makes them vulnerable to movements of mobile capital. It may be the case that at least in the 1980s and 1990s, the costs of capital mobility outweighed its benefits.

Political variables   Central bank independence had a significant negative effect on output growth during the first period of 1961–1981 and the entire period of 1961–2001. An increase in *CBI* from 0.14 to 0.68 (the lowest to highest in the sample) decreased growth by 4.2 percent during 1961–1981. In models without country dummies, CBI's negative effect is more modest (1.1 percent drop in growth for an equivalent increase in CBI). This is likely to be the result of a disinflationary monetary policy pursued by independent central banks during the 1960s and 1970s. As we have seen in the analysis of monetary policy, monetary policy was very tight in countries with independent central banks in 1961–1981 to curb inflationary pressures from expansionary fiscal policy by party governments (the dominant policy mix in countries with independent central banks in the 1960s and 1970s was a loose fiscal–tight monetary policy mix). The negative output effect of *CBI* disappears in the 1980s and 1990s (so the negative output effect of *CBI* for the entire period is likely to be mainly from the first period). This is because in the 1980s and 1990s, party governments' fiscal policy became disciplined, and central banks did not have to conduct a contractionary monetary policy, which had a positive effect on growth, as governments were able to avoid the deflationary effects of a contractionary monetary policy and to use monetary policy as a countercyclical tool. These results are consistent with my policy mix argument.

A notable finding here is that electoral cycles existed in economic growth during the second period of 1982–2001. Growth rates were 0.46 percent higher in election years.[35] The coefficient is not significant for the first period of 1961–1981 ($p = 0.49$) and the entire period ($p = 0.15$). The result shows that governments were able to generate electoral expansions in economic growth, despite the doubt cast by previous scholars on governments' ability to manipulate successfully output growth or even to maneuver economic policy for that purpose. The result is important from the standpoint of the debate on the effects of globalization. The globalization thesis claims that governments lose latitude in choosing economic policy and affecting economic outcomes in a globalized world. But this result here suggests that governments successfully generated economic expansions in election years in the 1980s and 1990s, when the alleged effects of globalization should have been stronger than in the previous decades. It shows that politics still mattered in the 1980s and 1990s and governments had not lost their propensity and ability to generate electoral expansions.

Also, this is a kind of empirical evidence that we would fail to detect if we only examined the entire period under study (1961–2001) without considering the possibility of time-variance of electoral cycles, as the coefficient for 1961–2001 is not significant.

There is evidence that countries with coordinated labor produced higher output growth in the second period of 1982–2001. Such an effect did not exist in the 1960s and 1970s, so they improved economic performance in the 1980s and 1990s. The evidence rejects the simplistic economic argument that strong labor is unconducive to economic performance as it creates price and market distortions – or, at least coordinated labor did not impair economic growth (note however that coordinated and strong labor is highly correlated). It also lends support to my argument that governments and political–economic actors that had previously been considered negative factors for economic performance changed their policy and/or effects and improved their performance in the 1980s and 1990s. As we have seen above, fiscal policy in countries with coordinated labor became generally disciplined in the 1980s and 1990s, shifting their economic policy toward a conservative policy regime (low spending, low tax).[36] Meanwhile, the result also suggests that fiscal discipline may have been conducive to economic growth, as factors that promote fiscal discipline generally tend also to produce positive economic outcomes (e.g. center governments).

Majority governments had higher growth rates than minority ones in the 1980s and 1990s. This is one of the very few pieces of evidence showing better performance by majority governments. There is no evidence that coalition governments caused low economic growth. If anything, coalition governments had significantly higher growth in 1982–2001 when *Fragmentation* is also entered in the models without country dummies, which is likely to be partly a result of their fiscal discipline in the same period.

Partisan impact and fragmentation   Table 4.17b reports partisan impact on output growth. The results show that partisan difference did exist in economic growth. Center governments recorded higher growth, and conservative (right) governments lower growth during the 1960s and 1970s and potentially throughout the

Table 4.17b Partisan impact on economic growth

Model	Economic growth		
	1961–1981	*1982–2001*	*1961–2001*
Left$_{t-1}$	0.00306	0.00114	0.00059
	(0.00542)	(0.00311)	(0.00270)
Center$_{t-1}$	0.011**	0.006	0.006*
	(0.006)	(0.005)	(0.003)
Right$_{t-1}$	–0.010**	–0.004	–0.004
	(0.005)	(0.003)	(0.003)

Notes
Only the results of the three government partisanship variables that were alternately entered in the basic models are reported.
OLS estimates with panel-corrected standard errors in parentheses.
***Significant at the 0.01 level.
**Significant at the 0.05 level.
*Significant at the 0.10 level.

entire period of 1961–2001. The signs of interventionist center and left governments are all positive (higher growth) for all three periods. While *Left* is never significant, *Center* is significant for 1961–1981 and 1961–2001. The positive coefficient for *Center* for the 1980s and 1990s is also not too far from significance ($p = 0.18$).

In contrast, the signs of *Right* are all negative (lower growth), and significant for 1961–1981 (for the entire period of 1961–2001, $p = 0.16$). Substantively, fully center governments (*Center* = 100) achieved 1.1 percent higher economic growth than governments with no center representation (*Center* = 0) during 1961–1981. By contrast, fully right governments (*Right* = 100) had 1 percent lower growth than non-right governments (*Right* = 0). These partisan results also suggest that fiscal discipline may have been conducive to economic growth, as high-growth center governments had fiscal discipline, and low-growth right governments suffered indiscipline.

As for the effect of party fragmentation (Table 4.17c), there is some evidence that economic growth may have been lower in countries with fragmented party systems in the second period of 1982–2001 and the entire period of 1961–2001. *Fragmentation* does not attain significance in the fixed-effect models, but is negative and significant in the models without country dummies (results not reported).[37] During 1982–2001, a one-party increase in the effective number of parliamentary parties lowered growth by 0.26 percent. In contrast, a one-party increase in the number of governing parties (*Coalition*) pushed up economic growth by 0.21 percent during the same period (significant). This result indicates that although a large number of *parliamentary parties* impaired economic growth, a large number of *governing parties* was not harmful for growth and may have even been conducive to it, refuting one of the claims about the weak government argument.

Table 4.17c Impact of party fragmentation on economic growth

Model	Economic growth		
	1961–1981	*1982–2001*	*1961–2001*
Fragmentation$_{t-1}$	−0.089	−0.159	−0.193
	(0.245)	(0.160)	(0.123)
Coalition$_{t-1}$	−0.130	0.188	0.087
	(0.177)	(0.126)	(0.109)

Notes
Only the results of *Fragmentation* and *Coalition* that were entered in the basic models are reported.
OLS estimates with panel-corrected standard errors in parentheses.
***Significant at the 0.01 level.
**Significant at the 0.05 level.
*Significant at the 0.10 level.

Inflation

Table 4.18 reports the results of inflation. Economic controls have the signs consistent with conventional understanding. Economic growth is associated with higher inflation in all periods. Unemployment decreased inflation in 1961–1981. In the models without country dummies, unemployment also reduced inflation during the entire period.

Trade openness had an upward effect on inflation (high inflation) in the first period of 1961–1981 and a downward effect (low inflation) in the second period of 1982–2001. This is probably partly because open-economy governments had an expansionary fiscal policy in the 1960s and 1970s, but conducted a conservative fiscal policy in the 1980s and 1990s (as we have seen in the analysis of fiscal spending and the primary balance above), providing another piece of evidence that governments' economic policy and outcomes changed in the 1980s and 1990s. A floating exchange rate regime has a negative sign (low inflation) during all periods, but nothing is significant.

Capital mobility has a negative sign (low inflation) in all three periods, and significant for the entire period of 1961–2001 and almost significant ($p = 0.11$) for the second period of 1982–2001. The explanation from my policy mix argument is that this is because monetary policy was tight in countries with great capital mobility, which in turn was the monetary policy authority's response to an expansionary fiscal policy by party governments in those countries. But the evidence is also consistent with the convergence thesis that capital mobility led governments to control inflation to maintain an antiinflation reputation, attract mobile capital, and improve economic performance. The results we have do not distinguish the validity of these two explanations.

Political variables   Inflation is not much affected by political factors. The results show that coalition governments had lower inflation during the first period of 1961–1981. It refutes the hypothesis from the weak government

Table 4.18 Determinants of inflation

Model	Inflation		
	1961–1981	*1982–2001*	*1961–2001*
Independent variables			
Inflation$_{t-1}$	0.767***	0.699***	0.774***
	(0.101)	(0.083)	(0.064)
Inflation$_{t-2}$	−0.100	0.010	−0.138**
	(0.104)	(0.079)	(0.066)
GDP$_{t-1}$	0.234***	0.322***	0.299***
	(0.073)	(0.064)	(0.054)
ΔUnemployment$_{t-1}$	−0.663***	0.083	−0.187
	(0.266)	(0.128)	(0.146)
Economic size$_{t-1}$	4.601*	2.989**	1.816
	(2.529)	(1.250)	(1.223)
Majority$_{t-1}$	−0.320	0.571*	0.309
	(0.526)	(0.348)	(0.303)
Coalition$_{t-1}$	−0.347**	−0.021	−0.147
	(0.179)	(0.129)	(0.103)
CBI$_{t-1}$	−2.908	−0.602	−1.531
	(5.592)	(1.187)	(1.650)
Labor$_{t-1}$	0.162	0.047	0.125
	(0.160)	(0.132)	(0.107)
Left$_{t-1}$	0.00104	0.00014	−0.00031
	(0.00608)	(0.00306)	(0.00266)
Election	−0.221	−0.101	−0.037
	(0.267)	(0.164)	(0.158)
Trade openness$_{t-1}$	0.072*	−0.029***	−0.024**
	(0.038)	(0.012)	(0.011)
Exchange rate$_{t-1}$	−0.021	−0.279	−0.209
	(0.487)	(0.364)	(0.270)
Capital mobility$_{t-1}$	−0.063	−0.189	−0.213***
	(0.206)	(0.121)	(0.082)
R^2	0.935	0.921	0.924
Observations	316	358	674

Notes
OLS estimates with panel-corrected standard errors in parentheses.
Country and time dummy variables not reported.
***Significant at the 0.01 level.
**Significant at the 0.05 level.
*Significant at the 0.10 level.

argument that coalition governments invite inflation from their expansionary fiscal policy (budget deficit). During this period, a one-party increase in the number of governing parties lowered inflation by 0.35 percent. *Coalition* also becomes significant for the entire period of 1961–2001 when *Fragmentation* is also entered in the model, so its downward effect on inflation potentially applies to the entire period. The results also suggest that majority governments had higher inflation (0.6 percent higher) than minority governments during the second period of 1982–2001, suggesting that minority governments did not perform poorly in controlling inflation.

The signs of election years are all negative and not significant. Unlike economic growth, inflation did not experience electoral cycles. Thus, the results deny the typical electoral-cycle argument that inflation tends to get higher in election years as a result of governments' attempts to generate electoral expansions. There is the possibility that electoral cycles are not detected in these models because such cycles are much more short-lived, as rational adaptation theory suggests (Alesina *et al.*, 1997). This possibility should be examined, but I defer it to later research.

The sign of *CBI* is all in the expected direction (negative = lower inflation), but none is significant. It indicates that independent central banks did not affect inflation (did not increase or decrease inflation). The interpretation of the results about coordinated labor is difficult, as the sign is positive and not significant in the fixed-effect models, but negative and significant without country dummies (results not reported). In the light of the possibility that country dummies can soak up the cross-national variance, I am inclined to count more heavily the results without country dummies, in which case the results show that coordinated labor recorded low inflation during the first period of 1961–1981 and the entire period of 1961–2001. This is consistent with the neocorporatist argument that countries with coordinated labor were better able to contain inflation with labor's wage restraint and coordination.

Partisan impact and fragmentation   Table 4.18b reports the results of partisan impact. There is little evidence that partisan differences affected inflation in any period. No coefficient is significant. Thus, the standard partisan thesis explaining that the left caused high inflation and the right low inflation does not

Table 4.18b Partisan impact on inflation

Model	Inflation		
	1961–1981	*1982–2001*	*1961–2001*
Left$_{t-1}$	0.00104	0.00014	–0.00031
	(0.00608)	(0.00306)	(0.00266)
Center$_{t-1}$	0.00688	–0.00413	0.00228
	(0.00468)	(0.00281)	(0.00250)
Right$_{t-1}$	–0.00271	0.00183	–0.00032
	(0.00523)	(0.00278)	(0.00265)

Notes
Only the results of the three government partisanship variables that were alternately entered in the basic models are reported.
OLS estimates with panel-corrected standard errors in parentheses.
***Significant at the 0.01 level.
**Significant at the 0.05 level.
*Significant at the 0.10 level.

receive empirical support. There is some chance that center governments may have contributed to higher inflation in 1961–1981 and lower inflation in 1982–2001, as the coefficients are not too far from significance ($p = 0.14$ for both periods). If this result is to be trusted, it suggests that center governments may have invited higher inflation in the 1960s and 1970s, but were able to contain it better than non-center governments in the 1980s and 1990s, lending some support to my argument that center governments became committed to antiinflationary economic policy and their economic policy became restrained in the recent two decades. It also suggests that left governments' loose monetary policy (reviewed above) did not result in inflation, because their fiscal policy was disciplined (reviewed above). In addition, right governments' loose fiscal policy (reviewed above) also did not create inflation because their monetary policy was tight.

The results reported in Table 4.18c show that during the entire period of 1961–2001, a large number of parliamentary parties (*Fragmentation*) caused high inflation, but a large number of governing parties (*Coalition*) produced lower inflation. This lends support to my argument that although party system fragmentation can cause undisciplined economic policy and poor economic outcomes, coalition governments are not necessarily weak performers. As we have seen above, fiscal policy in countries with fragmented party systems was undisciplined during the 1960s and 1970s, and their economic performance lagged (though their economic policy became more disciplined in the 1980s and 1990s). While an increase in the number of parliamentary parties may impair economic policy discipline and cause negative outcomes, coalition governments are more responsible economic managers and had more economic discipline, probably because coalition governments know that poor policy and outcomes will be attributed to their government action, whereas such an incentive is weaker for parliamentary parties unless they are in government. Thus, the simple argument that coalition governments and party fragmentation cause negative economic outcomes does not hold up in inflation.

Table 4.18c Impact of party fragmentation on inflation

Model	Inflation		
	1961–1981	*1982–2001*	*1961–2001*
Fragmentation$_{t-1}$	0.106	0.091	0.321***
	(0.220)	(0.131)	(0.112)
Coalition$_{t-1}$	−0.378**	−0.034	−0.255**
	(0.192)	(0.134)	(0.111)

Notes
Only the results of *Fragmentation* and *Coalition* that were entered in the basic models are reported.
OLS estimates with panel-corrected standard errors in parentheses.
***Significant at the 0.01 level.
**Significant at the 0.05 level.
*Significant at the 0.10 level.

Unemployment

Table 4.19 reports the results of unemployment. Economic controls have signs consistent with conventional understanding. Economic growth reduces and inflation increases unemployment in all three periods.

Trade openness increased unemployment during the first period of 1961–1981, suggesting that economic dislocations were severer in open economies and/or that open economies' expansionary compensatory economic policy during the period did not help reduce unemployment. But in 1982–2001, open economies achieved significantly lower unemployment than in closed economies. As reviewed above, open economies also recorded higher output growth. The possible reasons for their good economic performance are: the positive economic benefits of free trade; the expansionary effect of somewhat relaxed monetary policy in open-economy countries; the benefits of their low inflation, which enhances resource allocation efficiency and encourages investment and growth; or the positive economic benefits of fiscal discipline in open-economy countries, which enables governments to avoid the negative consequences of fiscal indiscipline, such as high deficits, inflation, high interest rates, and resulting low investment and output (see the sections on the fiscal balance, total spending, and total revenues: open-economy countries had fiscal discipline). Their good performance may also suggest that during the 1980s and 1990s, they were better able to cope with the shocks from the international economy or became more competitive. These factors probably combined to produce a good economic performance in open economies.

Exchange rate has a negative sign in all three periods, indicating that countries with a floating rate achieved low unemployment (significant only in the entire period of 1961–2001, but in the models with no country dummies, significant also in the first period of 1961–1981). As we have also seen in the results of the spending, tax revenue, and economic growth models, a floating exchange rate regime generally had favorable impacts on economic policy and outcomes – it led to fiscal discipline and high economic growth.

Capital mobility increased unemployment in all three periods. Capital mobility seems to cause more economic dislocations in the domestic economies than trade openness and the exchange rate regime, as it also caused low growth in the 1980s and 1990s. The negative result may come from international competition for capital, hollowing-out, capital flight, or other shocks from the international economy. The result suggests the possibility that the economic difficulty subsequently led governments to respond by conducting an expansionary policy (compensatory approach) in the 1980s and 1990s (as we have seen earlier, capital mobility induced higher spending, lower tax revenues, and fiscal deficit), or conversely that the fiscal indiscipline was unconducive to employment and to output growth. These governments with high capital mobility also conducted a contractionary monetary policy (as discussed in the analysis of monetary policy) to mitigate inflationary pressure from the expansionary fiscal policy, and it probably put deflationary pressure on their economies.

Table 4.19 Determinants of unemployment

Model	Unemployment		
	1961–1981	*1982–2001*	*1961–2001*
Independent variables			
Unemployment$_{t-1}$	0.739***	1.089***	1.160***
	(0.114)	(0.082)	(0.064)
Unemployment$_{t-2}$	0.083	−0.257***	−0.268***
	(0.119)	(0.080)	(0.066)
GDP$_{t-1}$	−0.066***	−0.191***	−0.091***
	(0.019)	(0.033)	(0.017)
Inflation$_{t-1}$	0.075***	0.059**	0.069***
	(0.014)	(0.025)	(0.016)
Economic size$_{t-1}$	−0.512	0.846	−0.010
	(0.341)	(0.616)	(0.351)
Majority$_{t-1}$	0.019	−0.455**	−0.131
	(0.129)	(0.199)	(0.123)
Coalition$_{t-1}$	0.038	−0.034	−0.005
	(0.061)	(0.053)	(0.037)
CBI$_{t-1}$	1.028	0.174	0.229
	(1.043)	(0.718)	(0.538)
Labor$_{t-1}$	0.009	−0.101	−0.004
	(0.051)	(0.067)	(0.044)
Left$_{t-1}$	0.00047	−0.00274**	−0.00121
	(0.00139)	(0.00116)	(0.00084)
Election	−0.005	−0.250***	−0.078
	(0.070)	(0.085)	(0.059)
Trade openness$_{t-1}$	2.250*	−1.948***	−0.807*
	(1.271)	(0.696)	(0.473)
Exchange rate$_{t-1}$	−0.116	−0.007	−0.228**
	(0.103)	(0.187)	(0.098)
Capital mobility$_{t-1}$	0.087**	0.160***	0.085***
	(0.040)	(0.049)	(0.025)
R^2	0.977	0.993	0.988
Observations	316	358	674

Notes
OLS estimates with panel-corrected standard errors in parentheses.
Country and time dummy variables not reported.
***Significant at the 0.01 level.
**Significant at the 0.05 level.
*Significant at the 0.10 level.

While their tight monetary policy enabled them to control inflation (as discussed earlier), it caused high unemployment (and low economic growth) in the 1980s and 1990s.

Political variables The results show that there were electoral cycles in unemployment. Unemployment rates were lower in election years by 0.25 percent during the second period of 1982–2001. Thus, governments successfully engineered expansions in employment in the 1980s and 1990s. The coefficients for the 1960s and 1970s and the entire period are also negative, but not significant.

The signs of *Coalition* are in the direction expected by my argument about improved performance by coalition governments in the 1980s and 1990s (changing from high to low unemployment), but they are not significant. The signs of coordinated labor also indicate the same pattern, but they are also not significant ($p = 0.13$ for 1982–2001). But the second period comes close to significance ($p = 0.11$) when *Left* is replaced with *Right*, and it suggests the possibility that coordinated labor may have achieved low unemployment in the 1980s and 1990s (it also recorded high growth during the period). The signs of *CBI* suggest that countries with independent central banks suffered high unemployment presumably because of their contractionary monetary policy, but these are also not significant. The results show that majority governments achieved low unemployment in the second period, lending support to the weak government argument. This is one of the few pieces of evidence that supports the claims of the argument.

Partisan impact and fragmentation   The results (Table 4.19b) show that left governments achieved low unemployment in the second period of 1982–2001. In the models without country dummies, it is also significant for the entire period of 1961–2001. Substantively, fully left governments (*Left* = 100) achieved 0.3 percent lower unemployment rates than non-left governments (*Left* = 0). The signs of *Right* are all positive (high unemployment), as expected by conventional partisan theory, but none is significant. Though only *Left* is significant, the patterns of the partisan results are largely consistent with partisan theory. But the results also show that contrary to the convergence thesis, partisan effects are clearer in the 1980s and 1990s than in the

Table 4.19b Partisan impact on unemployment

Model	Unemployment		
	1961–1981	*1982–2001*	*1961–2001*
Left$_{t-1}$	0.00047	−0.00274**	−0.00121
	(0.00139)	(0.00116)	(0.00084)
Center$_{t-1}$	−0.00078	0.00097	0.00047
	(0.00159)	(0.00208)	(0.00127)
Right$_{t-1}$	0.00026	0.00180	0.00084
	(0.00160)	(0.00140)	(0.00104)

Notes
Only the results of the three government partisanship variables that were alternately entered in the basic models are reported.
OLS estimates with panel-corrected standard errors in parentheses.
***Significant at the 0.01 level.
**Significant at the 0.05 level.
*Significant at the 0.10 level.

Table 4.19c Impact of party fragmentation on unemployment

Model	Unemployment		
	1961–1981	*1982–2001*	*1961–2001*
Fragmentation$_{t-1}$	0.031	0.057	0.055
	(0.061)	(0.075)	(0.045)
Coalition$_{t-1}$	0.029	−0.042	−0.024
	(0.060)	(0.055)	(0.040)

Notes
Only the results of *Fragmentation* and *Coalition* that were entered in the basic models are reported.
OLS estimates with panel-corrected standard errors in parentheses.
***Significant at the 0.01 level.
**Significant at the 0.05 level.
*Significant at the 0.10 level.

previous decades, indicating that the role of politics or partisan effects have not diminished in the recent decades despite globalization. Center governments are never significant.

The effective number of parliamentary parties (*Fragmentation*) is never significant, but its signs suggest that countries with party fragmentation had higher unemployment (Table 4.19c). In the models without country dummies, *Fragmentation* becomes close to significance ($p = 0.11$) for the entire period of 1961–2001, so there is a chance that party fragmentation caused high unemployment, which would support my argument that party fragmentation caused fiscal indiscipline and poor economic performance. If this result is to be trusted, it means that party fragmentation caused low growth, high inflation, and high unemployment. Thus, coalition governments did not cause poor economic outcomes, but party fragmentation did.

Summary and conclusion

I summarize the main messages of the empirical analysis of this chapter. First, independent central banks have disciplining effects on party governments' fiscal policy.[38] While independent central banks do not have control over fiscal policy, they help put pressure on party governments to raise sufficient revenues to finance their spending so that the governments will not create fiscal deficit and their fiscal policy will not be overly expansionary.

Second, the economic policy regime in industrial democracies changed from the 1960s and 1970s to the 1980s and 1990s. The policy shift was generally in the direction of neoliberal, conservative economic policy, characterized by fiscal discipline and monetary conservatism. Fiscal policy particularly became restrained in the past two decades. This policy shift was more conspicuous among the governments and political–economic regimes that had a prior reputation for fiscal indiscipline and/or economic inefficiencies, such as center governments, coalition governments, and countries with fragmented party systems or coordinated labor. Their economic policies became more market-conforming, and thus more compatible with neoliberal policy prescriptions embraced by central bankers.

The dominant economic policy mix in industrial democracies changed to a tight fiscal–neutral monetary policy mix in the 1980s and 1990s. In the 1960s and 1970s, party governments conducted an expansionary fiscal policy. This was not yet too much of a problem in the 1960s, as industrial democracies did not yet face detrimental inflation or have large government debt. Monetary policy in the 1960s was relaxed, but sufficiently tight for the purpose of maintaining low inflation. In the 1970s, however, monetary policy was not tight enough in the face of high inflation. As a result, for most of the 1970s, industrial governments' dominant policy mix was a loose fiscal–loose monetary policy mix. In the late 1970s and the beginning of the 1980s, governments became serious about containing inflation, and tightened their monetary policy; so they had a loose fiscal–tight monetary policy mix at the turn of the decade. During this period, central banks had to use monetary policy for controlling inflation because governments' fiscal policy was expansionary.

In the 1980s and 1990s, however, fiscal policy became more disciplined, with the increasing dominance of neoliberal antiinflationary economic policy thinking. As a result, once the inflation of the early 1980s was under control, central banks did not have to conduct a tight monetary policy to control inflation; thus, a tight fiscal–neutral (or relaxed) monetary policy mix in the second half of the 1980s and the 1990s. This released monetary policy from its role as a tool of inflation control to a certain extent, and governments could now use it for economic stimulus as well as price stability. This gave the governments and political–economic actors that achieved fiscal discipline an advantage in achieving positive economic outcomes, such as high economic growth or low unemployment without high inflation. This is so, partly because monetary policy – not fiscal policy – should be an effective demand stimulus tool under the conditions of capital mobility and a flexible exchange rate mechanism that characterized the economic environment for many industrial democracies in the 1980s and 1990s. That is, these governments could use an effective policy tool (monetary policy) in promoting economic performance, because they had fiscal discipline, which helped them keep inflation low. In contrast, fiscally profligate governments could not use the effective tool for economic stimulus because they had to use it for price stability. As a result, governments that achieved fiscal discipline generally attained positive economic outcomes in the 1980s and 1990s, including high economic growth, low inflation, and low unemployment.

The empirical analysis shows that there were also cross-national differences. During the 1960s and 1970s, countries with independent central banks had a tighter monetary policy than countries with only dependent central banks. Independent central banks used a tight monetary policy to respond to the inflationary effects of expansionary fiscal policy by party governments and to inflation itself. Dependent central banks did not or could not do the same due to their lack of independence from party governments.

But this contractionary response by independent central banks disappeared in the 1980s and 1990s (*CBI* not significant). The reason is that the economic policy of industrial democracies generally became antiinflationary, regardless of the independence of central banks. Party governments' fiscal policy became restrained, and central banks did not have to keep tight monetary policy to offset inflationary effects of fiscal policy. It is also because industrial democracies successfully controlled inflation and did not have to resort to a tight monetary policy. Thus, monetary policy during the second half of the 1980s and the 1990s was neutral, compared to the 1970s and the first half of the 1980s.

The results seem to suggest that fiscal discipline was conducive to positive economic outcomes. In many cases, the factors that induced fiscal discipline also helped produce good economic outcomes (*CBI* is an exception). Fiscal discipline lessens the need for a tight monetary policy. A tight monetary policy seems to be detrimental to output and employment, according to our results. So governments that can avoid a tight monetary policy seem to achieve good economic outcomes. Fiscal discipline also allows governments to avoid the negative consequences of fiscal indiscipline, such as high deficits, inflation, and high interest rates, which would in turn suppress investment and growth. Government deficits would also drain resources from the private economy. Further, inflation would create price distortions, resource allocation inefficiency, and economic uncertainties, which would impair investment and stifle growth.

Despite industrial democracies' general move toward a more neoliberal policy regime, however, different governments and institutions made policy adjustments in varied ways and to different degrees, contrary to the claims of the convergence thesis. The convergence thesis argues that the competitive pressures created by globalization have led to the convergence of economic policy pursued by governments of various ideological stripes and by different countries, and that, as a result, globalization and resulting convergence have diminished the role of politics in economic policy. But the empirical analysis of this chapter makes it clear that political impact on economic policy and outcomes had not diminished in the last two decades. If anything, the impacts of political factors on policy and performance were stronger in the 1980s and 1990s.

Third, left governments' economic policy regime shifted rightward (fiscal restraint) in the 1980s and 1990s and became closer to the one typically prescribed by central banks. And they became more willing to conduct economic policy along the lines of central banks' policy prescriptions. As a result, the policies positions of left governments and central banks became more compatible during the period.

Center governments also made a similar neoliberal shift in economic policy in the 1980s and 1990s. Their shift was stronger than the left's. In contrast, contrary to the conventional partisan explanation, right governments' policy regime was far from the conservative regime prescribed by central banks. Right governments' fiscal policy was more expansionary than the left or center for most of the period

1961–2001 and particularly so in the 1980s and 1990s. Right governments' policy was expansionary because when it comes to taxation, they taxed less than the left and center as consistent with the partisan explanation, but when it comes to spending, they were high spenders, naturally resulting in fiscal deficits.

Center governments during the 1980s and 1990s, in contrast, had fiscal policy patterns opposite to right governments. Their fiscal policy was conservative in that they had lower spending and higher tax revenues than other governments, producing a positive fiscal balance (more surplus or less deficit). This at least partly reflects the efforts by many governments (particularly those European governments that wished to qualify for the EMU) to reduce fiscal deficit and gross debt by curbing spending but maintaining or even increasing tax revenues. And center governments relied more on direct taxes, and left governments more on indirect taxes.

There is no reason to assume a priori that political parties and partisan governments have fixed, time-invariant policy positions. As I argued in Chapter 3, their policy changes when the environment changes, when economic conditions change, when their constituencies' policy preferences change, and when policy ideas about how the economy works change. In this sense, the assumption of the standard partisan theory that presumes partisan governments' time- or context-invariant policy preferences is too restrictive. Government partisanship affects both economic policy and outcomes. But the effect is contingent on time periods, the economic or political environment, and the institutional setting in which partisan governments make policy.

As for monetary policy, right governments experienced a tighter monetary policy than other partisan governments as a result of their relatively loose fiscal policy. Central banks' monetary policy responds to party governments' fiscal policy, as expected by my policy mix argument. Central banks conduct a tight monetary policy if party governments' fiscal policy is expansionary.

In contrast, monetary policy was looser under left governments because their fiscal policy was relatively tight in the 1980s and 1990s, so central banks did not have to mobilize their monetary policy to control inflation. This fits well with qualitative accounts showing that left party governments used monetary policy as a supply-side policy tool (e.g. low interest rates, cheap credit, currency devaluation) to promote economic growth and enhance the performance of the economy (e.g. Huber and Stephens, 1998). The difference from previous studies is that my analysis finds that left governments used such a monetary policy in the 1980s and 1990s, whereas previous studies suggested that such use of monetary policy came to an end during the period. Central banks' accommodating monetary policy under left governments during the 1980s and 1990s had a positive effect on economic outcomes. Left governments achieved significantly lower unemployment than other partisan governments during the period, as they did not have to face central banks' contractionary monetary policy that would put disinflationary pressures on the economy. Their fiscal discipline, thus, contributed to the generally positive economic outcomes. Fiscal discipline also helped their economic performance, as it allowed them to evade the negative consequences of fiscal indiscipline, such as high deficits, inflation, high interest rates, which would depress investment and growth.

Why does the analysis turn out the results showing that right governments were fiscally less disciplined than the left or center, when partisan theory has pointed out the opposite? Conservative governments' high spending is detected in government wage consumption, government investment, public subsidies, social security, total disbursement, and the fiscal balance. There are several reasons. First, it is true that when we examine only cross-sectional data on various spending items and partisan cabinet portfolios averaged across years (without controlling for other factors), right governments tend to have lower spending than left or center governments. But the often-discussed differences between right governments and the left and center are exaggerated. When we review the cross-national data averaged across years (see the Appendix to Chapter 3), the spending levels in conservative-dominant countries (liberal market economies) are only marginally lower than those in left- or center-dominant countries.

Second, anecdotal episodes suggest that many conservative governments in the last two decades were fairly expansionary. The U.S. Reagan administration accumulated large deficit in the 1980s. Japan's successive governments controlled by the conservative Liberal Democratic Party also conducted an extremely expansionary policy to end successive recessions and deflation throughout the 1990s, which pushed Japan's gross debt to the highest level among industrial countries. Conservative governments that occasionally replaced social democrats in Nordic countries also were unable to reduce spending. In the United States, the centrist Clinton administration reduced fiscal deficit, and the succeeding conservative Bush administration increased it (though the latter is outside the sample of this book). Third, as Figure 3.6 in Chapter 3 shows, the countries that are conventionally considered social-democratic-dominant and Christian-democratic-dominant actually have sizeable conservative-party representation in the executive branch. Conservative cabinet portfolios are as high as 40 percent in Denmark, 45 percent in France, and 33 percent in the Netherlands. This means that if these social-democratic-dominant or Christian-democratic-dominant countries ever have high levels of fiscal spending, chances are it will be reflected also in conservative-party governments' spending levels, as government spending changes only incrementally.

Turning back to the general findings of this chapter, fourth, governments engineered electoral expansions in both economic policy and outcomes. Furthermore, electoral cycles were stronger in the 1980s and 1990s than the 1960s and 1970s. This shows that the room for governments to maneuver economic policy and outcomes had not diminished in the past two decades, contrary to the views stressing the progressively reduced ability of governments to manipulate economic policy for political or economic purposes due to globalization, the rise of neoliberal economic orthodoxy, or central bank independence. The empirical results also suggest that governments' electoral expansions were created more by reducing tax revenues than by increasing spending.

Fifth, the evidence does not support the arguments that so-called weak governments and actors (e.g. coalition governments, interventionist center and left governments, minority governments, or labor) had undisciplined economic policy and poor economic performance. There are some sporadic signs of fiscal expansionism by some of these actors in some policy or performance indicators in the 1960s and 1970s. But even then, the supposedly weak governments and actors significantly disciplined their economic policy and improved their economic performance in the 1980s and 1990s.

Fiscal policy in countries with fragmented party systems was indeed often expansionary and undisciplined in the 1960s and 1970s. They also showed poor economic performance. While an increase in the number of parliamentary parties (party fragmentation) impaired economic policy discipline and caused negative economic outcomes in the 1960s and 1970s, however, there is little evidence that an increase in the number of governing parties created similar economic problems. Even in some minority of cases where it did, coalition governments significantly disciplined their economic policy and improved performance in the 1980s and 1990s. Thus, it is multiple parties *existing in the entire party system* that caused economic indiscipline and poor economic outcomes, but not multiple coalition parties *existing within a government*. Coalition governments were more restrained and responsible economic policy makers. This was probably partly because of their concern that poor economic management would be attributed to their government action and that there could be electoral retribution, whereas parliamentary parties did not face as strong concerns unless they were in government. But even the countries with party fragmentation restrained their economic policy in the 1980s and 1990s.

Finally, a clear overall picture comes out of the analysis of the effects on economic policy and performance of the three facets of globalization – trade openness, exchange rate regimes, and capital mobility. First, these different dimensions of globalization had different effects on economic policy and, second, the different economic policies induced by the different dimensions had varied impacts on economic outcomes (economic growth, inflation, and unemployment).

First, trade openness induced high spending and high taxes during the 1960s and 1970s. Such an expansionary fiscal policy consequently invited high inflation and high unemployment. (The effect of trade openness on economic growth is not clear because the results show that it had positive effects in fixed effect models, but negative effects in models without country dummies.) But in the 1980s and 1990s, open-economy governments' fiscal policy made a neoliberal turn and became conservative (they had low spending and low taxes). They sought to make their economic policy more market-conforming with a view to promoting economic efficiency and competitiveness. Partly as a result of the policy shift, open-economy countries were able to achieve low inflation, low unemployment, and high economic growth in the 1980s and 1990s. Thus, disciplined fiscal policy – and probably in combination with all other economic measures to increase economic competitiveness and efficiencies that accompanied fiscal conservatism – had positive impacts on economic outcomes, and open-economy countries showed markedly improved economic performance in the 1980s and 1990s. It probably also means that open economies were more successful in the second period in making their economies and industries competitive by upgrading technologies and human capital than in the 1960s and 1970s. The compensation policy tried by them in the 1960s and 1970s was not effective in producing good economic outcomes, but the neoliberal policy regime in the 1980s and 1990s was more successful.

Second, a floating exchange rate regime induced fiscal discipline for most of the entire period. Governments with a floating regime had lower spending and lower taxes throughout the period. As a result, they were able to avoid inflation (the coefficients are all negative but not significant, suggesting that the floating system did not cause inflation) and to achieve low unemployment and high economic growth. Their fiscal discipline may be a result of the ineffectiveness of fiscal expansions as a countercyclical tool in countries with a floating exchange rate system under capital mobility, which open economics argues should be the case. Governments therefore had a lower incentive to resort to fiscal expansions.

Third, contrary to the globalization thesis, capital mobility led governments to respond by conducting an expansionary fiscal policy (compensation approach) in the 1980s and 1990s. (Capital mobility induced higher spending and even lower tax revenues, consequently worsening the fiscal balance.) As a result, as my policy mix argument expects, those governments had to conduct a contractionary monetary policy to control inflation. While the tight monetary policy enabled them to control inflation, it caused lower economic growth and higher unemployment in governments with capital mobility in the 1980s and 1990s. The case of capital mobility thus provides a case in support of the hypothesis that fiscal indiscipline was unconducive to positive economic performance. Central banks' contractionary response to party governments' fiscal indiscipline exerts deflationary pressure. Governments cannot use monetary policy for economic stimulus. And fiscal indiscipline invites high deficits and interests, which suppress investment and output.

Thus, the evidence concerning globalization and economic policy in industrial democracies seems to suggest that the neoliberal (conservative) fiscal policy – probably accompanied by a host of other competitiveness- and efficiency-enhancing policy measures – produced better economic outcomes in economic growth, inflation, and unemployment. Part of the reason for this is that party governments' restrained fiscal policy releases central banks' monetary policy from its price stability role, and enables party governments and central banks to use monetary policy as a countercyclical policy tool, as my policy mix argument expects. Freed from inflationary concerns from party governments' expansionary fiscal policy, central banks can actively use monetary policy to promote economic growth. They do not have to conduct a contractionary monetary policy, which would drive up interest rates and suppress investment and growth.

Appendix: cyclically adjusted measures of discretionary fiscal and monetary policies

In examining the aggregate fiscal and monetary policy stances, I use cyclically adjusted measures of discretionary fiscal and monetary policies, as well as unadjusted primary balance and discount rates. Political scientists have in the past used conventional measures such as fiscal deficit and interest rates which are *cyclically unadjusted*.[39] But we are interested in the stance of *discretionary* policy that is a product of policy makers' intentional actions. To understand discretionary policy, it is advisable to examine *cyclically adjusted* policy stances. The reason is that (to take the case of fiscal policy) in the presence of automatic stabilizers, fiscal deficit can increase or decrease even if policy makers do nothing to change their fiscal policy stance when business cycles induce change in the tax bases and unemployment transfers. To tap the discretionary component of macroeconomic policy, it is necessary to remove the effects of automatic stabilizers that result from business cycles. But I also check the regression results with unadjusted policy stances by using cyclically unadjusted primary balance and central bank discount rates as dependent variables. The results from the adjusted and unadjusted measures do not radically change. But the use of the adjusted measures somewhat strengthens the results of political independent variables, although the results for government partisanship (*Left, Center, Right*) are significant somewhat more often in the unadjusted measures than in the adjusted measures.

It would be desirable also to analyze cyclically adjusted measures of discretionary policy for all disaggregate fiscal policy items. But although the OECD has begun to present such measures for spending and tax items, as of this writing, the coverage of countries, years, and fiscal policy items is too limited to be used for time-series cross-section analysis (OECD, 2003). So I had to forgo the line of analysis for disaggregate policy items in the current book. But such an analysis should be pursued as soon as data become available. The description of the cyclically adjusted policy stances follow.

Discretionary fiscal policy   For the measure of discretionary fiscal policy, I use cyclically adjusted primary balance as a percentage of potential GDP (this measure excludes interest payments). The source is OECD (2003). The OECD calculates cyclically adjusted fiscal balance as follows (van den Noord, 2000): Potential output is estimated by country-specific production functions. Elasticities of various taxation and expenditure components to output fluctuations are calculated. Then, they obtain the cyclical component of the budget balance by using the output gap and the elasticities, and subtract it from the actual balance. The OECD's measure empirically and directly derives the country-specific responses of taxation and expenditure to economic fluctuations and uses them to calculate cyclically adjusted balance.[40] This method is very similar to the ones used by the IMF and the European Commissions.

Discretionary monetary policy When measuring discretionary monetary policy, I also remove the effects of semi-automatic monetary policy responses by central banks that are considered normal reactions to business cycles in their effort to maintain price stability. I control for central banks' normal, automatic responses by using a Taylor-type rule and measuring the stance of their discretionary policy distinct from normal policy responses suggested by such rules (Taylor, 1993; Rothenberg, n.d.). I calculate discretionary monetary policy by subtracting the neutral interest rates suggested by the Taylor-type rule from the actual discount rates. The Taylor-type rule I use is as follows:

Taylor-rule implied discount rate$_{(t)}$ = 2 + inflation$_{(t-1)}$ + 0.5 * (inflation$_{(t-1)}$ – π*) + 0.5 * output gap$_{(t-1)}$ where the constant term 2 is the assumed long-run equilibrium real rate, and π* is the central bank's inflation target rate which is assumed to be 2 percent. The Taylor-type rule calculates a price-stability-conforming discount rate target from the past inflation rate, central banks' inflation target rate, the long-term real interest rate, and the gap between real and potential GDP. The inflation and discount rates data used for calculating the monetary policy stance are from the IMF (2003), and the output gap and potential GDP data are from OECD (2003).[41]

Note that I am not suggesting that central banks actually use Taylor rules in their conduct of monetary policy. All I assume here is that Taylor rules suggest a reasonable response of monetary policy to economic cycles given the goal of price stability, and that we can meaningfully study the deviations of monetary policy from a neutral stance by examining the gap between real rates and Taylor-rule rates.[42]

5 Party governments, central banks, and labor

Empirical evidence for interactive effects

The last chapter (Chapter 4) examined how political–economic factors individually affect economic policy and performance, without thinking about how they interact with each other and jointly affect outcomes. This chapter now analyzes their interactive effects. Specifically, I analyze how particular combinations of various party governments and central banks produce different economic policy and outcomes, when they interact with each other and operate under distinct policy making environments. As I explained in Chapter 2, party governments produce different policies and outcomes, depending on which partisan governments are in office, whether they are single-party or coalition governments, whether central banks are independent from party governments, and thus what kind of structural environment they face. Different party governments have distinct incentives and capacities in making economic policy and in responding to their central banks' monetary policy and thus fashioning a fiscal–monetary policy mix with central banks. The variation in their incentives and capacities results from their partisanship and structural composition, the independence of the central banks they face, and the policy making environment. This is so partly because the effectiveness and consequences of fiscal policy depend on the monetary policy concurrently implemented, and vice versa and, as a result, fiscal and monetary policy makers need to take into account each other's policy preferences and moves in deciding what policy they should respectively pursue and assessing what effects their policies will have on the economy in tandem with the other's policy.

I empirically show in this chapter that party governments produce distinct economic policy and outcomes, depending on their partisan and structural characters and the central banks they face. Coalition governments generate different policies and outcomes, depending on whether their central banks are independent from party governments. Center governments also create different policies and outcomes, depending on their central banks. So do left and right governments. I show also that labor affects economic policy and outcomes in different ways, depending on whether it is well coordinated and on whether it faces an independent or dependent central bank. Labor's influence on policy and outcomes also depends on which partisan government it faces. I also demonstrate that the presence of electoral cycles, too, is partly affected by whether central banks are independent or dependent, as well as by whether party governments are multiparty or single-party governments and by how many parties exist in the whole party system (fragmentation of the party system).

This chapter presents empirical results in a slightly different way from the last chapter. In the last chapter, I explained the results of the empirical analysis, policy by policy or performance indicator by indicator (i.e. by the dependent variable), to facilitate the ease of understanding the general patterns of the effects of the political–economic factors. In this chapter, I present the results about the interactive effects of a particular combination of policy makers and actors for all policy and performance indicators (i.e. by the independent variable), in turn. So, to begin with, I analyze the interactive effects of coalition governments and central banks for all policy and outcome indicators, and then, I examine the interaction of center governments and central banks for all indicators, and so forth (i.e. for left governments and central banks, for conservative governments and central banks, for electoral cycles conditioned by central banks, coalition governments, party fragmentation, for left governments and labor, and for labor and central banks).

The explanation of the results in this chapter is also different in another way. In this chapter, I simulate the results of regression estimation and compute the predicted values of the dependent variable when two independent variables of our interest (e.g. coalition governments and central banks) that are interacted are held at certain values. I then present and explain figures showing how two given factors (with their values held at different levels) together affect the dependent variable. The reason why I provide simulated results is the following.

The coefficients and significance for the constitutive and interactive variables in regression results do not give an immediately clear idea of how two given variables jointly affect the dependent variable. A common way to examine interactive effects is to calculate conditional coefficients and conditional standard errors. While conditional coefficients help understand the effect of one variable at a range of values for another variable, it is intuitively difficult to get a sense of how two factors jointly affect the dependent variable, because one can examine the effect of one variable at a time (with a range of the other variable). The difficulty increases especially when the units and measurements of two relevant variables are widely different. To facilitate a more immediate understanding of the results, I compute the predicted values of the dependent variable, when the relevant constitutive and interactive terms are held at certain values.[1]

Predicted values show how two factors jointly affect the dependent variable when they are manipulated to be at certain values. For instance, I calculate the predicated values of the dependent variable for the combinations of "a three-party coalition government with an independent central bank," "a single-party government with a dependent central bank," and so on. This way, the reader can understand more easily how two factors together affect the dependent variable.

Yet it does not immediately mean that the differences among different combinations of interacted variables are statistically significant and those different combinations indeed produce different values in the dependent variable. In order to show that different combinations of interacted factors produce significantly different outcomes in the dependent variable, I need to show that the differences in the predicted values between different combinations of two factors held at different values are statistically significant and therefore meaningful. Toward this end, I test whether the differences among different combinations of interacted variables are statistically significant. There is no easy way to present in the tables the results about the statistical significance of the differences among all cells, without causing a presentational mess. So I briefly explain whether the differences between the cells are statistically significant in the notes to the figures. In calculating the predicted values of the dependent variable, I only manipulated the two relevant constitutive terms and their interactive term. Therefore, the predicted values indicate how the two factors push up or down the dependent variable when they are held at certain values.

While the last chapter explained the results of all policy and outcome indicators (i.e. models for all dependent variables) regardless of the presence or absence of significant effects, in Chapter 5, I only report and explain the results for which the interactive effects of two relevant variables are statistically significant.

The data I analyze in this chapter are the same data used in Chapter 4 and are from 18 industrial democracies between 1961 and 2001. All data are annual data. The definitions and sources are the same as summarized in Tables 4.1 and 4.2 in Chapter 4. As in Chapter 4, the analysis of this chapter examines the determinants of economic policy and outcomes for the entire period of 1961–2001 and for the sub-periods of 1961–1981 and 1982–2001 to detect possible time-variant effects of political–economic factors and to uncover possible change in economic policy and outcomes and their determinants across time. This is a necessary analysis since, as I argue throughout the book, the nature of the international and domestic economies changed in the past two decades and it led governments to adjust their policy, and their impact on economic policy and outcomes changed. The estimation method is the same as in Chapter 4.

As in Chapter 4, I estimated all models both with and without country dummy variables. The inclusion and exclusion of country dummies produced essentially the same results sometimes and different results at some other times. Since it is difficult to judge across the board whether we should trust the results of the models with or without country dummies, I decided to utilize the results of both. This decision had to be made, partly, for the reason of my resource constraints – I estimated a large number of models and simulated their results in many ways, and it was near impossible to investigate whether I should trust the results of models with or without country dummies for each of all models. The decision was made also partly, and more importantly, because I wished not to dismiss potentially important and meaningful results just because the results of the models with and without country dummies differed. When their results differ, the disagreement is most often about statistical significance – e.g. in a fixed-effects model, a coefficient may not be significant, but in a model without country dummies, it is. Needless to say, I indicate whether a model is estimated with or without country dummies in reporting the results.

Finally, when I report the regression results in statistics tables (from which I calculate predicted values of dependent variables), I only report the results for the variables of our main interest – an interactive term and its constitutive terms in each section – since the other overall results do not change and do stay essentially the same as the results explained in Chapter 4 (the entire results are available from the author).

Coalition governments and central banks

I explained in Chapter 2 that coalition governments should be better able to conduct a restrained fiscal policy and achieve a fiscal–monetary policy mix conducive to good economic outcomes, if they have independent central banks. If they do not have independent central banks, their fiscal policy should be less disciplined and produce a policy mix unconducive to economic outcomes. In contrast, single-party governments should be less able to conduct a disciplined fiscal policy and achieve good economic outcomes when they have independent central banks.

Coalition governments have more potential veto players and more potential sources of policy conflict, due to their diverse constituencies, economic interests, and policy positions. Multiple governing parties have different sets of constituencies with distinct economic interests and policy preferences. The divergence in interests and policy preferences increases the number and magnitude of potential sources of policy conflict within coalition governments than in single-party governments (Bernhard, 2002). As a result, they have the greater urge to control their own policy conflict, enhance discipline in economic policy, and improve economic performance.

If they have independent central banks, coalition governments should be better able to conduct a restrained fiscal policy, because they can anticipate central banks' contractionary monetary response to an expansionary fiscal policy and like to avoid disinflationary pressures that could result from a contractionary monetary policy. So coalition governments should be more capable of fiscal restraint and of possibly realizing the economic benefits associated with it, if central banks are independent and control monetary policy (countries where party governments have delegated monetary policy control to central banks). If fiscal policy is disciplined and not expansionary, central banks do not have to conduct a contractionary monetary policy to offset inflationary pressures from fiscal policy. They can even mobilize monetary policy for countercyclical economic action, if the state of the economy calls for such stimulus. Thus, in the presence of fiscal discipline, central banks (or governments) can more flexibly employ monetary policy for economic stimulus. So if coalition governments have independent central banks, they should be better able to achieve fiscal discipline, and they and central banks together can fashion a tight fiscal–neutral (or relaxed) monetary policy mix and facilitate good economic outcomes.

If central banks are not independent, in contrast, it should be more difficult for coalition governments to achieve fiscal discipline. If coalition governments retain monetary policy autonomy, they face the temptation to expand economic growth and employment, which can create inflationary pressures. They can more easily resort to an expansionary economic policy since they do not have to worry about deflationary monetary response by central banks and can also use monetary or fiscal policy or both to stimulate the economy. So when they do not have independent central banks, coalition governments should have less fiscal discipline and a less favorable fiscal–monetary policy mix, possibly resulting in negative economic outcomes. If fiscal policy is expansionary this way, coalition governments and their dependent central banks may need to mobilize monetary policy to offset the inflationary pressures created by the former's expansionary fiscal policy, making monetary policy unavailable for countercyclical actions. A tight monetary policy can suppress investment, economic growth, and eventually employment. Coalition governments' use of fiscal policy – rather than monetary policy – for economic expansion under dependent central banks is more likely, because fiscal policy is more suited for targeted political or electoral distribution of government resources than monetary policy. Thus, I expect the combination of coalition governments and dependent central banks to produce a loose fiscal–tight monetary policy mix.

In contrast to coalition governments, single-party majority governments are often considered "strong" governments in terms of their ability to pursue their policy. They do not have many veto players or many potential sources of policy conflict, because they comprise member politicians of the same party whose policy positions are relatively homogeneous and cohesive, and because the economic interests and policy preferences of their constituencies are less diverse. As a result, they can carry out their policy more decisively or conduct a fiscal policy more easily that runs counter to the policy preferred by central banks. They also have less incentive to grant monetary policy control to central banks (Bernhard, 2002). If they can pursue their economic policies even by overriding central banks' policy preferences, they have the greater potential and ability to act on their temptation for an expansionary fiscal policy, even when central banks strongly oppose it for inflationary concerns. Thus, single-party governments should have less fiscal discipline and an unfavorable fiscal–monetary policy mix (or negative economic outcomes or both), when their central banks are independent.

If single-party governments can more easily implement a fiscal policy that conflicts with the policy preferences of central banks, it makes it difficult for central banks to conduct a monetary policy that would constitute a favorable fiscal–monetary policy mix, given the fiscal policy implemented by party governments. As a result, the combination of single-party governments and independent central banks can cause a conflictive or incompatible fiscal–monetary policy mix, where central banks and party governments use their policy instruments (monetary and fiscal policies, respectively) to counter each other's policy action. Namely, central banks raise interest rates to maintain price stability and to counteract party governments' expansionary fiscal policy, and party governments expand fiscal spending to boost output and employment and to undermine central banks' deflationary monetary policy, resulting in undesirable economic outcomes – high interest rates and high deficits, or lower output and higher inflation. I expect single-party governments to have less fiscal discipline and to cause an unfavorable fiscal–monetary policy mix, when their central banks are independent, potentially resulting in negative macroeconomic outcomes. I expect independent central banks to conduct a tight (contractionary) monetary policy to offset inflationary pressures created by single-party governments' expansionary fiscal policy, which can suppress investment and economic output. Therefore, the combination of single-party governments and independent central banks should produce a policy mix consisting of an expansionary fiscal policy and a tight monetary policy, and possibly negative economic outcomes.

When central banks are dependent, conversely, single-party governments do not necessarily have to implement an expansionary fiscal policy. When central banks are not independent, single-party governments can afford to conduct a conservative fiscal policy, because they have control over monetary policy and do not have to rely only on fiscal policy for economic stimulus and expansion. Compared to coalition governments, single-party governments have a lower need to resort to fiscal policy for electoral distributive politics, because of their relative homogeneity and cohesion in policy preferences and constituent interests. Since central banks are not independent, they can also use monetary policy to promote output growth and employment, and their fiscal policy does not have to be expansionary. Thus, single-party governments' fiscal policy under dependent central banks may be less expansionary than under independent central banks. But their monetary policy may be more expansionary than when central banks are independent. If this is the case, we should see a relatively tight (or neutral) fiscal policy and a relatively loose (or neutral) monetary policy under single-party governments with dependent central banks. This policy mix should be preferable for economic outcomes, since governments can avoid the negative macroeconomic consequences of fiscal indiscipline and a contractionary monetary policy. Further, if single-party governments face only dependent central banks and retain monetary policy control, they may be able to avoid a conflictive fiscal–monetary policy mix, since they control both fiscal and monetary policies and do not have to compete or conflict with independent central banks that could counter and offset the former's fiscal policy. That is, they can better coordinate fiscal and monetary policies and, as a result, produce a fiscal–monetary policy mix that is not conflictive, which may in turn result in good economic outcomes.

In this part of the chapter, I examine empirical data to see how the number of governing parties and central banks jointly affect economic policy and outcomes. The evidence below suggests that coalition governments achieved fiscal discipline and favorable economic outcomes, when they faced independent central banks. But in the absence of independent central banks, their fiscal policy became expansionary, and their economic outcomes negative. One of the significant aspects of the results is that the disciplining effects of central bank independence on coalition governments' fiscal policy are observed for a wide variety of policy tools and economic outcomes. In contrast, decisive single-party governments suffered lack of fiscal discipline when they faced independent central banks, resulting in negative economic outcomes.

Government wage consumption expenditures

Table 5.1a reports the predicted values of government wage consumption at different numbers of governing parties and different levels of central bank independence for the entire period of 1961–2001 (without country dummies).[2] The results show that coalition governments achieved lower spending than single-party governments, when central banks were independent. Independent central banks restrained coalition governments' spending. When central banks were independent, an increase in the number of governing parties led to a decrease in spending. When central banks were dependent (*CBI* = 0.14), additional governing parties contributed to higher spending, suggesting that in the absence of independent central banks' restraining effects, coalition governments' spending did become expansionary. Of all combinations, five-party governments with independent central banks (*CBI* = 0.68) achieved the lowest spending. By contrast, their spending was the highest of all, when central banks were dependent (*CBI* = 0.14). Their spending was 0.33 percent of GDP higher (2.9 percent of total wage consumption higher) when central banks were dependent than independent.

These results refute the argument that coalition governments' fiscal policy is undisciplined in this spending item; their spending depended on the central banks they faced, and was restrained when central banks were independent. Thus, the effect of coalition governments on government wage consumption was context-specific. Coalition governments' fiscal policy was expansionary if central banks were not independent, but was disciplined when central banks were independent. On the other hand, single-party governments' spending increased (the second highest of all) when they faced independent central banks. When central banks were independent (*CBI* = 0.68), single-party governments'

Table 5.1 Government wage consumption: regression results

1961–2001 (without country dummies)	
Coalition$_{t-1}$	0.082**
	(0.037)
CBI$_{t-1}$	0.526**
	(0.251)
Coalition$_{t-1}$ * CBI$_{t-1}$	−0.230**
	(0.105)

Notes
OLS estimates with panel-corrected standard errors in parentheses.
Only the results of the relevant variables are shown.
***Significant at the 0.01 level.
**Significant at the 0.05 level.
*Significant at the 0.10 level.

Table 5.1a Predicted values of government wage consumption

1961–2001	Dependent central banks (CBI = 0.14)	Independent central banks (CBI = 0.68)
Single-party governments	0.12	0.28
Three-party governments	0.22	0.13
Five-party governments	0.32	–0.01

Notes
Predicted values of government wage consumption calculated from the results in Table 5.1. The differences among the cells are all significant, except for the horizontal difference in the *Coalition* = 3 row.
In calculating the predicted values of the dependent variable, I only manipulated the two relevant constitutive terms and their interactive term. Therefore, the predicted values indicate how the two factors push up or down the dependent variable when they are held at certain values. I do not repeat this note for the rest of the simulation figures, but their values are calculated in the same manner.

spending was 0.29 percent of GDP higher (2.5 percent of total government wage consumption higher) than five-party governments'. Similar results are obtained also for the second period of 1982–2001 (fixed effects). No significant effect is detected for the first period of 1961–1981.

Government non-wage consumption expenditures

Government non-wage consumption follows the same pattern as wage consumption. Table 5.2a reports the predicted values of government non-wage consumption, conditional on the number of governing parties and central bank independence, for the first period of 1961–1981 (fixed effects). Coalition governments' spending was disciplined in the presence of independent central banks, but expansionary in their absence. Additional governing parties contributed to lower spending when central banks were independent. When central banks were independent (*CBI* = 0.68), five-party governments achieved the lowest spending

Table 5.2 Government non-wage consumption: regression results

1961–1981 (fixed effects)	
$Coalition_{t-1}$	0.211***
	(0.077)
CBI_{t-1}	2.143***
	(0.870)
$Coalition_{t-1} * CBI_{t-1}$	–0.698***
	(0.284)

Notes
OLS estimates with panel-corrected standard errors in parentheses.
Only the results of the relevant variables are shown.
***Significant at the 0.01 level.
**Significant at the 0.05 level.
*Significant at the 0.10 level.

Table 5.2a Predicted values of government non-wage consumption

1961–1981	Dependent central banks (CBI = 0.14)	Independent central banks (CBI = 0.68)
Single-party governments	0.41	1.19
Three-party governments	0.63	0.66
Five-party governments	0.86	0.13

Notes
Predicted values of government non-wage consumption calculated from the results in Table 5.2. The differences among cells are significant, except for the horizontal differences in the *Coalition* = 3 and 5 rows.

of all combinations, and single-party governments the highest – single-party governments' spending was higher than five-party governments' by 1.06 percent of GDP (14.2 percent of total non-wage consumption). When central banks were dependent (*CBI* = 0.14), additional governing parties contributed to higher spending. So coalition governments' spending was expansionary in the absence of independent central banks. Single-party governments' spending was 0.78 percent of GDP lower when central banks were dependent than independent. (The differences among cells are significant, except for the horizontal differences in the *Coalition* = 3 and 5 rows.) The simulation results for the second period (1982–2001, fixed effects) and the entire period of 1961–2001 (fixed effects) follow the same pattern.

Government investment

Central banks' disciplining effect on coalition governments' fiscal policy is also observed in government investment. Table 5.3a reports the predicted values of government investment for the entire period of 1961–2001, contingent on the number of governing parties and central bank independence (fixed effects). Additional governing parties contributed to lower spending when central banks were independent (*CBI* = 0.68). Under independent central banks, five-party governments achieved the second lowest spending of all combinations of the number of governing parties and central banks. Their spending was lower than single-party governments' by 0.40 percent of GDP (11.3 percent of total government investment). Single-party governments' spending under independent central banks was the highest of all. When central banks were dependent (*CBI* = 0.14), additional governing parties contributed to high spending. So coalition governments' spending was expansionary in the absence of independent central banks. Single-party governments recorded the lowest spending under dependent central banks, and their spending was 0.47 percent of GDP lower than when central banks were independent. Thus, single-party governments' spending sharply increased when they faced independent central banks, a pattern widely observed in many fiscal policy items. (The differences among the cells

Table 5.3 Government investment: regression results

1961–2001 (fixed effects)	
Coalition$_{t-1}$	0.097**
	(0.040)
CBI$_{t-1}$	1.157***
	(0.362)
Coalition$_{t-1}$ * CBI$_{t-1}$	−0.290***
	(0.109)

Notes
OLS estimates with panel-corrected standard errors in parentheses.
Only the results of the relevant variables are shown.
***Significant at the 0.01 level.
**Significant at the 0.05 level.
*Significant at the 0.10 level.

Table 5.3a Predicted values of government investment

1961–2001	Dependent central banks (CBI = 0.14)	Independent central banks (CBI = 0.68)
Single-party governments	0.21	0.68
Three-party governments	0.33	0.48
Five-party governments	0.44	0.28

Notes
Predicted values of government investment calculated from the results in Table 5.3. The differences among the cells are significant, except for the horizontal differences in the *Coalition* = 3 and 5 rows.

are significant, except for the horizontal differences in the *Coalition* = 3 and 5 rows.) The results for the first period (1961–1981) show the same pattern, but only half of the differences among the cells are significant.

Social security transfers paid by government

Social security transfers in the entire period of 1961–2001 show the same pattern, with coalition governments achieving low spending with independent central banks, and single-party governments high spending (without country dummies: results not reported). The differences among the cells are significant only in the vertical differences in the *CBI* = 0.14 column and the horizontal difference in the *Coalition* = 1 row. But if the results are to be trusted, consistent with other fiscal policy items, coalition governments had low spending when central banks were independent and high spending when central banks were dependent. By contrast, single-party governments had low spending under dependent central banks and high spending under independent central banks. An increase in central bank independence from 0.14 to 0.68

resulted in a 0.25 percent of GDP reduction for five-party governments' spending and in a 0.28 percent of GDP increase for single-party governments' spending. The highest spending of all combinations was recorded by single-party governments with independent central banks, and the lowest by single-party governments with dependent central banks and five-party governments under independent central banks.

Government subsidies to industries

Though the evidence is not conclusive, public subsidies are the only spending item that shows a pattern different from the rest of fiscal policy items. The results (not reported) show that during the first period of 1961–1981, an increase in central bank independence reduced single-party governments' spending but increased coalition governments'.[3] (The vertical differences among the cells are all significant, but the horizontal differences are not.) The pattern here is that additional governing parties pushed up spending when central banks were independent, and reduced it when central banks were dependent. As a result, the highest spending was recorded by five-party governments under independent central banks, and the lowest by single-party governments under independent central banks. The reason why only government subsidies had a different pattern from other fiscal policy items is not clear. This effect disappears in the second period of 1982–2001.

Government employment

Coalition governments' fiscal discipline under independent central banks is also observed in government employment. Table 5.4a shows the predicted values of government employment as a percentage of total employment for the entire period of 1961–2001, conditional on the number of governing parties and central banks (without country dummies). When central banks were independent,

Table 5.4 Government employment: regression results

1961–2001 (without country dummies)	
Coalition$_{t-1}$	0.100***
	(0.029)
CBI$_{t-1}$	0.427**
	(0.200)
Coalition$_{t-1}$ * CBI$_{t-1}$	−0.229***
	(0.079)

Notes
OLS estimates with panel-corrected standard errors in parentheses.
Only the results of the relevant variables are shown.
***Significant at the 0.01 level.
**Significant at the 0.05 level.
*Significant at the 0.10 level.

Table 5.4a Predicted values of government employment

1961–2001	Dependent central banks (CBI = 0.14)	Independent central banks (CBI = 0.68)
Single-party governments	0.12	0.23
Three-party governments	0.26	0.12
Five-party governments	0.40	0.01

Notes
Predicted values of government employment calculated from the results in Table 5.4. The differences among the cells are significant, except for the horizontal difference in the *Coalition* = 1 row where *p*-value is 0.15.

coalition governments recorded lower public employment than single-party governments. Five-party governments achieved the lowest public employment of all combinations under independent central banks (*CBI* = 0.68). Both three- and five-party governments had lower public employment under independent than dependent central banks. By contrast, additional governing parties contributed to higher public employment when central banks were dependent (*CBI* = 0.14). As a result, five-party governments had the highest public employment of all, providing another piece of evidence that coalition governments' spending was expansionary in the absence of independent central banks. (The differences among the cells are significant, except for the horizontal difference in the *Coalition* = 1 row where *p*-value is 0.15. The fixed-effects model has the same pattern but only the vertical differences in the *CBI* = 0.14 column are significant.)

Total government spending

The evidence for total government spending is weak, as only about half of the differences among the cells are significant. But the pattern of spending by coalition governments under different central banks follows that of other spending items, suggesting that coalition governments had low spending when central banks were independent, and single-party governments had high spending (Table 5.5a, the entire period of 1961–2001, fixed effects). Five-party governments' spending was 1.1 percent of GDP lower (2.4 percent of total spending lower) than single-party governments' when central banks were independent. The latter's spending was, in contrast, the highest of all combinations. Their total spending rises by 1.41 percent of GDP (3.2 percent of total spending) when it shifts from dependent to independent central banks. On the other hand, when central banks were dependent, additional governing parties pushed up total spending. As a result, coalition governments had high spending, and single-party governments had the lowest spending of all combinations, when central banks were dependent. Thus, independent central banks restrained coalition governments' total spending, as in other fiscal policy items. In the absence of independent central banks, however, coalition governments'

Table 5.5 Total government spending: regression results

1961–2001 (fixed effects)	
Coalition$_{t-1}$	0.384**
	(0.186)
CBI$_{t-1}$	3.554**
	(1.845)
Coalition$_{t-1}$ * CBI$_{t-1}$	−0.954**
	(0.489)

Notes
OLS estimates with panel-corrected standard errors in parentheses.
Only the results of the relevant variables are shown.
***Significant at the 0.01 level.
**Significant at the 0.05 level.
*Significant at the 0.10 level.

Table 5.5a Predicted values of total government spending

1961–2001	Dependent central banks (CBI = 0.14)	Independent central banks (CBI = 0.68)
Single-party governments	0.74	2.15
Three-party governments	1.24	1.62
Five-party governments	1.74	1.09

Notes
Predicted values of total government spending calculated from the results in Table 5.5. Only the vertical differences in the *CBI* = 0.14 column and the horizontal one in the *Coalition* = 1 row are significant, but the others are not. The significance level for the vertical differences in the *CBI* = 0.68 is 0.15.

spending became expansionary, showing that they could not achieve fiscal restraint under dependent central banks. (Only the vertical differences in the *CBI* = 0.14 column and the horizontal one in the *Coalition* = 1 row are significant, but the others are not. The significance level for the vertical differences in the *CBI* = 0.68 is 0.15.)

Total government tax revenues

Table 5.6a shows the predicted values of total revenues for the first period of 1961–1981 (fixed effects). The pattern of total tax revenues approximately follows that of various spending items. This is natural because when governments spend more, they need to raise more revenues to finance the spending, and when their spending is low, they only need to raise low revenues. The results show that single-party governments' revenues jumped when shifting from under dependent to independent central banks. This is a result of their expansionary spending when they faced independent central banks, as we have

Table 5.6 Total government tax revenues: regression results

1961–1981 (fixed effects)	
Coalition$_{t-1}$	0.628**
	(0.315)
CBI$_{t-1}$	2.690
	(3.663)
Coalition$_{t-1}$ * CBI$_{t-1}$	−1.814*
	(0.949)

Notes
OLS estimates with panel-corrected standard errors in parentheses.
Only the results of the relevant variables are shown.
***Significant at the 0.01 level.
**Significant at the 0.05 level.
*Significant at the 0.10 level.

Table 5.6a Predicted values of total government tax revenues

1961–1981	Dependent central banks (CBI = 0.14)	Independent central banks (CBI = 0.68)
Single-party governments	0.75	1.22
Three-party governments	1.49	0.01
Five-party governments	2.24	−1.20

Notes
Predicted values of total government revenues calculated from the results in Table 5.6. All vertical differences among the cells are significant, but the horizontal differences are not. The significance level for the horizontal difference in the *Coalition* = 5 is 0.14.

seen in various spending items above. As a result, they had to raise higher revenues.

Coalition governments had lower revenues, when central banks were independent than dependent. Five-party governments' revenues under independent central banks were the lowest of all combinations, and were 2.4 percent of GDP lower (5.8 percent of total revenues lower) than single-party governments' under the same independent central banks. Additional governing parties pushed down the revenues when central banks were independent, and pushed them up when central banks were dependent. As a result, when they faced dependent central banks, five-party governments had the highest revenues of all, reflecting their expansionary spending under dependent central banks. The low revenues by coalition governments under independent central banks could, under certain conditions, be a sign of fiscal indiscipline, but such is not the case here – coalition governments achieved the best fiscal balance (surplus) under independent central banks, as we will see below. (In Table 5.6a, all vertical differences among the cells are significant, but the horizontal differences are not. The significance level for the horizontal difference in the *Coalition* = 5 is 0.14.) We obtain the same results for the entire period of 1961–2001 (both with and without country dummies: results not reported).

The pattern of total tax revenues is also observed in the revenues from individual tax items. While there is no evidence that personal income tax was affected by the interaction of governing parties and central banks, consumption tax and social security contributions follow the same pattern of total tax revenues. Only corporate tax has a different pattern.

Consumption tax

The evidence for consumption tax is not strong (results not reported).[4] So the results should be viewed with caution. But if the results are to be trusted, during 1961–2001 (the entire period), under independent central banks, coalition governments had lower revenues than single-party governments, and under dependent central banks, higher revenues (fixed effects). Additional governing parties contributed to lower revenues when central banks were independent, and to higher revenues if central banks were dependent. Consumption tax revenues were the highest under single-party governments with independent central banks, and the lowest under single-party governments with dependent central banks. But independent central banks did not push down coalition governments' revenues so much that their revenues were still higher under independent than dependent central banks.

Social security contributions collected by government

Table 5.7a reports the predicted values of social security contributions for the second period of 1982–2001, under different combinations of governing parties and central banks (without country dummies). The pattern is the same as in total tax revenues. Coalition governments had lower contributions than single-party governments when central banks were independent, and higher contributions under dependent central banks. Five-party governments recorded the lowest contributions of all combinations under independent central banks. By contrast, single-party governments had the highest contributions of all under independent central banks. Five-party governments' contributions were 0.78 percent of GDP lower (7.7 percent of total contributions lower) than single-party governments' when central banks were independent. Five-party governments' contributions were 0.64 percent of GDP lower under independent central banks than when central banks were dependent. The differences among the cells are significant, except for the horizontal difference in the *Coalition* = 3 row. The same results are obtained for the second period (1982–2001) with country dummies and for the entire period of 1961–2001 (with and without country dummies), though statistical significance drops.

Table 5.7 Social security contributions: regression results

1982–2001 (without country dummies)	
Coalition$_{t-1}$	0.152**
	(0.070)
CBI$_{t-1}$	1.364***
	(0.463)
Coalition$_{t-1}$ * CBI$_{t-1}$	−0.511***
	(0.200)

Notes
OLS estimates with panel-corrected standard errors in parentheses.
Only the results of the relevant variables are shown.
***Significant at the 0.01 level.
**Significant at the 0.05 level.
*Significant at the 0.10 level.

Table 5.7a Predicted values of social security contributions

1982–2001	*Dependent central banks (CBI = 0.14)*	*Independent central banks (CBI = 0.68)*
Single-party governments	0.27	0.73
Three-party governments	0.43	0.34
Five-party governments	0.59	−0.05

Notes
Predicted values of social security contributions calculated from the results in Table 5.7. The differences among the cells are significant, except for the horizontal difference in the *Coalition =* 3 row.

Corporate income tax

Though the evidence is weak, corporate tax is the only exception in all tax revenue results. In all revenues but corporate tax, coalition governments achieved low revenues under independent central banks. This is because they had low spending levels to finance with tax revenues when facing independent central banks. Meanwhile, single-party governments had high tax revenues when they faced independent central banks because their spending was high and thus had high revenue needs. But in corporate tax, the reverse happens (without country dummies: results not reported). The results show that during 1961–2001, single-party governments recorded the lowest corporate tax revenues with independent central banks and the highest revenues with dependent ones. Additional governing parties contributed to higher revenues if central banks were independent, and to lower revenues if central banks were dependent – the opposite pattern from the other tax results. But the results are weak, so they should be viewed with caution (the differences among the cells are significant, except for the vertical differences in the *CBI* = 0.68 column and the horizontal difference in the *Coalition* = 5 row, and the significance level for the vertical differences in the *CBI* = 0.14 column is only 0.11). The same pattern is observed for the first period of 1961–1981 (without country dummies).

Fiscal balance

Table 5.8a reports the predicted values of the cyclically adjusted fiscal balance, contingent on the number of governing parties and central banks for the entire period of 1961–2001 (fixed effects). The disciplining effect of central banks on coalition governments is observed in the fiscal balance, as expected from the spending and tax results reviewed above. Independent central banks improved coalition governments' fiscal balance, while the absence of independent central banks made coalition governments' fiscal policy expansionary. Five-party governments under independent central banks achieved the best fiscal balance (surplus) of all combinations of the two variables. When central banks were independent, additional governing parties improved the fiscal balance. But with dependent central banks, additional governing parties deteriorated the fiscal balance. As a result, five-party governments under dependent central banks recorded the worst fiscal balance (deficit) of all combinations. Five-party governments' fiscal balance improved by 1.7 percent of potential GDP when moving from dependent (*CBI* = 0.14) to independent (*CBI* = 0.68) central banks. In contrast, an increase in central bank independence deteriorated single-party governments' fiscal balance. (The differences among the cells are significant, except for the vertical differences in the *CBI* = 0.68 column and the horizontal difference in the *Coalition* = 1 row, and the significance level for the *Coalition* = 3 row is only 0.17.)

The same disciplining effect of central bank independence on coalition governments is observed for the second period of 1982–2001 (fixed effects; not reported). Five-party governments under independent central banks achieved the best fiscal balance, and the worst balance with dependent central banks

Table 5.8 Fiscal balance: regression results

1961–2001 (fixed effects)	
Coalition$_{t-1}$	−0.383*
	(0.220)
CBI$_{t-1}$	−1.102
	(2.202)
Coalition$_{t-1}$ * CBI$_{t-1}$	0.881
	(0.565)

Notes
OLS estimates with panel-corrected standard errors in parentheses.
Only the results of the relevant variables are shown.
***Significant at the 0.01 level.
**Significant at the 0.05 level.
*Significant at the 0.10 level.

Table 5.8a Predicted values of the fiscal balance

1961–2001	Dependent central banks (CBI = 0.14)	Independent central banks (CBI = 0.68)
Single-party governments	–0.41	–0.53
Three-party governments	–0.93	–0.10
Five-party governments	–1.45	0.32

Notes
Predicted values of the fiscal balance calculated from the results in Table 5.8. The differences among the cells are significant, except for the vertical differences in the *CBI* = 0.68 column and the horizontal difference in the *Coalition* = 1 row, and the significance level for the *Coalition* = 3 row is only 0.17.

(single-party governments with dependent central banks also recorded the best balance). Thus, coalition governments' fiscal policy could be expansionary if central banks were not independent, while it was very disciplined if central banks were independent.

Monetary policy stance

My fiscal–monetary policy mix argument expects that monetary policy becomes tight when fiscal policy is too expansionary and becomes relaxed when fiscal policy is tight, other things being equal. Table 5.9a reports the predicted values of the monetary policy stance (cyclically adjusted discount rates) for the entire period of 1961–2001, conditional on the number of governing parties and central banks (fixed effects). The differences among the cells are not statistically significant (the significance level for the vertical differences is 0.16 for the *CBI* = 0.68 column and 0.26 for the *CBI* = 0.14 column, and *p*-values for the other differences are higher). So the results should be viewed as such with caution. But if the results are to be trusted, the predicted values suggest that monetary policy during 1961–2001 followed the pattern expected by the policy mix argument.

When central banks were independent, monetary policy loosened (lower values) with additional governing parties. This is because as we have seen above, under independent central banks, additional governing parties led to a tighter fiscal policy by party governments. Since fiscal policy was restrained, central banks did not have to conduct a contractionary monetary policy for price stability goals. In contrast, single-party governments' monetary policy under independent central banks was tight, because their fiscal policy was very expansionary when central banks were independent. As a result, single-party governments had the tightest monetary policy (highest discount rates) under independent central banks.

When central banks were dependent, on the other hand, monetary policy tightened with additional governing parties, because coalition governments'

Table 5.9 Monetary policy: regression results

1961–2001 (fixed effects)	
Coalition$_{t-1}$	0.607
	(0.447)
CBI$_{t-1}$	6.546
	(6.142)
Coalition$_{t-1}$ * CBI$_{t-1}$	−1.770
	(1.126)

Notes
OLS estimates with panel-corrected standard errors in parentheses.
Only the results of the relevant variables are shown.
***Significant at the 0.01 level.
**Significant at the 0.05 level.
*Significant at the 0.10 level.

Table 5.9a Predicted values of monetary policy

1961–2001	*Dependent central banks (CBI = 0.14)*	*Independent central banks (CBI = 0.68)*
Single-party governments	1.27	3.85
Three-party governments	1.99	2.66
Five-party governments	2.71	1.46

Notes
Predicted values of monetary policy calculated from the results in Table 5.9. The significance level for the vertical differences is 0.16 for the *CBI* = 0.68 column and 0.26 for the *CBI* = 0.14 column, and *p*-values for the other differences are higher. So the results should be viewed as such with caution.

fiscal policy under dependent central banks was expansionary, as we have seen above. Thus, five-party governments under dependent central banks had the second tightest monetary policy of all combinations of governing parties and central banks. By contrast, single-party governments' monetary policy under dependent central banks was the loosest of all, since their fiscal policy was disciplined when central banks were dependent, and central banks did not have to keep a tight monetary policy for price stability. Thus, we observe a case of counterbalancing between fiscal and monetary policies. But as I have mentioned, the differences among the cells are not statistically significant.

Economic growth

The benefits of central bank independence for coalition governments are not limited to economic policy. Similar benefits are also found in some economic outcomes. Table 5.10a reports the predicted values of economic growth rates for the first period of 1961–1981, contingent on the number of governing parties

Table 5.10 Economic growth (GDP): regression results

1961–1981 (fixed effects)	
Coalition$_{t-1}$	−1.156**
	(0.478)
CBI$_{t-1}$	−12.637***
	(4.784)
Coalition$_{t-1}$ * CBI$_{t-1}$	3.573**
	(1.598)

Notes
OLS estimates with panel-corrected standard errors in parentheses.
Only the results of the relevant variables are shown.
***Significant at the 0.01 level.
**Significant at the 0.05 level.
*Significant at the 0.10 level.

Table 5.10a Predicted values of economic growth (GDP)

1961–1981	*Dependent central banks (CBI = 0.14)*	*Independent central banks (CBI = 0.68)*
Single-party governments	−2.42	−7.31
Three-party governments	−3.73	−4.77
Five-party governments	−5.04	−2.22

Notes
Predicted values of economic growth calculated from the results in Table 5.10. The differences among the cells are significant, except for the horizontal differences in the *Coalition* = 3 and 5 rows.

and central bank independence (fixed effects). Five-party governments under independent central banks achieved the highest growth of all combinations of the number of governing parties and central banks. By contrast, single-party governments under independent central banks recorded the lowest growth rate of all. Five-party governments achieved a 5.1 percent higher growth rate than single-party governments under independent central banks. Additional governing parties increased growth rates under independent central banks. In contrast, more governing parties reduced growth rates when central banks were dependent. Under dependent central banks, five-party governments' growth was 2.6 percent lower than that of single-party governments. The differences among the cells are significant, except for the horizontal differences in the *Coalition* = 3 and 5 rows.

The same pattern of beneficial interaction between coalition governments and independent central banks also existed for the entire period of 1961–2001 (fixed effects: results not reported). As in the first period, additional governing parties contributed to higher economic growth rates under independent central banks, and to lower rates under dependent central banks. As a result, single-party governments registered the lowest growth of all combinations, when central banks were independent (as in the first-period results). But unlike the first-period simulation, independent central banks reduced growth rates at all numbers of governing parties between one and five. But the downward effect of central bank independence on output growth was smaller for coalition governments. Thus, when central banks were independent, five-party governments still had a 2 percent higher growth than single-party governments. The negative effect of central bank independence on economic growth was much larger for single-party governments than coalition governments. An increase of central bank independence from 0.14 to 0.68 reduced single-party governments' growth by 3.6 percent, but five-party governments' growth by only 0.85 percent. This case, thus, still shows the relative benefit of the combination of coalition governments and independent central banks for economic growth. (The differences among the cells are significant, except for the horizontal difference in the *Coalition* = 5 row, and the vertical ones in the *CBI* = 0.14 column where p = 0.15.)

Unemployment

The beneficial effect of central bank independence on coalition governments also manifests itself in unemployment rates – coalition governments achieved low unemployment when central banks were independent. Table 5.11a reports the predicted values of unemployment for the entire period of 1961–2001, conditional on the number of governing parties and central banks (without country dummies). Five-party governments' unemployment rate under independent central banks was the lowest of all combinations of governing parties and central banks. But when central banks were not independent, they recorded the highest unemployment of all. Thus, independent central banks improved the unemployment records of coalition governments. In contrast, single-party governments registered high unemployment under independent central banks, and low unemployment under dependent central banks. Thus, the incompatibility of single-party governments and independent central banks existed in unemployment as well as in economic policy and output growth we reviewed above. Under independent central banks, five-party governments achieved 0.46 percent lower unemployment than single-party governments. When central banks were independent, additional governing parties contributed to lower unemployment. When central banks were dependent, in contrast, additional parties led to higher unemployment. All governments, except for single-party governments, enjoyed lower unemployment under independent than dependent central banks. (The differences among the cells are significant, except for the vertical differences in the *CBI* = 0.14 column where p = 0.11 and the horizontal one in the *Coalition* = 1 row.)

The same pattern is also observed in the results of the fixed-effect models for the entire period (1961–2001) and the first period (1961–1981) and for the model with no country dummies for the first and second periods (1961–1981, 1982–2001). In all these results, the highest unemployment was recorded by single-party governments under independent central banks or five-party

Table 5.11 Unemployment: regression results

1961–2001 (without country dummies)	
Coalition$_{t-1}$	0.105**
	(0.050)
CBI$_{t-1}$	0.618*
	(0.329)
Coalition$_{t-1}$ * CBI$_{t-1}$	−0.328***
	(0.121)

Notes
OLS estimates with panel-corrected standard errors in parentheses.
Only the results of the relevant variables are shown.
***Significant at the 0.01 level.
**Significant at the 0.05 level.
*Significant at the 0.10 level.

Table 5.11a Predicted values of unemployment

1961–2001	Dependent central banks (CBI = 0.14)	Independent central banks (CBI = 0.68)
Single-party governments	0.14	0.30
Three-party governments	0.26	0.06
Five-party governments	0.38	−0.16

Notes
Predicted values of unemployment calculated from the results in Table 5.11. The differences among the cells are significant, except for the vertical differences in the *CBI* = 0.14 column where p = 0.11 and the horizontal one in the *Coalition* = 1 row.

governments under dependent central banks. But in these other results, only about half of the differences among the cells are significant.

Sum

Coalition governments' fiscal policy was very disciplined, when they had independent central banks. Their fiscal discipline is observed in a variety of spending and tax items. Coalition governments also achieved high output growth and low unemployment under independent central banks. The good economic outcome was partly attributable to the absence of a contractionary monetary policy under coalition governments and independent central banks that would have had to be mobilized if fiscal policy had not been disciplined. It was also partly because their fiscal discipline was conducive to economic growth and employment. Fiscal discipline allows governments to avoid negative economic consequences of fiscal indiscipline, such as high deficits, inflation, and high interest rates. Deficits can invite high interest rates and low savings, which depress investment and growth. Government deficits also drain resources from the private economy. Meanwhile, inflation caused by expansions can create price distortions, resource allocation inefficiency, and economic uncertainties, which impair investment and stifle growth (however, in this data, there is no evidence that the number of governing parties and central bank independence jointly had any effect on inflation). The case of coalition governments with independent central banks suggests that fiscal discipline and a relaxed monetary policy promoted economic performance.

In contrast, single-party governments' fiscal policy was expansionary, when they faced independent central banks. They also produced negative outcomes in economic growth and unemployment under independent central banks. Their fiscal indiscipline invited a contractionary monetary policy by central banks, which in tandem with the negative consequences of fiscal indiscipline adversely affected economic growth and employment. The fiscal indiscipline and poor economic performance by single-party governments under independent central banks suggest that there was an incompatibility in these two policy makers' economic policy actions.

But when they had only dependent central banks, single-party governments' fiscal policy was fairly disciplined, and their growth and employment records were also good. In contrast, coalition governments were unable to restrain their spending in the absence of independent central banks, and their fiscal policy was quite expansionary, and economic outcomes very negative.

We only had weak evidence for monetary policy, since the monetary policy results were not statistically significant. But if the pattern of the predicted values is to be trusted, it follows the pattern expected by the policy mix argument. The combination of coalition governments and independent central banks produces a tight fiscal–relaxed monetary policy mix and leads to good economic outcomes. Monetary policy does not have to be tight because coalition governments' fiscal policy is disciplined when central banks are independent. In contrast, coalition governments and dependent central banks produce a loose fiscal–tight monetary policy mix, resulting in poor economic outcomes. Coalition governments' fiscal policy is unrestrained in the absence of independent central banks, and monetary policy needs to be tightened for price stability.

Meanwhile, the combination of single-party governments and independent central banks leads to a loose fiscal–tight monetary policy and negative economic outcomes. In this configuration, fiscal policy is loose, and central banks use a tight monetary policy to offset inflationary pressures. And a contractionary monetary policy negatively affects economic outcomes by placing disinflationary pressures on the economy. But again, the monetary policy results are weak, so should be viewed with caution. Further research is much desired to investigate more thoroughly whether the interaction of coalition governments and central banks affects monetary policy.

Center governments and central banks

I argued in Chapter 2 that center governments had a great incentive to bring economic discipline in their economic management to achieve favorable economic outcomes in the recent decades. As a result of various changes in the international and domestic economies (e.g. the internationalization of capital and trade and increased international competition), governments of various types came under the competitive pressure to shift economic policy in a market-conforming direction. In order to attract mobile capital and promote the competitiveness of the national economies, governments with a prior reputation or record of fiscal expansionism and/or deficits (including center governments) particularly needed to show their commitment to price stability, restrain fiscal policy, and restructure the welfare system to reduce labor costs and curb welfare spending. In this economic environment, center governments had an incentive to seek to achieve fiscal discipline and improve economic performance by granting independence to central banks (Bernhard, 2002), gaining antiinflationary credibility, and implementing a fiscal policy along the lines of policy prescriptions by central banks and/or compatible with central banks' monetary policy.

Center governments also faced more potential sources of policy conflict (than the conservative governments), because the distance was large between their traditional interventionist policy and the neoliberal policy toward which they needed to shift their policy. They had to move their economic policy farther away from their traditional positions toward the right to make their policy more market-conforming. This potential for policy conflict led them to seek to achieve fiscal discipline and make a market-conforming policy shift by delegating monetary policy to central banks (Bernhard, 2002). They used independent central banks to make a neoliberal policy shift and fiscal austerity palatable to their pro-intervention and pro-welfare constituencies. This made it easier for center governments to justify their policy shift, because they could explain to their constituencies that the governments had no room for policy maneuvering in the presence of independent central banks and of the competitiveness and efficiency pressures of the global economy. Center governments also had much to gain from the constraints on their fiscal policy coming from independent central banks.

We should expect that center governments better achieve fiscal discipline and relatively good economic outcomes when they have independent central banks, because they are more willing, and have the incentive, to conduct a fiscal policy compatible with policy prescriptions by central banks. If their fiscal policy is disciplined, central banks do not need to employ a tight monetary policy to control inflation. They can thus avoid placing disinflationary pressures on the economy that would otherwise come from a tight monetary policy. The absence of a contractionary monetary policy facilitates economic growth and employment. Further, if center governments' fiscal policy is disciplined, central banks can also mobilize monetary policy countercyclically for economic stimulus if the state of the economy calls for it. So they should be better able to craft a fiscal–monetary policy mix with central banks that is conducive to good economic performance when central banks are independent.

If central banks are not independent, in contrast, center governments should have more difficulty maintaining fiscal discipline. If center governments control monetary policy, they face the temptation to expand economic growth and employment, as they do not need to fear a disinflationary response from central banks. Expansionary fiscal policy can create inflationary pressures. So in the absence of independent central banks, they should have less fiscal discipline and a less favorable fiscal–monetary policy mix, possibly resulting in negative economic outcomes. If fiscal policy is expansionary, center governments and their dependent central banks may need to mobilize monetary policy to offset inflationary pressures, making monetary policy unavailable for countercyclical use.

What do the empirical data say about center governments' economic policy and outcomes, when considered in the context of their interaction with central banks? Here is the summary of my main findings. Center governments, when they had independent central banks, had fairly high levels of public spending in the past two decades (1982–2001). While their spending was expansionary, however, their fiscal policy as a whole under independent central banks was very disciplined, as they did not produce fiscal deficit. To the contrary, center governments under independent central banks produced the highest fiscal balance (the largest surplus or smallest deficit) of all combinations of partisan governments and central banks for most of the period under study. This is because they raised sufficient tax revenues to finance their spending and did not create fiscal deficit. Thus, independent central banks helped discipline center governments' fiscal policy by exerting constraints on center governments to raise sufficient revenues to finance their spending and not to produce deficit (as I explained in Chapter 2, this does not mean that central banks had direct control over party governments' fiscal policy). Their fiscal discipline under independent central banks also contributed to very low inflation. Fiscal discipline and low inflation, in turn, helped them achieve very high economic growth during some periods, when they had independent central banks. Thus, independent central banks had beneficial effects on center governments' fiscal policy and economic outcomes, as was the case with coalition governments.

When central banks were not independent, however, center governments suffered the worst fiscal balance (highest deficit or lowest surplus) of all combinations of partisan governments and central banks. When they faced dependent central banks, their spending levels were low, and so were their tax revenues. However, they recorded the highest level of fiscal deficit, which in turn led to the highest level of inflation. It suggests that while their spending was low, they did not raise sufficient revenues.

The case of center governments also shows the presence of the differing effects of different partisan governments with distinct properties. While center governments successfully reduced deficit under independent central banks, they were not as successful in reducing spending in the 1980s and 1990s, due largely to their large fiscal commitments in social security and government services.[5] In addition to the competitive pressures of globalization, many center-dominant countries in Europe needed to reduce deficit and debt to qualify for the European Economic and Monetary Union in the 1990s. In the face of large fiscal commitments, which they were not immediately able to retrench for electoral reasons, they reduced deficit and debt by keeping high tax revenues. Thus, this is an indication that different partisan governments make varied adjustments to similar pressures emanating from change in the international and domestic economies.

Government wage consumption expenditures

Table 5.12a shows the predicted values of government wage consumption under different combinations of center governments and central banks during the second period of 1982–2001 (without country dummies). The results show that center governments had higher spending, when facing independent central banks, and lower spending when they had dependent central banks. Fully center governments (*Center* = 100) had the lowest spending of all combinations when central banks were dependent (*CBI* = 0.14). With independent central banks (*CBI* = 0.68), they had the second highest spending of all. The highest spending was recorded by non-center governments (*Center* = 0) under dependent central banks (it is not clear whether these non-center governments were left or right,

Table 5.12 Government wage consumption expenditures: regression results

1982–2001 (without country dummies)	
CBI_{t-1}	−0.311
	(0.256)
$Center_{t-1}$	−0.00636**
	(0.00295)
$Center_{t-1} * CBI_{t-1}$	0.011*
	(0.006)

Notes
OLS estimates with panel-corrected standard errors in parentheses.
Only the results of the relevant variables are shown.
***Significant at the 0.01 level.
**Significant at the 0.05 level.
*Significant at the 0.10 level.

Table 5.12a Predicted values of government wage consumption

	1982–2001	Dependent central banks (CBI = 0.14)	Independent central banks (CBI = 0.68)
Center governments (cabinet portfolios, %)	Center = 0	−0.04	−0.21
	Center = 50	−0.28	−0.17
	Center = 100	−0.53	−0.13

Notes
Predicted values of government wage consumption calculated from the results in Table 5.12. The differences among the cells are significant, except for the vertical differences in the *CBI* = 0.68 column and the horizontal ones in the *Center* = 0 and 50 rows.

because neither had significant effects when interacted with central banks). (The differences among the cells are significant, except for the vertical differences in the *CBI* = 0.68 column and the horizontal ones in the *Center* = 0 and 50 rows.)

It is not entirely clear why independent central banks pushed up center governments' wage consumption expenditures. As we saw in the last chapter, center governments themselves (when not interacted with central banks) had low spending during 1982–2001 across spending items, including wage consumption. But when interacted with central banks, center governments under independent central banks had high spending not just in wage consumption, but also in other spending items. They also had high tax revenues and the highest primary balance (i.e. fiscal surplus).

A likely explanation is that center governments that had high spending in social security and public services actively resorted to (or counted on) the disciplining effects expected from independent central banks to raise sufficient revenues and minimize fiscal deficit, exactly because they had high spending they had to fund. And independent central banks served as a source of disciplining pressure on center governments to have their high spending financed by sufficient revenues. Or it may have also been easier for center governments to increase spending because when they had independent central banks, high spending was not likely to result in deficit, because of the expected high revenues under independent central banks (as a result of the pressure imposed by the presence of independent central banks on them to achieve fiscal discipline). This is consistent with some available evidence that governments tend to spend more when they have more revenues to spend, for instance, as during economic booms (Lane, 2002). It is not clear whether high spending entailed high taxation or high taxation allowed high spending – most likely, these two processes probably took place simultaneously in a mutually reinforcing manner.

Government non-wage consumption expenditures

Center governments also produced relatively high spending in government non-wage consumption under independent central banks. Table 5.13a shows the predicted values of non-wage consumption at different levels of center governments and central banks for the second period of 1982–2001 (without country dummies). Center governments contributed to higher spending when central banks were independent, and to lower spending when central banks were dependent. And independent central banks pushed up spending at high levels of center representation. As a result, fully center governments had the second highest spending, when they had independent central banks.[6] The highest spending was registered by non-center governments (*Center* = 0) with dependent central banks, and the lowest by center governments (*Center* = 100) with dependent central banks. (These "non-center governments" for the 1980s and 1990s were left governments as we will see in the next part of the chapter.) (The differences among the cells are significant, except for the vertical differences in the *CBI* = 0.68 column where *p*-value is only 0.14 and the horizontal one in the *Center* = 50 row.)

Table 5.13 Government non-wage consumption expenditures:
regression results

1982–2001 (without country dummies)

CBI_{t-1}	−0.586***
	(0.191)
$Center_{t-1}$	−0.00739***
	(0.00241)
$Center_{t-1} * CBI_{t-1}$	0.013***
	(0.005)

Notes
OLS estimates with panel-corrected standard errors in parentheses.
Only the results of the relevant variables are shown.
***Significant at the 0.01 level.
**Significant at the 0.05 level.
*Significant at the 0.10 level.

Table 5.13a Predicted values of government non-wage consumption expenditures

	1982–2001	*Dependent central banks (CBI = 0.14)*	*Independent central banks (CBI = 0.68)*
Center governments	Center = 0	−0.08	−0.39
(cabinet portfolios, %)	Center = 50	−0.35	−0.31
	Center = 100	−0.63	−0.22

Notes
Predicted values of government non-wage consumption calculated from the results in Table 5.13.
The differences among the cells are significant, except for the vertical differences in the $CBI = 0.68$
column where p-value is only 0.14 and the horizontal one in the $Center = 50$ row.

Government subsidies to industries

Government subsidies during the second period of 1982–2001 show the same
pattern (results not shown).[7] When center governments faced independent
central banks, they had the highest spending of all combinations (*Center* = 100,
CBI = 0.68). In contrast, they had the lowest spending when central banks were
dependent (*CBI* = 0.14).[8] Independent central banks served to increase center
governments' public subsidies. Center governments, meanwhile, led to higher
spending under independent central banks, and to lower spending under dependent central banks.

Social security benefits paid by government

Table 5.14a shows the predicted values of social security benefits paid by governments for the second period of 1982–2001, conditional on center partisanship
and central banks (without country dummies). The combination of center
governments and independent central banks created high spending in social

Table 5.14 Social security transfers: regression results

1982–2001 (without country dummies)	
CBI_{t-1}	−0.414
	(0.391)
$Center_{t-1}$	−0.011**
	(0.005)
$Center_{t-1} * CBI_{t-1}$	0.023**
	(0.010)

Notes
OLS estimates with panel-corrected standard errors in parentheses.
Only the results of the relevant variables are shown.
***Significant at the 0.01 level.
**Significant at the 0.05 level.
*Significant at the 0.10 level.

Table 5.14a Predicted values of social security transfers

	1982–2001	*Dependent central banks (CBI = 0.14)*	*Independent central banks (CBI = 0.68)*
Center governments	Center = 0	−0.05	−0.28
(cabinet portfolios, %)	Center = 50	−0.45	−0.05
	Center = 100	−0.85	0.16

Notes
Predicted values of social security transfers calculated from the results in Table 5.14. The differences among the cells are significant, except for the horizontal row at *Center* = 0.

security transfers, as in the other spending items we have reviewed above. At higher center cabinet portfolios, an increase in central bank independence pushed up government spending on social security transfers. Meanwhile, when central banks were independent, center governments contributed to high spending, and to low spending under dependent central banks. (The differences among the cells are significant, except for the horizontal row at *Center* = 0.)

As a result, fully center governments (*Center* = 100) had the highest spending of all combinations, when central banks were independent (*CBI* = 0.68). And they recorded the lowest when central banks were dependent (*CBI* = 0.14). Fully center governments' spending under independent central banks was 1.01 percent of GDP higher (8.3 percent of total social security transfers higher) than under dependent central banks. As we will see in the next part of the chapter, left governments had the opposite effect – under independent central banks, left governments achieved the lowest spending level.

The results offer a counterintuitive finding. The conventional welfare state literature points out that Christian Democratic (center) governments (most of them being continental European countries) have the highest level of spending in social security transfers. The results here suggest, however, that their high spending was contingent on central bank independence. They had the highest spending if central banks were independent, but the lowest spending if central banks were not independent. Why? Judging from the results of center governments' spending, tax revenues, and fiscal balance, the answer is likely to be financeability – whether governments have the ability to secure sufficient funds to finance high spending. The results suggest that independent central banks seemed to serve as a source of disciplining pressure on center governments to have their generally high spending financed by sufficient revenues. As a result, center governments had the highest fiscal surplus (the lowest deficit) under independent central banks, and the lowest surplus (the highest deficit) under dependent central banks. Simply put, it is an explanation that center governments could not afford to have large social security spending if central banks were not independent. But a more definitive answer requires further research.

Corporate income tax

Table 5.15a shows the predicted values of corporate income tax revenues for the first period of 1961–1981 (without country dummies) at different levels of center cabinet portfolios and central bank independence. The results show that central bank independence reduced the revenues at all levels of center cabinet portfolios. This largely reflects the fact that central bank independence individually (when not interacted) induced low corporate tax revenues for most of the period under study (see Chapter 4). But the downward effect of central bank independence was progressively smaller at higher center portfolios. Center governments contributed to high revenues under independent central banks, and to low revenues with dependent central banks. But the upward pressure of the combination of center governments and independent central banks was relatively weak, compared to the results for consumption tax revenues (shown below), where the combination produced the highest revenues of all combinations of government partisanship and central banks. As a result, fully center governments

Table 5.15 Corporate income tax revenues: regression results

1961–1981 (without country dummies)	
CBI_{t-1}	−0.913***
	(0.310)
$Center_{t-1}$	−0.00408*
	(0.00251)
$Center_{t-1} * CBI_{t-1}$	0.00819
	(0.00519)

Notes
OLS estimates with panel-corrected standard errors in parentheses.
Only the results of the relevant variables are shown.
***Significant at the 0.01 level.
**Significant at the 0.05 level.
*Significant at the 0.10 level.

Table 5.15a Predicted values of corporate income tax revenues

	1961–1981	*Dependent central banks (CBI = 0.14)*	*Independent central banks (CBI = 0.68)*
Center governments	Center = 0	–0.12	–0.62
(cabinet portfolios, %)	Center = 50	–0.27	–0.54
	Center = 100	–0.42	–0.47

Notes
Predicted values of corporate income tax calculated from the results in Table 5.15. The differences among the cells are significant, except for the vertical differences in the *CBI* = 0.68 column and the horizontal one in the *Center* = 100 row.

had a medium level of corporate tax revenues with both independent and dependent central banks. This suggests that center governments' high total tax revenues under independent central banks (discussed below) may have come from consumption tax, rather than corporate tax observed here or personal income tax on which they did not exert any significant effect. During the same period, right governments had the lowest and left governments had the highest corporate tax revenues under independent central banks. (The differences among the cells are significant, except for the vertical differences in the *CBI* = 0.68 column and the horizontal one in the *Center* = 100 row.)

Consumption tax

The interaction of center governments and independent central banks shows a clear, strong pattern in consumption tax revenues for the entire period (1961–2001), the first period (1961–1981), and the second period (1982–2001). The pattern is identical across all periods and various specifications. Table 5.16a reports the predicted values of consumption tax revenues for the second period of 1982–2001 (fixed effects). Center governments had the highest consumption tax revenues of all combinations of partisan governments and central banks, when central banks were independent. By contrast, they recorded the lowest revenues of all, when central banks were dependent. Central bank independence pushed up the revenues from the medium to high values of center cabinet portfolios. Meanwhile, center cabinet portfolios contributed to high revenues under independent central banks, and to low revenues under dependent ones. As a result, fully center governments' consumption tax revenues were 1.27 percent of GDP higher (9.9 percent of total consumption tax revenues) when central banks were independent than dependent. We have seen above that center governments under independent central banks had high spending levels especially in the second period. These results together suggest that their high consumption tax revenues played a central role in financing their high spending, because they do not register high tax revenues in other tax items, except for total tax revenues. Although I do not report them, the consumption tax

Table 5.16 Consumption tax revenues: regression results

1982–2001 (fixed effects)	
CBI_{t-1}	−0.469
	(0.501)
$Center_{t-1}$	−0.016***
	(0.005)
$Center_{t-1} * CBI_{t-1}$	0.028***
	(0.009)

Notes
OLS estimates with panel-corrected standard errors in parentheses.
Only the results of the relevant variables are shown.
***Significant at the 0.01 level.
**Significant at the 0.05 level.
*Significant at the 0.10 level.

Table 5.16a Predicted values of consumption tax revenues

	1982–2001	Dependent central banks (CBI = 0.14)	Independent central banks (CBI = 0.68)
Center governments	Center = 0	−0.06	−0.31
(cabinet portfolios, %)	Center = 50	−0.65	−0.13
	Center = 100	−1.23	0.04

Notes
Predicted values of consumption tax revenues calculated from the results in Table 5.16. The differences among the cells are significant, except for the horizontal one in the *Center* = 0 row.

models yield the same results for all periods, with and without country dummies. (The differences among the cells are significant, except for the horizontal one in the *Center* = 0 row.)

Total government spending

As can be expected from the results of individual spending items, center governments under independent central banks had high total spending. Table 5.17a shows the predicted values of total government spending during the second period of 1982–2001, contingent on center cabinet portfolios and central banks (without country dummies). Only the vertical differences in the *CBI* = 0.14 column are statistically significant, so the results should be viewed with caution. But if trusted, the results indicate that center governments under independent central banks had the highest total spending of all combinations of partisan governments and central banks. Center governments contributed to high spending under independent central banks, but to low spending under dependent central banks. Central bank independence, meanwhile, contributed to high spending at medium to high values of center portfolios. As a result, the highest spending was

Table 5.17 Total government spending: regression results

1982–2001 (without country dummies)	
CBI_{t-1}	−1.343
	(1.046)
$Center_{t-1}$	−0.021*
	(0.013)
$Center_{t-1} * CBI_{t-1}$	0.043
	(0.027)

Notes
OLS estimates with panel-corrected standard errors in parentheses.
Only the results of the relevant variables are shown.
***Significant at the 0.01 level.
**Significant at the 0.05 level.
*Significant at the 0.10 level.

Table 5.17a Predicted values of total government spending

	1982–2001	*Dependent central banks (CBI = 0.14)*	*Independent central banks (CBI = 0.68)*
Center governments	Center = 0	−0.18	−0.91
(cabinet portfolios, %)	Center = 50	−0.95	−0.51
	Center = 100	−1.72	−0.11

Notes
Predicted values of total government spending calculated from the results in Table 5.17. Only the vertical differences in the *CBI* = 0.14 column are statistically significant. The significance levels for other differences are 0.12 for the horizontal differences in the *Center* = 100 row, 0.19 for the *Center* = 0 row, and 0.21 for the vertical ones in the *CBI* = 0.68 column.

recorded under fully center governments with independent central banks, and the lowest by the same governments with dependent central banks. (Only the vertical differences in the *CBI* = 0.14 column are statistically significant. The results should be viewed with caution. The significance levels for other differences are 0.12 for the horizontal differences in the *Center* = 100 row, 0.19 for the *Center* = 0 row, and 0.21 for the vertical ones in the *CBI* = 0.68 column.)

High total spending by center governments facing independent central banks, however, does not indicate fiscal indiscipline, because they had the highest fiscal balance (more surplus or less deficit) of all combinations of partisan governments and central banks throughout the periods under study. As we have seen above, this is because their spending was funded by sufficiently high tax revenues. The results of the analysis of inflation below also indirectly indicate that center governments' fiscal spending under independent central banks did not create inflationary pressures, since they achieved the lowest level of inflation among all combinations of partisan governments and central banks during the entire period of 1961–2001. There is no evidence that center governments created high total expenditures during any other periods in interaction with central banks.

Total government tax revenues

Center governments under independent central banks seemed to produce high total tax revenues in the 1960s and 1970s to finance their high spending. Table 5.18a reports the predicted values of total government revenues for 1961–1981 (without country dummies). (The results should be viewed with caution since the differences among the cells are significant only in the vertical differences in the CBI = 0.14 column and horizontal difference in the *Center* = 0 row. The *p*-value for the differences in the CBI = 0.68 column is only 0.20.) Center governments with independent central banks had the second highest total tax revenues of all combinations of partisan governments and central banks. Under independent central banks, center governments contributed to higher revenues. Under dependent central banks, they contributed to lower revenues. As a result, the highest revenues were recorded by

Table 5.18 Total government tax revenues: regression results

1961–1981 (without country dummies)	
CBI_{t-1}	−1.597*
	(0.851)
$Center_{t-1}$	−0.013*
	(0.007)
$Center_{t-1} * CBI_{t-1}$	0.027**
	(0.014)

Notes
OLS estimates with panel-corrected standard errors in parentheses.
Only the results of the relevant variables are shown.
***Significant at the 0.01 level.
**Significant at the 0.05 level.
*Significant at the 0.10 level.

Table 5.18a Predicted values of total government tax revenues

	1961–1981	Dependent central banks (CBI = 0.14)	Independent central banks (CBI = 0.68)
Center governments	Center = 0	−0.22	−1.08
(cabinet portfolios, %)	Center = 50	−0.70	−0.84
	Center = 100	−1.19	−0.61

Notes
Predicted values of total government tax revenues calculated from the results in Table 5.18. The differences among the cells are significant only in the vertical differences in the *CBI* = 0.14 column and horizontal difference in the *Center* = 0 row. The *p*-value for the differences in the *CBI* = 0.68 column is only 0.20.

non-center governments with dependent central banks (*Center* = 0, *CBI* = 0.14). The lowest revenues were registered by fully center governments with dependent central banks. These low revenues are a sign of fiscal indiscipline – as we will see below, center governments with dependent central banks recorded the lowest fiscal balance (highest deficit) of all combinations of partisan governments and central banks during the same period. This indicates that they were unable to raise enough revenues to fund their spending when central banks were not independent.[9] Independent central banks, in contrast, placed discipline on center governments' fiscal policy in such a way that the latter raised sufficient revenues to finance their spending and not to produce deficit. No significant effect of the interaction of center governments and central banks was detected for any other period.

Fiscal balance

The combination of center governments and independent central banks produced very favorable outcomes in the fiscal balance. Table 5.19a reports the predicted values of the fiscal balance (cyclically adjusted) for the entire period of 1961–2001, conditional on center cabinet portfolios and central banks (fixed

Table 5.19 Fiscal balance: regression results

1961–2001 (fixed effects)	
CBI_{t-1}	0.064
	(1.235)
$Center_{t-1}$	−0.032***
	(0.012)
$Center_{t-1} * CBI_{t-1}$	0.071***
	(0.023)

Notes
OLS estimates with panel-corrected standard errors in parentheses.
Only the results of the relevant variables are shown.
***Significant at the 0.01 level.
**Significant at the 0.05 level.
*Significant at the 0.10 level.

Table 5.19a Predicted values of the fiscal balance

	1961–2001	Dependent central banks (CBI = 0.14)	Independent central banks (CBI = 0.68)
Center governments (cabinet portfolios, %)	Center = 0	0.008	0.04
	Center = 50	−1.10	0.83
	Center = 100	−2.21	1.63

Notes
Predicted values of the fiscal balance calculated from the results in Table 5.19. All differences among the cells are significant, except for the horizontal difference in the *Center* = 0 row.

effects). The same results are also obtained for the first (1961–1981) and second (1982–2001), and the results are robust to the inclusion and exclusion of country dummies. Since the results are robust, I only report the results for the entire period.

The results show that fully center governments (*Center* = 100) achieved the highest fiscal balance (highest surplus or lowest deficit) of all combinations of partisan governments and central banks, when they had independent central banks (*CBI* = 0.68), and the lowest balance under dependent central banks (*CBI* = 0.14). Thus, independent central banks helped center governments achieve fiscal discipline. Independent central banks also improved the fiscal balance of non-center governments (*Center* = 0) and half-center governments (*Center* = 50), but the beneficial effects were the largest when governments were fully centrist (*Center* = 100). When central banks were independent, center governments' fiscal balance was 3.84 percent of potential GDP better than when central banks were not independent. Thus, we can see that although center governments facing independent central banks had high spending levels (particularly during 1982–2001), their overall fiscal policy was disciplined, as they did not create fiscal deficit. The results show that fully center governments' fiscal balance sharply deteriorated if they did not have independent central banks, suggesting that without independent central banks, center governments were indeed fiscally undisciplined. (All differences among the cells are significant, except for the horizontal difference in the *Center* = 0 row.)

In contrast to center governments that benefited from independent central banks, right governments suffered large fiscal deficit when facing independent central banks, as we will see later. This is another of many indications observed in the empirical analysis that the combination of right governments and independent central banks produced negative outcomes in economic policy and performance. The fiscal balance of left governments facing different central banks does not show any significant result.

Economic growth

No impact of the combination of center governments and central banks on economic growth is detected for the second period of 1982–2001. But for the first period (1961–1981), we have some evidence that they jointly had very favorable effects on output growth. Table 5.20a shows the predicted values of economic growth under different combinations of center governments and central banks for 1961–1981 (without country dummies). (The differences among the cells are statistically significant, except for the vertical differences in the *CBI* = 0.14 column and the horizontal differences in the *Center* = 50 and 100.) Center governments achieved higher economic growth when central banks were independent than dependent. Their growth rate was, in fact, the highest of all combinations, when central banks were independent (*CBI* = 0.68). Thus, the combination of center governments and independent central banks was conducive to economic growth.[10] Center governments' growth

Table 5.20 Economic growth (GDP): regression results

1961–1981 (without country dummies)

CBI_{t-1}	−3.138***
	(1.190)
$Center_{t-1}$	−0.00882
	(0.01041)
$Center_{t-1} * CBI_{t-1}$	0.045**
	(0.022)

Notes
OLS estimates with panel-corrected standard errors in parentheses.
Only the results of the relevant variables are shown.
***Significant at the 0.01 level.
**Significant at the 0.05 level.
*Significant at the 0.10 level.

Table 5.20a Predicted values of economic growth (GDP)

	1961–1981	Dependent central banks (CBI = 0.14)	Independent central banks (CBI = 0.68)
Center governments	Center = 0	−0.43	−2.13
(cabinet portfolios, %)	Center = 50	−0.56	−1.04
	Center = 100	−0.69	0.03

Notes
Predicted values of economic growth calculated from the results in Table 5.20. The differences among the cells are statistically significant, except for the vertical differences in the *CBI* = 0.14 column and the horizontal differences in the *Center* = 50 and 100.

under independent central banks was 0.7 percent higher than under dependent central banks. Central bank independence generally had a negative impact on economic growth (this was also what we observed in its individual effect in Chapter 4), but at a high level of center cabinet portfolios, it had a positive effect on economic growth. Center governments contributed to higher growth when central banks were independent, but to lower growth if central banks were dependent. Under independent central banks, fully center governments (*Center* = 100) achieved 2.16 percent higher economic growth than non-center governments (*Center* = 0). In contrast, economic growth for "non-center governments" (*Center* = 0) was the lowest of all, if central banks were independent. When we examine the interactive impact of left and right governments with central banks later in the chapter, we will observe that these "non-center governments" were actually left governments (see below). Left governments suffered the lowest growth rates when facing independent central banks during 1961–1981.

Inflation

There is the evidence that center governments and independent central banks jointly had a beneficial effect on price stability. Table 5.21a reports the predicted values of inflation at different levels of center cabinet portfolios and central banks for the entire period of 1961–2001 (without country dummies). Fully center governments (*Center* = 100) in the presence of independent central banks (*CBI* = 0.68) achieved the lowest rate of inflation of all combinations of partisan governments and central banks. If they had dependent central banks (*CBI* = 0.14), however, center governments suffered the highest inflation. Center governments' inflation rate under independent central banks (*CBI* = 0.68) was 1.4 percent lower than under dependent central banks (*CBI* = 0.14). Thus, independent central banks helped center governments maintain low inflation, while center governments were unable to keep inflation low if central banks were not independent. This is another piece of evidence that center governments performed poorly in the absence of independent central banks (the highest deficit),

Table 5.21 Inflation: regression results

1961–2001 (without country dummies)	
CBI_{t-1}	0.708
	(0.812)
$Center_{t-1}$	0.017**
	(0.008)
$Center_{t-1} * CBI_{t-1}$	−0.034**
	(0.016)

Notes
OLS estimates with panel-corrected standard errors in parentheses.
Only the results of the relevant variables are shown.
***Significant at the 0.01 level.
**Significant at the 0.05 level.
*Significant at the 0.10 level.

Table 5.21a Predicted values of inflation

	1961–2001	Dependent central banks (CBI = 0.14)	Independent central banks (CBI = 0.68)
Center governments	Center = 0	0.09	0.48
(cabinet portfolios, %)	Center = 50	0.68	0.15
	Center = 100	1.27	−0.16

Notes
Predicted values of inflation calculated from the results in Table 5.21. The vertical differences among the cells in the *CBI* = 0.14 column and the horizontal difference in the *Center* = 100 row are statistically significant. The significance level for the vertical differences in the *CBI* = 0.68 column is 0.12, and it is 0.14 for the horizontal difference in the *Center* = 50 row.

but achieved economic discipline and good economic outcomes in their presence. Independent central banks lowered inflation at medium to high levels of
center cabinet portfolios. Center governments contributed to low inflation when
central banks were independent, but to high inflation if central banks were
dependent. (The vertical differences among the cells in the *CBI* = 0.14 column
and the horizontal difference in the *Center* = 100 row are statistically significant.
The significance level for the vertical differences in the *CBI* = 0.68 column is
0.12, and it is 0.14 for the horizontal difference in the *Center* = 50 row.)

Sum

Center governments had an incentive to seek to achieve fiscal discipline and
improve economic performance by conducting a fiscal policy along the lines of
policy prescriptions by central banks and/or compatible with central banks'
monetary policy. In order to attract mobile capital and promote economic competitiveness and growth, they needed to show their commitment to price stability
and restrain fiscal policy. The evidence here shows that the combination of
center governments and independent central banks was conducive to fiscal
discipline and good economic outcomes. Though their spending was expansionary, their overall fiscal policy was not expansionary, as they achieved a very
favorable fiscal balance (higher surplus or lower deficit).

Center governments' fiscal discipline under independent central banks was
probably conducive to good economic outcomes (very high economic growth
during 1961–1981 and very low inflation during 1961–2001), as it allowed them
to avoid negative economic consequences of fiscal indiscipline, such as inflation,
high interest rates, and low savings, which depress investment and growth. Inflation (caused by deficits or otherwise) can create price distortions, resource allocation inefficiency, and economic uncertainties, which impair investment and
growth. Government deficits also drain resources from the private economy.
Fiscal discipline helps governments avoid or mitigate these problems.

Furthermore, since center governments' fiscal policy was disciplined when
central banks were independent, central banks did not have to employ a tight
monetary policy (the empirical results show that the interaction of center governments and central banks did not place upward or downward pressure on monetary policy). As a result, center governments did not have to suffer the
disinflationary consequences of a tight monetary policy, which would otherwise
depress economic growth and employment. Low inflation by center governments under independent central banks also did not come at the cost of high
unemployment (the interaction did not have positive or negative effects on
unemployment).

In contrast, when center governments only had dependent central banks, they
produced the highest levels of fiscal deficit and inflation. They were unable to
discipline their fiscal policy in the absence of independent central banks and
created the highest deficit. They also failed to contain inflation. Fiscal indiscipline and inflation kept them from attaining high economic growth.

We did not find any evidence that center governments and central banks jointly affected monetary policy. My policy mix argument expects that center governments would need to employ a tight monetary policy to mitigate inflationary pressures from their expansionary fiscal policy and control inflation in the absence of independent central banks. But the evidence suggests that they did not use a tight monetary policy even in the face of the expansionary fiscal policy. As a result, they suffered the highest inflation when central banks were not independent.

The findings also show some limits of the economic discipline that independent central banks can bring in party governments' fiscal policy. While center governments successfully reduced deficit under independent central banks, they were not successful in reducing their fiscal spending in the 1980s and 1990s, due to their large fiscal commitments in social security and government services. As the retrenchment of these commitments was politically difficult, they reduced deficit and debt by keeping high tax revenues.

While central bank independence improved center governments' economic policy and outcomes, it exerted unfavorable effects on right governments' inflation, as we will see later in the chapter – right governments recorded the highest inflation under independent central banks. The combination of right governments and independent central banks was generally unconducive to economic management, against the findings of a previous study (Way, 2000).

Left governments and central banks

Economic globalization and attendant changes in the international and domestic economies put competitive pressure on left governments (as on center governments) to shift economic policy in a market-conforming direction in the 1980s and 1990s. In order to attract mobile capital and promote economic competitiveness and growth, left governments needed to show their commitment to price stability, restrain fiscal policy, and restructure the welfare system to reduce labor costs and curb welfare spending. Thus, just like center governments, left governments had an incentive to seek to achieve fiscal discipline and improve economic performance by granting independence to central banks (Bernhard, 2002), gaining antiinflationary credibility, and implementing a fiscal policy along the lines of policy prescriptions by central banks and/or compatible with central banks' monetary policy.

Left governments, as with center governments, also faced more potential sources of policy conflict (than the conservative governments), because the distance was large between their traditional interventionist policy and the neoliberal policy toward which they needed to shift their policy. They had to move their economic policy farther away from their traditional positions toward the right to make their policy more market-conforming. This potential for policy conflict led them to seek to make a market-conforming policy shift by delegating monetary policy to central banks (Bernhard, 2002). They used independent central banks to make a neoliberal policy shift and fiscal austerity palatable to their pro-intervention and pro-welfare constituencies.

We should expect that left governments were better able to achieve fiscal discipline and relatively good economic outcomes in the 1980s and 1990s when they had independent central banks, because they were more willing, and had the incentive, to conduct a fiscal policy compatible with policy prescriptions by central banks. So, they should be better able to craft a favorable fiscal–monetary policy mix when central banks were independent. If central banks were not independent, in contrast, left governments should have more difficulty maintaining fiscal discipline in the 1980s and 1990s.

What does the empirical evidence tell us?

To preview the results, the following is a summary of my findings. In the 1960s and 1970s, left governments' fiscal spending, when they faced independent central banks, was generally expansionary. Left governments also experienced a tight monetary policy during the entire period of 1961–2001, when central banks were independent. Thus, during the 1960s and 1970s, the combination of left governments and independent central banks produced the outcome of a loose fiscal–tight monetary policy mix, an outcome expected by economists' game-theoretic models (Nordhaus, 1994; Bennett and Loayza, 2002; Demertzis *et al.*, 1998; Dixit and Lambertini, 2002). These economists explain that the policy preferences of party governments (not just leftist, but all party governments) and central banks clash and it leads to an expansionary fiscal policy by party governments that try to counter the tight monetary policy by independent central banks that seek to counteract the governments' inflationary fiscal policy to control inflation. Central banks and party governments, their explanation goes, use their policy instruments to counter each other's policy action – central banks raise interest rates to maintain price stability and to offset party governments' expansionary fiscal policy. Party governments increase their fiscal spending to boost output and employment even at the expense of higher inflation and to counter central banks' deflationary monetary policy, resulting in high deficits. This policy conflict intensifies when party governments are left-leaning, because their policy preferences and the monetary authority's positions diverge more than those of right governments and central banks, resulting in more undesirable outcomes.

My empirical results for the 1960s and 1970s presented below, thus, give some support to these economists' explanation, as left governments implemented a relatively expansionary fiscal policy during the 1960s and 1970s, and independent central banks conducted a tight monetary policy. There is also the evidence that this combination of the two policy makers or their policies produced negative outcomes in economic growth during the same period.

Yet, my analysis of the more recent 1980s and 1990s produces different results that run counter to this policy conflict explanation. Left governments' fiscal policy under independent central banks made a conservative shift (low spending) in the 1980s and 1990s and became more disciplined. The policy positions of left governments and central banks became more compatible in the last two decades, and their negative effect on economic growth also disappeared in the 1980s and 1990s.

But the beneficial economic effects of central bank independence on left governments' policy and outcomes were not as strong or as extensive as on center or coalition governments. We do observe the similar trends in left governments' policy and performance that center and coalition governments experienced. But the strength of the trends was weaker for left governments. The reason for this pattern may be that left governments' fiscal policy was more conservative, to begin with, as shown by recent studies (e.g. Boix, 1998; Sakamoto, 2003), than originally suggested by the conventional partisan theory. As a result, left governments may not have received as large economic discipline benefits from independent central banks as center or coalition governments did, because the former's fiscal policy was more restrained than the latter's in the first place.

Another reason may be that although left governments' economic policy generally experienced a neoliberal shift in the 1980s and 1990s, the growth strategy they chose (particularly in Nordic countries) was also different from that pursued by conservative or Christian democratic governments elsewhere. Instead of simply deregulating and liberalizing to leave economic decisions and resource allocation to market forces, social democratic governments have chosen to promote actively economic growth by making public investments in human capital formation (e.g. education, active labor market policy, job (re)training) and knowledge-intensive industries to facilitate technological advances and enhance the competitiveness and productivity of their economies and workers. Thus, while they have capitalized on the economic benefits of neoliberal market-conforming policy in the 1980s and 1990s, they have also consciously chosen to maintain a constructive role for government policy to play in the economy to promote economic growth; thus, less dramatic reductions in the size of government.

Meanwhile, when central banks were not independent, left governments showed different policy behavior. For instance, during the 1960s and 1970s, when central banks were not independent, left governments did not use an expansionary fiscal policy, probably since they retained control over monetary policy and could use an expansionary monetary policy as a countercyclical tool. The evidence suggests that left governments under dependent central banks conducted an expansionary monetary policy, but their fiscal policy was disciplined in the 1960s and 1970s. So they had a tight fiscal–loose monetary policy during the period, and achieved high economic growth in the absence of independent central banks.

Yet this pattern became reversed in the 1980s and 1990s. The fiscal policy by left governments under dependent central banks became expansionary. It shows that the policy positions and policy mix pursued by left governments and dependent central banks were not compatible in the 1980s and 1990s, and that left governments were unable to restrain their spending in the absence of independent central banks.

Government non-wage consumption expenditure

Table 5.22a reports the predicted values of government non-wage consumption for the first period of 1961–1981, conditional on left cabinet portfolios and central

Table 5.22 Government non-wage consumption expenditures: regression results

1961–1981 (fixed effects)	
CBI_{t-1}	0.985
	(0.754)
$Left_{t-1} * CBI_{t-1}$	0.00820**
	(0.00414)
$Left_{t-1}$	−0.00229
	(0.00188)

Notes
OLS estimates with panel-corrected standard errors in parentheses.
Only the results of the relevant variables are shown.
***Significant at the 0.01 level.
**Significant at the 0.05 level.
*Significant at the 0.10 level.

Table 5.22a Predicted values of government non-wage consumption

	1961–1981	Dependent central banks (CBI = 0.14)	Independent central banks (CBI = 0.68)
Left governments	Left = 0	0.13	0.66
(cabinet portfolios, %)	Left = 50	0.08	0.83
	Left = 100	0.02	0.99

Notes
Predicted values of government non-wage consumption calculated from the results in Table 5.22. The differences among the cells are statistically significant, except for the vertical differences in the CBI = 0.14 column and the horizontal one in the Left = 0 row.

bank independence (fixed effects). The results show that fully left governments under independent central banks had the highest spending of all combinations of partisan governments and central banks during the period (*Left* = 100, *CBI* = 0.68). Independent central banks pushed up spending at all levels of left cabinet portfolios. Meanwhile, left governments contributed to higher spending with independent central banks, and to lower spending with dependent central banks. The lowest spending was recorded by left governments under dependent central banks. During the 1960s and 1970s, left governments under dependent central banks generally conducted a tight fiscal policy. This is probably because when central banks were not independent, left governments did not have to rely on fiscal policy for countercyclical economic stimulus because they could use monetary policy for that goal. They indeed had an expansionary monetary policy during the period, as we will see below. The results also show that large public services spending by left governments assumed by standard partisan theory is contingent on central bank independence, and left governments actually had low spending levels in the 1960s and 1970s, if central banks were not independent.

When central banks were independent (*CBI* = 0.68), fully left governments had 0.97 percent of GDP higher (13 percent of total non-wage consumption higher) spending than when central banks were not independent. Left governments' fiscal policy in this category was expansionary when they faced independent central banks. This result shows that during the 1960s and 1970s, left governments and independent central banks produced the outcome of an expansionary fiscal policy as expected by economists' game-theoretic models. It supports the argument that during those two decades, the policy preferences of left governments and independent central banks conflicted with each other, and it led left governments to pursue an expansionary fiscal policy to counter a restrictive monetary policy by central banks. Since the combination of left governments and independent central banks induced a tight monetary policy by the latter, as we will see below, it lends support to the argument that the policy preferences of left governments and independent central banks clashed in the 1960s and 1970s and led to a loose fiscal–tight monetary policy mix. (The differences among the cells are statistically significant, except for the vertical differences in the *CBI* = 0.14 column and the horizontal one in the *Left* = 0 row.)

In the 1980s and 1990s, however, there is some possibility that there was a policy shift in left governments' non-wage consumption. Table 5.23a shows the predicted values of non-wage consumption for the second period of 1982–2001 (fixed effects). No differences among the cells are statistically significant (the vertical differences in the *CBI* = 0.14 column are not too far from significance (p = 0.12)). But if these results are to be trusted, they suggest that during this recent period, the combination of left governments and independent central banks led to low spending, and the combination of the left and dependent central banks to high spending, the opposite results from the 1960s and 1970s. Or at the least, we can conclude that the combination of left governments and independent central banks no longer caused high spending in non-wage consumption in the 1980s and 1990s, as there is no statistically significant result to suggest their continued high spending.

Table 5.23 Government non-wage consumption expenditures: regression results

1982–2001 (fixed effects)	
CBI_{t-1}	0.183
	(0.276)
$Left_{t-1} * CBI_{t-1}$	−0.00488
	(0.00313)
$Left_{t-1}$	0.00226
	(0.00140)

Notes
OLS estimates with panel-corrected standard errors in parentheses.
Only the results of the relevant variables are shown.
***Significant at the 0.01 level.
**Significant at the 0.05 level.
*Significant at the 0.10 level.

Table 5.23a Predicted values of government non-wage consumption

	1982–2001	*Dependent central banks (CBI = 0.14)*	*Independent central banks (CBI = 0.68)*
Left governments	Left = 0	0.02	0.12
(cabinet portfolios, %)	Left = 50	0.10	0.07
	Left = 100	0.18	0.01

Notes
Predicted values of government non-wage consumption calculated from the results in Table 5.23. No differences among the cells are statistically significant (the vertical differences in the *CBI* = 0.14 column are not too far from significance ($p = 0.12$)).

If these were the only results suggesting a possible change in left governments' economic policy, I would not put trust in them. But the same pattern (a conservative fiscal policy under left governments and independent central banks in the 1980s and 1990s) is observed also for government subsidies and social security transfers. In addition, the results of the analysis of the interaction between center governments and central banks and between right governments and central banks show that left governments had very low spending under independent central banks in the 1980s and 1990s (see previous parts of the chapter). It suggests that there was a shift in left governments' fiscal policy under independent central banks in the 1980s and 1990s, and their policy preferences became more compatible with each other.

Government subsidies to industries

Table 5.24a reports the predicted values of government subsidies to industries, conditional upon left cabinet portfolios and central bank independence, during the entire period of 1961–2001 (without country dummies). The results suggest that left governments contributed to higher spending under dependent central banks, but to lower spending under independent central banks. Independent central banks thus restrained fully left governments' spending on subsidies. Fully left governments had relatively high spending when central banks were not independent, but they achieved the lowest spending of all combinations when central banks were independent. The same results are obtained also for the 1980s and 1990s (both with and without country dummies). The significant effects observed for the entire period are likely to come from those for the 1980s and 1990s because we do not detect any effect for the 1960s and 1970s. If this is the case, it is an indication that left governments' spending was restrained in the 1980s and 1990s when they had independent central banks. (The differences among the cells are significant only in the vertical differences in the *CBI* = 0.68 column and the horizontal difference in the *Left* = 0 row. The significance level is 0.12 for the vertical differences in the *CBI* = 0.14, and 0.15 for the horizontal difference in the *Left* = 100 row.)

Table 5.24 Government subsidies to industries: regression results

1961–2001 (without country dummies)	
CBI_{t-1}	0.205*
	(0.114)
$Left_{t-1} * CBI_{t-1}$	−0.00407**
	(0.00188)
$Left_{t-1}$	0.00142*
	(0.00078)

Notes
OLS estimates with panel-corrected standard errors in parentheses.
Only the results of the relevant variables are shown.
***Significant at the 0.01 level.
**Significant at the 0.05 level.
*Significant at the 0.10 level.

Table 5.24a Predicted values of government subsidies to industries

	1961–2001	*Dependent central banks (CBI = 0.14)*	*Independent central banks (CBI = 0.68)*
Left governments	Left = 0	0.02	0.13
(cabinet portfolios, %)	Left = 50	0.07	0.07
	Left = 100	0.11	0.004

Notes
Predicted values of government subsidies calculated from the results in Table 5.24. The differences among the cells are significant only in the vertical differences in the $CBI = 0.68$ column and the horizontal difference in the $Left = 0$ row. The significance level is only 0.12 for the vertical differences in the $CBI = 0.14$, and only 0.15 for the horizontal difference in the $Left = 100$ row.

When central banks were independent, left governments' spending was about 0.11 percent of GDP lower (5.5 percent of total public subsidies lower) than when central banks were not independent. Meanwhile, "non-left governments" (*Left* = 0) had the highest spending under independent central banks (*CBI* = 0.68). (These "non-left governments" were center governments that had high spending under independent central banks. See previously about center governments.)

Social security transfers paid by government

Table 5.25a reports the predicted values of social security transfers, conditional on left partisanship and central bank independence, for the second period of 1982–2001 (without country dummies). The results show the same pattern as governments subsidies. Left governments contributed to high spending when central banks were dependent, but to low spending when central banks were independent. As a result, fully left governments under independent central banks achieved the

Table 5.25 Social security transfers: regression results

1982–2001 (without country dummies)

CBI_{t-1}	0.620*
	(0.324)
$Left_{t-1} * CBI_{t-1}$	−0.012*
	(0.006)
$Left_{t-1}$	0.00403*
	(0.00227)

Notes
OLS estimates with panel-corrected standard errors in parentheses.
Only the results of the relevant variables are shown.
***Significant at the 0.01 level.
**Significant at the 0.05 level.
*Significant at the 0.10 level.

Table 5.25a Predicted values of social security transfers

	1982–2001	*Dependent central banks (CBI = 0.14)*	*Independent central banks (CBI = 0.68)*
Left governments	Left = 0	0.08	0.42
(cabinet portfolios, %)	Left = 50	0.20	0.23
	Left = 100	0.32	0.04

Notes
Predicted values of social security transfers calculated from the results in Table 5.25. The differences among the cells are significant, except for the horizontal differences in the *Left* = 50 and 100 rows.

lowest spending of all combinations. Their spending was 0.28 percent of GDP lower (2.3 percent of total social security spending lower) than when central banks were not independent. This result shows that left governments' social security spending was restrained in the 1980s and 1990s when they had independent central banks (as in the results for government subsidies), providing another piece of evidence that left governments' fiscal policy became conservative in the 1980s and 1990s under independent central banks. In contrast, they had expansionary spending when central banks were dependent. (The differences among the cells are significant, except for the horizontal differences in the *Left* = 50 and 100 rows.)

The highest spending was registered by "non-left governments" (*Left* = 0) under independent central banks. The non-left governments were actually center governments, as they had the highest spending under independent central banks during the 1980s and 1990s (see earlier in the chapter).

The findings here show another important result. The conventional wisdom in the welfare state literature claims that left governments have high social security spending, although not as high as Christian democratic governments (center), with conservative (right) governments having the lowest spending. But the results here suggest that if left governments had independent central banks, their social security spending in the 1980s and 1990s was actually the lowest of all partisan governments – lower than center governments because the center had the highest spending under independent central banks (see earlier), and lower than right governments because the right did not have any effect on spending (not higher or lower than the others: see the next part of the chapter). Thus, first, partisan governments' social security spending is contingent on the independence of central banks, and second, the conventional understanding that conservative governments have the lowest social security spending is not correct, at least for the 1980s and 1990s, when central banks are also taken into account. In Chapter 4, we also saw that even if only the individual effects of partisan governments are examined, right governments' social security spending was not lower than the left or center.

Government employment

Table 5.26a reports the predicted values of government employment (as a percentage of total employment) for the entire period of 1961–2001, conditional on left partisanship and central bank independence (without country dummies). The results show that independent central banks restrained left governments' public employment as well. Fully left governments' public employment under independent central banks was 0.22 percent lower (1.3 percent of total public employment lower) than when central banks were dependent. Under dependent central banks, left governments contributed to higher public employment, and to lower public employment under independent central banks. As a result, the highest public employment ratio was experienced by fully left governments under dependent central banks, as consistent with the conventional explanation that left governments create large public employment and are expansionary. However, the results show that left governments had high public employment

Table 5.26 Government employment: regression results

1961–2001 (without country dummies)	
CBI_{t-1}	0.187
	(0.140)
$Left_{t-1} * CBI_{t-1}$	−0.00603**
	(0.00272)
$Left_{t-1}$	0.00366***
	(0.00113)

Notes
OLS estimates with panel-corrected standard errors in parentheses.
Only the results of the relevant variables are shown.
***Significant at the 0.01 level.
**Significant at the 0.05 level.
*Significant at the 0.10 level.

Table 5.26a Predicted values of government employment

	1961–2001	*Dependent central banks (CBI = 0.14)*	*Independent central banks (CBI = 0.68)*
Left governments (cabinet portfolios, %)	Left = 0	0.02	0.12
	Left = 50	0.16	0.10
	Left = 100	0.30	0.08

Notes
Predicted values of government employment calculated from the results in Table 5.26. The differences among the cells are significant, except for the vertical differences in the *CBI* = 0.68 column and the horizontal ones in the *Left* = 0 and 50 rows.

only when their central banks were not independent. When central banks were independent, left governments were not expansionary. (The differences among the cells are significant, except for the vertical differences in the *CBI* = 0.68 column and the horizontal ones in the *Left* = 0 and 50 rows.)

Personal income tax

Table 5.27a reports the predicted values of personal income tax revenues for the entire period of 1961–2001, conditional upon left cabinet portfolios and central bank independence (fixed effects). We obtain the same results for the second period of 1982–2001 (with and without country dummies). The results show that central bank independence pushed up the tax revenues at all levels of left portfolios. This is to be expected from the results reviewed in Chapter 4 of the individual impact of central bank independence on personal income tax, where we saw that CBI led to higher personal income tax revenues during all periods. While all partisan governments' tax revenues (*Left* = 0, 50, 100) were higher when central banks were independent, left governments contributed to higher

Table 5.27 Personal income tax revenues: regression results

1961–2001 (fixed effects)	
CBI_{t-1}	1.284***
	(0.498)
$Left_{t-1} * CBI_{t-1}$	−0.00540
	(0.00543)
$Left_{t-1}$	0.00336
	(0.00213)

Notes
OLS estimates with panel-corrected standard errors in parentheses.
Only the results of the relevant variables are shown.
***Significant at the 0.01 level.
**Significant at the 0.05 level.
*Significant at the 0.10 level.

Table 5.27a Predicted values of personal income tax revenues

	1961–2001	*Dependent central banks (CBI = 0.14)*	*Independent central banks (CBI = 0.68)*
Left governments	Left = 0	0.17	0.87
(cabinet portfolios, %)	Left = 50	0.31	0.85
	Left = 100	0.44	0.84

Notes
Predicted values of personal income tax calculated from the results in Table 5.27. The differences among the cells are statistically significant, except for the vertical differences in the *CBI* = 0.68 column and the horizontal difference in the *Left* = 100 row.

revenues under dependent central banks (significant) and to lower revenues under independent central banks (not significant). In fact, when central banks were independent, government partisanship did not make much difference (the differences are small and statistically insignificant). The high revenues by left governments under dependent central banks were due partly to their need to finance their high spending toward the 1980s and 1990s. (The differences among the cells are statistically significant, except for the vertical differences in the *CBI* = 0.68 column and the horizontal difference in the *Left* = 100 row.)

The highest revenues were achieved by "non-left governments" (*Left* = 0) with independent central banks, and the lowest by the same governments under dependent central banks. But the revenues by left governments under independent central banks were also close to the highest. When we examine the interaction of central banks and right and center governments, we observe that these non-left governments here are right governments, though their interaction does not produce significant results in their own models that estimate their effects.

Corporate income tax

Table 5.28a reports the predicted values of corporate income tax revenues for the first period of 1961–1981, conditional on left governments and central banks (fixed effects). Left governments' revenues were the highest of all combinations of partisan governments and central banks, when central banks were independent. In contrast, their revenues were the lowest of all, when central banks were not independent. Under independent central banks, left partisanship contributed to higher tax revenues (and to lower revenues if central banks were dependent). An increase in left cabinet portfolios from 0 percent to 100 percent led to a jump in the revenues by 0.48 percent of GDP (17.9 percent of total corporate tax revenues), if central banks were independent. This is a substantively large revenue increase. On the other hand, when central banks were not independent, the same jump in left portfolios decreased the revenues by 0.44 percent of GDP (16.4 percent of total corporate tax revenues), likewise a substantial effect. These results are consistent with the patterns of their spending. During the 1960s and

Table 5.28 Corporate income tax revenues: regression results

1961–1981 (fixed effects)	
CBI_{t-1}	−0.757
	(1.321)
$Left_{t-1} * CBI_{t-1}$	0.017**
	(0.007)
$Left_{t-1}$	−0.00674***
	(0.00263)

Notes
OLS estimates with panel-corrected standard errors in parentheses.
Only the results of the relevant variables are shown.
***Significant at the 0.01 level.
**Significant at the 0.05 level.
*Significant at the 0.10 level.

Table 5.28a Predicted values of corporate income tax revenues

	1961–1981	*Dependent central banks (CBI = 0.14)*	*Independent central banks (CBI = 0.68)*
Left governments	Left = 0	−0.10	−0.51
(cabinet portfolios, %)	Left = 50	−0.32	−0.27
	Left = 100	−0.54	−0.03

Notes
Predicted values of corporate tax revenues calculated from the results in Table 5.28. All vertical differences among the cells are significant, but the horizontal differences are not.

1970s, left governments' spending was expansionary when they had independent central banks, and they needed larger tax revenues to finance their high spending. In contrast, left governments' spending under dependent central banks was conservative, so did not need to raise as high tax revenues. But these effects disappeared in the 1980s and 1990s. (All vertical differences among the cells are significant, but the horizontal differences are not.)

Total government expenditures

Table 5.29a shows the predicted values of total government disbursement for the first period of 1961–1981, conditional on left governments and central bank independence (without country dummies). Half of the differences among the cells are not statistically significant, so the evidence is not strong. But if the results are to be trusted, they indicate that the combination of left governments and independent central banks produced relatively high total spending in the 1960s and 1970s.[11] Each of the two factors had the effect of reducing total spending in the relative absence of the other (i.e. when the other variable has a low value), but together they pushed up spending.[12] This is one of the signs of a

Table 5.29 Total government spending: regression results

1961–1981 (without country dummies)	
CBI_{t-1}	−2.567**
	(1.248)
$Left_{t-1} * CBI_{t-1}$	0.029**
	(0.014)
$Left_{t-1}$	−0.00909
	(0.00594)

Notes
OLS estimates with panel-corrected standard errors in parentheses.
Only the results of the relevant variables are shown.
***Significant at the 0.01 level.
**Significant at the 0.05 level.
*Significant at the 0.10 level.

Table 5.29a Predicted values of total government spending

	1961–1981	Dependent central banks (CBI = 0.14)	Independent central banks (CBI = 0.68)
Left governments (cabinet portfolios, %)	Left = 0	−0.35	−1.74
	Left = 50	−0.61	−1.22
	Left = 100	−0.86	−0.69

Notes
Predicted values of total government spending calculated from the results in Table 5.29. The vertical differences among the cells in the *CBI* = 0.68 column and the horizontal difference in the *Left* = 0 row are significant, but nothing else is.

policy conflict between left governments' and central banks' economic policies during the 1960s and 1970s – when facing left governments, independent central banks implemented a relatively tight monetary policy to counter the left's expansionary spending, and left governments conducted an expansionary fiscal policy to counter the central banks' contractionary monetary policy. Left governments had lower total spending when they had only dependent central banks. This is probably because they did not have to rely on fiscal policy for economic expansion, as they could use monetary policy as a countercyclical tool in the absence of independent central banks. So they had a tight fiscal–loose monetary policy (left governments under dependent central banks conducted an expansionary monetary policy, but their fiscal policy was disciplined). (The vertical differences among the cells in the *CBI* = 0.68 column and the horizontal difference in the *Left* = 0 row are significant, but nothing else is.)

Monetary policy stance

Table 5.30a reports the predicted values of the monetary policy stance for the entire period of 1961–2001, conditional upon left partisanship and central banks

Table 5.30 Monetary policy: regression results

1961–2001 (fixed effects)	
CBI_{t-1}	−1.604
	(3.713)
$Left_{t-1} * CBI_{t-1}$	0.055*
	(0.030)
$Left_{t-1}$	−0.028**
	(0.012)

Notes
OLS estimates with panel-corrected standard errors in parentheses.
Only the results of the relevant variables are shown.
***Significant at the 0.01 level.
**Significant at the 0.05 level.
*Significant at the 0.10 level.

Table 5.30a Predicted values of monetary policy

	1961–2001	*Dependent central banks (CBI = 0.14)*	*Independent central banks (CBI = 0.68)*
Left governments	Left = 0	−0.22	−1.09
(cabinet portfolios, %)	Left = 50	−1.24	−0.62
	Left = 100	−2.26	−0.15

Notes
Predicted values of monetary policy calculated from the results in Table 5.30. Only the vertical differences in the $CBI = 0.14$ column are statistically significant, so the evidence is not strong.

(fixed effects). Only the vertical differences in the $CBI = 0.14$ column are statistically significant, so the evidence is not strong. But if the results are to be trusted, they show that fully left governments under independent central banks produced the tightest monetary policy (highest discount rates) of all combinations. This suggests that central banks may have tightened monetary policy to offset the left's expansionary policy (remember that left governments' fiscal policy was expansionary when they faced independent central banks in the 1960s and 1970s).

An increase in central bank independence generally served to tighten monetary policy unless left cabinet portfolios were low (*Left* = 0). When central banks were not independent, left governments produced a loose monetary policy, and fully left governments (*Left* = 100) recorded the loosest monetary policy under dependent central banks. This is probably because left governments retained monetary policy control under dependent central banks and preferred to use an expansionary monetary policy as a supply-side economic strategy to promote output growth (Boix, 1998; Huber and Stephens, 1998). Under independent central banks, however, left governments contributed to a tighter monetary policy, probably because independent central banks controlled monetary policy and they tried to contain inflationary pressure from an expansionary fiscal policy by left governments. Even if left governments wanted to create monetary expansions, they had more difficulty doing so because they did not control monetary policy under independent central banks. Thus, left governments exploited monetary policy when they had monetary policy control, but they could not when central banks were independent, in which case they resorted to an expansionary fiscal policy, instead; hence, their loose fiscal policy when central banks were independent. (In this case of monetary policy, the non-left governments (*Left* = 0) were right governments that had a loose monetary policy if central banks were independent, and a tight monetary policy when central banks were not independent, as we will see below.)

Economic growth

Table 5.31a reports the predicted values of economic growth for the first period of 1961–1981, conditional upon left governments and central bank independence (fixed effects). Fully left governments had the lowest output growth of all combinations of partisan governments and central banks when they had independent

Table 5.31 Economic growth (GDP): regression results

1961–1981 (fixed effects)	
CBI_{t-1}	−5.736
	(4.047)
$Left_{t-1} * CBI_{t-1}$	−0.074**
	(0.032)
$Left_{t-1}$	0.029**
	(0.012)

Notes
OLS estimates with panel-corrected standard errors in parentheses.
Only the results of the relevant variables are shown.
***Significant at the 0.01 level.
**Significant at the 0.05 level.
*Significant at the 0.10 level.

Table 5.31a Predicted values of economic growth (GDP)

	1961–1981	Dependent central banks (CBI = 0.14)	Independent central banks (CBI = 0.68)
Left governments (cabinet portfolios, %)	Left = 0	−0.80	−3.90
	Left = 50	0.11	−4.97
	Left = 100	1.03	−6.05

Notes
Predicted values of economic growth calculated from the results in Table 5.31. All differences among the cells are significant, except for the horizontal difference in the *Left* = 0 row where $p = 0.15$.

central banks, but the highest growth of all when their central banks were not independent. Left governments generated the highest economic growth, as long as central banks were not independent. According to these calculations, left governments' growth rate was 7 percent higher when central banks were dependent than independent. Central bank independence lowered output growth at all levels of left partisanship, but its negative effect was larger at higher levels of left cabinet portfolios. This suggests two things: first, central bank independence was generally unconducive to economic growth during the 1960s and 1970s, regardless of government partisanship; but, second, the negative effect was much larger for left governments, indicating some incompatibility of left governments and independent central banks for output growth. (All differences among the cells are significant, except for the horizontal difference in the *Left* = 0 row where $p = 0.15$.)

This type of incompatibility is consistent with the signs of policy clash between left governments and independent central banks observed for some economic policies for the same period. During the 1960s and 1970s, the combination of left governments and independent central banks led to a loose fiscal–tight monetary policy mix – the former conducted an expansionary fiscal policy to boost growth and employment and to counter a contractionary policy that the latter implemented to offset the inflationary pressures from the expansionary fiscal policy. The result suggests that this particular policy mix was unconducive to economic growth in the 1960s and 1970s. But such a negative impact on output growth disappears in the 1980s and 1990s – we do not detect any significant effect of their interaction on growth during the 1980s and 1990s. This suggests that the policies of left governments and central banks became more compatible in the 1980s and 1990s, and did not cause negative outcomes at least in economic growth.

Sum

The interactive effect of left governments and central banks on economic policy and outcomes was not as extensive or as strong as that of center governments and central banks. The difference suggests that center governments were more forthcoming in conducting fiscal policy compatible with central banks' monetary policy or their economic policy preferences in general than left governments, and that central bank independence benefited center governments more than the left. This probably results from center governments' general fiscal indiscipline when there were no constraints on their fiscal policy. My results show that center governments' fiscal policy was very expansionary in the absence of independent central banks, though it was very disciplined in their presence. Center governments were more fiscally undisciplined than left governments and had a greater incentive to bring fiscal discipline in their economic management and improve their economic performance. To achieve the goal, they were probably more willing than left ones to conduct a conservative fiscal policy along the lines of central banks' prescriptions or to coordinate economic policy with central banks and fashion a favorable fiscal–monetary policy mix.

Nevertheless, left governments' fiscal policy became disciplined in the 1980s and 1990s, when they had independent central banks, and their economic policy became one that was closer to the policy prescriptions by central banks. There is no evidence that left governments were fiscally expansionary in the recent two decades, when they had independent central banks. But they were unable to restrain their spending, when they lacked independent central banks that could put restraint on the former's spending policy.

Conservative governments and central banks

I explained in Chapter 2 that conservative (right) governments had a weaker incentive to use central bank independence to manage economic policy than center or left governments. They had less to gain from granting independence to central banks and following conservative economic policy prescriptions by central banks, since they had better antiinflationary credibility than left and center governments (even though, as I showed in the empirical analysis in Chapter 4, right governments were higher spenders than previously thought). The competitive pressure from the globalized economy and the resulting need for a neoliberal policy shift also did not pose as great obstacles to right governments as to the center or left governments that had pro-welfare interventionist constituencies. Thus, conservative governments had less incentive to conduct a fiscal policy compatible with a given monetary policy pursued by central banks.

I then explained that center and left governments can achieve fiscal discipline and good economic outcomes under independent central banks, because they have the willingness and incentive to conduct a fiscal policy compatible with a monetary policy pursued by central banks. They can, thus, craft a fiscal–monetary policy mix conducive to economic performance when central banks are independent. In contrast, the combination of right governments and independent central banks either does not produce positive results in fiscal discipline and economic outcomes or even may result in fiscal indiscipline and negative outcomes.

I also showed in Chapter 3 that conservative governments are more likely (than center or left governments) to be single-party majority governments, which can more easily implement a fiscal policy that conflicts with the policy preferences of central banks than coalition governments. This makes it difficult for central banks to conduct a monetary policy that would constitute a favorable fiscal–monetary policy mix, given the fiscal policy implemented by single-party governments. If conservative governments can pursue their own economic policies even by overriding central banks' policy preferences, they also have the greater potential and ability to act on their temptation for an expansionary fiscal policy, when central banks oppose it for inflationary concerns. As a result, the combination of conservative governments and independent central banks is likely to cause fiscal indiscipline and an unconducive policy mix (and potentially poor economic outcomes).

Here, I investigate the empirical validity of these assertions. To anticipate the findings, conservative governments, when they faced independent central banks, generated an expansionary fiscal policy, as indicated by their low fiscal balance (higher deficits or lower surpluses). They also potentially had an expansionary monetary policy. As a result of expansionary fiscal and monetary policies, conservative governments under independent central banks generated the highest inflation of all combinations of partisan governments and central banks. When they faced only dependent central banks, by contrast, their fiscal policy was very disciplined, and they achieved very low inflation.

Government non-wage consumption

There is some (though somewhat weak) evidence that right governments under independent central banks – a combination that, according to the standard partisan explanation, should produce a conservative fiscal policy – indeed had low non-wage consumption spending during the 1960s and 1970s, but produced very expansionary spending in the 1980s and 1990s. Table 5.32a shows the predicted values of government non-wage consumption during the first period of 1961–1981, conditional upon right partisanship and central bank independence

Table 5.32 Government non-wage consumption expenditures: regression results

1961–1981 (without country dummies)	
CBI_{t-1}	0.403*
	(0.228)
$Right_{t-1}$	0.00226
	(0.00142)
$Right_{t-1} * CBI_{t-1}$	−0.00727**
	(0.00354)

Notes
OLS estimates with panel-corrected standard errors in parentheses.
Only the results of the relevant variables are shown.
***Significant at the 0.01 level.
**Significant at the 0.05 level.
*Significant at the 0.10 level.

Table 5.32a Predicted values of government non-wage consumption

	1961–1981	Dependent central banks (CBI = 0.14)	Independent central banks (CBI = 0.68)
Right governments (cabinet portfolios, %)	Right = 0	0.05	0.27
	Right = 50	0.11	0.14
	Right = 100	0.18	0.005

Notes
Predicted values of government non-wage consumption calculated from the results in Table 5.32. The differences among the cells are significant only in the *CBI* = 0.68 column vertically and in the *Right* = 0 row horizontally, but not in the others.

(without country dummies). Not all differences among the cells are statistically significant, so the results should be viewed with caution. But if the results are to be trusted, right governments had the lowest spending of all combinations of partisan governments and central banks, when central banks were independent. Independent central banks restrained right governments' spending. Right governments, meanwhile, contributed to lower spending under independent central banks, and to higher spending under dependent central banks. As a result, right governments' spending was high when they had only dependent central banks. The highest spending was recorded by non-right governments under independent central banks (we previously learned that these non-right governments were left governments).

By contrast, during the second period of 1982–2001 (Table 5.33a, fixed effects), right governments had the highest spending level of all combinations of partisan governments and central banks, when central banks were independent. Independent central banks pushed up right governments' spending, and right partisanship contributed to higher spending under independent central banks, and to lower spending under dependent central banks – completely the opposite

Table 5.33 Government non-wage consumption expenditures: regression results

1982–2001 (fixed effects)	
CBI_{t-1}	−0.283
	(0.286)
$Right_{t-1}$	−0.00318*
	(0.00176)
$Right_{t-1} * CBI_{t-1}$	0.00855**
	(0.00411)

Notes
OLS estimates with panel-corrected standard errors in parentheses.
Only the results of the relevant variables are shown.
***Significant at the 0.01 level.
**Significant at the 0.05 level.
*Significant at the 0.10 level.

Table 5.33a Predicted values of government non-wage consumption

	1982–2001	*Dependent central banks (CBI = 0.14)*	*Independent central banks (CBI = 0.68)*
Right governments (cabinet portfolios, %)	Right = 0	−0.03	−0.19
	Right = 50	−0.13	−0.06
	Right = 100	−0.23	0.07

Notes
Predicted values of government non-wage consumption calculated from the results in Table 5.33. All vertical differences among the cells are significant. The horizontal difference in the *Right* = 100 row is close to significance (0.14), but the other horizontal differences are not significant.

pattern from the first period. As a result, right governments recorded the lowest spending of all combinations with dependent central banks, and the highest spending with independent central banks.[13] This marks a contrast to left governments reviewed previously that produced high non-wage consumption spending under independent central banks in the 1960s and 1970s, but very restrained spending in the 1980s and 1990s.

Low spending by right governments under dependent central banks takes place probably because with only dependent central banks, right governments did not necessarily have to employ an expansionary fiscal policy, as they controlled monetary policy and could use it for economic or electoral purposes. The results here, however, need to be viewed with caution, since the first-period results are obtained from a model without country dummies, and the second-period results with a fixed-effects model.

As we will see here, right governments' fiscal policy in the 1980s and 1990s when facing independent central banks was generally expansionary. This is contrary to the expectations of the standard partisan theory, and lends support to my argument that the economic policies of right governments and independent central banks conflicted with each other (at least during the 1980s and 1990s). As we saw in Chapter 4, when individual (uninteracted) effects are examined, right governments' fiscal policy was also more expansionary than the left or center in the 1980s and 1990s, regardless of central bank independence. (In the first-period results, the differences among the cells are significant only in the $CBI = 0.68$ column vertically and in the $Right = 0$ row horizontally, but not in the others. In the second-period results, all vertical differences among the cells are significant. The horizontal difference in the $Right = 100$ row is close to significance (0.14), but the other horizontal differences are not significant.)

Social security transfers paid by government

Table 5.34a reports the predicted values of social security transfers paid by government during the first period of 1961–1981, contingent upon right partisanship and central bank independence (fixed effects). The results show an interesting pattern. Fully right governments ($Right = 100$), when they had independent central banks, had the highest social security spending of all combinations of partisan governments and central banks in the 1960s and 1970s. This runs counter to the common wisdom in the literature on welfare spending and government partisanship that conservative (right) parties have the lowest welfare spending of all partisan governments, and that high social security transfers are recorded by Christian democratic governments and to a lesser extent by left governments. If one looks at only cross-national data (i.e. when time-series are collapsed and averaged or not taken into account), the pattern still holds true (see Appendix to Chapter 3). But the results here show that, first, partisan influence on social security spending was contingent on the independence of central banks that party governments faced (at least during the 1960s

Table 5.34 Social security transfers: regression results

1961–1981 (fixed effects)	
CBI_{t-1}	1.420
	(1.389)
$Right_{t-1}$	−0.00473
	(0.00368)
$Right_{t-1} * CBI_{t-1}$	0.017**
	(0.009)

Notes
OLS estimates with panel-corrected standard errors in parentheses.
Only the results of the relevant variables are shown.
***Significant at the 0.01 level.
**Significant at the 0.05 level.
*Significant at the 0.10 level.

Table 5.34a Predicted values of social security transfers

	1961–1981	Dependent central banks (CBI = 0.14)	Independent central banks (CBI = 0.68)
Right governments	Right = 0	0.19	0.96
(cabinet portfolios, %)	Right = 50	0.08	1.31
	Right = 100	−0.03	1.66

Notes
Predicted values of social security transfers calculated from the results in Table 5.34. The differences among the cells are statistically significant, except for the vertical differences in the *CBI* = 0.14 column and the horizontal difference in the *Right* = 0 row.

and 1970s). Second, when central banks were independent, conservative governments actually produced the highest level of social security transfers. Right governments contributed to higher spending under independent central banks. In contrast, when central banks were dependent (*CBI* = 0.14), they recorded the lowest spending, which is consistent with the welfare literature.[14] Interestingly, central bank independence contributed to higher spending at all levels of partisanship. (The differences among the cells are statistically significant, except for the vertical differences in the *CBI* = 0.14 column and the horizontal difference in the *Right* = 0 row.)

But this effect of conservative governments disappeared in the 1980s and 1990s. In the second period of 1982–2001, when central banks were independent, left governments recorded the lowest spending, and center governments the highest (see previously). But right governments did not exert a significant effect (meaning their spending was higher than the left's but lower than the center's).

Government employment

Table 5.35a reports the predicted values of government employment as a percentage of total employment for the entire period of 1961–2001, conditional upon right partisanship and central bank independence (without country dummies).[15] The results show that the combination of right governments and independent central banks created the largest public employment of all combinations of government partisanship and central bank independence. When central banks were independent, right partisanship contributed to higher public employment. When central banks were not independent, it contributed to lower public employment. As a result, public employment was the lowest when right governments faced dependent central banks. (The differences among the cells are statistically significant, except for the horizontal difference in the *Right* = 50 row where $p = 0.16$.)

This result is contrary to the conventional understanding in the welfare state literature that expects left governments to have large public employment, but not conservative governments. In fact, as we saw previously, left governments had very low public employment when they had independent central banks, while

Table 5.35 Government employment: regression results

1961–2001 (without country dummies)

CBI_{t-1}	−0.385***
	(0.150)
$Right_{t-1}$	−0.00502***
	(0.00120)
$Right_{t-1} * CBI_{t-1}$	0.011***
	(0.003)

Notes
OLS estimates with panel-corrected standard errors in parentheses.
Only the results of the relevant variables are shown.
***Significant at the 0.01 level.
**Significant at the 0.05 level.
*Significant at the 0.10 level.

Table 5.35a Predicted values of government employment

	1961–2001	*Dependent central banks (CBI = 0.14)*	*Independent central banks (CBI = 0.68)*
Right governments (cabinet portfolios, %)	Right = 0	−0.05	−0.26
	Right = 50	−0.22	−0.13
	Right = 100	−0.40	−0.01

Notes
Predicted values of government employment calculated from the results in Table 5.35. The differences among the cells are statistically significant, except for the horizontal difference in the *Right* = 50 row where $p = 0.16$.

they had the highest public employment when facing dependent central banks. Thus, as with non-wage consumption and social security transfers, the results of public employment indicate that, for one, the conventional explanation that the left has large and the right has small public employment is not accurate and, for another, the size of government employment depended not only on government partisanship but also on central bank independence. And importantly, conservative governments recorded the largest public employment when they faced independent central banks.

Corporate income tax

Table 5.36a reports the predicted values of corporate income tax revenues for the first period of 1961–1981, conditional on right partisanship and central bank independence (fixed effects). The pattern of the results here is more consistent with the conventional partisan thesis. Fully conservative governments (*Right =* 100) under independent central banks recorded the lowest revenues of all

Table 5.36 Corporate income tax revenues: regression results

1961–1981 (fixed effects)	
CBI_{t-1}	−0.965
	(1.051)
$Right_{t-1}$	0.00702**
	(0.00355)
$Right_{t-1} * CBI_{t-1}$	−0.016*
	(0.009)

Notes
OLS estimates with panel-corrected standard errors in parentheses.
Only the results of the relevant variables are shown.
***Significant at the 0.01 level.
**Significant at the 0.05 level.
*Significant at the 0.10 level.

Table 5.36a Predicted values of corporate income tax revenues

	1961–1981	*Dependent central banks (CBI = 0.14)*	*Independent central banks (CBI = 0.68)*
Right governments	Right = 0	−0.13	−0.65
(cabinet portfolios, %)	Right = 50	0.10	−0.84
	Right = 100	0.34	−1.02

Notes
Predicted values of corporate income tax revenues calculated from the results in Table 5.36. The differences among the cells are statistically significant, except for the vertical differences in the *CBI* = 0.68 column (*p*-value = 0.17), the horizontal one in the *Right* = 50 row (*p*-value = 0.12), and the horizontal one in the *Right* = 0 row.

combinations of partisan governments and central banks. The standard partisan thesis postulates that right governments (and central banks) have pro-market and anti-interventionist policy preferences and are more hospitable to business. In this view, thus, they should produce low tax revenues, particularly lower corporate tax revenues than left or center governments. The results partly conform to these expectations, and corporate tax by right governments in the 1960s and 1970s is one of only a few policy items that support the standard partisan thesis. Central bank independence reduced corporate tax revenues at all levels of right partisanship, but the downward effect was stronger at higher values of right partisanship.[16]

However, conformity is only partial because under dependent central banks, right governments contributed to high revenues and as a result, fully right governments under dependent central banks recorded the highest corporate tax revenues of all combinations of partisan governments and central banks, which is not consistent with the standard partisan thesis. Right governments did not necessarily have low corporate tax revenues across the board – their low revenues were conditional upon independent central banks.

As we saw previously, left governments recorded the highest corporate tax revenues in the 1960s and 1970s when central banks were independent, also consistent with the partisan thesis. But these effects entirely disappear in the 1980s and 1990s for all partisan governments. Therefore, in the 1980s and 1990s, conservative governments no longer had lower corporate tax revenues than the left or center, when considered with their interaction with central banks. And as we saw in Chapter 4, there is no evidence that conservative governments (without interaction) had lower corporate tax revenues than left or center governments. If anything, left governments had lower corporate tax revenues than the right or center in the 1980s and 1990s. These results thoroughly refute the view or assumption that conservative governments had low corporate tax revenues in the globalized economy of the 1980s and 1990s (when considered with or without central banks). (The differences among the cells are statistically significant, except for the vertical differences in the *CBI* = 0.68 column (*p*-value = 0.17), the horizontal one in the *Right* = 50 row (*p*-value = 0.12), and the horizontal one in the *Right* = 0 row.)

Fiscal balance

Table 5.37a reports the predicted values of the fiscal balance (+ surplus/– deficit) under the different combinations of partisan governments and central banks for the entire period of 1961–2001 (fixed effects).[17] The results show that right governments' fiscal policy was expansionary, when they faced independent central banks. Central bank independence improved all partisan governments' fiscal balance, except when party governments were fully right. Right governments contributed to a better fiscal balance, when central banks were not independent. But when central banks were independent, right governments' fiscal balance deteriorated significantly. As a result, fully right governments under independent central banks produced the second worst fiscal balance of all combinations of

Table 5.37 Fiscal balance: regression results

1961–2001 (fixed effects)	
CBI_{t-1}	3.493***
	(1.299)
$Right_{t-1}$	0.015**
	(0.008)
$Right_{t-1} * CBI_{t-1}$	−0.046***
	(0.018)

Notes
OLS estimates with panel-corrected standard errors in parentheses.
Only the results of the relevant variables are shown.
***Significant at the 0.01 level.
**Significant at the 0.05 level.
*Significant at the 0.10 level.

Table 5.37a Predicted values of the fiscal balance

	1961–2001	Dependent central banks (CBI = 0.14)	Independent central banks (CBI = 0.68)
Right governments	Right = 0	0.48	2.37
(cabinet portfolios, %)	Right = 50	0.92	1.58
	Right = 100	1.36	0.79

Notes
Predicted values of the fiscal balance calculated from the results in Table 5.37. The differences among the cells are significant, except for the horizontal differences in the *Right* = 50 and 100 rows.

partisan governments and central banks. The best fiscal balance was recorded by non-right governments under independent central banks, and the worst balance by non-right governments under dependent central banks. From our analysis of center and left governments previously, we know that these non-right governments were center governments that registered very favorable fiscal balances when facing independent central banks.

Thus, independent central banks restrained most partisan governments' fiscal policy, but they clashed with conservative governments and produced negative outcomes in the fiscal balance (larger deficits or smaller surplus). This lends support to my argument that the combination of right governments and independent central banks creates fiscal indiscipline and negative economic outcomes. (The differences among the cells are significant, except for the horizontal differences in the *Right* = 50 and 100 rows.)

Monetary policy stance

Table 5.38a presents the predicted values of the monetary policy stance for the entire period of 1961–2001, conditional on right partisanship and central bank

Table 5.38 Monetary policy: regression results

1961–2001 (fixed effects)	
CBI$_{t-1}$	1.961
	(4.026)
Right$_{t-1}$	0.032**
	(0.015)
Right$_{t-1}$ * CBI$_{t-1}$	−0.062*
	(0.034)

Notes
OLS estimates with panel-corrected standard errors in parentheses.
Only the results of the relevant variables are shown.
***Significant at the 0.01 level.
**Significant at the 0.05 level.
*Significant at the 0.10 level.

Table 5.38a Predicted values of monetary policy

	1961–2001	*Dependent central banks (CBI = 0.14)*	*Independent central banks (CBI = 0.68)*
Right governments	Right = 0	0.27	1.33
(cabinet portfolios, %)	Right = 50	1.46	0.84
	Right = 100	2.64	0.35

Notes
Predicted values of monetary policy calculated from the results in Table 5.38. Only the vertical differences in the *CBI* = 0.14 column are significant, so the evidence is weak.

independence (fixed effects). Only the vertical differences in the *CBI* = 0.14 column are significant, so the evidence is weak. But if the results are to be trusted, they suggest that the combination of right governments and independent central banks produced a loose (expansionary) monetary policy. The discount rate (cyclically adjusted) under fully right governments (*Right* = 100) was 2.3 percent lower (more expansionary) when they faced independent central banks than when facing dependent central banks. Fully right governments recorded the highest discount rate (least expansionary policy) under dependent central banks. The lowest rate (most expansionary monetary policy) was registered with non-right governments (*Right* = 0) under dependent central banks, and from previously, we know that these non-right governments were left governments. Central bank independence loosened monetary policy at higher levels of right cabinet portfolios. Right governments contributed to an expansionary monetary policy when central banks were independent, and to a tight monetary policy when central banks were dependent.[18]

As we have seen in the fiscal balance results (Table 5.37a), the combination of right governments and independent central banks led to an expansionary fiscal policy. Since the same combination also produced a loose monetary policy, it means that the combination of right governments and independent central banks created a loose fiscal–loose monetary policy mix, which might be appropriate during recessions, but might be too inflationary under other economic conditions. In fact, this expansionary policy mix matches the inflation record by right governments under independent central banks. As we will see next, right governments under independent central banks created the highest inflation of all combinations of partisan governments and central banks during the entire period of 1961–2001. It is reasonable to suspect that the high inflation was at least partly a result of their expansionary fiscal–monetary policy mix. By contrast, the combination of right governments and dependent central banks produced a tight fiscal–tight monetary policy mix, which resulted in the lowest inflation.

Inflation

The cost of the expansionary fiscal and monetary policies by right governments under independent central banks can be seen in their high inflation. Table 5.39a reports the predicted values of inflation for the entire period of 1961–2001 (without country dummies). Fully conservative governments (*Right* = 100) had the highest inflation of all combinations of partisan governments and central banks, when they faced independent central banks. In contrast, they achieved the lowest inflation of all, when they had dependent central banks. This is another area where we find relatively good economic outcomes by right governments if central banks were not independent. Right governments' inflation under independent central banks was 1.2 percent higher than under dependent central banks. Further, when central banks were independent, inflation under fully right governments was 0.89 percent higher than that under non-right governments (*Right* = 0). We know from the analysis of center and left governments previously that these non-right governments

Table 5.39 Inflation: regression results

1961–2001 (without country dummies)	
CBI_{t-1}	−1.484**
	(0.738)
$Right_{t-1}$	−0.016***
	(0.006)
$Right_{t-1} * CBI_{t-1}$	0.037**
	(0.016)

Notes
OLS estimates with panel-corrected standard errors in parentheses.
Only the results of the relevant variables are shown.
***Significant at the 0.01 level.
**Significant at the 0.05 level.
*Significant at the 0.10 level.

Table 5.39a Predicted values of inflation

	1961–2001	Dependent central banks (CBI = 0.14)	Independent central banks (CBI = 0.68)
Right governments	Right = 0	–0.20	–1.00
(cabinet portfolios, %)	Right = 50	–0.76	–0.56
	Right = 100	–1.31	–0.11

Notes
Predicted values of inflation calculated from the results in Table 5.39. The differences among the cells are statistically significant, except for the horizontal difference in the *Right* = 50 row.

were center governments that achieved the lowest inflation of all under independent central banks, and the highest inflation under dependent central banks.

Central bank independence contributed to lower inflation only when right cabinet portfolios were zero (*Right* = 0), and it led to higher inflation at higher levels of right cabinet portfolios. Right governments contributed to lower inflation when central banks were dependent, but to higher inflation when central banks were independent. Thus, right governments' expansionary fiscal and monetary policies under independent central banks led to the high inflation outcome. In contrast, center governments carried out a conservative fiscal policy when they faced independent central banks, and it enabled them to achieve the lowest inflation. (The differences among the cells are statistically significant, except for the horizontal difference in the *Right* = 50 row.) The combination of right governments and independent central banks did not significantly affect economic growth or unemployment in any period.

Sum

Conservative governments – when they faced independent central banks – conducted an expansionary fiscal policy, at least as measured by the fiscal balance for the entire period of 1961–2001. They also produced an expansionary fiscal policy in government non-wage consumption (1982–2001), social security transfers (1961–1981), and government employment (1961–2001). Their high spending in these spending items is noteworthy, because they are all policy items in which the standard partisan theory has long assumed left or center governments have high spending and right governments have low spending. The standard partisan theory – expecting the expansionary left and the conservative right – does not hold up empirically.

There is some, though weak, evidence that the combination of conservative governments and independent central banks also induced an expansionary monetary policy. Combined with the results of the fiscal balance analysis, this means that conservative governments and independent central banks conducted a loose fiscal–loose monetary policy mix. And this expansionary policy mix resulted in the highest level of inflation. There is, however, no evidence that fiscal indiscipline and high inflation under right governments and independent central banks produced low economic growth or high unemployment. Thus, they apparently avoided the adverse macroeconomic consequences of their high deficits and high inflation.

In contrast, conservative governments under dependent central banks conducted a tight fiscal–tight monetary policy mix, producing low inflation outcomes. Thus, conservative governments better achieved fiscal discipline and low inflation when they retained control over both fiscal and monetary policies. But the combination of right governments and independent central banks was not compatible with fiscal discipline and low inflation. This suggests that there was an incompatibility between conservative governments and independent central banks either in their policy preferences or in the actual policies they implemented.

My policy mix argument expects that the combination of right governments and independent central banks produces a loose fiscal–tight monetary policy mix. The expectations of my argument were correct about their fiscal indiscipline, but incorrect about the monetary policy component of the policy mix. The argument expects independent central banks' contractionary response to right governments' expansionary fiscal policy. But the data suggest that the former accommodated the latter's fiscal expansion with a relatively lax monetary policy. Central banks should use a tight monetary policy to mitigate the inflationary pressures of an expansionary fiscal policy. But they did not, and as a result, invited high inflation. It is not clear why independent central banks did not respond with a contractionary monetary policy to right governments' expansionary fiscal policy. This needs further investigation, so we will find out what exactly happens in their interaction in economic policy making.

Central bank independence and electoral cycles

When we entertain the possibility that the presence or nature of electoral cycles may be contingent on other factors, we begin to observe electoral cycles we do not detect by simply examining the independent effect of elections (without interaction). Electoral cycles can be conditional partly on such factors as central banks, the number of governing parties, and party fragmentation. Here we look at electoral cycles and central banks, followed in the next part of the chapter by electoral cycles and coalition governments, and then by electoral cycles and fragmented party systems.

We have seen in this book that independent central banks restrain party governments' fiscal policy. If so, it is reasonable to suspect that electoral cycles – which, if they exist, are created by politicians and political parties – may be conditional on the independence of central banks. If independent central banks constrain party governments' fiscal policy, the latter may be able to generate electoral cycles only when central banks are not independent. I find evidence that party governments create electoral expansions when central banks are not independent. But the results also show that party governments do not always use electoral expansions, even if their fiscal policy is not constrained by independent central banks.

Government non-wage consumption

Table 5.40a reports the predicted values of government non-wage consumption for the second period of 1982–2001, conditional upon election years and central bank independence (without country dummies). The results show that when central banks were not independent, electoral expansions did take place, and when central banks were independent, electoral contractions took place. As a result, non-wage consumption spending recorded the highest level in election years under dependent central banks. In contrast, the lowest spending was recorded in election years under independent central banks. Thus, independent central banks constrained party governments' electoral expansions, and the latter created electoral expansions only if central banks were not independent.

Table 5.40 Government non-wage consumption expenditures: regression results

1982–2001 (without country dummies)	
CBI_{t-1}	−0.093
	(0.128)
CBI_{t-1} * Election	−0.591***
	(0.239)
Election	0.204**
	(0.099)

Notes
OLS estimates with panel-corrected standard errors in parentheses.
Only the results of the relevant variables are shown.
***Significant at the 0.01 level.
**Significant at the 0.05 level.
*Significant at the 0.10 level.

Table 5.40a Predicted values of government non-wage consumption

1982–2001	*Non-election years (Election = 0)*	*Election years (Election = 1)*
Dependent central banks (*CBI* = 0.14)	−0.01	0.10
Independent central banks (*CBI* = 0.68)	−0.06	−0.26

Notes
Predicted values of government non-wage consumption calculated from the results in Table 5.40. The differences among the cells are significant, except for the vertical difference in the *Election* = 0 column.

In election years, spending was 0.36 percent of GDP higher (4.8 percent of total non-wage consumption spending) when central banks were dependent than when they were independent. Thus, in the absence of independent central banks, party governments took advantage of their latitude in fiscal policy making (since there was little constraint coming from central banks) and expanded spending in election years. But party governments' spending in election years was restrained in the presence of independent central banks. (The differences among the cells are significant, except for the vertical difference in the *Election* = 0 column. We obtain the same results for the entire period of 1961–2001 (without country dummies).)[19] In Chapter 4 where we examined the independent effect of elections (without interaction), we did not detect any significant electoral cycle. The result here suggests that electoral cycles did exist in government non-wage consumption and were conditional on central bank independence.

Government subsidies to industries

Government subsidies to industries show a pattern identical to that of non-wage consumption expenditures, though the evidence is not strong. The results (not reported) show that as in non-wage consumption, public subsidies experienced electoral expansions if central banks were not independent and contractions if central banks were independent, during the entire period of 1961–2001 (without country dummies). As a result, the highest spending was recorded in election years with dependent central banks, and the lowest in non-election years with independent central banks. We obtain the same results for the first period of 1961–1981. But the evidence is weak, and the results should be viewed as such. In both periods, the horizontal difference in the *CBI* = 0.14 row is significant, but nothing else.

Total government spending

There is some evidence that electoral cycles also existed in total government spending. Table 5.41a shows the predicted values of total spending for the entire period of 1961–2001, conditional upon election years and central bank independence (without country dummies). Electoral expansions took place if central banks were not independent. If central banks were independent, electoral contractions happened. As a result, total spending was the highest in election years in the absence of independent central banks, and the lowest in election years in the presence of independent central banks. Thus, party governments increased total spending in election years when they were not under constraints from independent central banks, but they did not increase it when central banks were independent. (Only the vertical difference in the *Election* = 1 column is significant, but the horizontal differences in the *CBI* = 0.14 and 0.68 rows are close to significance (*p*-value = 0.11 and 0.12).) In Chapter 4 where we examined the individual effects of CBI and elections without their interaction, neither variable had a statistically significant effect. But the result here suggests that electoral cycles did exist in total spending and were conditional on central bank independence.

Table 5.41 Total government spending: regression results

1961–2001 (without country dummies)	
CBI_{t-1}	0.173
	(0.561)
CBI_{t-1} * Election	−1.568*
	(0.881)
Election	0.624*
	(0.366)

Notes
OLS estimates with panel-corrected standard errors in parentheses.
Only the results of the relevant variables are shown.
***Significant at the 0.01 level.
**Significant at the 0.05 level.
*Significant at the 0.10 level.

Table 5.41a Predicted values of total government spending

1961–2001	*Non-election years (Election = 0)*	*Election years (Election = 1)*
Dependent central banks ($CBI = 0.14$)	0.02	0.42
Independent central banks ($CBI = 0.68$)	0.11	−0.32

Notes
Predicted values of total government spending calculated from the results in Table 5.41. Only the vertical difference in the *Election* = 1 column is significant, but the horizontal differences in the $CBI = 0.14$ and 0.68 rows are close to significance (*p*-value = 0.11 and 0.12).

Monetary policy stance

Our measure of the monetary policy stance is central bank discount rates (cyclically adjusted). Table 5.42a reports the predicted values of discount rates for the first period of 1961–1981, conditional upon central bank independence and election years (higher rates = a tighter monetary policy, lower rates = a looser policy) (without country dummies). (The differences among the cells are significant, except for the horizontal difference in the $CBI = 0.68$ row and the vertical one in the *Election* = 1 column.) The results should be viewed with caution since not all differences are significant. But if the results are to be trusted, they indicate a few noteworthy things. First, monetary policy was tighter under independent than dependent central banks, as consistent with the conventional understanding, in both election and non-election years. But, second, in election years, electoral contractions took place in monetary policy if central banks were dependent (significant), and expansions if central banks were independent (not significant), though even with monetary expansions, independent central banks kept a tighter monetary policy than dependent central banks. Central bank discount rates in countries without independent central banks were

Table 5.42 Monetary policy: regression results

1961–1981 (without country dummies)	
CBI_{t-1}	12.194**
	(5.186)
CBI_{t-1} * Election	−10.197***
	(4.144)
Election	5.575***
	(2.015)

Notes
OLS estimates with panel-corrected standard errors in parentheses.
Only the results of the relevant variables are shown.
***Significant at the 0.01 level.
**Significant at the 0.05 level.
*Significant at the 0.10 level.

Table 5.42a Predicted values of monetary policy

1961–1981	Non-election years (Election = 0)	Election years (Election = 1)
Dependent central banks ($CBI = 0.14$)	1.70	5.85
Independent central banks ($CBI = 0.68$)	8.29	6.93

Notes
Predicted values of monetary policy calculated from the results in Table 5.42. The differences among the cells are significant, except for the horizontal difference in the $CBI = 0.68$ row and the vertical one in the *Election* = 1 column.

4 percent higher (tighter monetary policy: statistically significant) during election years than in non-election years. This is counterintuitive: it would be easy to imagine that countries with dependent central banks would experience electoral expansions since party governments had control over monetary policy, but that countries with independent central banks would not create expansions because party governments did not control monetary policy. But the result here suggests the reverse was the case – independent central banks induced expansions, and dependent ones contractions.

The result becomes easier to understand if we pay attention to what usually happened in fiscal policy during election years. As we have seen in this and previous chapters, electoral expansions happened in various spending and tax policy items and in economic outcomes (i.e. what we observed in the results of the variables *Election* and *CBI * Election*). So fiscal policy tended to become expansionary in election years under all countries. We have also observed that independent central banks restrained fiscal policy in general (i.e. what we observed in the results of the variable *CBI*). We have also observed here that independent central banks restrained electoral fiscal expansions in some spending items (*CBI * Election*). So, (1) controlling for central bank independence, governments tended to conduct an expansionary fiscal policy in election years, and (2) controlling for election years, if governments did not have independent central banks, their fiscal policy tended to be less restrained. This means that fiscal policy is expected to be expansionary under governments without independent central banks during election years. My fiscal–monetary policy mix explanation expects that if fiscal policy is expansionary, monetary policy may need to be tight to curb inflationary pressures from an expansionary fiscal policy. According to the explanation, this is why we observe monetary contractions during election years in governments without independent central banks (their fiscal policy in election years is likely to be expansionary in the absence of central banks).

On the other hand, fiscal policy is expected to be restrained in countries with independent central banks in election and non-election years. If fiscal policy is disciplined, then monetary policy need not be kept restrictive in these countries with independent central banks. Since they have less inflationary pressures from fiscal policy, they may even be able to conduct monetary expansions, be it for electoral or economic purposes. My policy mix explanation speculates that this is why we observe electoral expansions in countries with independent central banks (but this expansion is, as I mentioned, not significant).

However, electoral cycles in monetary policy conditional on central banks disappeared in the second period of 1982–2001. This is probably because in the 1980s and 1990s, price stability became a policy priority in many governments, and monetary policy became increasingly neutral (politically and electorally neutral, that is); hence, the presence of electoral cycles in fiscal policy in the 1980s and 1990s, but not in monetary policy. In the 1980s and 1990s, fiscal policy became generally more disciplined in industrial democracies and as a result, central banks did not have to use a contractionary monetary policy to curb inflationary pressures as much as before.

We detected no evidence that the interaction of central bank independence and election years affected the fiscal balance or economic performance.

Coalition governments and electoral cycles

We observe some electoral expansions by coalition governments in a few spending items. Their electoral expansions are, however, not frequent and are limited to only a few spending items.

Government wage consumption

Table 5.43a shows the predicted values of government wage consumption expenditures for the second period of 1982–2001, conditional upon the number of governing parties and election years (fixed effects). The results show that coalition governments created electoral expansions. They also had higher spending than single-party governments in election years. But in non-election years, they had

Table 5.43 Government wage consumption: regression results

1982–2001 (fixed effects)	
Coalition$_{t-1}$	−0.054*
	(0.030)
Coalition$_{t-1}$ * Election	0.083**
	(0.041)
Election	−0.172*
	(0.091)

Notes
OLS estimates with panel-corrected standard errors in parentheses.
Only the results of the relevant variables are shown.
***Significant at the 0.01 level.
**Significant at the 0.05 level.
*Significant at the 0.10 level.

Table 5.43a Predicted values of government wage consumption

1982–2001	Non-election years (Election = 0)	Election years (Election = 1)
Single-party governments	−0.05	−0.14
Three-party governments	−0.16	−0.08
Five-party governments	−0.26	−0.02

Notes
Predicted values of government wage consumption calculated from the results in Table 5.43. The differences among the cells are significant, except for the vertical differences in the *Election* = 1 column, the horizontal difference in the *Coalition* = 3 row, and the horizontal one in the *Coalition* = 1 where *p*-value is 0.11.

lower spending than single-party governments. While five-party governments' spending in non-election years was the lowest of all combinations of the number of governing parties and election years, their spending in election years was the highest of all. Their spending was 0.24 percent of GDP higher (2.1 percent of total wage consumption expenditures higher) in election years than in non-election years. In non-election years, five-party governments' spending was 0.21 percent of GDP lower (1.8 percent of total spending) than single-party governments'. (The differences among the cells are significant, except for the vertical differences in the *Election* = 1 column, the horizontal difference in the *Coalition* = 3 row, and the horizontal one in the *Coalition* = 1 where *p*-value is 0.11.)

In Chapter 4, we estimated the individual effects of election years and the number of coalition parties without their interaction and did not detect any electoral cycle. We also observed in Chapter 4 that coalition governments had lower spending than single-party governments in this spending item in the second period. But the result here suggests that electoral cycles existed in government wage consumption and were conditional on the number of governing parties. It also suggests that although coalition governments recorded lower spending than single-party governments when considered independent of election years, they generated electoral expansions that probably drove up their spending above single-party governments' spending in election years. So in this limited sense, the evidence here lends some support to the weak government argument that coalition governments are expansionary. A possible explanation for this election-specific result would be that the pressure to expand spending to boost electoral prospects is greater for multiple parties in coalition governments than for single-party governments, although the pressure is successfully suppressed in non-election years. That is, there may be more pressure for credit-claiming on coalition governments in election years, because coalition parties have to compete in elections as separate political parties. Another explanation would be that coalition governments may be better able to increase spending in election years, because their fiscal policy is generally very disciplined and has some room for expansions in election years. But the answer to this question needs further research.

Government non-wage consumption

Government non-wage consumption expenditures display a pattern similar to that of wage consumption, and the results point to the presence of electoral cycles. Table 5.44a shows the predicted values of government non-wage consumption, conditional on the number of governing parties and election years, during the second period of 1982–2001 (fixed effects). Spending increased in election years at higher numbers of governing parties. Spending by single-party governments, by contrast, decreased in election years. Thus, coalition governments tended to experience electoral expansions in this spending item, but not single-party governments. In election years, five-party governments had the highest spending of all combinations, and single-party governments had the lowest of all. The former's spending in election years was 0.27 percent of GDP higher (3.6 percent of total non-wage consumption expenditures) than the

Table 5.44 Government non-wage consumption expenditures: regression results

1982–2001 (fixed effects)	
Coalition$_{t-1}$	−0.00583
	(0.02622)
Coalition$_{t-1}$ * Election	0.078***
	(0.031)
Election	−0.181**
	(0.080)

Notes
OLS estimates with panel-corrected standard errors in parentheses.
Only the results of the relevant variables are shown.
***Significant at the 0.01 level.
**Significant at the 0.05 level.
*Significant at the 0.10 level.

Table 5.44a Predicted values of government non-wage consumption

1982–2001	Non-election years (Election = 0)	Election years (Election = 1)
Single-party governments	−0.005	−0.10
Three-party governments	−0.01	0.03
Five-party governments	−0.02	0.17

Notes
Predicted values of government non-wage consumption calculated from the results in Table 5.44. The differences among the cells are significant, except for the vertical differences in the *Election* = 0 column, and the horizontal one in the *Coalition* = 3 row where *p*-value = 0.15.

latter's. We obtain essentially the same results from the models without country dummies. (The differences among the cells are significant, except for the vertical differences in the *Election* = 0 column, and the horizontal one in the *Coalition* = 3 row where *p*-value = 0.15.)

In Chapter 4, we examined the individual impact of election years and the number of coalition parties alone without their interaction, but did not detect any electoral cycle. But the result here (as in wage consumption) suggests that electoral cycles existed in government non-wage consumption and were conditional on the number of governing parties. Further, although coalition governments recorded lower spending than single-party governments when considered independent of election years, they generated electoral expansions that drove up their spending above single-party governments' spending in election years. So as in wage consumption, the evidence here lends partial support to the weak government argument in this qualified sense.

Social security transfers paid by government

Social security transfers during the second period of 1982–2001 also show a similar pattern. The results (not reported) show that electoral expansions took place at higher numbers of governing parties, and contractions happened with single-party governments.[20] Spending by five-party governments in election years was 0.34 percent of GDP higher (2.8 percent of total social security spending higher) than in non-election years. In contrast, single-party governments' spending in election years was 0.15 percent of GDP lower (0.12 percent of total social security spending higher) than in non-election years. However, coalition governments still recorded lower spending than single-party governments in both election and non-election years. But in election years, the difference between them was practically nonexistent since the vertical difference in the *Election* = 1 column is small and not statistically significant. The highest spending was registered by single-party governments in non-election years, and the lowest spending by five-party governments in non-election years. The simulation results of the entire period of 1961–2001 (both fixed effects and without country dummies) display similar patterns, but these results show that coalition governments had higher spending than single-party governments in election years, providing one of a few pieces of evidence to support the weak government argument.

In Chapter 4, we learned that coalition governments had lower social security spending during the second period of 1982–2001 than single-party governments. But the result here shows that coalition governments' social security spending depended also on election years. We also found in Chapter 4 that social security spending did not experience electoral cycles when election years were entered in the models alone (without an interactive term). But the result here suggests that electoral cycles did exist and were contingent on the number of governing parties. It is interesting to note that I originally did not expect electoral cycles in social security spending because social security is hard to manipulate in the short term. But the result indicates that politicians did manipulate social security spending in election years.

Social security contributions received by government

There is some weak evidence that coalition governments raised more social security contributions in election years during the second period of 1982–2001 (fixed effects: results not reported). Coalition governments' receipt of contributions was lower than single-party governments in both election and non-election years. But five-party governments' receipt of contributions increased in election years and was 0.16 percent of GDP higher (1.6 percent of total social security contributions) than in non-election years. In contrast, single-party governments reduced contributions in election years. (Only the vertical differences in the *Election* = 0 column and the horizontal difference in the *Coalition* = 1 row are significant.) Coalition governments' increase in the social security contributions they collected in election years is a result of their increase in social security benefits they paid in election years, as we saw previously. An increase of social security contributions in election years, when considered alone, would sound electorally self-defeating. But when we keep in mind that coalition governments also increased social security benefits in election years, it becomes easier to understand. In the presence of increases in social security benefits, voters may not be as hostile to accompanying contributions increases.

Fragmented party systems and electoral cycles

Here, we examine the interactive effect of party fragmentation and elections. In Chapter 4, we found that, during the 1960s and 1970s, countries with fragmented party systems (i.e. many parties in parliament) were fiscally very expansionary (high spending, low tax revenues), but in the 1980s and 1990s, their fiscal policy became conservative and disciplined (low spending, high tax revenues, positive fiscal balance). Fragmented systems also generated negative outcomes in economic growth, inflation, and unemployment. But the effects of party fragmentation on economic policy may also be conditional on political parties' electoral incentives. It may be the case that electoral cycles are affected by party fragmentation, and countries with fragmented party systems experience more electoral cycles, perhaps because the larger number of competitors in securing reelection and government control forces parties to engage in distributive politics for credit-claiming. In the following, we indeed find that fragmented systems did cause electoral expansions in some policy items, but in other policy and outcome indicators, non-fragmented systems induced expansions. So a simple weak government argument that party fragmentation creates electoral expansions is not supported, and such electoral manipulation is also policy specific.

Government wage consumption

Table 5.45a shows the predicted values of government wage consumption expenditures for the second period of 1982–2001, conditional on fragmented party systems and election years (fixed effects). The results show that the presence of a larger number of parties in the party system (fragmented party systems) induced electoral expansions, and also increased the size of

Table 5.45 Government wage consumption expenditures: regression results

1982–2001 (fixed effects)	
Fragmentation$_{t-1}$	0.039
	(0.035)
Fragmentation$_{t-1}$ * Election	0.045**
	(0.021)
Election	−0.178*
	(0.094)

Notes
OLS estimates with panel-corrected standard errors in parentheses.
Only the results of the relevant variables are shown.
***Significant at the 0.01 level.
**Significant at the 0.05 level.
*Significant at the 0.10 level.

Table 5.45a Predicted values of government wage consumption

1982–2001	*Non-election years (Election = 0)*	*Election years (Election = 1)*
Two-party system	0.07	−0.01
Five-party system	0.19	0.24
Nine-party system	0.35	0.57

Notes
Predicted values of government wage consumption calculated from the results in Table 5.45. The differences among the cells are significant, except for the vertical differences in the *Election* = 0 column, the horizontal differences in the *Fragmentation* = 5, and the horizontal difference in the *Fragmentation* = 2 where the *p*-value is only 0.13.

expansions. Spending by nine-party systems was 0.22 percent of GDP higher (1.9 percent of total wage consumption spending) in election years than in non-election years. As a result, nine-party systems registered the highest spending level in election years of all combinations of the number of parliamentary parties and election years. The lowest level was recorded by two-party systems in election years. Fragmented systems pushed up spending in both election and non-election years. (The differences among the cells are significant, except for the vertical differences in the *Election* = 0 column, the horizontal differences in the *Fragmentation* = 5, and the horizontal difference in the *Fragmentation* = 2 where the *p*-value is only 0.13.) In Chapter 4, we did not find electoral cycles in government wage consumption. The result here indicates that electoral cycles did exist but were conditional on party fragmentation.

Government non-wage consumption

The analysis of government non-wage consumption expenditures generates some evidence that the presence of many parties in the party system induced electoral expansions during the entire period of 1961–2001 and the second period of 1982–2001 (results not reported). However, fragmented systems recorded lower spending than non-fragmented systems in both election and non-election years. So while party fragmentation did cause electoral expansions, a simplistic version of the weak government argument does not receive support, because fragmented systems achieved lower spending in both election and non-election years. In Chapter 4, we did not find electoral cycles in government non-wage consumption. The result here indicates that electoral cycles did exist but were conditional upon party fragmentation.

Government subsidies to industries

Government subsidies to industries yield interesting results.[21] The results (not reported) show that less fragmented party systems (fewer parties) generated electoral expansions, and more fragmented systems (more parties) electoral contractions. In fact, nine-party systems' spending in election years was the lowest of all combinations of the number of parties and election years, and two-party systems' the highest. In election years, additional parliamentary parties contributed to lower spending. In non-election years, fragmented systems had slightly higher spending (though this vertical differences in the *Election* = 0 column are not significant). Thus, party fragmentation not only contributed to lower spending, but also induced electoral contractions, refuting the simplistic argument that fragmentation causes fiscal indiscipline.

Social security transfers paid by government

The results of social security transfers show the existence of electoral expansions in countries with fragmented party systems. Table 5.46a reports the predicted values

Table 5.46 Social security transfers: regression results

1982–2001 (without country dummies)	
Fragmentation$_{t-1}$	−0.023
	(0.022)
Fragmentation$_{t-1}$ * Election	0.079**
	(0.036)
Election	−0.335**
	(0.151)

Notes
OLS estimates with panel-corrected standard errors in parentheses.
Only the results of the relevant variables are shown.
***Significant at the 0.01 level.
**Significant at the 0.05 level.
*Significant at the 0.10 level.

Table 5.46a Predicted values of social security transfers

1982–2001	*Non-election years (Election = 0)*	*Election years (Election = 1)*
Two-party systems	−0.04	−0.22
Five-party systems	−0.11	−0.05
Nine-party systems	−0.20	0.16

Notes
Predicted values of social security transfers calculated from the results in Table 5.46. The differences among the cells are significant, except for the vertical differences in the *Election* = 0 column and the horizontal difference in the *Fragmentation* = 5 row.

of social security payments for the second period of 1982–2001, conditional on party system fragmentation and election years (without country dummies). Nine-party systems recorded electoral expansions, while two-party systems experienced electoral contractions. As a result, nine-party systems in election years registered the highest spending of all combinations. Their spending in election years was 0.38 percent of GDP higher (3.1 percent of total social security transfers higher) than that of two-party systems. Their spending in election years was also 0.36 percent of GDP higher (3 percent of total social security transfers) than their spending in non-election years. Additional parties in the party system contributed to lower spending in non-election years, but to higher spending in election years. (The differences among the cells are significant, except for the vertical differences in the *Election* = 0 column and the horizontal difference in the *Fragmentation* = 5 row.) We also obtain similar results from the fixed effect models and from the all-period model without country dummies. In Chapter 4 where we estimated the individual effects of party fragmentation and election years without their interaction, we did not detect any evidence for electoral cycles in social security transfers or for the effect of fragmentation for the second period. The result here shows that electoral cycles did exist in the second period but were conditional upon party fragmentation.

Corporate income tax

The results (not reported) show that fragmented party systems experienced electoral expansions (low tax revenues) in corporate income tax.[22] In countries with
fragmented party systems, the revenues were lower in election years than in
non-election years. The revenues by nine-party systems in election years were
0.39 percent of GDP lower (14.6 percent of total corporate tax revenues lower)
than in non-election years. Their revenues in election years were also 0.64
percent of GDP lower (23.9 percent of total corporate tax revenues) than the revenues by two-party systems in election years. The lowest revenues were
recorded by nine-party systems in election years, and the highest by two-party
systems in election years. Fragmented party systems produced lower revenues in
both election and non-election years and thus were expansionary. The results
suggest that a large number of parties existing in the party system created pressure for electoral expansions in corporate tax (although a larger number of
parliamentary parties does not immediately mean a larger number of governing
parties and fiscal policy makers). The low tax revenues in election years may be
due to stronger electoral competition among multiple parties in fragmented
systems than in non-fragmented ones. It is not clear why fragmented systems
created electoral expansions in corporate tax but not in individual income tax. In
Chapter 4, we did not detect electoral cycles in corporate tax revenues when the
individual effect of election years were examined. Thus, electoral cycles in
corporate tax existed but were contingent on party fragmentation.

Total government spending

In Chapter 4, I presented the basic results of the determinants of total government spending, where we did not detect any significant individual effects of
party fragmentation or election years for any period. But when we examine the
interaction of fragmentation and election years, we detect the evidence of the
presence of electoral cycles in total spending. The predicted values of total
government spending for the entire period of 1961–2001, conditional upon party
fragmentation and election years (without country dummies: results not
reported), show that fragmented party systems experienced electoral expansions,
while two-party systems recorded electoral contractions. Spending by nine-party
systems in election years was 0.94 percent of GDP higher (2.1 percent of total
spending) than in non-elections. Their spending in election years was also 1.1
percent of GDP higher (2.4 percent of total spending) than spending by two-
party systems in election years. Nine-party systems in election years recorded
the highest spending of all combinations, and two-party systems in election
years registered the lowest spending. (The differences among the cells are
significant, except for the vertical differences in the *Election* = 0 column and the
horizontal difference in the *Fragmentation* = 5 row.) Thus, electoral cycles in
total government spending was contingent on party fragmentation, as in wage
consumption and social security benefits. We obtain similar results for the

second period of 1982–2001 (without country dummies). But we do not observe any electoral cycles in total government revenues.

Fiscal balance

The analysis of the government fiscal balance (cyclically adjusted) reveals the evidence that fragmented party systems produced electoral expansions in both the first period of 1961–1981 and the entire period of 1961–2001 in similar manners. But there was also significant change in the effects of party fragmentation between the first and entire periods. While party fragmentation created electoral expansions in both periods, fragmented party systems during 1961–2001 achieved a better fiscal balance (more surplus or less deficit) than non-fragmented systems in both election and non-election years. But during the first period of 1961–1981, they produced a worse balance (more deficit or less surplus) than non-fragmented systems in both election and non-election years. Thus, although fragmented systems generated electoral expansions in both periods, their fiscal policy was more disciplined (conservative) than non-fragmented systems when the entire period is considered, and was more expansionary than non-fragmented systems when only the first period of 1961–1981 is considered. This is because, as we saw in the basic analysis of the primary balance and other fiscal policy items in Chapter 4, although party fragmentation contributed to an expansionary fiscal policy in the 1960s and 1970s, it contributed to a disciplined fiscal policy in the 1980s and 1990s. Thus, as I argued in Chapter 3, the governments and political actors that were conventionally considered weak economic performers made a conservative shift in their economic policy in the 1980s and 1990s, and their economic policy became disciplined and outcomes improved, supporting my argument in Chapters 2 and 3. In the empirical analysis in Chapter 4, we detected a better fiscal balance for fragmented systems for the entire period of 1961–2001 and the second period of 1982–2001. We did not detect any significant effect of fragmentation in the first period. But the analysis here shows that fragmented systems' lack of fiscal discipline during 1961–1981 was contingent on election years.

Table 5.47a reports the predicted values of the primary balance for the first period of 1961–1981, conditional upon party fragmentation and election years (fixed effects). In election years (compared to non-election years), two-party systems' primary balance improved, and fragmented party systems' balance deteriorated. That is, in election years, fiscal contractions took place in two-party systems, and expansions happened in fragmented systems. In election years, nine-party systems' balance was 2.6 percent of potential GDP lower (more deficit or less surplus) than two-party systems'. The size of expansions also increased with party fragmentation (the larger the number of effective parties, the larger expansions). Nine-party systems' balance was 1.14 percent lower in election years than in non-election years (fiscal expansion). Regardless of election or non-election years, additional parties contributed to a negative fiscal balance (more deficit or less surplus). The lowest (worst) balance was recorded

Table 5.47 Fiscal balance: regression results

1961–1981 (fixed effects)	
Fragmentation$_{t-1}$	−0.126
	(0.191)
Fragmentation$_{t-1}$ * Election	−0.247*
	(0.134)
Election	1.086**
	(0.527)

Notes
OLS estimates with panel-corrected standard errors in parentheses.
Only the results of the relevant variables are shown.
***Significant at the 0.01 level.
**Significant at the 0.05 level.
*Significant at the 0.10 level.

Table 5.47a Predicted values of fiscal balance

1961–1981	Non-election years (Election = 0)	Election years (Election = 1)
Two-party systems	−0.25	0.33
Five-party systems	−0.62	−0.78
Nine-party systems	−1.13	−2.27

Notes
Predicted values of the fiscal balance calculated from the results in Table 5.47. The differences among the cells are significant in the vertical differences in the *Election* = 1 column and the horizontal one in the *Fragmentation* = 2 row. The *Fragmentation* = 5 row is significant at 0.12 level. But no other difference is statistically significant.

by nine-party systems in election years, and the highest (best) balance by two-party systems in election years. (The differences among the cells are significant in the vertical differences in the *Election* = 1 column and the horizontal one in the *Fragmentation* = 2 row. The *Fragmentation* = 5 row is significant at 0.12 level. But no other difference is statistically significant.)

During the entire period of 1961–2001, electoral expansions took place at most numbers of effective parties, and more fragmented systems experienced larger electoral expansions. However, fragmented systems' fiscal balance was better (more disciplined, less expansionary) than non-fragmented systems' in both election and non-election years. Table 5.48a reports the predicted values of the primary balance for 1961–2001, conditional upon fragmentation and election years (fixed effects). Nine-party systems' balance in election years was 0.97 percent worse than in non-election years, showing that they created expansions in election years. In contrast, two-party systems did not experience much change between election and non-election years. But regardless of election or non-election years, fragmented systems achieved a higher (better)

Table 5.48 Fiscal balance: regression results

1961–2001 (fixed effects)	
Fragmentation$_{t-1}$	0.246**
	(0.120)
Fragmentation$_{t-1}$ * Election	−0.135*
	(0.083)
Election	0.255
	(0.351)

Notes
OLS estimates with panel-corrected standard errors in parentheses.
Only the results of the relevant variables are shown.
***Significant at the 0.01 level.
**Significant at the 0.05 level.
*Significant at the 0.10 level.

Table 5.48a Predicted values of the fiscal balance

1961–2001	*Non-election years* *(Election = 0)*	*Election years* *(Election = 1)*
Two-party systems	0.49	0.47
Five-party systems	1.22	0.80
Nine-party systems	2.21	1.24

Notes
Predicted values of the fiscal balance calculated from the results in Table 5.48. The differences among the cells are significant, except for the vertical differences in the *Election* = 1 column and the horizontal difference in the *Fragmentation* = 2 row. We obtain the same results without country dummies.

balance than non-fragmented systems. Nine-party systems' balance was 1.7 percent higher (better) than two-party systems' in non-election years, and was 0.77 percent higher (better) than two-party systems' in election years. The best balance was achieved by nine-party systems in non-election years, and the worst by two-party systems in election years. (The differences among the cells are significant, except for the vertical differences in the *Election* = 1 column and the horizontal difference in the *Fragmentation* = 2 row. We obtain the same results without country dummies.)

In sum, party fragmentation created electoral fiscal expansions in both the entire period and the first period. But it led to a disciplined fiscal policy in the entire period, while it induced a loose fiscal policy in the first period. This difference between the two periods results from fragmented systems' conservative shift in their fiscal policy in the 1980s and 1990s, which affects the results for the entire period. This is indicated by the regression results for the 1980s and 1990s that are not significant but show that the effects of fragmentation and election years changed from the 1960s and 1970s. The interaction of party fragmentation and election years does not have significant impact on monetary policy.

Economic growth

Economic growth experiences electoral cycles, conditional on party fragmentation and election years. The predicted values of economic growth for the second period of 1982–2001 show the following pattern (fixed effects: results not reported).[23] Two-party systems' growth was higher in election years than in non-election years by 1.17 percent. In contrast, nine-party systems experienced lower growth in election years than in non-election years by 1.05 percent. Thus, non-fragmented systems experienced electoral expansions, and fragmented systems electoral contractions. As a result, the lowest growth was recorded by nine-party systems in election years, and the highest rate by two-party systems in election years – the latter's growth was 2.7 percent higher than the former's in election years. Party fragmentation reduced growth in both election and non-election years, but its negative impact was larger in election years. Also, as we observed in Chapter 4, governments managed to generate electoral expansions in output growth, but the result here indicates that they were able to do so if their party systems were not very fragmented. We also obtain the same results for the entire period of 1961–2001 (with and without fixed effects).

Why did two-party systems have higher growth in election years, and fragmented systems lower growth? There is no clear answer. The explanation that makes some sense would be that the low number of parties in two-party systems did not impair party governments' ability to create electoral expansions, while the policy competition among multiple parties in fragmented systems reduced governments' ability to do so due, for instance, to policy inconsistency or fiscal indiscipline caused by party fragmentation. But the real answer awaits further research.

Sum

Electoral cycles exist in some policy and performance indicators during some period. The particular cycles we reviewed here are also conditional on central bank independence, coalition governments, or party fragmentation. But such electoral cycles are not ubiquitous. The economic policy and performance items I reviewed are the only areas where electoral cycles are present. The other policy and performance items either do not show any statistically significant electoral cycles conditional on the three interacting factors or do exhibit electoral contractions. Thus, electoral cycles are policy- and context-specific. Coalition governments and fragmented systems produce electoral expansions in some policy or performance indicators for some time periods. In this qualified sense, the weak government argument receives some empirical support. Yet, they create electoral expansions only in a few areas – In the other areas, they either do not have any electoral cycles, do produce electoral contractions, or do create expansions, but their spending is lower than single-party governments or non-fragmented systems. So empirical support for the simplistic weak government argument is fairly weak.

Left governments and coordinated labor: social democratic neocorporatist regimes

In the 1980s and 1990s, the combination of left governments and coordinated labor brought fiscal discipline and some good economic outcomes. The policy positions and actions of left governments and coordinated labor regime were compatible and conducive to fiscal discipline in the most recent decades. Their fiscal discipline marks a contrast with the combination of independent central banks and coordinated labor, which produced fiscal indiscipline and negative macroeconomic outcomes, including high inflation, high unemployment, and low growth, part of which probably resulted from their fiscal indiscipline. Here, I examine the economic policy and outcomes of countries with left governments and coordinated labor. I will then study the policy and outcomes of countries with independent central banks and coordinated labor.

Government non-wage consumption

Table 5.49a reports the predicted values of government non-wage consumption expenditures for the second period of 1982–2001, conditional upon left cabinet portfolios and labor coordination (without country dummies). The results show that the left–labor regime (*Left* = 100, *Labor* = 5) jointly helped reduce this spending, and actually achieved the lowest spending of all combinations of partisan governments and labor coordination. But each of the two factors individually contributed to higher spending, when the other factor was weak. As a result, the highest spending was recorded by left governments with uncoordinated labor (*Left* = 100, *Labor* = 1). Non-left governments with coordinated labor (*Left* = 0, *Labor* = 5) also recorded high spending.

Thus, left governments and coordinated labor produced fiscal discipline in the 1980s and 1990s. It was probably because they could better cooperate and

Table 5.49 Government non-wage consumption expenditures: regression results

1982–2001 (without country dummies)	
$Left_{t-1} * Labor_{t-1}$	−0.00090**
	(0.00043)
$Labor_{t-1}$	0.035**
	(0.018)
$Left_{t-1}$	0.00309**
	(0.00155)

Notes
OLS estimates with panel-corrected standard errors in parentheses.
Only the results of the relevant variables are shown.
***Significant at the 0.01 level.
**Significant at the 0.05 level.
*Significant at the 0.10 level.

Table 5.49a Predicted values of government non-wage consumption expenditures

	1982–2001	Uncoordinated labor (Labor = 1)	Intermediately coordinated labor (Labor = 3)	Coordinated labor (Labor = 5)
Left governments	Left = 0	0.03	0.10	0.17
(cabinet	Left = 50	0.14	0.12	0.10
portfolios, %)	Left = 100	0.25	0.14	0.03

Notes
Predicted values of government non-wage consumption calculated from the results in Table 5.49. The differences among the cells are significant, except for the vertical differences in the *Labor* = 3 column and the horizontal ones in the *Left* = 50 row. The significance level of the vertical differences in the *Labor* = 5 column is only 0.11.

coordinate their actions, due to the proximity of their policy preferences and political relationship. As we will see below, the left–labor regime in the 1980s and 1990s generally achieved fiscal discipline in other policy instruments as well. (The differences among the cells are significant, except for the vertical differences in the *Labor* = 3 column and the horizontal ones in the *Left* = 50 row. The significance level of the vertical differences in the *Labor* = 5 column is only 0.11.)

By contrast, the combination of left governments and uncoordinated labor produced an expansionary fiscal policy in the 1980s and 1990s, suggesting that left governments were unable to discipline their fiscal spending in the absence of labor that could effectively coordinate their action to cooperate or coordinate with the former. Non-left governments facing coordinated labor also were unable to discipline their spending, probably because their policy preferences diverged and could not cooperate or coordinate their actions sufficiently to bring down spending. Or non-left governments may have been unable to resist strong labor's spending demands.

The result of low government non-wage spending by the left–labor regime is noteworthy, because the welfare state literature points out that social democratic neocorporatist regimes have high spending on the provision of government services, such as health care, education, and daycare, and such extensive provision of public services should show in both wage and non-wage components of government final consumption. But the left–labor regime actually recorded the lowest spending in non-wage consumption in the 1980s and 1990s. Further, we do not detect any significant effect of the left–labor regime in wage consumption for any period. And the regime did not exert any significant effects on non-wage consumption in the 1960s and 1970s.

Government employment

There is some indication that left governments had high public employment ratios when labor was uncoordinated, but low public employment when labor was coordinated (the left–labor regime). This evidence also runs counter to the conventional social democratic neocorporatist literature arguing that left governments with organized labor created large public employment to provide jobs for union workers and to counter unemployment. Table 5.50a shows the predicted values of government employment as a percentage of total employment for the first period of 1961–1981, conditional upon left cabinet portfolios and labor coordination (fixed effects). The results show that when labor was uncoordinated, left governments led to high public employment. Fully left governments with uncoordinated labor (*Left* = 100, *Labor* = 1) had the highest public employment of all combinations of the two factors. In contrast, coordinated labor contributed to low public employment ratios, particularly when left cabinet portfolios were high. The lowest public employment was recorded by the left–labor regime (*Left* = 100, *Labor* = 5: to be precise, the values in the *Labor* = 5 column do not differ and are not significant). We obtain similar results for the second period of 1982–2001. (The differences among the cells are significant, except for the vertical differences in the *Labor* = 5 column and the horizontal ones in the *Left* = 0 row.)

This result goes against the social democratic neocorporatist literature, but consistently comes up in my analysis of the left–labor regime's spending on government services. The results of government wage and non-wage consumption expenditures above yielded no evidence that the left–labor regime had high spending in government services. The exact reason why the left–labor corporatist regime had low public employment is not clear. But one plausible explanation is that the left–labor regime generated relatively good macroeconomic outcomes – high growth, low inflation, and neither high nor low unemployment, as we will see below (though during different periods) – and as a result, did not have to create large public employment as an employment policy. In contrast, macroeconomic performance by left governments with uncoordinated labor was unfavorable – low output growth and high inflation; as a result, they may have needed to create large public employment. Consistent with this explanation, the

Table 5.50 Government employment: regression results

1961–1981 (fixed effects)	
$Left_{t-1} * Labor_{t-1}$	–0.00174***
	(0.00064)
$Labor_{t-1}$	–0.00792
	(0.02913)
$Left_{t-1}$	0.00876***
	(0.00285)

Notes
OLS estimates with panel-corrected standard errors in parentheses.
Only the results of the relevant variables are shown.
***Significant at the 0.01 level.
**Significant at the 0.05 level.
*Significant at the 0.10 level.

Table 5.50a Predicted values of government employment

	1961–1981	*Uncoordinated labor (Labor = 1)*	*Intermediately coordinated labor (Labor = 3)*	*Coordinated labor (Labor = 5)*
Left governments (cabinet portfolios, %)	Left = 0	–0.007	–0.02	–0.03
	Left = 50	0.34	0.15	–0.03
	Left = 100	0.69	0.33	–0.03

Notes
Predicted values of government employment calculated from the results in Table 5.50. The differences among the cells are significant, except for the vertical differences in the *Labor* = 5 column and the horizontal ones in the *Left* = 0 row.

regime of left governments with uncoordinated labor generally produced an expansionary fiscal policy in the 1980s and 1990s.

Individual income tax

The combination of left governments and coordinated labor (the left–labor regime) led to low individual income tax revenues in the entire period of 1961–2001. Table 5.51a reports the predicted values of the revenues from personal income tax, contingent on left cabinet portfolios and labor coordination (1961–2001, fixed effects). They show that the left–labor regime (*Left* = 100, *Labor* = 5) recorded very low income tax revenues. The left–labor regime's revenues were 0.42 percent of GDP lower (3.8 percent of total personal income tax revenues lower) than those of fully left governments with uncoordinated labor (*Left* = 100, *Labor* = 1). The latter's revenues were the highest of all combinations of left partisanship and labor coordination. The pattern here is that labor coordination contributed to low revenues, and the downward effect was larger

Table 5.51 Personal income tax revenues: regression results

1961–2001 (fixed effects)	
$Left_{t-1} * Labor_{t-1}$	–0.00066
	(0.00061)
$Labor_{t-1}$	–0.042
	(0.037)
$Left_{t-1}$	0.00364
	(0.00228)

Notes
OLS estimates with panel-corrected standard errors in parentheses.
Only the results of the relevant variables are shown.
***Significant at the 0.01 level.
**Significant at the 0.05 level.
*Significant at the 0.10 level.

Table 5.51a Predicted values of personal income tax revenues

	1961–2001	*Uncoordinated labor (Labor = 1)*	*Intermediately coordinated labor (Labor = 3)*	*Coordinated labor (Labor = 5)*
Left governments (cabinet portfolios, %)	Left = 0	−0.04	−0.12	−0.20
	Left = 50	0.10	−0.04	−0.19
	Left = 100	0.25	0.04	−0.17

Notes
Predicted values of personal income tax revenues calculated from the results in Table 5.51. The differences among the cells are significant, except for the vertical ones in the *Labor* = 5 column and the horizontal ones in the *Left* = 0 row.

when left cabinet portfolios were high. Left governments, by contrast, contributed to higher revenues when labor was not well coordinated. Thus, left governments had lower personal income tax revenues when they had coordinated labor, but in its relative absence, they had higher revenues.

We saw in Chapter 4 that labor coordination itself had downward effects on personal income tax revenues. The result here about the left–labor regime suggests that labor wanted and gained low personal income tax, but had its demands met better when it was well coordinated and had left governments that were supportive of and sympathetic to labor. The left–labor regime also better achieved fiscal discipline (as we see here for non-wage consumption and total spending) and, as a result, better reduced tax revenues because of their cooperative relationship and the compatibility of their policy preferences. By contrast, left governments could not well achieve fiscal discipline when they faced uncoordinated labor, because of the relative incompatibility of the two actors' policy preferences and the reduced ability to coordinate and achieve cooperation. As partial evidence, we have seen above that left governments facing uncoordinated labor had expansionary spending in government non-wage consumption expenditures and public employment in the 1980s and 1990s. As we will see below, the left–labor regime also recorded generally low tax revenues in the 1980s and 1990s (total tax revenues and social security contributions), suggesting that its fiscal policy profile shifted from a high spending, high taxing regime to a low spending, low tax one in the 1980s and 1990s. Left governments facing uncoordinated labor, in contrast, collected larger tax revenues (total tax revenues and social security contributions) in the 1980s and 1990s to finance their expansionary spending. (The differences among the cells are significant, except for the vertical ones in the *Labor* = 5 column and the horizontal ones in the *Left* = 0 row.)

Corporate income tax

The results of corporate income tax revenues for the first period of 1961–1981 (not reported) show that the left–labor regime registered the highest revenues of all combinations of government partisanship and labor.[24] The left–labor regime's (*Left* = 100, *Labor* = 5) revenues were 1.1 percent of GDP higher (41 percent of total corporate tax revenues higher) than those of fully left governments with uncoordinated labor (*Left* = 100, *Labor* = 1). This is a substantively large difference. The pattern here is that left governments contributed to lower revenues if labor was not well coordinated. Coordinated labor contributed to higher revenues, for the most part, particularly if they had left governments. Non-left governments with uncoordinated labor also had very high revenues (*Left* = 0, *Labor* = 1).

One plausible explanation for this pattern in the results is that labor preferred high corporate tax to high individual income tax and was able to materialize its preference when it was buttressed by supportive left governments. This explanation is consistent with the results of individual income tax discussed above, which show that coordinated labor achieved low income tax when facing left governments. When labor was not coordinated, in contrast, left governments reduced corporate tax and increased personal income tax instead, presumably because they only faced uncoordinated labor and could better go against its tax preferences. But when labor was well coordinated, it appears that they met labor's demand for low individual tax and/or high corporate tax. Left governments may also have had to raise corporate tax to finance low individual income tax under coordinated labor.

The results are also consistent with the general results of the left–labor regime's economic policy, showing that it had an expansionary fiscal policy regime in the 1960s and 1970s, but a conservative fiscal policy in the 1980s and 1990s. The left–labor regime did not have high corporate tax revenues in the 1980s and 1990s, as indicated by the results for the second period (1982–2001) that show that the regime did not have upward or downward effects on corporate tax revenues.

Consumption tax

The results of consumption tax revenues follow the patterns of other tax revenues that suggest that the left–labor regime was high taxing in the 1960s and 1970s but low taxing in the 1980s and 1990s. Table 5.52a shows the predicted values of the revenues from consumption tax for the first period of 1961–1981, conditional on left cabinet portfolios and labor coordination (without country dummies). The results show that the left–labor regime (*Left* = 100, *Labor* = 5) had the highest revenues of all combinations of partisan governments and labor coordination. This is consistent with the conventional wisdom that consumption tax is an important revenue source for many social democratic welfare states. The left–labor regime's revenues were 0.96 percent of GDP higher (7.5 percent of total consumption tax revenues) than those of left governments with uncoordinated labor (*Left* = 100, *Labor* = 1), which registered the lowest revenues of all. This is the same pattern as those for corporate tax and total revenues for the first period of 1961–1981. This effect disappeared in the 1980s and 1990s, as we do not detect any statistically significant effects for the second period of

1982–2001. This is another piece of evidence suggesting that during the 1960s and 1970s, the left–labor regime had a high spending, high tax regime but made a transition to a low spending, low tax regime in the 1980s and 1990s.

Part of the reason for this change between the two periods is the change in the effect of coordinated labor. As we saw in Chapter 4, coordinated labor contributed to high spending and high tax revenues in the 1960s and 1970s and to low spending and low revenues in the 1980s and 1990s. The left–labor regime needed larger revenues in the 1960s and 1970s to finance larger government programs, which labor tended to prefer in general. But in the 1980s and 1990s, the regime did not need as large revenues because its spending became less expansionary.

According to the results in Table 5.52a, during the 1960s and 1970s, coordinated labor led to high revenues unless left portfolios were very low, and its upward impact on the revenues was larger as left portfolios were higher. Left governments' impact was to reduce revenues unless labor was highly coordinated in which case left governments also led to high revenues. One might wonder why labor or left governments did not oppose high consumption

Table 5.52 Consumption tax revenues: regression results

1961–1981 (without country dummies)	
$Left_{t-1} * Labor_{t-1}$	0.00276***
	(0.00111)
$Labor_{t-1}$	−0.031
	(0.032)
$Left_{t-1}$	−0.010**
	(0.004)

Notes
OLS estimates with panel-corrected standard errors in parentheses.
Only the results of the relevant variables are shown.
***Significant at the 0.01 level.
**Significant at the 0.05 level.
*Significant at the 0.10 level.

Table 5.52a Predicted values of consumption tax revenues

	1961–1981	*Uncoordinated labor (Labor = 1)*	*Intermediately coordinated labor (Labor = 3)*	*Coordinated labor (Labor = 5)*
Left governments	Left = 0	−0.03	−0.09	−0.15
(cabinet	Left = 50	−0.40	−0.18	0.02
portfolios, %)	Left = 100	−0.76	−0.28	0.20

Notes
Predicted values of consumption tax revenues calculated from the results in Table 5.52. The differences among the cells are significant, except for the horizontal differences in the *Left* = 0 row, and the vertical differences in the *Labor* = 3 column where *p*-value is only 0.15.

tax, because consumption tax is usually regressive and the burdens of high consumption tax should be felt more strongly among low-income workers and families. But social democratic neocorporatist regimes have conventionally had high consumption tax, and it shows, at least empirically, that the left–labor regime did not mind high consumption tax if it was in exchange for generous government programs and services that workers and families received. Combined with the results of individual income tax, corporate tax, and total receipts, the results here suggest that during the 1960s and 1970s, the left–labor regime financed its expansionary spending by raising high revenues from corporate and consumption tax but keeping individual income tax low. (The differences among the cells are significant, except for the horizontal differences in the *Left* = 0 row, and the vertical differences in the *Labor* = 3 column where *p*-value is only 0.15.)

Social security contributions received by government

The results of social security contributions received by governments for the entire period of 1961–2001 (not reported) show that the left–labor regime (*Left* = 100, *Labor* = 5) recorded the lowest contributions of all combinations of partisan governments and labor coordination.[25] Its contributions were 0.4 percent of GDP lower (3.9 percent of total social security contributions lower) than left governments with uncoordinated labor, which collected the highest social security contributions. Considering that the results for the second period (1982–2001) had the same pattern (though not significant) and that the first period (1961–1981) had a different pattern and no significant effect detected, this pattern here for the entire period is likely to come from the second period. If so, the result is consistent with the patterns of the rest of the revenues by the left–labor regime – the left–labor regime was low taxing in the 1980s and 1990s.

The observed pattern here is that coordinated labor contributed to lower social security contributions, particularly as governments became more leftist. Left governments also led to lower contributions when labor became more coordinated. This pattern exists probably because coordinated labor preferred lower social security contributions, and achieved the goal better when it had left governments that were more supportive of labor's cause. There is an alternative explanation – the welfare state literature would explain that social democratic neocorporatist regimes do not have the highest level of social security spending or contributions, because their provision of welfare is more through provision of public services. But this explanation runs into a small problem, at least, in light of the empirical results of this book – the left–labor regime did not have large spending on public services, as discussed above.

The high social security contributions by left governments with uncoordinated labor are also consistent with the results for other revenues and spending items – when labor was uncoordinated, left governments' fiscal policy regime was characterized by high-spending and high-tax revenues in the 1980s and 1990s. This was probably because of the relative incompatibility of the two actors' policy preferences and the reduced ability to coordinate and achieve cooperation.

Total government spending

The results of total government spending do not provide strong evidence for the interactive effects of the left–labor regime, since most differences among predicted values are not significant (results not reported). So we have to conclude that the left–labor regime did not affect total spending. But the pattern of the coefficients shows that the left–labor regime had a relatively high level of total spending in the first period (1961–1981), but the lowest spending in the second period (1982–2001) (without country dummies). The pattern of the left–labor regime's total spending is thus consistent with its patterns of other spending items – the left–labor regime's fiscal policy was expansionary in the 1960s and 1970s, but became disciplined in the 1980s and 1990s. On the other hand, the combination of strong left governments and uncoordinated labor induced an expansionary fiscal policy in the 1980s and 1990s. When labor was not coordinated, left governments were unable to restrain fiscal spending, probably because of the relative incompatibility of the two actors' policy preferences and the reduced ability to coordinate and achieve cooperation.

Total government receipts

The evidence shows that the left–labor regime had high tax revenues in the 1960s and 1970s, but low revenues in the 1980s and 1990s, suggesting that its fiscal policy regime experienced a shift between the two periods. Tables 5.53a and 5.54a report the predicted values of total government revenues, contingent upon left cabinet portfolios and labor coordination, for the first (1961–1981) and the second periods (1982–2001), respectively (without country dummies). Table 5.53a shows that the left–labor regime (*Left* = 100, *Labor* = 5) had the

Table 5.53 Total government revenues: regression results

1961–1981 (without country dummies)	
$Left_{t-1}$ * $Labor_{t-1}$	0.00593**
	(0.00252)
$Labor_{t-1}$	0.173**
	(0.074)
$Left_{t-1}$	−0.021*
	(0.011)

Notes
OLS estimates with panel-corrected standard errors in parentheses.
Only the results of the relevant variables are shown.
***Significant at the 0.01 level.
**Significant at the 0.05 level.
*Significant at the 0.10 level.

Table 5.53a Predicted values of total government revenues

	1961–1981	*Uncoordinated labor (Labor = 1)*	*Intermediately coordinated labor (Labor = 3)*	*Coordinated labor (Labor = 5)*
Left governments	Left = 0	0.17	0.51	0.86
(cabinet	Left = 50	−0.58	0.34	1.28
portfolios, %)	Left = 100	−1.35	0.18	1.71

Notes
Predicted values of total government revenues calculated from the results in Table 5.53. The differences among the cells are statistically significant, except for the vertical ones in the *Labor* = 3 column.

highest revenues of all combinations of left cabinet portfolios and labor coordination in the 1960s and 1970s. During this period, coordinated labor put significant upward pressure on government revenues (regardless of government partisanship), and the upward pressure was stronger as left portfolios increased. It suggests that left governments with coordinated labor needed to raise large revenues to finance large public spending under the left–labor regime. Meanwhile, left governments contributed to lower revenues if labor was not coordinated and to higher revenues if labor was well-coordinated. This suggests that in the absence of coordinated labor, left governments did not raise large revenues or were able to reduce tax revenues, probably because labor was not coordinated or strong enough to place effectively demands on left governments' spending or because left governments without coordinated labor were low spenders for another reason. In fact, fully left governments recorded the lowest revenues of all combinations when labor was not coordinated (*Left* = 100, *Labor* = 1) in the 1960s and 1970s. It also suggests that when labor was coordinated, left governments were unable to keep tax revenues low, probably because labor placed upward pressure on spending, and left governments could not resist labor demands and therefore had to collect large tax revenues to finance their expansionary spending. This pattern of high revenues by the left–labor regime in the 1960s and 1970s is consistent with the expectations of the conventional neocorporatist thesis that social democratic corporatist regimes had high spending and revenues.

This pattern, however, gets completely reversed in the second period of 1982–2001 (Table 5.54a). During this period, the left–labor regime (*Left* = 100, *Labor* = 5) recorded the lowest revenues of all combinations of partisan governments and labor. By contrast, fully left governments with uncoordinated labor (*Left* = 100, *Labor* = 1) registered the highest revenues of all, whereas in the previous decades, they had the lowest revenues. In the 1980s and 1990s, labor coordination contributed to low revenues, and the downward effect was larger, as left cabinet portfolios increased. This is consistent with the pattern of the individual effect of labor we reviewed in Chapter 4, where labor coordination had

Table 5.54 Total government revenues: regression results

1982–2001 (without country dummies)	
Left$_{t-1}$ * Labor$_{t-1}$	−0.00257**
	(0.00112)
Labor$_{t-1}$	0.013
	(0.050)
Left$_{t-1}$	0.00778**
	(0.00365)

Notes
OLS estimates with panel-corrected standard errors in parentheses.
Only the results of the relevant variables are shown.
***Significant at the 0.01 level.
**Significant at the 0.05 level.
*Significant at the 0.10 level.

Table 5.54a Predicted values of total government revenues

	1982–2001	Uncoordinated labor (Labor = 1)	Intermediately coordinated labor (Labor = 3)	Coordinated labor (Labor = 5)
Left governments	Left = 0	0.01	0.03	0.06
(cabinet	Left = 50	0.27	0.04	−0.19
portfolios, %)	Left = 100	0.53	0.04	−0.44

Notes
Predicted values of total government revenues calculated from the results in Table 5.54. The differences among the cells are significant, except for the vertical differences in the *Labor* = 3 column and the horizontal ones in the *Left* = 0 row.

downward effects on total revenues in the 1980s and 1990s. Left governments contributed to high revenues if labor was not coordinated, but to low revenues when labor was coordinated. As a result, left governments successfully contained tax revenues when labor was coordinated. The high tax revenue outcome under left governments with uncoordinated labor is also consistent with the results of other spending and tax policy items where their policy regime changed from a low spending, low taxing regime in the 1960s and 1970s to a high spending, high tax regime in the 1980s and 1990s. (In Table 5.53a, the differences among the cells are statistically significant, except for the vertical ones in the *Labor* = 3 column. In Table 5.54a, the differences among the cells are significant, except for the vertical differences in the *Labor* = 3 column and the horizontal ones in the *Left* = 0 row. The results for the models with country dummies for the entire period of 1961–2001 and the second period follow the pattern of the second-period results.)

All in all, these spending and tax results suggest that the left–labor regime raised high revenues to finance its expansive government programs in the 1960s and 1970s, but it restrained fiscal spending and reduced tax revenues in the 1980s and 1990s. This lends support to one of my arguments in this book – the governments and actors that had helped produce an expansionary fiscal policy regime in the 1960s and 1970s restrained their economic policy and behavior in the 1980s and 1990s.

Economic growth

The left–labor regime – whose fiscal policy shifted to a low spending, low tax policy regime in the 1980s and 1990s – achieved high economic growth during the same period. Table 5.55a reports the predicted values of output growth for the second period of 1982–2001, conditional on left cabinet portfolios and labor coordination (without country dummies). The results show that the left–labor regime (*Left* = 100, *Labor* = 5) achieved the highest economic growth of all combinations of partisan governments and labor. In contrast, fully left governments that faced uncoordinated labor (*Labor* = 1) recorded the lowest growth of

Table 5.55 Economic growth (GDP): regression results

1982–2001 (without country dummies)	
$Left_{t-1}$ * $Labor_{t-1}$	0.00406**
	(0.00180)
$Labor_{t-1}$	−0.127
	(0.104)
$Left_{t-1}$	−0.013**
	(0.006)

Notes
OLS estimates with panel-corrected standard errors in parentheses.
Only the results of the relevant variables are shown.
***Significant at the 0.01 level.
**Significant at the 0.05 level.
*Significant at the 0.10 level.

Table 5.55a Predicted values of economic growth (GDP)

	1982–2001	*Uncoordinated labor (Labor = 1)*	*Intermediately coordinated labor (Labor = 3)*	*Coordinated labor (Labor = 5)*
Left governments (cabinet portfolios, %)	Left = 0	−0.12	−0.38	−0.63
	Left = 50	−0.58	−0.43	−0.28
	Left = 100	−1.05	−0.49	0.06

Notes
Predicted values of economic growth calculated from the results in Table 5.55. The differences among the cells are significant, except for the horizontal differences in the *Left* = 0 and 50 rows and the vertical ones in the *Labor* = 3 column.

all, suggesting the incompatibility of left governments and uncoordinated labor for economic growth. The left–labor regime's growth was 1.1 percent higher than that for fully left governments facing uncoordinated labor. (We have seen above that the same combination of left governments and uncoordinated labor produced an expansionary fiscal policy regime in the 1980s and 1990s.)

The pattern here is that labor coordination contributed to lower growth when left cabinet portfolios were low, but to higher growth when left portfolios were high. Thus, coordinated labor produced high growth under left governments. Left governments, likewise, led to low growth if labor was uncoordinated, but to high growth when labor was highly coordinated. (The differences among the cells are significant, except for the horizontal differences in the *Left* = 0 and 50 rows and the vertical ones in the *Labor* = 3 column.)

The results here are largely consistent with the conventional social democratic neocorporatist thesis arguing that the left–labor regime attained favorable economic outcomes. But the results here also differ from the conventional thesis in an important way. In the thesis, the left–labor regime should achieve good economic outcomes during the heyday of social democracy in the 1960s and 1970s, but the favorable result should weaken in the 1980s and 1990s when the neocorporatist arrangements allegedly started breaking down. But my results indicate that the left–labor regime achieved high growth in the 1980s and 1990s, not in the 1960s and 1970s when the neocorporatist arrangements were intact. And we do not find any significant effect of the left–labor regime for the first period of 1961–1981, suggesting that the left–labor regime did not bring about higher economic growth than other combinations of government partisanship and labor. Thus, my analysis shows that the left–labor regime had beneficial effects on economic growth during the 1980s and 1990s, when the beneficial attributes and arrangements of social democratic neocorporatist systems allegedly waned. My analysis also does not detect any significant employment benefits of the left–labor regime for any period, which runs counter to the neocorporatist thesis.

The evidence here also supports Garrett's (1998) regime coherence thesis, because both "strong left–uncoordinated labor" regimes and "weak left–coordinated labor" regimes produced low economic growth, and both "strong left-coordinated labor" regimes and "weak left–uncoordinated labor" regimes produced high growth.

Inflation

The evidence indicates that the left–labor regime achieved low inflation during the 1960s and 1970s (results not reported).[26] The combination of left governments and coordinated labor served to reduce inflation, and the left–labor regime (*Left* = 100, *Labor* = 5) recorded the second lowest inflation of all combinations of partisan governments and labor. (We obtain similar results with the models without country dummies, and in there, the left–labor regime recorded the lowest inflation of all.) In contrast, fully left governments that faced uncoordinated labor

(*Left* = 100, *Labor* = 1) registered the highest inflation of all. The left–labor regime's inflation was 3.3 percent lower than left governments with uncoordinated labor. This suggests that left governments had difficulty keeping inflation low in the absence of labor that could coordinate its action and achieve wage restraint or cooperate with left governments. It likewise shows that coordinated labor did not help keep inflation low when it did not have left governments whose policy preferences were similar to labor's, and which could coordinate and achieve cooperation with labor and make favorable policies toward labor in exchange for labor's wage restraint. These patterns are perfectly consistent with the conventional neocorporatist literature.

The pattern here is that labor coordination contributed to lower inflation when left cabinet portfolios were high, but to higher inflation when left portfolios were very low. Thus, labor coordination was conducive to low inflation, but the downward effect on inflation was contingent on government partisanship. Left governments, meanwhile, contributed to higher inflation when labor coordination was low, but to lower inflation when labor was highly coordinated.

The results also qualify the price stability benefits of the left–labor regime in that we detect the beneficial effects only in the 1960s and 1970s, not in the 1980s and 1990s. In the last two decades, the combination of left partisanship and labor coordination did not affect inflation at all (this means that their inflation in the 1980s and 1990s was not high, either). Thus, the price stability benefits of the left–labor regime disappeared in the recent decades. Overall, the evidence here supports the conventional social democratic neocorporatist thesis for the 1960s and 1970s – coordinated labor provided wage restraint and contributed to low inflation when left governments existed to make policy favorable to labor. But in the absence of sympathetic left governments, labor did not produce low inflation. From the perspective of governments, left governments were able to achieve low inflation as long as labor was coordinated enough to provide wage restraint, but otherwise, they failed to achieve low inflation. Lastly, as far as the 1960s and 1970s are concerned, Garrett's (1998) regime coherence thesis gains empirical support, because both "strong left–coordinated labor" and "weak left–uncoordinated labor" regimes registered low inflation. But Garrett's study itself provides the empirical result that the left–labor regime produced the highest inflation.

Sum

The left–labor regime's fiscal policy was relatively expansionary in the 1960s and 1970s, but became disciplined in the 1980s and 1990s. Its fiscal policy profile shifted from a high spending, high tax regime to a low spending, low tax one in the 1980s and 1990s. Thus, social democratic neocorporatist countries' high spending and high tax policy regime depicted in the past literature was specific to the 1960s and 1970s and no longer existed in the 1980s and 1990s. The combination of left governments and uncoordinated labor, in contrast, produced a generally disciplined fiscal policy in the 1960s and 1970s, but created an expansionary fiscal policy in the 1980s and 1990s. The left–labor regime's shift in its fiscal policy regime is consistent with my argument that the governments and actors that produced an expansionary fiscal policy regime in the 1960s and 1970s made a conservative shift in their economic policy or their effects on policy changed in a conservative direction in the 1980s and 1990s.

In the 1980s and 1990s, left governments were unable to discipline their fiscal spending in the absence of labor that could effectively coordinate its action to cooperate or coordinate with the former. But left governments and coordinated labor were better able to cooperate and coordinate their actions and achieve fiscal discipline, due to the proximity and compatibility of their policy positions and relationship. Furthermore, the left–labor regime's fiscal discipline helped produce high economic growth in the 1980s and 1990s. Fiscal discipline allowed the left–labor regime to avoid negative economic consequences of fiscal indiscipline, such as high deficits, inflation, high interest rates and low savings, which could depress investment and economic growth. In contrast, left governments' fiscal indiscipline under uncoordinated labor led to low growth in the same period.

Why did the same left–labor regime not produce fiscal discipline in the 1960s and 1970s? Part of the reason lies in change in the effects of labor between those two decades and the 1980s and 1990s. As we saw in Chapter 4, coordinated labor induced a relatively expansionary fiscal policy in the 1960s and 1970s, but in the 1980s and 1990s, coordinated labor helped create fiscal discipline. Coordinated labor was one of the actors whose effect on economic policy was expansionary in the 1960s and 1970s, but made a conservative shift in the 1980s and 1990s. In the 1960s and 1970s, left governments were unable to restrain fiscal spending, facing labor that preferred and demanded large public spending. But in the 1980s and 1990s, left governments were better able to achieve fiscal discipline in the presence of labor that was more receptive to the importance of fiscal discipline and that could effectively coordinate their action to cooperate with the governments.

Another noteworthy finding is the absence of evidence for the left–labor regime's high spending on the provision of government services in any period, and the presence of the evidence showing that the left–labor regime actually had low spending on government services during some periods. The standard welfare state literature points out that social democratic neocorporatist regimes have high spending on the provision of government services, such as health care, education, and daycare. Extensive provision of public services by the left–labor regime should show in its wage and non-wage components of government final consumption and government employment. But we do not detect any significant effect of the left–labor regime in wage consumption for any period. Further, the left–labor regime also did not exert any significant effect on non-wage consumption in the 1960s and 1970s. And the regime actually recorded the lowest spending in non-wage consumption in the 1980s and 1990s. Moreover, the left–labor regime had the lowest public employment ratios during both periods. Thus, there is absolutely no evidence of the regime's high spending on government services. However, the evidence does show that the combination of left governments and uncoordinated labor led to very large spending on government services. Thus, left governments' large spending on government services was contingent on the absence of coordinated labor.

Why the large spending by left governments with uncoordinated labor? The empirical results suggest two possibilities. One is that it was a result of their poor economic performance. The combination of left governments and uncoordinated labor led to the lowest economic growth in the 1980s and 1990s and the highest inflation in the 1960s and 1970s. They may have had to increase spending on government services and employment to respond to their poor economic performance (though there is no evidence that they had high unemployment). Left governments with coordinated labor, on the other hand, produced favorable economic outcomes and therefore may not have needed to have large spending on government services and employment. The other possibility is that left governments were unable to restrain spending on public services in the absence of labor that could effectively coordinate their action and cooperate with the governments, and the fiscal discipline led to poor economic performance, like low growth and high inflation. The current analysis cannot tell which of the two explanations is actually the case.

Labor and central banks

We have seen in this chapter that central bank independence improved fiscal discipline and some economic outcomes for coalition and center governments (and left governments, to a lesser extent). But the empirical analysis of this part of the chapter shows that independent central banks caused negative outcomes in economic policy and outcomes for coordinated labor (i.e. countries with coordinated labor). The combination of coordinated labor and independent central banks was not a compatible one for economic policy and outcomes. This combination generally produced high spending, high taxation, and unfavorable macroeconomic outcomes – high unemployment, high inflation, and possibly low economic growth.

Government non-wage consumption

Table 5.56a reports the predicted values of government non-wage consumption expenditures for the second period of 1982–2001, conditional upon labor coordination and central bank independence (without country dummies). The results show that the combination of coordinated labor and independent central banks produced high spending. The observed pattern is that each of the two factors reduced spending in the relative absence of the other, but they together created expansionary spending. Independent central banks reduced this spending if labor was not coordinated, but when labor was coordinated, they increased

Table 5.56 Government non-wage consumption expenditures: regression results

1982–2001 (without country dummies)	
CBI_{t-1}	−2.016***
	(0.502)
$CBI_{t-1} * Labor_{t-1}$	0.455***
	(0.123)
$Labor_{t-1}$	−0.160***
	(0.050)

Notes
OLS estimates with panel-corrected standard errors in parentheses.
Only the results of the relevant variables are shown.
***Significant at the 0.01 level.
**Significant at the 0.05 level.
*Significant at the 0.10 level.

Table 5.56a Predicted values of government non-wage consumption expenditures

1982–2001	Dependent central banks (CBI = 0.14)	Independent central banks (CBI = 0.68)
Uncoordinated labor (Labor = 1)	−0.37	−1.22
Intermediately coordinated labor (Labor = 3)	−0.57	−0.92
Coordinated labor (Labor = 5)	−0.76	−0.62

Notes
Predicted values of government non-wage consumption calculated from the results in Table 5.56. The differences among the cells are significant, except for the horizontal difference in the *Labor* = 5 row where *p*-value is 0.13.

spending. Similarly, coordinated labor reduced spending when central banks were not independent. But when central banks were independent, coordinated labor pushed up spending. (Note that neither central banks nor labor makes fiscal policy. Thus, we are here talking about the effects they may have on spending levels decided by governments. The same applies throughout this part of the chapter.)

This is a pattern common to the results of many spending items for the two actors, suggesting that coordinated labor and independent central banks clashed and induced negative outcomes. (The differences among the cells are significant, except for the horizontal difference in the *Labor* = 5 row where *p*-value is 0.13.) The results are very similar for the entire period of 1961–2001 (with and without country dummies). But for the entire period, the combination of coordinated labor and independent central banks recorded close to the highest spending of all combinations of labor and central banks.

Government investment

Government investment for the second period (1982–2001, fixed effects) follows the same pattern as non-wage consumption, though the evidence is weaker (results not reported).[27] The results show that the combination of coordinated labor and independent central banks produced high spending. Each of the two variables reduced spending in the relative absence of the other, but they together generated expansionary spending. Independent central banks restrained this spending if labor was not coordinated, but when labor was coordinated, they contributed to high spending. Coordinated labor likewise produced restrained spending when central banks were not independent. But when central banks were independent, coordinated labor pushed up spending.[28]

Social security transfers paid by government

Social security transfers also follow the same pattern (the entire period of 1961–2001, fixed effects: results not reported).[29] The combination of coordinated labor and independent central banks produced the highest spending. Each of the two variables reduced spending in the relative absence of the other, but they together caused expansionary spending. When central banks were dependent, labor reduced spending, and central bank independence reduced spending if labor was not coordinated.

Government subsidies to industries

Government subsidies to industries show a different pattern (the entire period of 1961–2001 without country dummies: results not reported).[30] Here, each factor pushed up spending in the relative absence of the other. In contrast, the combination of coordinated labor and independent central banks led to low spending.[31] It is not clear why the spending level was the highest with independent central banks and uncoordinated labor.

Government employment

Government employment as a percentage of total employment follows the pattern of government subsidies to industries for the second period of 1982–2001 (results not reported).[32] The combination of coordinated labor and independent central banks led to the lowest public employment of all combinations. But in the relative absence of the other factor, each pushed up public employment. We obtain similar results for the entire period of 1961–2001 (without country dummies).

Individual income tax

Table 5.57a shows the predicted values of personal income tax revenues for the second period of 1982–2001, conditional on labor and central banks (fixed

Table 5.57 Personal income tax revenues: regression results

1982–2001 (fixed effects)	
CBI_{t-1}	3.125***
	(1.194)
$CBI_{t-1} * Labor_{t-1}$	−0.684**
	(0.338)
$Labor_{t-1}$	0.168
	(0.122)

Notes
OLS estimates with panel-corrected standard errors in parentheses.
Only the results of the relevant variables are shown.
***Significant at the 0.01 level.
**Significant at the 0.05 level.
*Significant at the 0.10 level.

Table 5.57a Predicted values of personal income tax revenues

1982–2001	*Dependent central banks (CBI = 0.14)*	*Independent central banks (CBI = 0.68)*
Uncoordinated labor (Labor = 1)	0.50	1.82
Intermediately coordinated labor (Labor = 3)	0.65	1.23
Coordinated labor (Labor = 5)	0.79	0.63

Notes
Predicted values of personal income tax revenues calculated from the results in Table 5.57. The differences among the cells are significant, except for the vertical differences in the *CBI* = 0.14 column and the horizontal one in the *Labor* = 5 row.

effects: we also obtain the same results for the entire period of 1961–2001). The combination of coordinated labor and independent central banks produced very low revenues. This reflects labor's generally downward effect on personal income tax. Central bank independence generally increased revenues, but when labor was coordinated, it helped reduce them. Labor coordination, likewise, contributed to lower revenues when central banks were independent. The highest revenues were recorded by the combination of independent central banks and uncoordinated labor. (The differences among the cells are significant, except for the vertical differences in the *CBI* = 0.14 column and the horizontal one in the *Labor* = 5 row.)

Consumption tax

The combination of independent central banks and coordinated labor produced relatively high consumption tax revenues during the second period of 1982–2001

(Table 5.58a: without country dummies). This is the opposite pattern from personal income tax. Each of the two factors reduced revenues when the other was weak. When central banks were dependent, labor reduced revenues, and central bank independence reduced revenues if labor was not coordinated. But each of them served to increase revenues at high values of the other. The highest revenues were collected by dependent central banks with uncoordinated labor. (The differences among the cells are significant, except for the horizontal differences in the *Labor* = 3 and 5 rows.)

This result suggests that consumption tax revenues played an important role in financing high fiscal spending in countries with independent central banks and coordinated labor, as these countries had low personal income tax revenues, and the other tax revenues were not high (except for social security contributions).

Social security contributions received by government

There is some evidence (though not strong) that the combination of coordinated labor and independent central banks also led to high social security contributions. The results for the second period of 1982–2001 (not shown) show the following pattern.[33] Each of the two factors reduced the contributions when the other was weak. When central banks were dependent, coordinated labor led to low contributions, and central bank independence reduced the contributions if labor was not coordinated. But each of them served to increase contributions when the other factor was strong. As a result, the combination of coordinated labor and independent central banks recorded almost the highest social security contributions. The lowest contributions were registered by independent central banks with uncoordinated labor. Similar results are obtained for the models for the entire period of 1961–2001 (fixed effects) and the second period of 1982–2001 (fixed effects).[34]

Table 5.58 Consumption tax revenues: regression results

1982–2001 (without country dummies)	
CBI_{t-1}	−1.332**
	(0.660)
$CBI_{t-1} * Labor_{t-1}$	0.325**
	(0.163)
$Labor_{t-1}$	−0.132*
	(0.071)

Notes
OLS estimates with panel-corrected standard errors in parentheses.
Only the results of the relevant variables are shown.
***Significant at the 0.01 level.
**Significant at the 0.05 level.
*Significant at the 0.10 level.

Table 5.58a Predicted values of consumption tax revenues

1982–2001	Dependent central banks (CBI = 0.14)	Independent central banks (CBI = 0.68)
Uncoordinated labor (Labor = 1)	–0.27	–0.81
Intermediately coordinated labor (Labor = 3)	–0.44	–0.64
Coordinated labor (Labor = 5)	–0.62	–0.46

Notes
Predicted values of consumption tax revenues calculated from the results in Table 5.58. The differences among the cells are significant, except for the horizontal differences in the *Labor* = 3 and 5 rows.

Total government spending

The combination of coordinated labor and independent central banks drove up total government spending in both the first (1961–1981) and second (1982–2001) periods. Table 5.59a shows the predicted values of total government spending, conditional upon labor coordination and central bank independence, for the 1980s and 1990s (without country dummies). The results for the 1960s and 1970s are not shown but are essentially the same as those for the 1980s and 1990s. In both periods, each of the two factors helped reduce spending when the other factor was weak – coordinated labor and independent central banks, respectively, were conducive to restrained fiscal spending if the other factor was weak. When central banks were dependent, labor contributed to low spending. Central bank independence reduced spending if labor was not coordinated. But each of them served to increase spending when the other factor was also strong. As a result, the combination of coordinated labor and independent central banks produced

Table 5.59 Total government spending: regression results

1982–2001 (without country dummies)	
CBI_{t-1}	–3.086*
	(1.823)
$CBI_{t-1} * Labor_{t-1}$	0.733
	(0.457)
$Labor_{t-1}$	–0.197
	(0.193)

Notes
OLS estimates with panel-corrected standard errors in parentheses.
Only the results of the relevant variables are shown.
***Significant at the 0.01 level.
**Significant at the 0.05 level.
*Significant at the 0.10 level.

Table 5.59a Predicted values of total government spending

1982–2001	Dependent central banks (CBI = 0.14)	Independent central banks (CBI = 0.68)
Uncoordinated labor (Labor = 1)	−0.52	−1.79
Intermediately coordinated labor (Labor = 3)	−0.71	−1.19
Coordinated labor (Labor = 5)	−0.90	−0.59

Notes
Predicted values of total government spending calculated from the results in Table 5.59. The differences among the cells are significant, except for the vertical differences in the *CBI* = 0.14 column and the horizontal differences in the *Labor* = 3 and 5 rows.

moderately high spending in the first period, and the second highest spending in the second. Thus, the combination of coordinated labor and independent central banks led to an expansionary fiscal policy regime. It was beneficial to have either coordinated labor or independent central banks for fiscal discipline, but not both or neither.

What the results of total spending and other spending items reviewed above suggest is the following. Each of coordinated labor and independent central banks functioned to restrain spending in the relative absence of the other. But when labor was coordinated and central banks were independent, they together pushed up spending and created an expansionary fiscal policy. Meanwhile, the most conservative (disciplined or contractionary) spending regime was achieved under independent central banks facing uncoordinated labor. Thus, independent central banks helped restrain spending if labor was uncoordinated, but were unable to do so if labor was coordinated and was probably politically powerful. (In the first-period results (not shown), the differences among the cells are significant, except for the vertical differences in the *CBI* = 0.14 column and the horizontal difference in the *Labor* = 5 row. In the second-period results, the horizontal difference in the *Labor* = 3 row is also not significant.)

Total government revenues

There is some (though weak) indication that the combination of coordinated labor and independent central banks led to relatively high total tax revenues. This is consistent with the results of total spending described above – if spending was high, revenues would be high to finance it. The results for the 1980s and 1990s (not reported) show that each factor reduced revenues if the other factor was weak.[35] So when the other factor was weak, each factor led to the lowest revenues, respectively. But when labor was coordinated and central banks were independent, they served to increase revenues. As a result, the combination of coordinated labor and independent central banks led to large tax revenues. The highest revenues were recorded under dependent central banks and uncoordinated labor, as with the total spending results.

Economic growth

Though the evidence is weak, there is some indication that the combination of coordinated labor and independent central banks produced low economic growth during the entire period of 1961–2001. If these results (not reported) are to be trusted, they suggest that the combination of coordinated labor and independent central banks produced the lowest growth of all combinations of labor coordination and central bank independence.[36] The pattern of the variation in output growth here is that each factor contributed to higher growth if the other factor was weak. But when both were strong, they contributed to low growth. Uncoordinated labor and dependent central banks yielded equally low growth. The highest growth was recorded by independent central banks with uncoordinated labor, and the second highest by dependent central banks and coordinated labor. Thus, if the results are to be trusted, the combination was unconducive to economic growth. This suggests some incompatibility between coordinated labor and independent central banks. As we will see below, they also generated negative outcomes in inflation and unemployment.

Unemployment

There is the evidence that the combination of coordinated labor and independent central banks created high unemployment in the first period of 1961–1981. Table 5.60a reports the predicted values of unemployment for 1961–1981, conditional on labor coordination and central bank independence (fixed effects). The results show that coordinated labor (*Labor* = 5) and independent central

Table 5.60 Unemployment: regression results

1961–1981 (fixed effects)	
CBI_{t-1}	−1.489
	(1.857)
$CBI_{t-1} * Labor_{t-1}$	0.764*
	(0.427)
$Labor_{t-1}$	−0.300*
	(0.179)

Notes
OLS estimates with panel-corrected standard errors in parentheses.
Only the results of the relevant variables are shown.
***Significant at the 0.01 level.
**Significant at the 0.05 level.
*Significant at the 0.10 level.

Table 5.60a Predicted values of unemployment

1961–1981	Dependent central banks (CBI = 0.14)	Independent central banks (CBI = 0.68)
Uncoordinated labor (Labor = 1)	−0.40	−0.79
Intermediately coordinated labor (Labor = 3)	−0.78	−0.35
Coordinated labor (Labor = 5)	−1.17	0.08

Notes
Predicted values of unemployment calculated from the results in Table 5.60. The differences among the cells are significant in the vertical differences in the *CBI* = 0.68 column and the horizontal difference in the *Labor* = 5 row. The vertical differences in the *CBI* = 0.14 column were close to significance ($p = 0.11$).

banks (*CBI* = 0.68) led to the highest unemployment rate of all combinations of labor and central banks. Each of the two factors contributed to lower unemployment when the other factor was weak. When central banks were dependent, coordinated labor produced lower unemployment. And when labor was not coordinated, central bank independence contributed to lower unemployment. But when both were strong, it led to high unemployment. Coordinated labor's (*Labor* = 5) unemployment was 1.25 percent higher when central banks were independent (*CBI* = 0.68) than dependent (*CBI* = 0.14). Unemployment under independent central banks (*CBI* = 0.68) was 0.87 percent higher when labor was highly coordinated (*Labor* = 5) than not coordinated (*Labor* = 1). The lowest unemployment was achieved by countries with coordinated labor and dependent central banks (*Labor* = 5, *CBI* = 0.14).[37] (The differences among the cells are significant in the vertical differences in the *CBI* = 0.68 column and the horizontal difference in the *Labor* = 5 row. The vertical differences in the *CBI* = 0.14 column were close to significance ($p = 0.11$).) In Chapter 4 where we estimated independent effects of CBI or labor (without their interaction) on unemployment, we did not detect any significant effect of either factor. The result here shows that the effects of the two factors on unemployment was contingent on their interaction. But these effects disappeared in the 1980s and 1990s.

Inflation

The combination of coordinated labor and independent central banks produced relatively high inflation during all three periods under study. Table 5.61a reports the predicted values of inflation for the entire period of 1961–2001 under different combinations of labor coordination and central bank independence (without country dummies). We obtain the same results for the first (1961–1981) and second (1982–2001) periods with and without country dummies. The results are very stable across different periods and specifications. The predicted values

Table 5.61 Inflation: regression results

1961–2001 (without country dummies)	
CBI_{t-1}	−7.727***
	(2.181)
$CBI_{t-1} * Labor_{t-1}$	1.839***
	(0.479)
$Labor_{t-1}$	−0.826***
	(0.200)

Notes
OLS estimates with panel-corrected standard errors in parentheses.
Only the results of the relevant variables are shown.
***Significant at the 0.01 level.
**Significant at the 0.05 level.
*Significant at the 0.10 level.

Table 5.61a Predicted values of inflation

1961–2001	Dependent central banks (CBI = 0.14)	Independent central banks (CBI = 0.68)
Uncoordinated labor (Labor = 1)	−1.65	−4.82
Intermediately coordinated labor (Labor = 3)	−2.78	−3.97
Coordinated labor (Labor = 5)	−3.92	−3.13

Notes
Predicted values of inflation calculated from the results in Table 5.61. All differences among the cells are statistically significant.

show that each of the two factors contributed to low inflation if the other factor was weak. So the lowest inflation was recorded by countries with independent central banks and uncoordinated labor. Inflation in countries with dependent central banks and coordinated labor was likewise very low. In countries with uncoordinated labor (*Labor* = 1), an increase of central bank independence from 0.14 to 0.68 brought down inflation by 3.2 percent. In countries with dependent central banks (*CBI* = 0.14), an increase of labor coordination from 1 to 5 reduced inflation by 2.3 percent. But when both factors were strong, they pushed up inflation.[38] The highest inflation was experienced in countries with dependent central banks and uncoordinated labor. In countries with independent central banks (*CBI* = 0.68), an increase in labor coordination from 1 to 5 pushed up inflation by 1.7 percent.

These patterns suggest that each of coordinated labor and independent central banks was conducive to low inflation in the relative absence of the other factor, as more or less consistent with the corporatist literature and the central bank independence literature, respectively. Independent central banks brought inflation down as long as labor was not coordinated. Likewise, coordinated labor contributed to low inflation if central banks were not independent. But independent central banks and coordinated labor, when combined together, caused some forces that drove up inflation, suggesting their incompatibility for economic outcomes and policy. (All differences among the cells are statistically significant.)

Sum

The combination of coordinated labor and independent central banks produced generally negative outcomes in economic policy and performance. It induced relatively high spending, high tax revenues, high inflation, high unemployment, and possibly low economic growth.[39] Although independent central banks helped improve economic policy and outcomes for other actors such as coalition, center, and left governments, they clashed with coordinated labor and resulted in unfavorable outcomes. This is another case that shows that fiscal indiscipline was unconducive to good macroeconomic performance.

This general picture of the effects of central bank independence and labor coordination resembles the theoretical conclusions of economists' non-cooperative game-theoretic models that expect fiscal expansionism by party governments and contractionary monetary policy by central banks, creating low output and high inflation (Nordhaus, 1994; Bennett and Loayza, 2002; Demertzis et al., 1998; Dixit and Lambertini, 2002). To apply their logic to labor and central banks, labor values employment and economic growth more than price stability, but central banks value price stability more than the former. As a result, labor causes an expansionary fiscal policy (but labor does not make policy; it only makes demands and puts pressure on governments to meet its demands), and central banks counter it with a contractionary monetary policy. This policy mix leads to high deficits and high interest rates, which in turn create high inflation and low economic growth. (But according to the results of my empirical analysis, the interaction of labor and central banks did not affect the fiscal balance or monetary policy.)

As we saw in Chapter 4, coordinated labor itself contributed to fiscal discipline and positive economic outcomes in the 1980s and 1990s. But it is also mostly during these two decades that the combination of coordinated labor and independent central banks produced fiscal indiscipline and negative economic outcomes. Thus, the conclusion from our empirical analysis should be that although labor itself was conducive to fiscal discipline and favorable macroeconomic outcomes in the 1980s and 1990s, there was an incompatibility or conflict between coordinated labor and independent central banks in their economic goals, policy preferences, or actions, and that led to negative outcomes in economic policy and performance. To lend support to this explanation, our empirical results show also that independent central banks, when they faced uncoordinated labor, led to relative fiscal discipline and good economic outcomes (high growth, low inflation, low unemployment), and so did coordinated labor when it faced only dependent central banks. The effects of labor coordination were, thus, contingent on central bank independence.

The exact reason why labor and central banks produced negative economic outcomes – when central bank independence was generally beneficial for coalition, center, and left governments – is not clear. But one possible explanation would be that it was less difficult for party governments to achieve (unintentional or intentional, implicit or explicit) policy agreement and/or coordination with central banks than for labor, because the former were smaller in size and more cohesive in policy positions and actions, whereas labor unions were much larger in size and number and were more diverse in their policy goals and actions. The large size and multiplicity of labor unions may make it difficult for them to attain (intentional or unintentional) policy agreement, cooperation, and coordination with central banks. And it was also abundantly clear to party governments that they were jointly responsible for economic management and performance with central banks, and any policy mistake, economic mismanagement, or poor performance would be attributed to them. That kind of sense of responsibility and accountability and the capacity to act responsibly may be weaker for labor unions.

Conclusion

Economic policy and outcomes vary, depending on which governments make policy and which other political or economic actors have influence on their policy making. Economic policy and outcomes also change, depending on the environment under which governments and other actors operate. Thus, economic policy and outcomes are partly context-specific. Different governments produce distinct economic policy and outcomes, depending on their own characteristics and their environment.

The changing globalized economy left its marks on the economic policy of industrial democracies, and the impact of the competitive pressure it produces was visible in many results reviewed in this chapter. Governments, generally, shifted their economic policy in a neoliberal direction. So we observed change in their economic policy and outcomes from the 1960s–1970s to the 1980s–1990s. But the particular ways different governments made the adjustments also varied, depending on who they were and on their policy making environment. Different party governments had varied ways of adjusting to the new economic environment and the competitive pressures from the globalized economy.

Coalition governments significantly reduced spending and achieved fiscal discipline and positive economic outcomes, if they had independent central banks. Likewise, when buttressed by independent central banks, center governments successfully reduced deficit. But they were unable to reduce spending, so had high levels of public spending even in the 1980s and 1990s. In the face of their large fiscal commitments in social security and government services, which they were not immediately able to retrench, they reduced deficit by keeping high tax revenues. The economic policy of left governments facing independent central banks also became disciplined. But the benefits of independent central banks for left governments were not as extensive as for center governments. In contrast, the combination of conservative (right) governments and independent central banks was not a very favorable one and resulted in expansionary fiscal policy and monetary policies and subsequent inflation.

The left–labor regime's fiscal policy was relatively expansionary in the 1960s and 1970s, but became disciplined in the 1980s and 1990s. Its fiscal discipline helped yield high economic growth in the 1980s and 1990s. The combination of left governments and uncoordinated labor, by contrast, produced a generally disciplined fiscal policy in the 1960s and 1970s, but an expansionary fiscal policy and low economic growth in the 1980s and 1990s. Meanwhile, the combination of coordinated labor and independent central banks was not a very compatible one for economic policy and outcomes, and generally produced relatively high spending, high taxation, and unfavorable macroeconomic outcomes – high unemployment, high inflation, and possibly low economic growth. In contrast, independent central banks, when they faced only uncoordinated labor, led to relative fiscal discipline and good economic outcomes (high growth, low inflation, low unemployment). So did coordinated labor when it faced only dependent central banks. The effects of labor coordination were, thus, contingent on central bank independence.

6   Conclusion

I close this book by discussing some implications of the findings of the book for the understanding of the comparative political economy of industrial democracies. I also explain what more we need to do to understand better the workings of the political economies.

In this book, we observed various patterns that exist in economic policy and outcomes, and learned how political and economic factors affect them. We also learned the patterns of the impact of those factors. For instance, we found that central banks extensively affect party governments' fiscal policy, though they do not control fiscal policy. Independent central banks have the effect of disciplining party governments' fiscal policy. They also restrain party governments' electoral expansions. Economic policy is also affected by a host of other political–economic factors and their interaction – such as government partisanship, the structure of governments, that of party system, labor coordination, and elections. Different partisan governments conduct different economic policy and produce disparate outcomes, because they have distinct incentive and capacity and make policy under different policy making environments.

Yet, it does not mean that the findings of this book will remain the same or true in the future. For I have also explained that the impact of these factors can be time- and context-variant. There is no reason to assume a priori that political parties and partisan governments have fixed, time-invariant policy positions. As I argued in Chapter 3, their policy changes when the environment changes, when economic conditions change, when their constituencies' policy preferences change, and when policy ideas about how the economy works change. In this sense, the assumption of the standard partisan theory that presumes partisan governments' time- or context-invariant policy preferences is too restrictive. Government partisanship affects both economic policy and outcomes, but the effect is contingent on time periods, the economic or political environment, and the institutional setting in which partisan governments make policy. Politics affects economic policy and outcomes, but it does so in a specific time period and in a specific structural environment. Thus, we need to take into account time and environment in thinking about political impact on policy and outcomes.

There is very little that is deterministic about the nature and magnitude of the impact of these factors. Economic policy and outcomes, political events, and political behavior are a product of contingencies, interactions, situational environments of policy making, and thus history.[1] Politicians and policy makers are adaptive, learning actors, and they can change their policy behavior by learning. The granting of independence to central banks in many countries in the 1990s was an example of a result of learning by party governments and economic policy makers that central bank independence stabilizes inflation expectations, helps governments gain the market's confidence, and brings discipline in economic policy. Or they may also be able to learn to discipline their fiscal policy regardless of whether they have independent or dependent central banks. The potential for politicians and policy makers to be willing and able to change economic policy making is also clearly observed in the conservative policy shift they orchestrated into the 1980s and 1990s that we revealed in Chapters 4 and 5 of this book. Even prior to the period under study (1961–2001), political parties and their governments changed their economic policy regime in the mid-twentieth century to the one represented by the Keynesian welfare state after the Great Depression and World War II (Gourevitch, 1986). So we have much evidence showing that policy makers change their economic policy, particularly when their previous economic policy is rendered ineffective by real-world economic crises, such as the Great Depression and the oil crises in the 1970s.

The neoliberal shift in the 1980s and 1990s was more conspicuous among the governments and political–economic regimes that had a prior reputation for fiscal indiscipline and/or economic inefficiencies, such as center governments, coalition governments, and countries with fragmented party systems or coordinated labor. But the potential for policy shift does not have to be limited to those actors. For instance, we have seen in this book that conservative governments were not fiscally disciplined policy makers during the period under study, and their economic outcomes were not so favorable. We have also seen that conservative governments, when they faced independent central banks, generated unfavorable economic policy and outcomes. Yet, this does not have to be the way they always will be. They, too, can change. Such a change may require the realization on their part that their policy does not work well. Or it may require economic crises. But if they face a need to change their policy, they can potentially change their policy and improve economic outcomes.

Such potential for change among conservative governments is manifest in the neoliberal, market-conforming economic reforms implemented in some countries led by conservative governments. Both the United Kingdom and New Zealand drastically cut spending in the 1980s and 1990s and implemented numerous reforms to bring market principles into their economies (though the latter's reform was also carried out by the leftist Labour Party). (The U.S. Reagan administration's reform was also along these lines, but differed from the first two countries because it was accompanied by massive government deficits.) Another case is provided by the Japanese government led by the conservative Liberal Democratic Party (LDP) that has been trying to carry out market reform in the past several years. Their reform effort was a response to the financial crisis and economic stagnation that had lasted for 15 years from the beginning of the 1990s. It was precipitated by their realization that their heavily regulated economic regime governed by a powerful bureaucracy and the alliance between the conservative LDP, the bureaucracy, and their client groups was poorly fit to cope with their economic problems and to recover a vigorous, viable economy. Japan's conservative government tried to ride out economic recessions in the 1990s with Keynesian economic stimulus, but conventional Keynesian spending did not pull its stagnant economy out of recessions and deflation. True, the progress in Japan's reforms has been extremely slow, because of political opposition by traditional LDP politicians and their constituencies to the reform, but it has been moving in the neoliberal, market-conforming direction.[2]

Meanwhile, we also found that the fiscal policy of conservative governments is especially different from the expectation of the standard partisan theory and is expansionary. We need to reconsider the standard assumptions of conventional partisan explanations about the economic policy positions of political parties. Some may counter by saying that the expansionary nature of conservative governments' policy is unduly influenced by the "untypical" experiences of expansionary conservative governments in the 1980s and 1990s in some countries such as the United States and Japan. But if these episodic or qualitative accounts are accurate and conservative governments in the two countries were fiscally expansionary in the 1980s and 1990s, that means that, at least in these countries, conservative governments were expansionary for two decades, half of the entire period of 1961–2001 under study.

In a sense, the U.S. Reagan administration and Japan's conservative LDP governments may have been anomalies or aberrations for conservative governments. Yet if anomalies lasted for two decades and in the world's two largest economies, they should not be treated as anomalies.[3] Otherwise, we could assume away as anomalies most of the things that happen in our lifetime. Thus, it is time for researchers to reconsider and refine the economic policy preferences of different political parties and governments. It makes much sense to re-examine and re-map parties' policy preferences, especially because many center and left governments have modified their economic policy positions in the past two decades. Part of such efforts has been underway (e.g. Budge *et al.*, 2001). But what we need is a remapping of the policy positions and preferences of political parties that are measured – as much as possible – in terms of what policy they actually pursue, rather than their self-proclaimed policy platforms, in which they "say" what they plan or hope to do.[4] In any event, the conventional conception of the policy preferences of right and left parties (e.g. Hibbs, 1977), which was built perhaps from the empirical observations of their policy preferences during the first two-and-a-half decades of the postwar period, should be submitted to re-examination and refinement in order to analyze more meaningfully party governments and their economic policy.

Trends in spending and tax policies and future prospects

One of the goals of the analysis of this book was to examine the effects of political and economic factors on a broad range of economic policy tools. The goal was important, because the analysis of individual disaggregate spending and tax items has rarely been done in the previous literature. Even the studies that did analyze a broad range of policy tools (Garrett, 1998; Clark, 2003) did not really pay attention to the different properties of those policy tools and the effect those differences have on the impact of partisan governments and the structural features of government.

But such a broad analysis of the multitude of policy tools has a cost. Because of the large number of policy tools, I was unable to conduct a detailed analysis of the properties of each of many policy tools and the implications they have for the existence and nature of the impact of political and economic factors in each of the policy tools. We have observed in this book varied patterns across the individual disaggregate policy tools. We have seen that some of the patterns are explicable with relative ease. But we have also found the patterns that are not easily explicable. An analysis of the properties of different economic policy tools and the varying roles political and economic factors have in those policy tools is imperative to our systematic understanding of the effects of political and economic factors on economic policy. We need to investigate more deeply what the patterns and mechanisms are. This avenue of research should be pursued, and it will be the task of my next research. What follows below is my observations of the trends we can observe in each of the policy tools I analyzed in this book and the implications of the trends for the role of governments and political parties in shaping or utilizing those policies. Though they are in no way a full-blown analysis of those policies, we can start from there.

Different disaggregate economic policy tools – e.g. government consumption expenditure, government fixed capital formation, public subsidies to industries, social security payments – have different characteristics and consequences and may be used by party governments and politicians in different ways. If party governments or politicians use economic policies to promote their economic, electoral, or other goals, they do so because of the specific effects they expect those policies produce. If different policy tools have different properties and create different consequences, then politicians should use disparate policy tools differently. They use policy tools that will produce desirable effects from their point of view.

For example, it has previously been pointed out that fiscal policy should be a better policy tool for politicians targeting particular constituents than monetary policy (e.g. Clark and Hallerberg, 2000; Bearce, 2002). But this book finds that distinct patterns exist also across different fiscal policy tools.

Government consumption

Of all spending and tax items, government final consumption expenditures (spending on the provision of government services) are most often affected by various party governments and other political factors. One of the reasons for the frequent manipulation of government consumption by political parties is that it – combining its wage and non-wage components – represents the largest spending item in total government spending. Government consumption occupies 19 percent of GDP (11.5 percent of GDP for its wage component, and 7.5 percent of GDP for its non-wage component) and is even larger than another large government spending item – social security transfers (12.2 percent of GDP). In terms of its share of total government budgets, total government final consumption (combining both wage and non-wage consumption) comprises 43 percent of total government spending. Likewise, wage consumption occupies 26 percent of total government spending, and non-wage consumption 17 percent.

As a result, government consumption presents a great opportunity for political parties to use economic policy to promote their political or electoral goals as well as to mold the shape of government services, the welfare system, and society, and the well-being of their citizens. The provision of government services is also very visible to and appreciated by citizens and other constituency groups, and can directly contribute to the popularity of economic policy by party governments and of party governments themselves.

The manipulation of government consumption can be a very effective electoral and political tool. One of the socioeconomic groups that greatly benefit from government services is low- and medium-income workers and families. The utility of government services as public policy and as an electoral/political tool is demonstrated by the historical use of government services by left parties (labor and social democratic parties). But low-income workers and families are not the only group to prefer large government services. Even wealthy citizens can prefer certain government services. In countries that have national health services, conservative party governments have had difficulty retrenching spending on health care, because even wealthy citizens enjoy the benefits of public health care and oppose its retrenchment or privatization, as in the British Conservative governments' failure to privatize health care. So this leaves room also for conservative governments to use the provision of government services as a political or electoral tool.[5] Thus, government consumption is a useful and easy policy tool for political parties to use for political purposes, because it is the largest spending item and visible to constituency groups.

The two components of government final consumption spending – wage and non-wage components – have shown distinct trends in the recent decades. Most governments – including leftist, centrist, and rightist ones – have high wage consumption spending, except the United States and Japan (see Figure 2.6, page 45). But wage consumption has been declining in almost all countries since around 1980. Countries such as the United Kingdom, Australia, Ireland, the Netherlands, New Zealand, and Sweden, particularly, have drastically reduced this spending. Governments have been successful in reducing wages for government employees engaged in the provision of public services (though the decline of government employees as a percentage of total employment has been much more gradual and smaller).[6]

But as Figure 2.5 (page 44) shows, governments have been unable to reduce non-wage consumption spending. In many countries, this spending is still on the gradual rise, though the rate of the increase slowed down since around 1980 or the spending has leveled off in some countries. This shows that governments have been successful in reducing the wage component of government services, but have been unable to reduce the spending on government services themselves. Non-wage spending is also as high in countries with frequent conservative governments (e.g. Japan, France, the United Kingdom, Canada, New Zealand) as in those with left or center governments, as consistent with the results of my analysis pointing to right governments' expansionary fiscal policy.

Party governments will continue to have difficulty drastically reducing government consumption. This spending funds one of the most important functions of government. The neoliberal orthodoxy in many countries will continue to put pressures on government to reduce government consumption spending. But its reductions will be gradual. As a result, government consumption will remain the largest spending item, and continue to represent a policy area where party governments have the greatest maneuvering room and abilities in manipulating economic policy. It will also remain a policy area where the impact of partisan governments is felt strongly.

There is another reason government consumption will remain the most important and attractive economic policy tool for party governments. That is, demand is likely to increase for a more active government involvement in promoting human capital formation and technological advances with a view to enhancing the productivity and competitiveness of their national economies and maximizing economic growth. This is a result of the awareness among governments and policy makers that governments can actively promote economic growth by facilitating technological advances. Government investment in human capital and technology is likely to increase in importance in many countries, because international economic competition is getting ever stronger, and their industries and corporations vie for profits and market shares and strive to win competition in developing new technologies. Since their industries and corporations are exposed to harsh competition in the global economy, the demand by the private sector and the public is likely to rise for increased government involvement in assisting the private economy in the development of technological advances and human capital and enhancing the productivity and competitiveness of the national economies. I would not be surprised to see increased government spending on education and R&D to assist technological advances and improve human capital. The performance of industries and corporations has direct bearings on the performance of the national economies.

But at the same time, two opposing forces are at work to affect the use of government consumption by party governments and the strength and nature of the impact of other political factors in the future. The first dynamic is that political impact will continue to be felt strongly in government consumption in this area, because it will represent a large and important spending item and, as a result, preserve much room for political, economic, and ideological contestation among different political parties and partisan governments. But the second is that partisan impact may decrease in importance in this policy area, because the productivity and competitiveness of the national economy and economic growth are equally important to all political parties, and they will have to promote those economic goals, regardless of their partisan differences. Such economic pressures exert some converging effects on the economic policy of different governments, as represented by the recent shift among industrial democracies toward a neoliberal, market-conforming policy regime.

Yet, so far, industrial democracies have preserved differences in their economic growth strategies, and partisan differences in policy have remained. The experience of industrial democracies shows that the American-style free market economy with minimal government intervention is not the only way to promote economic growth. The cases of Scandinavian countries, such as Sweden and Denmark, show that governments can actively implement public policy to simultaneously promote the well-being of citizens *and* economic competitiveness and growth. U.S. policy, overall, has sought to achieve the latter at the cost of the former. But countries like Sweden and Denmark have sought to achieve both goals through the active government provision of public services – education, health care, active labor market policy, job (re)training, and investments in knowledge-intensive industries and R&D (most of these expenditures belong to government final consumption). These policy and institutional differences can be sticky and tend to persist.

Social security transfers

Social security transfers are the second largest spending item, next to government wage and non-wage consumption expenditures combined. It comprises 12.2 percent of GDP (28 percent of total government spending). Countries with frequent center- and left-party governments have high social security transfers, but those with frequent right-party governments – such as France, the United Kingdom, and New Zealand – also have high spending levels (see Figure 2.7, page 47), as consistent with my result pointing out large social security transfers by right governments (see Chapter 4). The trend in social security transfers shows that most governments have had difficulty reducing spending. Social security transfers have steadily risen, while the rate of the increases slowed down in the 1980s and 1990s. Reductions of social security spending are difficult since the aged populations have been expanding in all countries and because most citizens enjoy the benefits of social security, and political parties have difficulty retrenching popular entitlement programs. But several countries – such as Belgium, Canada, Denmark, Finland, the Netherlands, New Zealand, Norway, Sweden, and the United Kingdom – have managed to reduce this spending in the 1990s.

Social security transfers are another spending item that this book finds is affected much by political factors. Social security benefits are also very visible to citizens and directly affect their financial conditions, so in that sense, they are an attractive policy tool for political parties to manipulate. But I originally expected that party governments would not often use social security spending for political purposes, because although it may be tempting to manipulate social security spending for political goals, it would be difficult for them to readjust the spending in the near future when, for instance, fiscal discipline requires retrenchment. In fact, most governments are currently under tremendous pressure to control the expansion of social security spending to make their social security system solvent and self-sustaining and maintain fiscal discipline. In this environment, it would be tempting to increase social security benefits for political goals, but party governments would find it not particularly convenient nor plausible to do so because of their long-term need to restrain social security spending. For once in place, citizens become used to the level of current benefits, and political parties have difficulty retrenching such entitlements. But surprisingly, my empirical analysis finds that party governments do often manipulate social security spending. Social security is apparently easier to manipulate than I originally expected.

The future trend will be for governments to have to control social security spending. But exactly because it needs to be controlled and in many cases retrenched, it will open space for intense partisan and political conflict by political parties over who should bear the costs of retrenchment and how it should be done. In this sense, partisan governments are likely to continue to affect social security spending in the foreseeable future.

Government subsidies

By contrast, government subsidies to industries do not represent an extremely attractive tool for political parties' political manipulation of economic policy. Their spending level is very low – only 1.9 percent of GDP (4.4 percent of total government spending). And the trend in almost all countries has been for government subsidies to decrease further (see Figure 4.2 on page 117). This spending has steadily been declining since the 1970s or 1980s. As a result, there is not much room for political parties to use this spending for political purposes (although it of course does not preclude politicians' use of government subsidies to give particularized benefits and favors to their client industries and regions). The size of the spending is small, and its effects would be small and limited to a narrow range of industries and constituency groups, and party governments cannot expect to derive the sizeable political benefits that they would like to gain from manipulating economic policy. This may be a reason why government subsidies show different patterns than other fiscal policy tools (see Chapter 4). Government subsidies are not likely to increase their size in the future. Sizeable increases in government subsidies are not likely especially under the dominance of neoliberal economic thinking that encourages the exit of government intervention from the private economy. In this environment, party governments are also not likely to use them extensively for political manipulations.

As can be seen in Figure 4.2, government subsidies have experienced large spending cuts of all major expenditure items. It suggests that the electoral costs of the retrenchment of subsidies to industries are relatively small, and governments have had relative ease cutting them down. Government subsidies probably affect electoral votes less directly than other spending items.

Government investment

Government investment (see Figure 4.1 on page 114) has also continuously declined since the end of 1960s in most countries (except in Japan), and is a small spending item (3.5 percent of GDP or 8 percent of total government spending). Its small size and continuous reduction do not give political parties much space for political maneuvering. However, in contrast to public subsidies, government investment has the potential to experience some boost in spending levels and in the importance of partisan impact, for the same reason that government spending on human capital formation and technology may increase in importance. As mentioned above, governments and policy makers are increasingly aware that they can constructively promote economic growth by making public investments to improve the factors of production for the national economy, facilitate technological advances, and enhance economic productivity and competitiveness, as long as public investments are made in a way not to impair resource allocation efficiencies and cause market distortions. In a globalized economy where industries and firms are exposed to harsh international competition, calls for government policy to help enhance the factors of production and promote growth are likely to become strong. While its small size within the total budget sets natural limits to the size of political manipulation by party governments, partisan differences in the conception of optimal growth strategies are likely to be reflected in the way public investment is employed in economic management.

Total spending and revenues

When we look at total government spending and revenues, we see that many governments have significantly reduced total spending in the 1980s and 1990s. As Figure 6.1 shows, total spending has been on the decline in most countries since the 1980s and 1990s. This reflects governments' effort to reduce deficit and debt and bring fiscal discipline, make their economic policy more market-conforming, promote resource allocation efficiency, and increase the productivity and competitiveness of their national economies.

But as Figure 6.2 shows, governments have not reduced total tax revenues – they have reduced spending, but have kept the previous revenue levels or slowed the pace of revenue increases. With the exceptions of the Netherlands, Ireland, New Zealand, and Finland, total revenues have not declined at all, though they leveled off in the 1980s and 1990s. This reflects the effort by these governments – including those that wished to join the EMU – to reduce deficit and gross debt by reducing spending but not reducing revenues. Their effort has certainly led to improvements in their primary balance as well as their gross debt levels.[7] In total

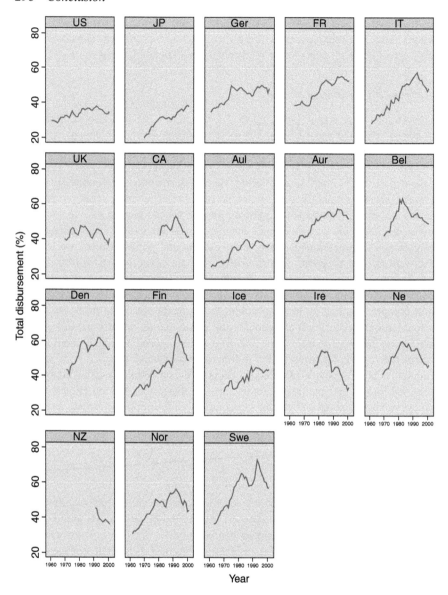

Figure 6.1 Total government spending as a percentage of GDP (sources: see variables, definitions, and sources in Table 4.1 and 4.2).

tax revenues, we do not see any "race to the bottom" envisioned by proponents of the globalization or convergence thesis. The rise of tax revenues slowed down or leveled off, but total revenues have not declined, with the exception of some countries such as the Netherlands, where we see a clear long-term downward trend in the total revenues.

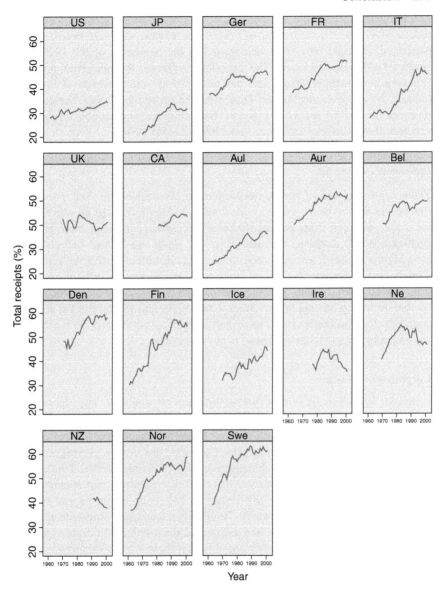

Figure 6.2 Total government revenues as a percentage of GDP (sources: see variables, definitions, and sources in Table 4.1 and 4.2).

Direct tax

As with total government revenues, there is no sign that direct tax revenues have experienced decline in industrial economies in the 1980s and 1990s (individual and corporate income tax combined). The general trend is for the direct tax revenues to continue their gradual rise. The only exceptions are Japan and New

Zealand in the 1990s – but in Japan's case, it is not all its government's effort to reduce government revenues. Japan's direct tax revenues declined because of its protracted, multiple recessions that started in the beginning of the 1990s and lasted for a decade and a half. The recessions depressed revenues from personal and corporate income taxes, and the governments' countercyclical tax cuts reduced the tax revenues further. Thus, with the exception of New Zealand, the revenues from direct taxes continued to rise, and there is no support for the convergence thesis that expects a race to the bottom in tax policy.

Individual income tax

There is also no sign of revenue reductions in personal income tax, except for Ireland, the Netherlands, and New Zealand (see Figure 6.3). In all other countries, the revenues from personal income tax either continued their gradual, small, but steady increase or leveled off in the 1980s and 1990s.[8] Left countries have high revenues from individual income tax. But all countries with frequent conservative governments (except Japan and France) also have large revenues from this tax item. Ireland, the Netherlands, and New Zealand experienced substantial decline in income tax revenues in the 1980s and 1990s. But for all other countries, income tax revenues have not declined. And the race to the bottom envisaged by the globalization thesis is not observable.

Corporate income tax

Corporate tax revenues show a different pattern (Figure 6.4). They have more variations among industrial democracies as well as more dramatic fluctuations than individual income tax. But the changes are not exactly the kind of change envisaged by the convergence thesis. Corporate tax revenues progressively declined in many countries in the course of the 1960s and 1970s. This is consistent with the convergence thesis. But the only countries that steadily kept the decline in the 1980s and 1990s (when globalization deepened and spread) are the United States and Germany. In all other countries, corporate tax revenues sharply increased in the late 1980s and the 1990s.[9] The figures are tax revenues – not tax rates – so it is possible that there were widespread cuts in corporate tax rates (which are documented by many studies and sources), but a broadening of the tax bases more than made up for revenue reductions from the tax rate cuts. Still, the revenues from corporate income tax do not look like a race to the bottom.

Tax policy may become an area where politics and partisan governments exert an important influence in the coming years. I make this speculation for the following reason. As we have seen above, governments have cut spending sizeably in the recent past. But they have not slashed tax revenues. This is probably a result of many governments' effort to reduce not only deficit but also gross debt. In the economic policy environment of fiscal conservatism, it is not easy for governments to use spending increases for political purposes. But since they

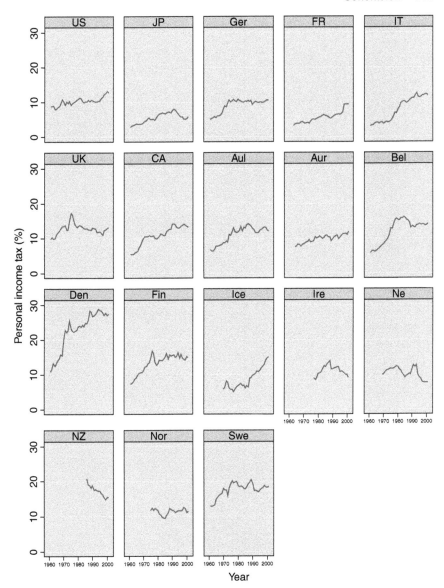

Figure 6.3 Personal income tax as a percentage of GDP (sources: see variables, definitions, and sources in Table 4.1 and 4.2).

have not significantly reduced tax revenues, there is some room for governments
to use tax cuts politically, assuming that they have enough revenues to finance
their spending and not create budget deficit. This may be why electoral expansions by party governments existed only in total government revenues, but not in
total spending during the 1980s and 1990s (Chapter 4). Direct tax (individual

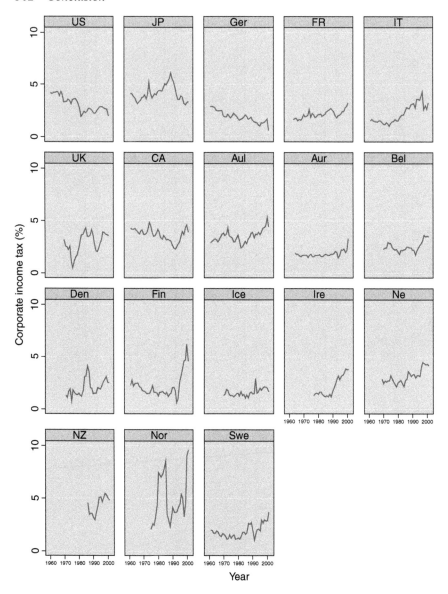

Figure 6.4 Corporate income tax revenues as a percentage of GDP (sources: see variables, definitions, and sources in Table 4.1 and 4.2).

and corporate income taxes), particularly, has not declined and may present an opportunity for governments to use economic policy for political goals. Existing spending commitments naturally restrict the ability of governments to implement tax reductions, especially since population aging places serious strains on social security programs and government finance in general. But the question of who should bear tax burdens has always been a source of partisan conflict, and it will likely continue to affect partisan governments' economic policy in the future.

Indirect tax

Government revenues from indirect taxes (mostly consumption tax) show a slow long-term rise in many countries (Figure 6.5). Italy, Australia, the Netherlands, New Zealand, and Sweden experienced substantial rises in indirect tax revenues (Ireland, in contrast, significantly reduced the revenues). There is a trend among industrial economies to increase their reliance on consumption tax. The trend is likely to continue. Consumption tax could potentially be a source of partisan conflict because of its regressive nature, but the partisan use of consumption tax has not seemed to be as strong as one would expect. This is partly because a small increase in consumption tax rates can achieve much larger revenue increases than can an equivalent increase in individual income tax rates, and as a result, voters may not be as averse to consumption tax increases as income tax increases, and politicians can carry out tax increases with relative ease using consumption tax. This explains the continuous increases of consumption tax revenues in many countries. Consumption tax is likely to remain a low-intensity issue in many countries and provide a relatively easy means of revenue increases for governments. And partisan impact on consumption tax is not likely to be strong, if the past is an indication.

Social security contributions

Social security contributions (see Figure 2.8 on 48) are a major revenue source for industrial democracies (10 percent of GDP or 23 percent of total government revenues). As with social security spending, social security contributions have been on the long-term rise in many countries. But as a result of governments' effort to contain the expansion of social security spending, social security contributions leveled off in many countries in the 1980s and 1990s. In some countries, social security contributions have even declined (France, Italy, Finland, the Netherlands, and Norway). But drastic decreases in social security contributions in the future are not likely for many countries, because of aging, resulting increases in social security spending needs, and the political difficulty of reducing social security benefits.

Issues we need to investigate

There are many things we do not know about the economic policy and performance of industrial democracies. At the end of this book, I would like to briefly mention some of the issues into which we need to inquire, so that we will have a better understanding of governments' economic policy, its determinants, and its effects on the national economy and the well-being of the public.

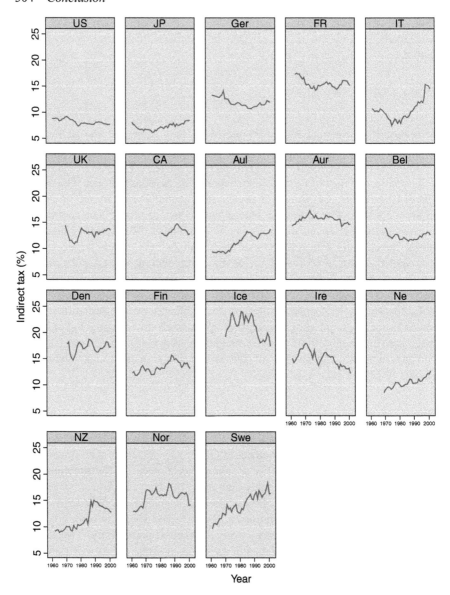

Figure 6.5 Indirect tax as a percentage of GDP (sources: see variables, definitions, and sources in Table 4.1 and 4.2).

First, we need to study the qualitative nature of various economic policy tools, rather than focusing merely on the quantitative level and change of government spending, as this book has done. The book has sought to understand the broad patterns existing in many policy instruments across countries and time and their political determinants. As such, it focused on the quantitative properties of policy tools. But the level and change of government spending in various policy areas are only half of the story. As Esping-Andersen (1990) has shown in the study of welfare policy, the qualitative nature of policy is equally important. It may be the case that political impact on policy manifests itself more strongly in the nature of policy governments implement than its quantity. Or political impact on the nature of policy may be different from that on its quantity. Thus, it is important to study exactly on what programs governments spend money and whether and how politics affects the way governments spend money.

Second, and relatedly, we need to examine more disaggregated policy tools than I have done in this book. I studied spending items such as government final consumption, investment, subsidies, social security transfers, and various tax revenue sources. Yet, each of these items comprises many more disaggregated and specific policies. Government consumption encompasses public spending on education, health care, active labor market policy, and many other government services. Social security includes old-age pension, unemployment, disability, income assistance, and other cash transfers. Different governments have different approaches to these policy areas and use distinct types and combinations of policies. It is very likely that political impact varies across different policy tools. Thus, we need to study these disaggregated policy tools and the political impact therein. Such studies will undoubtedly produce informative results.

Third, while this book has focused on public spending and political impact therein, there is an urgent need to direct analytic attention to private spending on equivalent policy targets, such as education, health care, and social security. In countries with low public spending on these programs (particularly in liberal market economies such as the United States and Japan), much of these programs is funded privately, and private and public funding together finances those programs with different policy targets.[10] So the fact that, for instance, the United States has low levels of public spending on these programs does not mean that the overall level and quality of its education, health care, and social security are also correspondingly low. In fact, Adema and Ladaique (2005) find that when both public and private spending is taken into account, net social spending levels are not so different across industrial democracies, and liberal market economies such as the United States and Japan spend almost as much as social democratic governments in Scandinavia and continental European countries. In many cases, such private funding is mandated by laws or regulations and comprises the overall social or welfare system together with government spending. And as with government policy and spending, privately funded systems and programs are shaped and affected by governments and other political–economic factors. Therefore, we can get a different picture of government policy and spending if we also take private spending and programs into account. Research on the public–private mix of social and welfare policy is much desired.

Fourth, we need to investigate how different policies implemented by different governments affect various aspects of the national economy and the well-being of citizens, such as income distribution, the nature and degree of the economic well-being of families and children, and the effectiveness of public policy in reducing long-term unemployment and poverty and in providing competitive education to prepare students and workers for productive professional careers in the new competitive economy. Much research has been conducted on these issues in the past. But in light of the recent changes in the international and domestic economies, government policy, and political impact demonstrated in this book, there must be changes in these previously well-researched areas, and they should be subjected to re-examination.

Lastly, one thing I was unable to do in this book is the analysis of the EMU and European Central Bank (ECB) and their implications for domestic economic policy and outcomes in European countries. Part of the reason for this omission is that the delegation of monetary policy autonomy to the ECB took place in 1999, and so we would only have two or three years of the ECB to analyze its impact, since the time period of this study ends in 2001. But since the ECB now determines monetary policy for all member states, its analysis is imperative. I intend to embark on such an analysis.

In a similar vein, I was unable to examine the interactive effect of economic globalization and domestic political–economic institutions, in the way Garrett (1998) and Clark (2003) do. I studied the individual effects of the two separately. But if we want to investigate their possible interactive effect, we need to study explicitly their interactive effect by including their interactive terms in the models I analyzed in this book. These remain the task of my future research.

Notes

1 Introduction

1 The countries under study are 18 industrial democracies of the United States, Japan, Germany, France, Italy, the United Kingdom, Canada, Australia, Austria, Belgium, Denmark, Finland, Ireland, the Netherlands, New Zealand, Norway, Sweden, and Switzerland. Their economic policy and performance are analyzed for the 40-year period from 1961 to 2001.

2 See Franzese (2002b) for an excellent review of the implications of the interaction of these different factors for partisan and electoral cycles in macroeconomic policy and outcomes.

3 For studies that analyze the political determinants of economic policy, see Hibbs, 1977; Goldthorpe, 1984; Grilli, *et al.*, 1991; Alesina *et al.*, 1997; Boix, 1998, 2000; Garrett, 1998; Lohmann, 1998; Kitschelt *et al.*, 1999a; Iversen, 1999; Iversen *et al.*, 2000; Clark and Hallerberg, 2000; Poterba and von Hagen, 1999; Hall and Soskice, 2000; Pierson, 2001; Franzese, 2002a, 2002b; Swank, 2002; Clark, 2003; Hallerberg, 2004. For the role of institutions in politics in general: March and Olsen, 1989; Elster, 1989; North, 1990; Weaver and Rockman, 1993; Steinmo *et al.*, 1992; Lijphart, 1999. For the effect of electoral system on politicians' behavior in general, see Duverger, 1954; Rae, 1967; Katz, 1980; Grofman and Lijphart, 1986; Taagepera and Shugart, 1989; Lijphart, 1994.

4 Roubini and Sachs, 1989a, 1989b; Grilli *et al.*, 1991; Edin and Ohlsson, 1991; Borrelli and Royed, 1995; Crepaz, 1996; Hallerberg and Basinger, 1998; Steinmo and Tolbert, 1998; Lijphart, 1999; Poterba and von Hagen, 1999; Sakamoto, 2001, 2005.

5 The antiinflationary benefits of central bank independence may come at a cost; central banks' restrictive monetary policy can place deflationary pressures on the national economy, suppressing economic output and employment, depending on the circumstances and the particular political environment they face (e.g. Iversen, 1999; Franzese and Hall, 2000; Down, 2004).

6 Melitz (1997) is an empirical study of the subject. Iversen (1999), Iversen and Soskice (1999), Way (2000), and Bearce (2002) also touch lightly on the subject.

7 In political science, there is much evidence to suggest that left governments are not more expansionary than right ones. Such is also the findings of this book. See, for instance, Boix (1998). Boix argues that left governments' fiscal restraint gives them the fiscal maneuverability to carry out its supply-side economic policy.

8 Christian democrats' relatively large welfare spending results from their traditional Catholic sense of social responsibility to take care of the weak and poor of society (Esping-Andersen, 1990).

9 It is, of course, preferable to model directly the effects of substantively specific time-variant variables as independent variables, instead of conducting analysis by dividing the entire period into separate sub-periods. I enter some of such factors in the models, such as capital mobility, trade openness, and exchange rate regimes. But there are

also other time-variant factors that are hard to model directly, but that affect economic policy and outcomes importantly. The specific factors I have in mind are the degree of the acceptance of dominant economic policy ideas among policy makers and politicians, political parties' changing policy positions, other aspects of structural changes in the international and domestic economy than capital and trade openness, and the policy-making "atmosphere" or environment such changes create. Economic policy is affected partly by policy makers' understanding of how the economy works and of what is an effective policy solution to economic problems. It is also affected by policy makers' and citizens' conceptions of what is an acceptable policy or an acceptable policy cost. But such cognitive factors are hard to measure and quantify, though not impossible. So as a second best alternative, I examine change in political impact on policy and outcomes by studying it across different periods. This is an approach widely adopted (e.g. Alesina *et al.*, 1997; Cusack, 1999; Boix, 2000; Gali and Perotti, 2003). But it is important to measure directly and model such cognitive and other factors. It will remain my future research task. I thank an anonymous reviewer for calling my attention to this legitimate concern.

2 Party governments–central banks interaction: the fiscal–monetary policy mix

1 For a discussion of goal-seeking political parties and politicians that purposefully determine central bank independence and exchange rate mechanisms to promote their own political interests, see Bernhard (2002), and various chapters in Bernhard *et al.* (2003).

2 For instance, German political parties tried unsuccessfully to reduce the independence of their Bundesbank in the 1950s and 1990s (Bernhard, 2002). Both attempts were blocked by the *Bundesrat* (the upper house).

3 Economists' studies on the fiscal–monetary policy mix have been limited almost exclusively to theoretical exposition of what policy mixes are likely to be used by policy makers. They typically employ noncooperative game-theoretic models, and conclude that conflict between fiscal and monetary authorities' policy preferences generates a loose fiscal–tight monetary policy mix and, as a result, produces suboptimal outcomes; higher deficits and higher interest rates, or lower output and higher inflation. In their game-theoretic models, this undesirable outcome results because fiscal and monetary policy makers respectively use their own policy tool to undermine each other.

4 To a certain extent, this is what happened in Japan in the 1990s where the Bank of Japan's reputation was damaged when it was criticized for causing and prolonging the post-Bubble recessions by not loosening monetary policy early enough or sufficiently.

5 Japan's Koizumi administration and his governing party (the Liberal Democratic Party), for instance, began threatening to change the central bank laws to deprive the Bank of Japan of its monetary policy independence in late 2005, when the Bank of Japan started considering a reversal of an expansionary monetary policy against the administration's wishes.

6 We here have an endogeneity problem, and I do not have a solution to it. Many things in politics are endogenous in reality.

7 In the 1960s and 1970s, party governments carried out relatively expansionary fiscal policy. Fiscal policy was not particularly conservative even in countries with independent central banks.

8 The judgment about the tightness or looseness of monetary policy is, generally, not immediately easy, because it is determined partly by reference to inflation. For instance, no matter how tight a monetary policy at one time point is considered, the

same monetary policy could be regarded as not tight enough (or loose) if high inflation then took place (though probably not likely because of the monetary policy).

9   Many EU countries adopted pegged currency regimes (EMS) in the post-Bretton Woods period, and in their case, the use of monetary policy was restricted by their exchange rate system.

10 For instance, the Conservative government in the United Kingdom blocked a reform attempt to increase the independence of the Bank of England in the early 1990s. The Labour Party opposed it, too (Bernhard, 2002).

11 A more detailed explanation of what differences single-party and coalition governments produce is provided in the second part of Chapter 3.

12 In Tsebelis's (1995, 1999) original thesis on veto players, not only the number of veto players but also their ideological distance and configuration matter jointly.

13 To avoid confusion in terminology, we will refer to left, center, and right governments as "partisan" governments to distinguish them from the term "party" governments we have used to refer to the executive and legislative branches that politicians and political parties control.

14 Christian democrats' relatively large welfare spending results from their traditional Catholic sense of social responsibility to take care of the weak and poor of society (Esping-Andersen, 1990).

15 For a thesis contrary to mine, see Way (2000). He argues that left governments when combined with independent central banks produce low inflation but at the cost of high unemployment, because (1) their policy preferences conflict with each other, (2) left governments' expansionary fiscal policy meets with central banks' contractionary monetary policy, and (3) this conflictual policy mix and economic uncertainty impair economic performance. In contrast, in his view, right governments and the central bank share similar policy preferences, and this relative accord helps them achieve low inflation without causing increasing unemployment. As I will show in the empirical analysis (Chapter 5), this thesis does not receive empirical support.

16 See Franzese (2002b) for an excellent exhaustive review and discussion of previous studies of electoral cycles.

17 There are other theoretical considerations. For one, open-economy economics tells us that the effectiveness of fiscal and monetary policies for countercyclical economic stimulus is subject to the combination of a country's level of capital mobility and exchange rate regime (Mundell, 1963). Under perfect capital mobility, fiscal policy is an effective policy tool of demand management if a country has a fixed exchange rate mechanism, but monetary policy is ineffective. In contrast, if a country has a floating exchange rate system, monetary policy is effective under perfect capital mobility, but fiscal policy is not. Following this thesis, Clark (2003) argues that electoral cycles exist only when and where these constraints do not interfere with the availability and effectiveness of fiscal and monetary policies as tools of electoral expansion. But what we do not know is the following: if fiscal or monetary policy is not effective, will party governments not use it because it is not effective, or will they still try to use it for electoral purposes, if not for economic outcomes? For all we know, the ineffectiveness of either economic policy does not have to prevent party governments from using fiscal or monetary policy for electoral purposes even if it is not effective in stimulating aggregate demand; economically ineffective policy manipulations may still win voters. Voters and constituents could potentially be pleased just with spending increases or tax cuts even if they do not stimulate the macroeconomy. Or even if such economic policy fails to win votes, politicians believe or wish that it will increase votes. Party governments can potentially use these policy tools to court voters and constituents, knowing their limitations as tools of demand management. The presence of electoral cycles under different combinations of capital mobility and exchange rate mechanisms is an important and interesting question to be probed, but I have to make it the task of my future research, largely because this book already has

the results of many interactive effects to report and partly also due to my resource constraints. The inclusion of capital mobility and exchange rate regimes would entail four- and five-way interactions in this study, and it would make it difficult to analyze the effects of other political–economic variables I am interested in. Another consideration is the potential effect of politicians' electoral prospects on their use of electoral manipulations (Franzese, 2002a, 2002b). This also needs to await my next research.

18 Or, relatedly, there may have been little need for governments' economic expansions because economic performance was already good without expansions by policy prior to the oil crises.

3 Change in the economic environment, political actors, and adjustment

1 There is no inevitability in actors adjusting to a new environment. I am not arguing that every actor will adjust and adapt. It is possible that some actors do not or cannot adapt. Some actors that do not adjust may still survive in the new environment. Some others may not survive in the new environment and weaken or perish. For instance, some political parties survive in party competition for a long time, and others disappear.

2 Many social scientists feel uncomfortable with this sort of accidental view of human behavior and social events. But from the perspective of astrobiology or evolutionary biology, one can easily see that even the origin of human life on Earth owes itself to many contingencies, coincidences, and luck. As far as we know so far, it was rather a rare event that Earth developed to provide a favorable environment for life like it did; that complex life with intelligence emerged, and that life was human beings; that human beings had the physical features of two eyes, one nose, two ears, two arms, and two legs; and that human civilizations developed the way they did. There is no natural- or physical-law-like inevitability in the emergence of any of these phenomena. One can find a functional reason for just about anything that exists on Earth, but the point is that it would not have had to be that way, and there were many other possibilities that could have materialized. Political behavior and phenomena we observe today, likewise, would not have had to develop the way they did. They could have taken other forms. They are the way they are now because of the particular environment, history, and their interaction they have had with other actors and events.

3 Kitschelt (1999, 2001) argues that the likelihood of left governments' implementation of market-conforming reform depends not only on their policy positions but also on their strategic locations in electoral competition with other political parties.

4 The years and countries of reform are from Bernhard and Leblang (2003).

5 The list of institutional differences scholars have studied is long: parliamentary vs. presidential democracies; the structure of parliament (bicameral vs. unicameral parliaments, symmetric vs. asymmetric power relations between lower and upper houses); electoral system; federal vs. unitary systems; coordinated market economies vs. liberal market economies; the mode of interest aggregation (pluralist and corporatist systems); strong vs. weak bureaucracy. The following studies provide a good introduction for the reader who wishes to study the role of institutions in politics: March and Olsen, 1989; Elster, 1989; North, 1990; Weaver and Rockman, 1993; Steinmo *et al.*, 1992; Lijphart, 1999. For the effects of institutions on economic policy and outcomes, see Goldthorpe, 1984; Kitschelt *et al.*, 1999a; Iversen *et al.*, 2000; Hall and Soskice, 2000; Pierson, 2001. For the effect of electoral system on politicians' behavior in general, see Duverger, 1954; Rae, 1967; Katz, 1980; Grofman and Lijphart, 1986; Taagepera and Shugart, 1989; Lijphart, 1994.

6 Fiscal rules and procedures, and the role of the financial minister have also been argued to affect fiscal policy. But I defer the analysis of their effects to future

research, as the inclusion of these factors in the current study would make the presentation of my theoretical arguments and empirical tests intractable.

7 See also Weaver and Rockman, 1993; Tsebelis, 1995, 1999. None of these studies are simplistic enough to conclude that multiple veto players generate disadvantages under any circumstances. The contributors in Weaver and Rockman agree that the multiplicity of veto players generally decreases government capabilities of policy innovation, but note that it is only one of many factors and its effect is contingent on other factors. In Tsebelis's thesis, not only the number of veto players but also their ideological distance and configuration matter jointly.

8 A majority of empirical studies have been done on the relationship between government types and fiscal policy (Borrelli and Royed, 1995; Clark and Hallerberg, 2000; Edin and Ohlsson, 1991; Grilli *et al.*, 1991; Hallerberg and Basinger, 1998; Poterba and von Hagen, 1999; Roubini and Sachs, 1989a, 1989b; Sakamoto, 2001; Steinmo and Tolbert, 1998). But there are some recent studies that investigate the effects of government attributes on unemployment, inflation, and economic growth (Crepaz, 1996; Lijphart, 1999).

9 Single-member district (SMD) systems create (approximately) two-party systems and single-party majority governments, producing a few veto players within government and (allegedly) facilitating a greater ability of governments to pursue their policies. Proportional representation (PR) systems tend to produce multiparty systems and coalition governments, creating multiple veto players within government and increasing the likelihood of policy disagreement.

10 Other scholars challenge the hypothesis about "undisciplined" coalition governments, and argue that coalition governments may actually perform better than single-party governments. Crepaz (1996) argues that multiparty governments with PR produce better macroeconomic outcomes because they enjoy wider popular government support than single-party majority governments and this makes the former's policies "more responsible" (although his independent variable is consensus democracy – not exactly the same as coalition governments). He argues that coalition governments (which show a correlation with consensus democracy) produce more stable, steady, and predictable policy than single-party majority governments. Single-party governments are often in two-party systems, where government responsibility alternates between two major parties and, in his view, the magnitude of policy change or reversal is large. In multiparty systems, by contrast, the scale of policy change is smaller because one or two coalition parties are replaced by other small parties (see also Lijphart, 1999).

11 In political science, there is much evidence to suggest that left governments are not more expansionary than right ones (see, for instance, Boix, 1998). Boix argues that left governments' fiscal restraint gives them the fiscal maneuverability to carry out its supply-side economic policy.

12 Christian democrats' relatively large welfare spending results from their traditional Catholic sense of social responsibility to take care of the weak and poor of society (Esping-Andersen, 1990).

13 But in the past decade or so, a new partisan theory called the rational partisan theory challenged the Hibbsian explanation and its empirical validity (Alesina *et al.*, 1997). The rational partisan model explains that distinct partisan outcomes exist only in the short run because rational agents adjust to new conditions, whereas the Hibbsian model argues for the existence of long-term partisan outcomes. The rational partisan model is not considered in this book.

14 Garrett's (1998) theory predicts that the combination of conservative rule and weak labor also leads to coherent economic policy and good performance.

15 Calmfors and Driffill (1988) explain that in countries where wage negotiations take place at the firm or national level, inflation and unemployment performance is better than in countries where wages are determined at the industry level. This is because nationally

coordinated union leaders take into account the inflationary and unemployment effects of their militant wage behavior and restrain their wage demands. But this thesis is not well supported by empirical evidence (OECD, 1997).

16 In this sense, right governments had a right reputation as fiscally conservative, though they are not as fiscally disciplined as believed by many, as I show in the empirical analysis.

17 As explained in Chapter 2, conservative governments had a weaker need to use central bank independence to manage economic policy in a competitive globalized world.

18 Center governments are the least likely to be single-party majority governments of all partisan governments. Center governments are also more likely to have independent central banks than left or right governments. Thus, center governments are likely to be coalition governments and have independent central banks. Left governments are more often minority governments than right or center governments.

19 In contrast, central bank independence affects the fiscal policy of center and left governments. But central bank independence does restrain the monetary policy of right as well as center governments (Sakamoto, 2003).

20 Germany's Christian Democratic governments are treated as center governments in this book. But in the general literature, they are also often treated as conservative governments. If they were classified as conservative governments, they would be added to the list of the fiscally expansionary right governments, as they ran an expansionary fiscal policy in the 1990s under Chancellor Helmut Kohl due to economic difficulties after German unification. Likewise, Italy's successive Christian Democratic governments produced large deficit and debt and would be added to the list, though in this book, they are classified as center governments.

4 The political–economic determinants of economic policy and outcomes: basic empirical results

1 The countries included are the United States, Japan, Germany, France, Italy, the United Kingdom, Canada, Australia, Austria, Belgium, Denmark, Finland, Ireland, the Netherlands, New Zealand, Norway, Sweden, and Switzerland. Iceland and Luxembourg are not included due to the paucity of economic data. Portugal and Spain are excluded because of their shorter experience with democracy and economic development, which makes them different from the other industrial democracies in some ways.

2 I thank Bill Bernhard and David Leblang for generously sharing their data.

3 The sources for the political variables are Woldendorp *et al.*, 1993, 1998; Mackie and Rose, 1991, 1997; *European Journal of Political Research, Political Data Yearbook*, various years; *Keesing's Record of World Events*, various years. In coding *Coalition*, if the number of governing parties changed during the course of a year, these scores were weighted by quarter, and annual averages were computed. In the case of *Majority*, if two or more governments of different categories existed in a given year, the category of the government that stayed in office longer in that year was chosen for the value of the year. In coding the coalition/majority status of U.S. governments, I judged that U.S. divided government should not be treated as minority government. So, following Borrelli and Royed (1995), I coded split control of the executive and legislative branches in the United States as an instance of coalition majority governments (1 for *Majority*, 2 for *Coalition*) where the president and Congress jointly make decisions. Democratic control of both branches was coded as a single-party majority government (1 for *Majority*, and 1 for *Coalition*).

4 These partisanship data are almost identical to the data by Swank (n.d.) in definitions. The correlation between Armingeon *et al.*'s (2002) and Swank's left variables is very high (0.99). But Armingeon *et al.*'s center includes both Christian democratic and

non-Christian democratic centrist parties, and Swank separates them. As a result, the correlation of the former's center and the latter's Christian democratic variables is only 0.61. This difference comes mainly from the fact that Armingeon *et al.*'s center includes the U.S. Democrats and the Canadian Liberals, whereas Swank's Christian democratic variable does not include them. The only other major difference is that Armingeon *et al.* classify the German Christian Democratic Union as a center party, and Swank as a right party.

5 More specifically, Kenworthy's (2001) scores represent: 1 = fragmented wage bargaining; 2 = industry- and firm-level bargaining with little pattern setting; 3 = industry-level bargaining with irregular pattern setting, or government wage arbitration; 4 = centralized bargaining by peak confederations or government imposition of a wage schedule without a peace obligation; 5 = centralized bargaining by peak confederations or government imposition of a wage schedule with a peace obligation, or extensive pattern setting with coordination by large firms.

6 I made minor modifications to Boix's (2000) coding with regard to Germany, Japan, and Switzerland, following Soskice (1990) who justifiably underscores the role of employers' associations in wage coordination.

7 Ideally, I should also analyze the effect of labor, using different operationalizations of labor coordination or centralization. But given the already large number of variables and models I need to estimate, this option was not pursued.

8 I thank Quinn for generously sharing his data.

9 I thank Carles Boix for suggestions on this variable's measurement.

10 I thank Rob Franzese, Neal Beck, and Tom Fomby for so patiently teaching me much about unit roots, cointegration, and single-equation ECMs.

11 Franzese (2002a) uses single-equation ECMs in his analysis of social security payments and government debt.

12 Many previous studies use full fixed-effect models (Alesina *et al.*, 1997; Franzese, 2002a; Garrett, 1998; Bearce, 2002; Clark, 2003); Boix (1998) estimates his models both with and without country dummies.

13 I also use period dummy variables in the entire-period models to control for some unknown effects accruing to particular time periods. I experimented with period dummies with three periods (1961–1973, 1974–1984, 1986–2001: 1985 = reference year) and four periods (1961–1972, 1973–1981, 1983–1990, 1991–2001: 1982 = reference year), which are all reasonable period divisions from theoretical and empirical perspectives in one way or another. Since the choice of period division does not change the main results, I only report the results of the models with three period dummies.

14 Gali and Perotti (2003) find a global trend toward more countercyclical fiscal policy among OECD countries in the post-Maastricht period, though their period refers only to the most recent several years after the European Economic and Monetary Union (EMU).

15 There is still the possibility that, as Garrett (1998) argues, the independent effect of increasing trade is to reduce spending, but the interactive effect of left–labor corporatist regimes and increasing trade is to push up spending and deficits.

16 There is still the possibility that strong (organized or centralized) labor may put upward pressure on spending, but coordinated labor does not.

17 But this loses significance in the models without country dummies.

18 When *Fragmentation* is entered in the models, *Coalition* becomes positive and significant in 1961–1981, suggesting that coalition governments may have had higher spending during the first period. Further, *Coalition* is negative and significant for 1982–2001 in models without country dummies, suggesting coalition governments may have had lower spending.

19 Germany's Christian Democratic governments are treated as center governments in this book. But in the general literature, they are also often treated as conservative

governments. If they were classified as conservative governments, they would be added to the list of the fiscally expansionary right governments, as they ran an expansionary fiscal policy in the 1990s under Chancellor Helmut Kohl due to economic difficulties after German unification. Likewise, Italy's successive Christian Democratic governments produced large deficit and debt and would be added to the list, though in this book, they are classified as center governments.

20 Party fragmentation did not affect social security transfers in either period (results not reported). Though none is significant, the signs of *Fragmentation* are negative for both periods, but turned positive in the models without country dummies. To erase the possibility of multicollinearity with *Coalition*, I removed *Coalition* from the model, but nothing is significant except the first period without country dummies where *Fragmentation* has a positive (higher spending) sign. But the same coefficient is positive and insignificant in the fixed effect models.

21 The results of the models without the country dummies, however, show that CBI significantly affected public employment positively in 1961–1981 and negatively in 1982–2001. This supports my argument that independent central banks restrained public spending by party governments in the second period.

22 Another possibility is that tax revenues are expressed as percentages of GDP, and both the denominator and numerator expand during high growth periods. But this does not explain the increases in tax revenues in response to high GDP growth in the first period.

23 Tom Fomby suggested to me these possible explanations about the effects of inflation in this paragraph in personal communications. I thank him for his explanations.

24 The dependent variable is indirect taxes, which also include excise tax in addition to consumption (sales) tax. But it approximates consumption tax because most indirect tax revenues are from consumption tax.

25 If governments ever have to increase taxes, consumption tax increases are an attractive option for politicians, because a small percentage increase in consumption tax rates can raise more revenues than the same percentage increases in personal or corporate income tax rates.

26 Remember that this is a first difference of unemployment, not its level. See the explanation of the methods at the beginning of this chapter.

27 There is no evidence that minority governments caused fiscal indiscipline in any period. If anything, the models of unadjusted primary balance show that majority governments were fiscally undisciplined compared to minority governments, and they are significant.

28 In the primary balance models with country dummies, *CBI* gets dropped in the first period, because its values do not change much during this period for many countries, and this time-invariant variable and country dummies together cause perfect multicollinearity, making it impossible to estimate fixed models with country dummy variables. So we estimate models with no country dummies to examine the role of *CBI*.

29 Two notes are in order about the monetary policy models. First, I had to remove the variable *Inflation* from the models. The reasons is as follows. When I include inflation in the models, it creates a level of autocorrelation that cannot be eliminated by the inclusion of lagged dependent variables. (Even with the first through tenth lags of the dependent variables, autocorrelation remains very high (0.57).) The exclusion of inflation and the inclusion of the first to third lags of the dependent variable eliminates autocorrelation. Second, *CBI* gets dropped in the first-period, fixed-effects regressions of the monetary policy stance for the following reason. The calculation of "Taylor-rule suggested discount rates" uses output gap as one element, and the data for output gap are missing for early years. As a result, the first period has fewer observations during which central bank independence did not change, and this time-invariant variable cannot be estimated with similarly time-invariant country dummy variables because of perfect multicollinearity.

30 The observations for *Discount rates* for the first period are limited because one of the elements for the calculation of the variable – *Output gap* – is missing for earlier years.

31 This is also the conclusion of Franzese (1999).

32 Iversen (1999) argues also that if monetary policy is nonaccommodating, higher nominal wages will translate into higher real wages and unemployment.

33 The relatively accommodating monetary policy under left governments during the 1980s and 1990s also seemed to have a favorable effect on their economic outcomes, as we will see below – left governments achieved significantly lower unemployment during the period in the absence of a contractionary monetary policy, which would put deflationary pressures on the economy.

34 *Unemployment* is a lagged first difference of unemployment rates.

35 This result is robust to the inclusion and exclusion of country dummies.

36 One qualification is necessary. Fiscal policy in countries with coordinated labor became generally low spending and low taxing when we examine the individual dis-aggregate spending and tax items. However, when we consider the aggregate fiscal balance, their fiscal policy may have been expansionary in the 1980s and 1990s, in that the coefficient is negative and significant in the models without country dummies. But this result is inconclusive, since in the fixed-effect models, no period is statistically significant, indicating that labor did not affect the fiscal balance upward or downward.

37 The results do not change when *Coalition* is removed.

38 Government non-wage consumption in the 1960s and 1970s is the exception.

39 The exceptions are Cusack (2001) and some economists (e.g. Alesina and Perotti, 1995; Gali and Perotti, 2003; Perotti and Kontopoulos, 1998).

40 The use of potential output as a reference point is not without problems and is subject to debate, because of the issue of the reliability of its measurement. Alesina and Perotti (1995) and Buti and van den Noord (2003) also correctly point out that cyclically adjusted primary balance does not take inflation into account. But I use this measure because it is still a reasonable, useful measure of discretionary fiscal policy stance, data availability is large, and this is widely used by the OECD and others (Gali and Perotti, 2003). See Alesina and Perotti (1995) on alternative measures of discretionary fiscal policy.

41 When observations for discount rates are missing in a small number of cases, the data are augmented by money market rates and then treasury bills rates.

42 The use of the Taylor-type rule is also not without problems. The rule assumes that both the long-run real interest rate and central banks' inflation target rate are 2 percent. But the calculation of the long-run real interest rate is problematic, and it is questionable that the equilibrium real interest rate and the inflation target rate are constantly 2 percent across countries and over time (Hetzel, 2000; Kozicki, 1999). In addition, the reliable measurement of potential output is not easy. But in the absence of better measures, the measure based on the Taylor-type rule is a sensible choice.

5 Party governments, central banks, and labor: empirical evidence for interactive effects

1 Even with figures showing only predicted values of the dependent variable when two variables are set at given values, conditional coefficients for the variables manipulated in the calculation of predicted values are understandably significant most of the time, when the differences between the predicted values of the dependent for different combinations of two variables are statistically significant.

2 The differences among the cells are all significant, except for the horizontal difference in the *Coalition* = 3 row.

3 The predicted values of government subsidies for the first period of 1961–1981, conditional on the number of governing parties and central banks (fixed effects).

4 The vertical differences among the cells in the *CBI* = 0.68 column and the horizontal difference in the *Coalition* = 5 row are not significant. And the significance level of the vertical differences in the *CBI* = 0.14 column is only 0.14.

5 The conventional wisdom is that Christian democratic (center) governments in Europe have high transfer payments. But my results show that they had both high social security transfers and government services, when they had independent central banks, in the 1980s and 1990s.

6 Center governments under independent central banks also had high spending in the first period (1961–1981, fixed effects).

7 The predicted values of government subsidies to industries for the second period of 1982–2001 (without country dummies). The differences among the cells are significant, except for the vertical differences in the *CBI* = 0.14 column and the horizontal one in the *Center* = 0 row.

8 This result takes place partly because independent central banks individually (when not interacted) had an upward effect on public subsidies in the second period, as we saw in Chapter 4.

9 Center governments under dependent central banks generally had low spending, low revenues, the highest level of fiscal deficit, and the highest rate of inflation.

10 It suggests that center governments' fiscal discipline was conducive to economic growth during the 1960s and 1970s, though the beneficial effect disappeared in the 1980s and 1990s.

11 But a similar interactive effect of left governments and central banks is not observed for total government tax revenues or the fiscal balance, suggesting that their high spending level was not accompanied by high revenue or a worsening of the fiscal balance.

12 The highest spending was recorded by non-left governments with dependent central banks, and the lowest by non-left governments with independent central banks. The simulated results of right governments and central banks reveal (below) that these non-left governments are right governments (though the differences among the cells are not significant).

13 The results for the entire period 1961–2001 follow the pattern of the second period.

14 This result is interesting also because when the individual effects of right partisanship and central bank independence are examined (without interaction), neither variable has a statistically significant effect on social security transfers in the 1960s and 1970s. One detects the existence of their effects only when one inspects their interactive effect.

15 The results are robust for the entire period and the first period (1961–1981) with and without country dummies. So I only report the results of the entire period model without country dummies.

16 Independent central banks' downward impact on corporate tax revenues is also confirmed in the models estimating their individual (not interacted) effect, as we saw in Chapter 4.

17 The results are stable across specifications. We obtain the same results for the entire period without country dummies and for the second period (1982–2001) with country dummies.

18 In the first period results without country dummies, the pattern is similar, but the combination of right governments and independent central banks did not produce as loose a monetary policy as in the entire period results. In the first period (1961–1981), right governments' monetary policy was tighter when they had independent central banks than dependent ones. This matches my policy mix argument that right governments under dependent central banks should have a tight fiscal–loose monetary policy, and right governments with independent central banks a loose fiscal–tight monetary mix. But as with the entire-period model in Table 5.38a, right governments contributed to a looser monetary policy when central banks were

independent, and to a tighter monetary policy when central banks were dependent. Central bank independence tightened monetary policy at all levels of right cabinet portfolios, but the upward effect was the smallest under fully right governments (i.e. independent central banks did not tighten right governments' monetary policy nearly as much as non-right governments' monetary policy).

19 In the entire-period model with country dummies, electoral expansions under depend- ent central banks and electoral contractions under independent central banks take place, but spending is the highest in non-election years under independent central banks. The same happens in the first-period model with country dummies and without country dummies. In the second-period results with country dummies, electoral expansions under dependent central banks and contractions under independent central banks are observed, but only the difference among the cells in the *CBI* = 0.68 row is significant.

20 The predicted values of social security transfers paid by governments, conditional on the number of governing parties and elections, for the second period of 1982–2001 (fixed effects). The vertical differences among the cells in the *Election* = 0 column and the horizontal differences in the *Coalition* = 1 and 5 are significant, but not the others.

21 The predicted values of government subsidies for the first period of 1961–1981 (without country dummies), conditional on party fragmentation and election years. The differences among the cells are significant, except for the vertical differences in the *Election* = 0 column and the horizontal difference in the *Fragmentation* = 5.

22 The predicted values of corporate income tax revenues for the first period of 1961–1981, conditional on party fragmentation and election years (without country dummies). The differences among the cells are statistically significant, except for the vertical differences in the *Election* = 0 column and the horizontal difference in the *Fragmentation* = 2. We obtain the same results for the fixed-effects models.

23 The differences among the cells are significant, except for the vertical differences in the *Election* = 0 column and the horizontal difference in the *Fragmentation* = 5 row.

24 The predicted values of corporate income tax revenues for the first period of 1961–1981, conditional on left cabinet portfolios and labor coordination (fixed effects). The differences among the cells are significant, except for the horizontal ones in the *Left* = 0 row, and in the vertical differences in the *Labor* = 5 column where *p*-value is 0.12. We obtain the same results with the model without country dummies.

25 The predicted values of social security contributions received by governments for the entire period of 1961–2001, conditional upon left cabinet portfolios and labor coordination (fixed effects). The differences among the cells are significant, except for the vertical differences in the *Labor* = 1 and 3 columns and the horizontal ones in the *Left* = 0 row.

26 The predicted values of inflation, conditional on left partisanship and labor coordination, for the first period of 1961–1981 (fixed effects). The differences among the cells are significant, except for the horizontal differences in the *Left* = 50 row, and the vertical differences in the *Labor* = 5 column where *p*-value is 0.13.

27 The differences among the cells are significant only in the *Labor* = 1 row and close to significance (0.12) in the *CBI* = 0.68 column.

28 The results for the first period (1961–1981 without country dummies) suggest that the combination of coordinated labor and independent central banks helped restrain spending. It suggests that there was some change in the interactive effect of labor and central banks between the two periods.

29 Only the vertical differences in the *CBI* = 0.14 column are significant. So the results should be viewed with caution.

30 The differences among the cells are significant in the vertical differences in the *CBI* = 0.14 column and the horizontal difference in the *Labor* = 1 row. The vertical differences

in the *CBI* = 0.68 column are close to significance (*p*-value = 0.11), and the *p*-value for the horizontal difference in the *Labor* = 3 row is 0.14.

31 In the entire-period model (1961–2001), this combination produced the lowest spending.

32 The predicted values of government employment for the second period of 1982–2001, conditional on labor coordination and central bank independence (without country dummies). The differences among the cells are significant, except for the horizontal differences in the *Labor* = 1 and 3 rows.

33 The predicted values of social security contributions for the second period of 1982–2001, conditional upon labor coordination and central bank independence (without country dummies). The differences among the cells are significant in the vertical differences in the *CBI* = 0.68 column and the horizontal difference in the *Labor* = 5 row. The significance levels for the differences among the cells in the *Labor* = 1 row and the *CBI* = 0.14 column were 0.14 and 0.15.

34 Though more than half of the differences among the cells are not significant, the results for the first period of 1961–1981 (without country dummies) show the opposite pattern – the combination of coordinated labor and independent central banks led to low contributions. So there is a chance that the impact of labor coordination and central bank independence changed between the two periods.

35 The predicted values of total government revenues for the second period of 1982–2001, conditional on labor coordination and central bank independence (without fixed effects). Only the vertical differences in the *CBI* = 0.14 column are statistically significant, but no other was. The results of the first period (1961–1981) were not significant.

36 The predicted values of output growth for the entire period of 1961–2001, conditional upon labor coordination and central bank independence (without country dummies). The differences among the cells are significant only in the horizontal difference in the *Labor* = 5 row and close to significance (*p*-value = 0.11) in the vertical differences in the *CBI* = 0.14 column (the *p*-value for the vertical differences in the CBI = 0.68 column is 0.18).

37 These unemployment results are largely consistent with Iversen's (1999) findings.

38 This is for the most part consistent with Iversen (1999) and different from the findings by Franzese and Hall (2000).

39 This result is also consistent with Iversen's (1999) thesis.

6 Conclusion

1 This is how Gould (1987) describes the evolution of life. I believe that the nature and development of economic policy making are similar to the evolution of life described by Gould. The difference is that the evolution of life takes place over a much, much longer time span than that of economic policy or any political phenomena, and that humans have control over the development of economic policy, but cannot control the evolution of their own life.

2 One could speculate that Japan's reform would not have happened if it had not been for enormously popular, pro-reform Prime Minister Koizumi and the landslide victory of his LDP in the 2005 general election. But the point is it has been happening.

3 Germany's Christian Democratic governments are treated as center governments in this book. But in the general literature, they are also often treated as conservative governments. If they were classified as conservative governments, they would be added to the list of the fiscally expansionary right governments, as they ran an expansionary fiscal policy in the 1990s under Chancellor Helmut Kohl due to economic difficulties after reunification.

4 Of course, if we measure political parties' policy positions from their actual policy and use them to predict the parties' policy, we end up making tautological arguments.

But to the extent that we are interested in what policy they actually pursue, this is an unavoidable methodological flaw. In addition, with this approach, we cannot measure the policy positions of political parties that never participate in government.

5 Social security pensions are another spending item that is so popular among middle and upper classes that political parties have had difficulty retrenching, though they are not government consumption.

6 Government employment is relatively flat throughout the period under study, except for several countries that experienced wide fluctuations. The United Kingdom drastically reduced public employment since the early 1980s (the Thatcher administration). Germany, Ireland, the Netherlands, and New Zealand have also reduced public employment substantially, though to a much lesser extent than the United Kingdom. In contrast, social democratic countries (Denmark, Finland, Norway, Sweden) experienced sharp rises in government employment up to the 1980s, but the increases have leveled off in the 1980s and 1990s.

7 Japan is an exception. Its gross debt exploded as a result of successive recessions for over a decade and the government's Keynesian countercyclical spending.

8 Japan's revenue reduction is again due to its recessions.

9 Japan steadily increased corporate tax revenues until the 1990s when recessions started decreasing their tax revenues.

10 I thank an anonymous reviewer for pointing this out.

References

Adema, Willem and Maxime Ladaique. 2005. "Net Social Expenditure, 2005 Edition: More Comprehensive Measures of Social Support." OECD Social, Employment and Migration Working Papers No. 29. Paris: OECD.

Alesina, Alberto and Roberto Perotti. 1995. "Fiscal Expansions and Adjustments in OECD Countries." *Economic Policy* 21 (October): 205–248.

Alesina, Alberto and Nouriel Roubini with Gerald D. Cohen. 1997. *Political Cycles and the Macroeconomy.* Cambridge, MA: MIT Press.

Armingeon, Klaus, Michelle Beyeler, and Sarah Menegale. 2002. Comparative Political Data Set 1960–2001. Institute of Political Science, University of Berne.

Bearce, David H. 2002. "Monetary Divergence: Domestic Political Institutions and the Monetary Autonomy–Exchange Rate Stability Trade-Off." *Comparative Political Studies* 35 (2): 194–220.

Beck, Nathaniel. 1992. "Comparing Dynamic Specifications: The Case of Presidential Approval." *Political Analysis* 3: 51–87.

Beck, Nathaniel and Jonathan N. Katz. 1995. "What To Do (and Not To Do) with Time-Series Cross-Section Data." *American Political Science Review* 89 (3): 634–647.

Beck, Nathaniel and Jonathan N. Katz. 1996. "Nuisance vs. Substance: Specifying and Estimating Time-Series–Cross-Section Models. *Political Analysis* 6: 1–34.

Bennett, Herman and Norman Loayza. 2002. "Policy Biases When the Monetary and Fiscal Authorities Have Different Objectives." In *Monetary Policy: Rules and Transmission Mechanisms*, eds. Norman Loayza and Klaus Schmidt-Hebbel. Santiago, Chile: Central Bank of Chile: 299–330.

Bernhard, William. 2002. *Banking on Reform: Political Parties and Central Bank Independence in the Industrial Democracies.* Ann Arbor, MI: University of Michigan Press.

Bernhard, William and David Leblang. 2003. "Political Parties and Monetary Commitments." In *The Political Economic of Monetary Institutions: A Special Issue of International Organization*, eds. William T. Bernhard, J. Lawrence Broz, and William Roberts Clark. Cambridge, MA: MIT Press: 111–138.

Bernhard, William T., J. Lawrence Broz, and William Roberts Clark. Eds. 2003. *The Political Economic of Monetary Institutions: A Special Issue of International Organization.* Cambridge, MA: MIT Press.

Blais, André, Donald Blake, and Stéphane Dion. 1993. "Do Parties Make A Difference? Parties and The Size of Government in Liberal Democracies." *American Journal of Political Science* 37 (1): 40–62.

Boix, Carles. 1998. *Political Parties, Growth and Equality: Conservative and Social Democratic Economic Strategies in the World Economy*. Cambridge: Cambridge University Press.

Boix, Carles. 2000. "Partisan Governments, the International Economy, and Macroeconomic Policies in Advanced Nations, 1960–1993." *World Politics* 53 (1): 38–73.

Borrelli, Stephen A. and Terry J. Royed. 1995. "Government 'Strength' and Budget Deficits in Advanced Democracies." *European Journal of Political Research* 28 (2): 225–260.

Budge, Ian, Hans-Dieter Klingemann, Andrea Volkens, Judith Bara, and Eric Tanenbaum. 2001. *Mapping Policy Preferences: Estimates for Parties, Electors, and Governments 1945–1998*. New York, NY: Oxford University Press.

Buti, Marco and Paul van den Noord. 2003. "Discretionary Fiscal Policy and Elections: The Experience of the Early Years of EMU." Economics Department Working Paper No. 351, Paris: OECD.

Calmfors, Lars and John Driffill. 1988. "Bargaining Structure, Corporatism and Macroeconomic Performance." *Economic Policy* 6: 14–61.

Cameron, David R. 1978. "The Expansion of the Public Economy: A Comparative Analysis." *American Political Science Review* 72 (4): 1243–1261.

Cameron, David. 1984. "Social Democracy, Corporatism, Labor Quiescence and the Representation of Economic Interest in Advanced Capitalist Society." In *Order and Conflict in Contemporary Capitalism*, ed. John H. Goldthorpe. New York, NY: Oxford University Press: 143–178.

Clark, William Roberts. 2003. *Capitalism, Not Globalism: Capital Mobility, Central Bank Independence, and the Political Control of the Economy*. Ann Arbor: University of Michigan Press.

Clark, William Roberts and Mark Hallerberg. 2000. "Mobile Capital, Domestic Institutions, and Electorally Induced Monetary and Fiscal Policy." *American Political Science Review* 94 (2): 323–346.

Crepaz, Markus M.L. 1996. "Consensus Versus Majoritarian Democracy: Political Institutions and Their Impact on Macroeconomic Performance and Industrial Disputes." *Comparative Political Studies* 29 (February): 4–26.

Cukierman, Alex. 1992. *Central Bank Strategy, Credibility, and Independence*. Cambridge, MA: MIT Press.

Cusack, Thomas R. 1999. "Partisan Politics and Fiscal Policy." *Comparative Political Studies* 32 (4), 464–486.

Cusack, Thomas R. 2001. "Partisanship in the Setting and Coordination of Fiscal and Monetary Policies." *European Journal of Political Research* 40 (1): 93–115.

Demertzis, Maria, Andrew Hughes Hallett, and Nicola Viegi. 1998. "Can the ECB be Truly Independent? Should It?" Unpublished typescript. September.

Dixit, Avinash and Luisa Lambertini. 2002. "Interactions of Commitment and Discretion in Monetary and Fiscal Policies." Unpublished typescript. September.

Down, Ian. 2004. "Central Bank Independence, Disinflations, and the Sacrifice Ratio." *Comparative Political Studies* 37 (4): 399–434.

Duverger, Maurice. 1954. *Political Parties*. New York, NY: John Wiley and Sons.

Edin, Per-Anders and Henry Ohlsson. 1991. "Political Determinants of Budget Deficits: Coalition Effects versus Minority Effects." *European Economic Review* 35 (December): 1597–1603.

Elster, Jon. 1989. *The Cement of Society*. Cambridge: Cambridge University Press.

Esping-Andersen, Gosta. 1990. *The Three Worlds of Welfare Capitalism*. Princeton, NJ: Princeton University Press.

Franzese, Robert J. Jr. 1999. "Partially Independent Central Banks, Politically Responsive Governments, and Inflation." *American Journal of Political Science* 43 (3): 681–706.

Franzese, Robert J. Jr. 2002a. *Macroeconomic Policies of Developed Democracies.* Cambridge: Cambridge University Press.

Franzese, Robert J. Jr. 2002b. "Electoral and Partisan Cycles in Economic Policies and Outcomes." *Annual Reviews of Political Science* 5: 369–421.

Franzese, Robert J. Jr. and Peter A. Hall. 2000. "Institutional Dimensions of Coordinating Wage Bargaining and Monetary Policy." In *Unions, Employers, and Central Banks: Macroeconomic Coordination and Institutional Change in Social Market Economies,* eds. Torben Iversen, Jonas Pontusson, and David Soskice. Cambridge: Cambridge University Press: 173–204.

Frieden, Jeffry A. 1991. "Invested Interests: The Politics of National Economic Policies in a World of Global Finance" *International Organization* 45 (4): 425–451.

Gali, Jordi, and Roberto Perotti. 2003. "Fiscal Policy and Monetary Integration in Europe." Paper prepared for the "Economic Policy" meeting, Athens, April.

Garrett, Geoffrey. 1998. *Partisan Politics in the Global Economy.* Cambridge: Cambridge University Press.

Golden, Miriam, and Michael Wallerstein. 1994. "Trade Union Organization and Industrial Relations in the Postwar Era in Sixteen Nations." Paper delivered at the annual meeting of the American Political Science Association, New York.

Goldthorpe, John H. Ed. 1984. *Order and Conflict in Contemporary Capitalism.* New York, NY: Oxford University Press.

Gould, Stephen Jay. 1987. *An Urchin in the Storm.* New York, NY: W.W. Norton & Company.

Gourevitch, Peter. 1986. *Politics in Hard Times: Comparative Responses to International Economic Crises.* Ithaca, NY: Cornell University Press.

Grilli, Vittorio, Donato Masciandaro, and Guido Tabellini. 1991. "Political and Monetary Institutions and Public Financial Policies in the Industrial Countries." *Economic Policy* 13 (October): 341–392.

Grofman, Bernard and Arend Lijphart. Eds. 1986. *Electoral Laws and Their Political Consequences.* New York, NY: Agathon Press.

Hall, Peter A. 1993. "Policy Paradigms, Social Learning, and the State: The Case of Economic Policy-Making in Britain." *Comparative Politics* 25 (3): 275–296.

Hall, Peter and David Soskice. Eds. 2000. *Varieties of Capitalism: The Institutional Foundations of Comparative Advantage.* Cambridge: Cambridge University Press.

Hallerberg, Mark. 2003. "Veto Players and the Choice of Monetary Institutions." In *The Political Economic of Monetary Institutions: An International Organization Reader,* eds. William T. Bernhard, J. Lawrence Broz, and William Roberts Clark. Cambridge, MA: MIT Press: 83–110.

Hallerberg, Mark. 2004. *Domestic Budgets in a United Europe: Fiscal Governance from the End of Bretton Woods to EMU.* Ithaca, NY: Cornell University Press.

Hallerberg, Mark and Scott Basinger. 1998. "Internationalization and Changes in Tax Policy in OECD Countries: The Importance of Domestic Veto Players." *Comparative Political Studies* 31 (June): 321–352.

Hetzel, Robert L. 2000. "The Taylor Rule: Is It a Useful Guide to Understanding Monetary Policy?" Federal Reserve Bank of Richmond, *Economic Quarterly* 86 (2): 1–33.

Hibbs, Douglas A. 1977. "Political Parties and Macroeconomic Policy." *American Political Science Review* 71 (December): 1467–1487.

Huber, Evelyne and John D. Stephens. 1998. "Internationalization and the Social Democratic Model." *Comparative Political Studies* 31 (3): 353–397.

Huber, Evelyne and John D. Stephens. 2001. *Development and Crisis of the Welfare State: Parties and Policies in Global Markets*. Chicago, IL: University of Chicago Press.

International Monetary Fund. 2003. *International Financial Statistics*. CD-ROM. Washington, DC: IMF.

International Monetary Fund. Various years. *Exchange Arrangements and Exchange Restrictions*. Appendix. Washington, DC: IMF.

Iversen, Torben. 1999. *Contested Economic Institutions: The Politics of Macroeconomics and Wage Bargaining in Advanced Democracies*. Cambridge: Cambridge University Press.

Iversen, Torben and David Soskice. 1999. "Monetary Integration, Partisanship, and Macroeconomic Policy." Paper prepared for the annual meeting of the American Political Science Association, Atlanta.

Iversen, Torben and Anne Wren. 1998. "Equality, Employment, and Budgetary Restraint: The Trilemma of the Service Economy." *World Politics* 50 (4) (July): 507–546.

Iversen, Torben, Jonas Pontusson, and David Soskice. Eds. 2000. *Unions, Employers, and Central Banks: Macroeconomic Coordination and Institutional Change in Social Market Economies*. Cambridge: Cambridge University Press.

Katz, Richard S. 1980. *A Theory of Parties and Electoral Systems*. Baltimore, MD: Johns Hopkins University Press.

Katzenstein, Peter J. 1985. *Small States in World Markets: Industrial Policy in Europe*. Ithaca, NY: Cornell University Press.

Keefer, Philip and David Stasavage. 2003. "Checks and Balances, Private Information, and the Credibility of Monetary Commitments." In *The Political Economic of Monetary Institutions: An International Organization Reader*, eds. William T. Bernhard, J. Lawrence Broz, and William Roberts Clark. Cambridge, MA: MIT Press: 59–82.

Kenworthy, Lane. 2001. Wage Setting Coordination Scores. Dataset. Department of Sociology, Emory University. June 17.

Kenworthy, Lane. 2004. *Egalitarian Capitalism: Jobs, Incomes, and Growth in Affluent Countries*. New York, NY: Russell Sage Foundation.

Keohane, Robert O. and Helen V. Milner. Eds. 1996. *Internationalization and Domestic Politics*. Cambridge: Cambridge University Press.

Kitschelt, Herbert. 1999. "European Social Democracy between Political Economy and Electoral Competition." In *Continuity and Change in Contemporary Capitalism*, eds. Herbert Kitschelt, Peter Lange, Gary Marks, and John D. Stephens. Cambridge: Cambridge University Press: 317–345.

Kitschelt, Herbert. 2001. "Political–Economic Context and Partisan Strategies in the German Federal Elections." In *Germany: Beyond the Stable State*, eds. Herbert Kitschelt and Wolfgang Streeck. London: Frank Cass: 125–152.

Kitschelt, Herbert, Peter Lange, Gary Marks, and John D. Stephens. Eds. 1999a. *Continuity and Change in Contemporary Capitalism*. Cambridge: Cambridge University Press.

Kitschelt, Herbert, Peter Lange, Gary Marks, and John D. Stephens. 1999b. "Convergence and Divergence in Advanced Capitalist Democracies." In *Continuity and Change in Contemporary Capitalism*. eds. Herbert Kitschelt, Peter Lange, Gary Marks, and John D. Stephens. Cambridge: Cambridge University Press: 427–460.

Kittel, Bernhard. 1999. "Sense and Sensitivity in Pooled Analysis of Political Data." *European Journal of Political Research* 35 (2): 225–253.

Kozicki, Sharon. 1999. "How Useful Are Taylor Rules for Monetary Policy?" Federal Reserve Bank of Kansas City *Economic Review* 84 (second quarter): 5–33.

Kurzer, Paulette. 1993. *Business and Banking*. Ithaca, NY: Cornell University Press.

Laakso, Markku and Rein Taagepera. 1979. "Effective Number of Parties: A Measure with Application to West Europe." *Comparative Political Studies* 12 (1) (April): 3–27.

Lane, Philip R. 2002. "The Cyclical Behaviour of Fiscal Policy: Evidence from the OECD." Unpublished manuscript. Institute for International Integration Studies, Trinity College Dublin, February.

Lange, Peter, Michael Wallerstein, and Miriam Golden. 1995. "The End of Corporatism? Wage Setting in the Nordic and Germanic Countries." *The Workers of Nations: Industrial Relations in a Global Economy*, ed. Sanford M. Jacoby. Oxford: Oxford University Press.

Lijphart, Arend. 1994. *Electoral Systems and Party Systems: A Study of Twenty-Seven Democracies 1945–1990*. Oxford: Oxford University Press.

Lijphart, Arend. 1999. *Patterns of Democracy: Government Forms and Performance in Thirty-Six Countries*. New Haven, CT: Yale University Press.

Lohmann, Susanne. 1998. "Federalism and Central Bank Independence: The Politics of German Monetary Policy, 1957–92." *World Politics* 50 (3) (April): 401–446.

Mackie, Thomas T. and Richard Rose. 1991. *The International Almanac of Electoral History*. (3rd rev. edn.) Washington, DC: Congressional Quarterly.

Mackie, Thomas T. and Richard Rose. 1997. *A Decade of Electoral Results: Updating the International Almanac*. Glasgow: Centre for the Study of Public Policy, University of Strathclyde.

McNamara, Kathleen R. 1998. *The Currency of Ideas: Monetary Politics in the European Union*. Ithaca, NY: Cornell University Press.

Manow, Philip. 2001. "Comparative Institutional Advantages of Welfare State Regimes and New Coalitions in Welfare State Reforms." In *The New Politics of the Welfare State*, ed. Paul Pierson. Oxford: Oxford University Press.

March, James G. and Johan P. Olsen. 1989. *Rediscovering Institutions*. New York, NY: Free Press.

Melitz, Jacques. 1997. "Some Cross-Country Evidence about Debt, Deficits and the Behaviour of Monetary and Fiscal Authorities." Discussion Paper No. 1653, Centre for Economic Policy Research, May.

Moser, Peter. 1999. "Checks and Balances, and the Supply of Central Bank Independence." *European Economic Review* 43 (8): 1569–1593.

Mundell, Robert A. 1963. "Capital Mobility and Stabilization Policy under Fixed and Flexible Exchange Rates." *Canadian Journal of Economics and Political Science* 29 (November): 475–485.

Nordhaus, William D. 1994. "Policy Games: Coordination and Independence in Monetary and Fiscal Policies." *Brookings Papers on Economic Activity* 2: 139–199.

North, Douglass C. 1990. *Institutions, Institutional Change and Economic Performance*. Cambridge: Cambridge University Press.

Oatley, Thomas. 1999. "How Constraining Is Capital Mobility? The Partisan Hypothesis in an Open Economy." *American Journal of Political Science* 43 (4): 1003–1027.

OECD. 1993. *Employment Perspectives 1993*. Paris: OECD.

OECD. 1997. "Economic Performance and the Structure of Collective Bargaining." In *Employment Outlook*. Paris: OECD: 63–92.

OECD. 2003. *Economic Outlook: Statistics and Projections*. CD-ROM. Vol. 2003/2, No. 74 (December). Paris: OECD.

OECD. Various years. *Employment Outlook*. Paris: OECD.

OECD. Various years. *Labor Force Statistics*. Paris: OECD.

Perotti, Roberto and Yianos Kontopoulos. 1998. "Fragmented Fiscal Policy." Unpublished manuscript.

Pierson, Paul. Ed. 2001. *The New Politics of the Welfare State*. Oxford: Oxford University Press.

Poterba, James M. and Jurgen von Hagen. eds. 1999. *Fiscal Institutions and Fiscal Performance*. Chicago, IL: University of Chicago Press.

Quinn, Dennis. 1997. "The Correlates of Change in International Financial Regulations." *American Political Science Review* 91 (3): 531–552.

Rae, Douglas W. 1967. *The Political Consequences of Electoral Laws*. New Haven, CT: Yale University Press.

Rogoff, Kenneth. 1985. "The Optimal Degree of Commitment to An Intermediate Monetary Target." *Quarterly Journal of Economics* 100 (4): 1169–1190.

Rogowski, Ronald. 1989. *Commerce and Coalitions: How Trade Affects Domestic Political Alignments*. Princeton, NJ: Princeton University Press.

Rothenberg, Alexander D. (n.d.). "The Monetary–Fiscal Policy Mix: Empirical Analysis and Theoretical Implications." Unpublished typescript.

Roubini, Nouriel and Jeffrey D. Sachs. 1989a. "Political and Economic Determinants of Budget Deficits in the Industrial Democracies." *European Economic Review* 33 (2): 903–938.

Roubini, Nouriel and Jeffrey Sachs. 1989b. "Government Spending and Budget Deficits in the Industrial Countries." *Economic Policy* 8 (April): 99–132.

Sakamoto, Takayuki. 2001. "Effects of Government Characteristics on Fiscal Deficits in 18 OECD Countries, 1961–1994." *Comparative Political Studies* 34 (June): 527–554.

Sakamoto, Takayuki. 2003. "Fiscal–Monetary Policy Mix: An Investigation of Political Determinants of Macroeconomic Policy Mixes." Unpublished manuscript. Southern Methodist University.

Sakamoto, Takayuki. 2005. "Economic Performance of 'Weak' Governments and Their Interaction with the Central Bank and Labor: Deficits, Economic Growth, Unemployment, and Inflation, 1961–1998," *European Journal of Political Research* 44 (6): 801–836.

Scharpf, Fritz W. 1991. *Crisis and Choice in European Social Democracy*. Ithaca, NY: Cornell University Press.

Schmidt, Vivien A. 2002. *The Futures of European Capitalism*. Oxford: Oxford University Press.

Soskice, David. 1990. "Wage Determination: The Changing Role of Institutions in Advanced Industrialized Countries." *Oxford Review of Economic Policy* 6 (December): 36–61.

Steinmo, Sven and Caroline J. Tolbert. 1998. "Do Institutions Really Matter? Taxation in Industrialized Democracies." *Comparative Political Studies* 31 (April): 165–187.

Steinmo, Sven, Kathleen Thelen, and Frank Longsreth. Eds. 1992. *Structuring Politics*. Cambridge: Cambridge University Press.

Strom, Kaare. 1990. *Minority Government and Majority Rule*. Cambridge: Cambridge University Press.

Swank, Duane. 2002. *Global Capital, Political Institutions, and Policy Change in Developed Welfare States*. Cambridge: Cambridge University Press.

Swank, Duane. n.d. Comparative Parties Data Set. Marquette University.

Taagepera, Rein and Matthew Soberg Shugart. 1989. *Seats and Votes: The Effects and Determinants of Electoral Systems*. New Haven, CT: Yale University Press.

Taylor, John B. 1993. "Discretion versus Policy Rules in Practice." *Carnegie-Rochester Conference Series on Public Policy* 39 (December): 195–214.

Traxler, Franz. 1994. *The Level and Coverage of Collective Bargaining: A Cross-National Study of Patterns and Trends*. Paris: OECD.

Tsebelis, George. 1995. "Decision Making in Political Systems: Veto Players in Presidentialism, Parliamentarism, Multicameralism and Multipartyism." *British Journal of Political Science* 25 (July): 289–325.

Tsebelis, George. 1999. "Veto Players and Law Production in Parliamentary Democracies: An Empirical Analysis." *American Political Science Review* 93 (September): 591–608.

van den Noord, Paul. 2000. "The Size and Role of Automatic Fiscal Stabilizers in the 1990s and Beyond." Economics Department Working Papers No. 230, Paris: OECD.

Way, Christopher. 2000. "Central Banks, Partisan Politics, and Macroeconomic Outcomes." *Comparative Political Studies* 33 (2): 196–224.

Weaver, R. Kent and Bert A. Rockman. Eds. 1993. *Do Institutions Matter? Government Capabilities in the United States and Abroad*. Washington, DC: The Brookings Institution.

Woldendorp, Jaap, Hans Keman, and Ian Budge. 1993. *Handbook of Democratic Government: Party Government in 20 Democracies (1945–1990)*. Dordrecht: Kluwer Academic.

Woldendorp, Jaap, Hans Keman, and Ian Budge. 1998. "Party Government in 20 Democracies: An Update (1990–1995)." *European Journal of Political Research* 33 (January): 125–164.

Index

Adema, Willem 305
adjustments, in response to economic crises 63–5
Alesina, Alberto 41
Armingeon, Klaus 92–4
Australia: government wage consumption expenditures 293; indirect tax 303; single-party majority governments 79
Austria: fixed exchange rates 59; left governments 58

Bank of England 24, 309n10
Bank of Italy 24, 34
Bank of Japan 308n4, 308n5
Belgium: central bank independence 59; fixed exchange rates 59; frequent coalition governments with large public debt 66; social security transfers 295
Bernhard, William 19–20, 22, 24, 32–4, 40, 59, 67, 78, 80, 92, 179–80, 199, 215, 308n1, 308n2, 309n10, 310n4
Boix, Carles 4–6, 31, 60, 72, 74, 96, 98, 125, 217, 228, 307n3, 307n7, 308n9, 311n11, 313n6, 313n12
Bretton Woods system 28–9, 100, 309n9
Bundesbank 19–21, 308n2
Bush administration 24, 80, 121, 171

Canada: government non-wage consumption expenditure 294; single-party majority governments 79; social security transfers 295
capital, internationalization of 4, 38, 55, 61–2, 73, 81, 127, 199; *see also* capital mobility; globalization
capital mobility 5, 17, 28–9, 35, 41, 94, 96, 98, 100, 103–4, 125–7, 139–40, 147–9, 157, 160, 164–5, 168, 172–3, 307n9, 309n17; constraints 5, 35; *see also* capital; globalization

capital mobility constraints 5, 35
CBI (central bank independence) *see* central banks
center governments 2, 11, 24, 37–40, 59, 62–3, 72–3, 76, 79–80, 95, 105, 107, 109, 120, 129, 132–3, 134, 137–8, 144, 150–5, 158–9, 163, 167, 169–71, 176–7, 198–215, 221–5, 230–1, 235, 238–42, 276, 287–90, 294, 312n18, 312n19, 312n20, 313n19, 316n5, 316n6, 316n9, 316n10, 318n3; variable for 92–6; *see also* Christian democratic parties or governments; interactions
central bank independence (CBI) *see* central banks
central banks 5, 12, 17, 23–4, 32, 40–1, 47–50, 75, 79, 92, 109, 112, 142, 153, 157, 171, 181–6, 192–8, 204–7, 212, 215–18, 220–48, 260–1, 276–90, 307n5, 308n1, 312n17, 312n19, 314n29, 316n14, 317n18, 318n32, 318n33, 318n34, 318n35, 318n36; *see also* interactions
Christian democratic parties or governments 5, 8, 24, 30, 34, 37–9, 62, 71, 79, 92, 95, 121, 138, 171, 204, 217, 222, 234, 312n20, 312n4, 313n19, 316n5, 318n3; *see also* center governments
Clark, William Roberts 5–6, 10, 31, 41, 74, 98, 292, 306, 307n3, 309n17, 311n8, 313n12
Clinton administration 80, 121, 171
coalition governments: possibility of party conflict 33; veto players 32–7; "weak government" argument 3, 11, 65–9, 75–7, 107–8, 154, 159–60, 163, 172; *see also* interactions
compensation policy or hypothesis 63, 103–4, 125–7, 139–40, 147, 157, 173; *see also* convergence thesis

For Product Safety Concerns and Information please contact our EU
representative GPSR@taylorandfrancis.com
Taylor & Francis Verlag GmbH, Kaufingerstraße 24, 80331 München, Germany

www.ingramcontent.com/pod-product-compliance
Ingram Content Group UK Ltd.
Pitfield, Milton Keynes, MK11 3LW, UK
UKHW021622240425
457818UK00018B/694